WE ARE THE CHAMPIONS:
THE POLITICS OF SPORTS AND POPULAR MUSIC

To my parents
Don McLeod and Louise Rapson

We are the Champions: The Politics of Sports and Popular Music

KEN MCLEOD
University of Toronto, Canada

ASHGATE

Published by
Ashgate Publishing Limited
Wey Court East
Union Road
Farnham
Surrey, GU9 7PT
England

Ashgate Publishing Company
Suite 420
101 Cherry Street
Burlington
VT 05401-4405
USA

www.ashgate.com

British Library Cataloguing in Publication Data
McLeod, Ken.
  We are the champions : the politics of sports and popular
  music. -- (Ashgate popular and folk music series)
  1. Music and sports.
  I. Title II. Series
  780'.0796-dc22

Library of Congress Cataloging-in-Publication Data
McLeod, Ken, 1964-
  We are the champions : the politics of sports and popular music / Ken McLeod.
      p. cm. -- (Ashgate Popular and folk music series)
  Includes bibliographical references and index.
   ISBN 978-1-4094-0864-2 (hardcover) 1. Music and sports. 2. Popular music--Social
aspects. 3. Sports in popular culture I. Title.
  ML3916.M38 2011
  781.5'94--dc22

                                                                            2011004229

ISBN 9781409408642 (hbk)
ISBN 9781409431442 (ebk)

MIX
Paper from
responsible sources
FSC® C018575
www.fsc.org

Printed and bound in Great Britain by the
MPG Books Group, UK.

Contents

General Editor's Preface

The upheaval that occurred in musicology during the last two decades of the twentieth century has created a new urgency for the study of popular music alongside the development of new critical and theoretical models. A relativistic outlook has replaced the universal perspective of modernism (the international ambitions of the 12-note style); the grand narrative of the evolution and dissolution of tonality has been challenged, and emphasis has shifted to cultural context, reception and subject position. Together, these have conspired to eat away at the status of canonical composers and categories of high and low in music. A need has arisen, also, to recognize and address the emergence of crossovers, mixed and new genres, to engage in debates concerning the vexed problem of what constitutes authenticity in music and to offer a critique of musical practice as the product of free, individual expression.

Popular musicology is now a vital and exciting area of scholarship, and the *Ashgate Popular and Folk Music Series* presents some of the best research in the field. Authors are concerned with locating musical practices, values and meanings in cultural context, and draw upon methodologies and theories developed in cultural studies, semiotics, poststructuralism, psychology and sociology. The series focuses on popular musics of the twentieth and twenty-first centuries. It is designed to embrace the world's popular musics from Acid Jazz to Zydeco, whether high tech or low tech, commercial or non-commercial, contemporary or traditional.

Professor Derek B. Scott
Professor of Critical Musicology
University of Leeds

Acknowledgments

It was while watching a televised broadcast of the 2002 World Cup co-hosted by Japan and Korea that I was first inspired to write this book. Over the top of the announcers' voices and the general din of the cheering fans was the clearly audible and nearly constant presence of the tune to the Village People's "Go West." The precise words, other than the emphatic chorus "Go West", were indistinguishable to me; however, in subsequent broadcasts I heard the melody being sung repeatedly. Although I was well aware of the proclivity of soccer supporters to chant and sing it still struck me as a rather incongruous setting in which to hear this song—a gay anthem, an ode to the Western state of California, being sung in Korea by tens of thousands of Asian soccer fans. As I gave the matter more thought, I realized that a host of pop anthems from "We Are the Champions" to "Rock and Roll Part 2" are played or sung regularly at sporting events around the world and that, particularly in those contexts, they are often important in constructing and problematizing various identities. From there I began to understand that music and sports intersect on many levels and that, almost invariably, this nexus served to construct, contest and/or promote one identity or another. For me, this realization was significant, in that it represented a potentially important fusion of the seemingly disparate realms of athletic and artistic cultures that, despite a recent emphasis on academic interdisciplinarity, are typically only addressed in discreet studies. I offer this work in the hopes that it will add one more piece to the puzzle of understanding the full scope and reach of music's powers.

This book would not have been possible without the continuing support and encouragement of my parents, family, friends, and colleagues. In particular I would like to thank Julie Cumming, James Deaville, William Renwick, and Ellen Harris for their unflagging support of my work, despite the fact that I veered away from my original research on eighteenth-century English music and into the realm of popular music studies. I am also grateful to Susan McClary, whose graduate seminar at McGill initially inspired my interest in pursuing popular music studies. I would like to thank my former colleague Richard Hoffman for his stimulating insights into science, sports and music. I also wish to express my appreciation to the moderators, panels and audiences at the AMS, IMS, IASPM and ICSS meetings, and to my graduate seminar students at the University of Toronto, all of whom have provided invaluable feedback on various aspects of this project.

I would also like to express my sincerest gratitude to my parents, my grandparents, and my sister Ann for their love and support throughout my life.

Above all, I am deeply grateful to my wife, Alison McQueen, who read and discussed numerous aspects of the manuscript with me.

I would like to acknowledge the Social Sciences and Humanities Research Council of Canada for supporting this research with a Standard Research Grant.

Introduction: Warming Up

This book examines the intersections of popular music and sports primarily, although not exclusively, in North America and Europe from the late eighteenth century to the present. This region and period represents the development of history's largest international music and sporting markets. In particular I seek to examine the historical connections between music and sports and to analyze how such synergies construct, contest, reinforce, and re-envision gender, racial, and national identities in both abstract aesthetic and explicit political contexts. While there is a body of scholarship that has addressed the socio-cultural meanings of sports and music as discrete fields of inquiry, there has been no study of their important cross-pollinations or of their combined and often mutually reinforcing cultural impact. This project seeks to rectify these lacunae and will offer a much more complete understanding of the breadth and meaning of this cultural nexus.

The central thesis of this study is that sports and music are fundamentally connected, not only through cross-marketing tactics, metaphoric similarities of aesthetic and stylistic approaches, and issues of spectatorship, but also through their often active influence on each other's performative strategies and content and their action as synergistic agents in the construction of identity and community. Though music and sports are usually considered in isolation from one another, connections between the two cultures occur on a wide variety of levels. These include music used to enhance sporting events (anthems, chants or cheers, and intermission entertainment), music that is used as an active part of the athletic event (as in figure skating, exercise classes, and gymnastic routines), and music that has been written about or that is associated with sports (for example, the *Hockey Night in Canada* theme or "Take Me Out to the Ball Game"). There are also connections in the comparative, competitive aspects of music (as in *American Idol* and other current and historical musical competitions), the use of music in sports movies and video games, the importance of mutually influential stylistic approaches (as evidenced by improvisational links between jazz and basketball and baseball among other instances), and the important, though critically under-acknowledged, similarities regarding spectatorship, practice, and performance that have often stereotyped various communities (for instance, in the connections between rap, basketball, and the construction of African American masculinity). Despite the extensive history of such confluences, the extraordinary impact of the interrelationship of music and sports on popular culture has remained almost completely unrecognized. My work ties together several influential threads of popular culture and fills a significant void in our understanding of the construction and communication of identity in the late twentieth and early twenty-first centuries.

Specific questions that are addressed in this work include the following: What is the historical relationship of sports and music, and how did it evolve throughout Europe and North America? In what ways do athletics influence our experience of and relationship to music, and how does music inform our experience of and relationship to athletics? In what ways have sports and music combined to reinforce class, racial, gender, and sexual identities and stereotypes? How has the relationship between sports and music informed our understanding of national and global identities? In what ways have sports and music been combined in other media—including film, television, and video games—to construct identity?

A complete history of the relationship between sports and music is beyond the scope of this single volume. Future scholars may profitably expand this project to incorporate detailed analysis of sports–music relationships in other eras and geographic regions and to include other agendas. In the current work, however, I offer a broad overview of the historical connections to contextualize my concentration on the period of roughly 1850 to the present. Documenting every notable score or recording referencing athletics is not possible. I intend, however, to provide readers with a substantive overview of such works in order to produce a meaningful analysis of trends in song types, lyrical topics, and content.

Current scholarship addresses the individual roles of sports and music in shaping national and social identities, but there is no scholarly study of the convergences and mutual reinforcement of these cultures in constructing such identities. Similarly, the important connection between the musical representation of sports in film, television, and video and the construction of masculinity has received little critical attention. My work seeks to rectify these omissions and offers a comprehensive understanding of the breadth and socio-cultural function of the historical synergy between sports and popular music. This project responds to recent shifts in humanities research. Intersections, synergistic connections, and exchanges have become central questions not just in music history but in the humanities generally. In pursuit of a greater understanding of the cultural web, scholars are increasingly focusing on connected histories, the liminal, borders, and topics that are shared by multiple disciplines.

Among other objectives this project will address the general lack of scholarly recognition for the important relationship between music and sports in constructing identity. Works by Epstein, Redhead (editor), Straw, and Gracyk, for example, specifically address the notion of identity in popular music without ever noting the significant role played by the symbiotic relationship of music and sports.[1] Recently, authors such as Aaron Baker, David Zang, Stanley Eitzen,

---

[1]   Jonathan Epstein, *Youth Culture: Identity in a Postmodern World* (Oxford: Blackwell, 1998); Steve Redhead, Derek Wynne and Justin O'Connor (eds), *The ClubCultures Reader: Reading in Popular Cultural Studies* (Oxford: Blackwell, 1997); Will Straw, *Popular Music—Style and Identity* (Montreal: Centre for Research on Canadian Cultural Industries

John Sugden and Alan Tomlinson (editors), Joseph Maguire (editor), Richard Giulianotti, John Horne, and Howard L. Nixon have begun to analyze the considerable social significance of contemporary sports.[2] These and other studies have, however, thus far completely overlooked the important and, in many cases, formative connections between sports and music.

As scholarly attention to the study of popular music is becoming increasingly significant, old paradigms of the discipline of music history are challenged and new methodologies for the study of music are being developed. The social analysis of popular music is an increasingly important aspect of cultural studies. There have been several major contributions to this field in recent years, including works by Richard Middleton, Robert Walser, David Brackett, and Sheila Whiteley.[3] My book builds on these studies, as well as on the works of Susan McClary, Simon Frith, Timothy Taylor, and others whose scholarship has focused on aspects of popular music, cultural studies, and identity and who seek to develop new strategies for analyzing this material.[4] I am particularly interested in approaching music as a cultural practice and in understanding its role in shaping identity.

Though sports and popular music together account for a large part of the entertainment industry and are integrally connected in popular culture, there has been almost no scholarly work that addresses the significance of their interrelationships. Exceptions to this are studies by David Rowe, Don Cusic, Todd Boyd, Gina Caponi-Tabery (2008), and Anthony Bateman and John Bale

---

and Institutions, 1995); Theodore Gracyk, *I Wanna Be Me: Politics and Identity in Rock Music* (Temple University Press, 2001).

[2]   Aaron Baker, *Contesting Identities: Sports in American Film* (University of Illinois Press, 2003); David Zang, *Sports Wars: Athletes in the Age of Aquarius* (Fayetteville: University of Arkansas Press, 2001); D. Stanley Eitzen (ed.), *Sport in Contemporary Society* (New York: Worth, 2001); John Sugden and Alan Tomlinson (eds), *Power Games: A Critical Sociology of Sports* (London: Routledge, 2002); Joseph Maguire (ed.), *Power and Global Sport: Zones of Prestige, Emulation and Resistance* (London: Routledge, 2005); Richard Giulianotti, *Sport: A Critical Sociology* (Cambridge, UK: Polity, 2005); John Horne, *Sport in Consumer Culture* (New York: Palgrave Macmillan, 2006); Howard L. Nixon, *Sport in a Changing World* (London: Paradigm, 2008).

[3]   Richard Middleton, *Studying Popular Music* (Milton Keynes: Open University Press, 1990) and *Reading Pop: Approaches to Textual Analysis in Popular Music* (New York: Oxford University Press, 2000); Robert Walser, *Running With the Devil: Power, Gender and Madness in Heavy Metal Music* (Hanover, NH: University Press of New England, 1993); David Brackett, *Interpreting Popular Music* (New York: Cambridge University Press, 1995); Sheila Whitely, *Sexing the Groove: Popular Music and Gender* (New York: Routledge, 1997).

[4]   Susan McClary, *Feminine Endings: Music, Gender, and Sexuality* (Minneapolis: University of Minnesota Press, 1995); Simon Frith, *Performing Rites: On the Value of Popular Music* (Cambridge, Mass: Harvard University Press, 1996); Timothy Taylor *Strange Sounds: Music, Technology and Culture* (New York: Routledge, 2001).

(2009).[5] Rowe's work, however, concentrates on corporate and commercial ties between sports and music with less emphasis on critical, musical, or sociological analysis. Cusic's and Boyd's works focus on the social connections between one sport (baseball and basketball respectively) and one musical style (country and rap). Caponi-Tabery's significant recent study of jazz and basketball also explores a single sport and musical style but in relationship to African American culture in the 1930s. Bateman and Bale's edited volume of essays is the most comprehensive study of the relationship between sports and music to date. Presenting a variety of case studies it is, however, often centred on psychological and psychophysical aspects of music's effect on sports. My work builds on and complements all of the aforementioned studies and extends the arguments into the tangible bonds between popular music, sports, and related politics—not just of the burgeoning study of masculinity, which forms a significant undercurrent to this study—but of identity and identity politics in general.

The book is organized as a series of essays covering the influence of the relationship of music and sports on various issues of identity and socio-cultural formation. Chapter 1, while not focused on a particular aspect of identity formation, provides a broad overview of the connections between music and sport in Western history. From the influence of music on sport in ancient Greece through to the present day, I have attempted to show the increasing "sportization" of society, including many musical practices, and the growing emphasis on the social connection between music and sports that has particularly occurred since the eighteenth century. Among other issues considered are the considerable interconnections between dance and athletics, and the evolution of an aristocratic dueling mentality that has continued to fuel and influence both athletic and musical competitions to the present day.

Chapter 2 looks at the use of music in exercise. Likely the most common and practical example of the use of music in conjunction with sports occurs in the context of exercise classes and personal fitness regimes. Whether broadcast to various aerobics classes, à la Jane Fonda's workout videos, or simply played on an iPod while jogging, music often forms an integral part of a personal fitness regime. This chapter particularly surveys the phenomenon of exercise music and analyzes the use of music by the exercise and fitness industry as a means of constructing notions of "ideal" female identity.

---

    [5]   David Rowe, *Popular Cultures: Rock Music, Sport and the Politics of Pleasure* (London: Sage Publications, 1995); Don Cusic, *Baseball and Country Music* (Madison WI: University of Wisconsin Press, 2003); Todd Boyd, *The Rise of the NBA, The Hip Hop Invasion and the Transformation of American Culture* (New York: Doubleday, 2003); Gina Caponi-Tabery, *Jump for Joy: Jazz, Basketball & Black Culture in 1930s America* (Amherst: University of Massachusetts Press, 2008); Anthony Bateman and John Bale (eds), *Sporting Sounds: Relationships Between Sports and Music* (London: Routledge, 2009).

Chapter 3 describes and analyzes the significance and influence of the rise of a specifically targeted sports–music business in general. I attempt to account for the increasing cross-marketing of popular music and sports. In addition, this chapter also addresses and connects issues surrounding performance enhancement that have scandalized both the sports and music industries and called into question the notion of "authentic" performance in each activity.

Chapter 4 looks at the place of music, particularly the repeated use of some pop songs in crowd sing-alongs, in the context of various sporting events. Among other issues this chapter posits the notion of homo-social bonding as an underlying presence in the enduring popularity of many "gay" themed sports anthems such as Queen's "We Are the Champions," and "We Will Rock You," or the Village People's "YMCA."

Chapter 5 analyzes the construction of African American masculinity through the interconnected aesthetics of African American approaches to sports and music. In particular, this chapter examines the shared notions of improvisation and spectacular performativity that have marked the exceptionalism characteristic of sports and musical stars. Both sports and music have fostered stereotypical notions of threatening, gangsta masculinity that have reinforced such identities within the black male community and that have been increasingly influential in the shaping and exportation of American image around the globe.

Chapter 6 looks at the combined role of sports and music in shaping various national and global communities. Whether it is merely through the singing of national anthems prior to a sporting event or whether it is a national identification with a sport or a music genre, sports and music often form a powerful allegiance in shaping notions of political communities on many levels. In addition to looking at the role of music and sports in constructing and maintaining national, regional or other fan communities, this chapter outlines the significant role of music in various non-Western traditional sports.

Chapter 7 presents a study of music and sports as they are combined in the visual media of movies, video games, and television. Sports movie soundtracks, sports video game soundtracks, and sports television themes have received little or no scholarly discussion, yet they represent some of the most pervasive and powerful signifiers of various class, gender, racial, and ethnic identities in popular culture. The themes from *Rocky* and from ABC's *Monday Night Football*—to name but two of the better-known examples—are indelibly marked on our collective conscious as moments of typically masculine encoded triumph and heroism. This chapter, in addition, looks at the increasingly popular use of interactive music video games, such as *Guitar Hero* and *Rock Band*, that combine graphic imagery, competitive game playing, and music.

This book attempts to advance our understanding of the relationship between music and society and the significant role of the integration of the physical and the psychic/aesthetic in shaping identity and ideology. I seek to reclaim an important, but overlooked, aspect of music history and its web of influence. Popular music and sport cultures mutually "play off" each other in an isomorphic exchange of style, ideologies, and forms. Posing unique challenges to notions of mind–body dualities, nationalism, and codes of gender, class, race and sexual orientation, this book aims to illuminate the paradoxical and often conflicting relationships associated with these forms of leisure and entertainment, and to demonstrate that they are not culturally or ideologically distinct but are increasingly interconnected modes of contemporary social practice.

Chapter 1

"Take Me Out to the Ball Game": A Brief History of Music, Sports, and Competition

As demonstrated by the recent focused marketing and popularity of sports music, sports and music have become closely intertwined cultural expressions of the modern and postmodern era. Athletic competition and music, however, have long been connected. At some point in ancient history the idea of rivalry and competition became important to human socialization. The straightforward idea of the hunt was refined such that those members of a society who most effectively administered a kill were elevated in status. As sports historian Ellis Cashmore has outlined, "Competition between individuals or groups added a new and apparently appealing dimension to an already perilous activity."[1]

Such rivalry and competition eventually extended to other cultural activities, including music, which thereby gained a wide appeal, both for participants seeking to express their physical or intellectual dominance and for audiences who were enraptured by the spectacle of humans competitively displaying physical or technical abilities. Through what Norbert Elias has termed "the civilizing process," humans gradually replaced the physical dangers of hunting and warfare with the vicarious thrills of less dangerous physical displays.[2] The seemingly inherent human need for pleasurable excitement and entertainment was a common rationale for the early inception of both sports and music.

This chapter provides a historical overview of the relationship between sports and music in Western society for the past 2,000 years. It is not intended as a complete documentation and narrative of the socio-cultural evolution of the historical connection between sports and music, the volume of which would necessitate a separate study. Rather, this overview is intended to provide an outline of the breadth and depth of the issue. Before commencing the survey, however, it will be helpful to understand some of the historical debates regarding the relationship of sports, not just to music, but to the arts in general.

---

[1]   Ellis Cashmore, *Making Sense of Sports* (London: Routledge, 2000), 62.

[2]   Norbert Elias, *The Quest for Excitement: Sport and Leisure in the Civilizing Process* (Oxford: Blackwell, 1986).

The Sports–Music Aesthetic

On a general level the concept of aesthetic beauty in sports and its relationship to the arts has been the subject of considerable inquiry and contemplation. The link between athletics and music in Western society is founded upon the ancient Greek notion that the union of strength and beauty is the hallmark of the ideal man.[3] As outlined in *Politics*, Aristotle believed that both music and gymnastics were fundamental to the education of boys and wondered whether music is "capable of producing a certain quality of character just as gymnastics are capable of producing a certain quality of body."[4] In contrast to our contemporary Western notion of the two spheres existing in isolation from one another, for the ancient Greeks sports and the arts, including music, were intimately bound together in the cultivation of a complete individual. Many festivals, notably the Pythian Games held in Delphi in the sixth century BC, subsequently encouraged musical as well as athletic competition. If not incorporating actual musical competition, many athletic events were accompanied by music, often by reed flutes, and victors could be honored by ceremonial hymns. The poet Pindar's tenth Olympic ode, for example, proclaims:

> All the precinct rang with music
> Sung at the feast
> In the mode of praise

For the ancient Greeks the athletic body—though this was limited to the male body—was held to be the aesthetic ideal of symmetry and proportion. Throughout the succeeding centuries painters and sculptors often used the subject of sports and the associated athletic body in their works.[5] Perhaps the most famous example of this is Myron's *Discus Thrower (Discobolus)*, a bronze sculpture from the fifth century BC that is typically praised for its symmetry and proportion. As the historian John Fairs stated, "The perfectly proportioned body was the beautiful body and for the Greeks the beautiful body was the good body."[6]

More recent aesthetic analysis of the athletic body maintains such a notion of unity and symmetry but adds the element of technical mastery. The ideal body of the athlete, according to Paul Weiss, writing in 1969, makes him "a man apart." "The beauty and grace of his body, his coordination, responsiveness, alertness, efficiency, his devotion and accomplishments, his splendid unity with

---

[3] For a more detailed discussion of this point see Benjamin Lowe, *The Beauty of Sport: A Cross-Disciplinary Inquiry* (Englewood Cliffs, New Jersey: Prentice Hall, 1977).

[4] Aristotle, *Politics*, Book 8, Part IV, H. Rackham (trans.), (Cambridge, Mass.: Harvard University Press, 1990), 651.

[5] For a detailed listing and discussion of sports-related works of art, see Lowe, *The Beauty of Sport*.

[6] J.R. Fairs, "When was the golden age of the body?" *Journal of the Canadian Association of Health, Physical Education and Recreation*, 37/1 (1970), 11–24, 15.

his equipment, all geared to produce a result at the limits of bodily possibility, set him over against the rest of men."[7] Despite the rather dated patriarchal tone of such language, it is language that, however unintentionally, applies equally well to bodies involved in musical performance.

The need to delineate a distinction between sports and art has preoccupied scholars from the time of Plato and Aristotle. The Aristotelian position was that sports should be determined by the beauty of nature. In his *De rebus naturalibus* Aristotle states, "Nature is the cause of motion in natural things, not only in the body itself in which it is (immanent motion) but also on another external body (transeunt motion)."[8] Thus what distinguishes art, for Aristotle, is that the principle of motion comes from forces external to the object, caused by man, whereas in sports the principle of motion comes from within. More recently, in attempting to delineate a similar distinction between art and sports, the Organizing Committee of the 1972 Munich Olympics published a paper entitled *The Scientific View of Sport*. Among other issues the paper promoted the following opinion:

> Art and sports are both to be distinguished from play through the quality of earnestness; they demand hard work, and intense effort which can only be made by total commitment, and a great deal of expenditure of will. The seriousness of sport is stressed by the presence of spectators. The spectator has a "connection" with the athlete, a "participation," which might be understood as a sort of initiating reproduction of the movements he makes. The "participation" is accompanied by a "distancing" (distanciation), for the spectator "never in fact intends to take part in the action." Both "participation" and "distancing" are equally characteristic of the reception of works of art: the latter can only be and has to be reproduced by the observer.
>
> The earnestness of the athlete and the presence of spectators [are] explained by the fact that sporting, just like artistic activity, is directed towards an end; both are directed towards a *result*. But what corresponds in sport to the work of art (oeuvre)?[9]

The paper stresses the similarities between art and sports that stem from the participant's effort and hard work and the common "participation" and "distancing" experienced by the spectators of both activities. As expressed in the final line above, the committee ultimately failed to answer its own question. Nonetheless the similarities between art and sports have been noted in a variety of sources.

---

[7]   Paul Weiss, *Sports: A Philosophic Inquiry* (Carbondale: Southern Illinois University Press, 1969).

[8]   Cited in Lowe, 17.

[9]   Organizing Committee for the Games of the XXth Olympiad, Munich, 1972, *The Scientific View of Sport* (New York: Springer Verlag, 1972), 39.

In his book *Soccer: The World Game*, Geoffrey Green saw strong aesthetic commonalities between sports and art:

> In order to appreciate the possibilities of aesthetic compensation in the sphere of sport and to grasp the meaning of the latter—especially the simple and beautiful pattern movements created in football—one can point to the very real nearness of sport to art.
>
> The two have three important things in common. Strong, emotional excitement; a system of conventions and rules by which an appropriate sphere of human experience is delimited and dominated, and which are just as serious and valid in their own particular way as the intellectual categories of the philosopher and the physicist; and last, exercise and creativeness within such a sphere.
>
> The essential difference between art and sport is that the latter is more external and everyday, more materialist and matter-of-fact.[10]

To be sure, one might argue that the difference between an aesthetic of sports and one of music, or of any other art for that matter, is that there is a closer empathetic relationship between the spectator and the sport as an art form. Indeed, one might expect a sports aesthetic to correlate most closely with an aesthetic of dance, owing to their common kinesthetic element. Indeed, given the aesthetic description of the well-proportioned athletic body as outlined by Fairs and Weiss above, it seems clear that one of the strongest connections between athletic and musical pursuits is the social value placed on disciplining and regulating the body.

In recent years the world of sports has become increasingly aestheticized in a postmodern pastiche of advertising logos, television and publicity images, and various symbols of consumer capitalism. Even the body parts of athletes have been subject to hypercommodification (think of the often-remarked-upon size of Shaquille O'Neal's feet in basketball or the emphasis placed on Rafael Nadal's muscular biceps in tennis), such that they become mere extensions of the larger self, alienated, disembodied—appendages, as it were. Sports theorist Genevieve Rail goes so far as to claim that athletes' bodies are "disappearing under the weight of social power."[11] Such a proposal is resonant of arguments, addressed in Chapter 3, surrounding the increasing removal of the body in musical culture stemming from various technologies that allow virtual experience of both "live" performance and listening.

---

[10]   Geoffrey Green, *Soccer: The World Game* (London: The Phoenix House, 1953), 214–15. Also cited in Lowe, 30.

[11]   Genevieve Rail, "Seismography of the postmodern condition: Three theses on the implosion of sports," in Rail (ed.), *Sport and Postmodern Times* (New York: State University of New York Press, 1998), 155–6.

Dance and Athleticism and Competition

As previously intimated, one of the most pervasive manifestations of the commonality between music and athletics occurs through the practice of dance. A central characteristic of dancing is that it always involves physical human movement and exertion and is fundamentally accompanied by musical sound. For the ancient Greeks, in fact, music, dance, and poetry were represented by the single term *mousikē* (art of the Muses). The Greeks used dance in education and to some degree, as a form of gymnastics—a fact that impelled Plato (in *The Republic* and in more detail in *The Laws*) to recommend strict state control over the forms of dancing to be permitted. Free Hellenic citizens, he suggested, should concentrate on stately dances such as the *emmeleia*, which he deemed to impart grace to body and soul alike.[12]

As dance has evolved throughout history, the connection to exercise or athletics has never been far from central. William McNeill has studied dance from the standpoint of what he terms "muscular bonding," its role in creating "social cohesion among any and every group that keeps together in time, moving big muscles together and chanting, singing ... ."[13] In this sense dance has often been linked to militarism, both in the sense of rehearsing group battle formation and in preparing soldiers for the physical exertion of human combat.

In the middle ages and early Renaissance, one of the most common dances was the saltarello, an athletic dance form involving a vigorous jump or leap. Slightly later in the Renaissance, athletic dances such as high-vaulting voltas and energetic galliards were common entertainments mingled with exercise. Thoinot Arbeau's dance manual *Orchésographie* (1588) lauded the practice of dancing both for health reasons and as part of the pleasurable search for a mate. Arbeau explained at some length the many possible variations of the galliard; the basic pattern consisted of the dancer hopping onto the ball of one foot while moving the other forward in the air "as if to kick someone."[14] Men would attempt to impress their female partners with athletically and technically impressive virtuoso "tricks," including fast footwork, competitive hitch-kicks to a tassel raised high above the floor, pirouettes, or rapid air turns or beats ("capers"). Men and women, when dancing hand in hand, suited their styles to each other, but when dancing separately, their styles were strongly differentiated according to sex, the gentlemen displaying strength, elevation, and athletic prowess, and the ladies grace and

---

[12]   Julia Sutton, et al., "Dance," in *Grove Music Online*, Oxford Music Online. www.oxfordmusiconline.com.myaccess.library.utoronto.ca/subscriber/article/grove/music/45795 (accessed May 19, 2009).

[13]   William McNeill, *Keeping Together in Time: Dance and Drill in Human History* (Cambridge, Mass.: Harvard University Press, 1995), 2.

[14]   Julia Sutton, "Arbeau, Thoinot," in *Grove Music Online*, Oxford Music Online. www.oxfordmusiconline.com.myaccess.library.utoronto.ca/subscriber/article/grove/music/01163 (accessed May 18, 2009).

charm. According to Kate van Orden, in "the galliarde ... the male dancer had the opportunity to show his strength, fiery nature, and even aggression."[15] Van Orden also looks at the military connections of the French theatrical *ballet de cour*, in which she claims "musicians and professional dancers [became] an infantry under the command of nobles who command from above ... [for whom] sweating it out together on stage was not far from the closeness that came from shared blood sports, fencing, jousts, and fighting together in battle."[16] Thus the athleticism exhibited and required in many dances of the day was closely connected to the competitive nature of war and likely served to keep aristocratic men physically active and fit between actual battles.

During the baroque period dancing skills were cultivated daily by the nobility and their middle-class emulators and typically taught by ubiquitous dancing masters. The enervated flirtation and the exhibition through dance of feminine charms and lusty male prowess were considered to be healthy and desirable aspects of social intercourse. All occasions of state, great or small, required celebration and entertainment, often by dance, while personal aggrandizement, physically and sartorially, were natural concomitants of the theatrical and socially competitive ambience of such public events.

The nineteenth century saw a more rigid division between socially motivated dance and competitive sports. The twentieth century, however, witnessed much more blurring of the sports–dance division. Several Olympic sports, such as men's and women's figure skating, ice dancing, women's gymnastics and rhythmic gymnastics, and synchronized swimming have routines and movements that are also heavily choreographed and dance-inspired.

Recent controversies over the suitability of some dance-related sports, particularly competitive ballroom dancing—commonly referred to as "DanceSport"—for inclusion in the Olympic Games would seem to reinforce the particularly blurry relationship between sports and performing art. Many traditionalists in the dance community prefer to maintain and think of ballroom dance as a "performing art," while others see it as an "artistic sport." For several years the governing body of DanceSport has lobbied for its inclusion as an Olympic sport, comparable to ice dancing. On September 4, 1997, the International Olympic Committee (IOC) granted full recognition to the International DanceSport Federation as the sport's governing body. Actions to obtain IOC acceptance of DanceSport as a medal sport are currently still in progress.

In addition to blurring the line between competitive sports and art, ballroom dance plays with several aspects of identity ranging from gender to class. Men who ballroom dance are often over-determined as "men" through their upper-class, tuxedoed costuming but are simultaneously required to adopt typically feminine

---

[15]   Kate van Orden, *Music, Discipline, and Arms in Early Modern France* (Chicago: University of Chicago Press, 2005), 103.

[16]   Ibid., 105, 119.

qualities of graceful movement. Similarly, women in ballroom dance are often hyper-feminized in terms of their similarly upper-class gowns and makeup but are required to exhibit stereotypically masculine attributes of strength, stamina, and power on the dance floor. Despite requiring such gender-crossing attributes, DanceSport nonetheless requires an overt reinforcement of traditional gender roles, as men must be seen to stoically "lead" and women to "follow," while allowed more room for facial and bodily expression. Caroline Picart has even postulated that different kinds of dance specialists reinforce and enact racial stereotypes. "If the standard smooth categories [of dance—for instance, foxtrot and quickstep] enshrine whiteness, then the Latin and rhythm divisions ambivalently glorify its racialized exotic other, and it is important to note that the two types of competitions form a binary opposition—one needs the other in order to mark its place within the overall system."[17] Indeed, dancers cultivating the Latin dance types often tan themselves, an act one observer has called "putting on brownface," and wear particularly hypersexualized, revealing costumes that promote an association with an exotic Latin stereotype.

In recent years contemporary dance has, like rap, been tied to the competitive athleticism associated with breakdancing. Such athletic competitiveness is also reinforced in televised talent competitions, such as Fox television's wildly popular *So You Think You Can Dance*. As such, the interconnection of dance with sports and related cultures of health and fitness is perhaps more overtly pronounced now than at any time in history.

In the case of classical music performance, notwithstanding the perhaps increased psychological pressure to achieve "perfection," to a large extent it is the participation in a physical pursuit of excellence that links art to sports. Musicians and athletes both must attempt to create mistake-free performances that require finely tuned neural and muscle control enabled by countless hours of practice. For both activities, disciplining the body and mind is central to achieving what is typically considered a successful performance. Indeed one might posit that one of the prime objectives of art, as in sports, is to win recognition for the artist/performer's technical physical ability. Thus, in essence, even music becomes a competition for performers, who compete against their own bodies, if not those of others, in attaining recognition for their performances.

A Brief History of the Relationship Between Music and Athletics

Music and Athletics from Ancient Greece to the Renaissance

The ancient Greeks are widely understood to have been the first culture to incorporate competition into civic life. The public recognition of one's supremacy

---

[17] Caroline Joan Picart, *From Ballroom to DanceSport: Aesthetics, Athletics, and Body Culture* (New York: State University of New York Press, 2006), 94.

through open contest with others was known as *agōn*. Almost every area of Greek life was invested with the spirit of competition and rivalry, ostensibly so that the citizens might systematically better themselves individually and thus collectively empower the state. The prime manifestation of this principle was the foundation of the Olympic Games in 766 BC. Various mythographers also cemented this principle, particularly as it related to music. Ovid's *Metamorphoses* (vi. 383–7), for example, tells the story of Marsyas' *aulos* (a double reed pipe) contest with Apollo. Apollo won the competition, as judged by the muses, and had the satyr flayed.

Outside the realm of myth, however, the ancient Greeks held many festivals that encouraged musical as well as athletic competition. As depicted on fifth-century BC vases, the primary instrument involved in these competitions was the *kithara*, a lyre-like stringed instrument. The performer usually wore an elaborate costume, and both the performance and the compositions (virtuosic narrative works called *nomoi*) were evaluated by appointed judges. The lyrical subjects of the *nomoi* were often themselves based on mythic contests, such as that between Apollo and Python.[18] One of the earliest of such musical competitions was held as part of the Spartan festival of the Carneia in 670 BC, said to have been won by the poet Terpander. Similar musical and athletic contests were held throughout the Hellenistic era.

As outlined above, for the Greeks sports and the arts, including music, were intimately bound together in the cultivation of the whole individual. This integration stands in contrast to our customary Western notion of the two spheres existing in mutual isolation as mind–body opposites. For the Greeks, musical contests were a means of expressing aggression in a socially acceptable form and, in association with athletic competitions, had the added benefit of molding a mentally and physically fit society.

In the succeeding Roman era, this humanistic commonality between music and athletics seems to have been largely lost. In ancient Rome and on into the Byzantine era, music was commonly used merely to supplement chariot races and gladiatorial contests. Much as with the elaborate ceremonies and musical productions surrounding the modern Olympics or the Super Bowl, such events were often held on a spectacular scale. Priests would bless the event and the emperor would signal the beginning of a race by dropping a handkerchief. The intervals between contests and races would be marked by exhibitions of exotic African beasts, decorated floats, and parades of musicians,[19]—spectacles echoed today in the music and antics of mascots and cheerleaders. An increasing interest in blood sports—animal baiting for example—seems to have precluded a significant music–sports relationship during the remainder of the classical period.

---

[18]   Thomas Mathiesen, "Nomos," *Grove Music Online*. L. Macy (ed.), www.grovemusic.com (accessed March 5, 2006).

[19]   Richard Mandell, *Sport: A Cultural History* (New York: Columbia University Press, 1984), 107.

By the late middle ages, however, the sports–music relationship became more pronounced. Some genres of music were even directly inspired by sports. For example, songs known in Italy as the *caccia* or in France as the *chace* flourished from roughly 1345 to 1370. Both the French and Italian words translate as "hunt." These musical works consisted of two voices in strict imitation, effectively echoing or chasing each other and thus evoking both a literal and figurative imitation of a hunt. The lyrics, likewise, described a hunt, a fishing party, or some other animated scene, though they also often contained none too subtle allusions to the "hunt" for physical pleasure.

An example of a relatively rare work from the middle ages that directly references sports is the secular musical play *Jeu de Robin et de Marion*, attributed to the famous trouvère Adam de la Halle and dating to about 1284. The simple plot involves the shepherd Robin and a knight vying for the favor of maid Marion. The two adversaries, however, pursue different sports that are representative of their relative social status. Robin, the common shepherd, arrives from a game of football, while the aristocratic knight comes from a tournament, as he proclaims in the song "Je me repairoire du tournoiement." Of course the *jeu*, or game, alluded to in the play's title is, like the *caccia*, a clear reference to the game of love.

In succeeding centuries music and sports increasingly began to be linked through their common status as leisure activities. Mathias Gerung's oil on wood painting *Melancholia* (1558), for example, depicts a number of sports such as archery, knightly combat, and bowling side by side with other recreational activities such as music. Jousting tournaments, which first gained popularity in the fifteenth century, were surrounded by considerable pomp and pageantry in which music played a supportive role. Trumpets would announce the jousts and often short songs or odes, likely based on the family motto, were also sung or recited as knights entered the arena.

As real combat began to disappear in the sixteenth and seventeenth centuries, musical "tourneys" became increasingly popular, particularly at the ducal courts of northern Italy. These quasi-operatic productions were often staged by squadrons of horsemen, though they could also be performed on foot. No actual combat was involved, but the lyrical subject matter of these events usually represented a verbal battle over the relative merits of the various contestants. As such, these tourneys can been seen as precursors of contemporary rap "battles." The introduction and conclusion to these spectacles were sung in operatic style, while the choreographed contest itself would often be accompanied by dance music, typically played on trumpets and drums.[20] These musical and dance spectacles are echoed today in the use of music to introduce events and punctuate breaks of play in many contemporary professional sports such as football and basketball. Indeed, the great tournaments of the medieval and Renaissance eras may be compared to the Olympic Games of ancient Greece and to today's sporting spectaculars such as the World Cup, in that

[20]   Colin Timms, "Opera-Torneo," *New Groves Online*. L. Macy (ed.), www.grovemusic.com (accessed May 16, 2006).

they all function as exceptional ceremonialized festivals that identify and reinforce regional loyalties or principles.

The Renaissance era also saw a marked rise in popularity of early forms of tennis and handball games such *palo della mano*, *rachetta*, *palette*, and *calico* (an early form of soccer).[21] These sports were predicated on the ideal of taking aesthetic pleasure from participating in and performing the activities rather than winning. As such, they were analogous to the similar aesthetic pleasure gained from the aristocratic participation in madrigal singing and in various instrumental consorts. The non-combative participation in both sports and music at this time also had the additional benefit of producing larger numbers of spectators who took aesthetic pleasure in watching.

Seventeenth- and Eighteenth-century Musical Competition and Contests

The competitive nature of music is generally overlooked in critical theory; however, musical skill competitions have long fascinated audiences. The dramatic nature of the competition provides a rough narrative for audiences to follow— suggesting that such events are not so much concerts or performances as they are expressions of social rivalry and politics. Such occasions also provide an opportunity for audiences to become a part of the performance by taking sides— casting a vote or cheering for their favorite piece or performer. In the wake of the human blood-sport mentality of Roman gladiatorial combat, the impetus for such competitions can be found in the European proclivity for more controlled and ritualized combat between individuals, commonly known as the duel.

Dueling as a means of settling an argument or point of honor had few, if any, counterparts in classical cultures. The Roman historian Tacitus in his *Germania* claims that the prehistoric Germans might pit a captive of a hostile tribe against a tribal champion with the resulting outcome interpreted as an omen for a potential war.[22] Wherever the historical roots of dueling lie, the European moral psyche has long been ingrained with the notion that the gods favor the brave and strong. In the Christian era, duels (such as the biblical one between David and Goliath) evolved into a form of moral trial in which it was assumed that God would intervene by granting victory to the more just of the two disputants. The resultant judicial duel became permissible throughout European feudal society and in many places entered customary law. The dueling code became a unique and accepted practice throughout European aristocratic culture. In seventeenth-century France, for example, dueling was institutionalized in fencing schools and until World War I, duels were authorized by the Prussian army code to settle grave cases of personal difference.[23] The long

---

[21]   Cashmore, 101.

[22]   See Richard Mandell, *Sport: A Cultural History* (New York: Columbia Press, 1984), 115.

[23]   See Robert Baldick, *The Duel: A History of Dueling* (London: Chapman & Hall, 1965).

history of dueling fraternities in German universities (which continues to this day) also speaks to the persistence of formal combat in the European mindset. Thus the fascination with musical competition that arose in the seventeenth and eighteenth centuries was merely a less physically dangerous extension of this way of thinking.

I have already described the *kithara* competitions that marked the athletic festivals of ancient Greece. Musical competitions, however, are found throughout the course of music history. The ancient tradition of competitive singing in medieval German cities is relatively well known. Richard Wagner's opera *Die Meistersinger* (1868) is based on just such a contest. Musical competitions, however, had already become particularly common during the seventeenth and eighteenth centuries—concomitant with the rise of aristocratic dueling. Composition contests, for example, were often a feature of baroque courtly life. Louis XIV, for example, regularly held competitions to fill the most important musical posts in his kingdom. One of the more spectacular occurred in 1683, when 35 candidates for the position of *sous-maître* to the *chapelle* from across France were summoned to Versailles to perform their motets.

Singing competitions were also common in the baroque period. In 1624 Francesca Caccini, for example, was involved in an improvising contest with the singer-composer Andreana Basile. Caccini was judged to have had the deeper musical knowledge, while Basile to have the better voice and vocal agility.[24] More informal and perhaps more hotly contested rivalries between singers were also not unknown. The most famous of these was between the two *prima donne* Faustina Bordoni and Francesca Cuzzoni. The rivalry was so intense that factions in support of each singer disrupted a performance of Bononcini's *Astianatte* for London's Royal Academy of Music in 1727 and eventually resulted in the abrupt cancellation of the entire season, as the singers could no longer be heard above the whistling and catcalling from the audience.

Perhaps the most infamous musical contests and rivalries in the eighteenth century, however, were the numerous hotly contested keyboard contests. Eighteenth-century biographer John Mainwaring describes a keyboard skills competition between Domenico Scarlatti and George Frederick Handel that took place in 1707. The contest was arranged by Cardinal Ottoboni, and Scarlatti was adjudged to "some preference" on the harpsichord, but on the organ, "Scarlatti himself declared the superiority of his protagonist."[25]

An even more infamous keyboard contest took place on December 24, 1784. On this date Muzio Clementi was asked by the Emperor Josef II of Vienna to enter into a piano playing contest with Mozart for the amusement of the emperor's guests, the Grand Duke (later Tsar Paul I) and Duchess of Russia. The two were called upon to improvise on the piano and perform selections from their own

---

[24]   Suzanne G. Cusick, "Caccini," *Grove Music Online*. L. Macy (ed.), www. grovemusic.com (accessed January 24, 2006).

[25]   John Mainwaring, *Memoirs of the Life of the Late George Frederick Handel* (London, 1760), 59–60.

compositions. At the suggestion of the Grand Duchess, they both sight-read some sonatas by Giovanni Paisiello, "poorly written out in his own hand," according to Mozart in a letter to his father.[26] The emperor declared the competition a tie, though in subsequent letters relating the event to his father, Mozart described Clementi as "not having a penny's worth of taste or feeling" and his abilities as "mere mechanicus."[27]

In addition to technical singing and keyboard skill competitions, composition contests were also common during the seventeenth and eighteenth centuries. Promoting English music in the wake of Henry Purcell's death, one of the more infamous composition contests was the Prize Musick competition of 1701. The unique nature of this contest is worthy of some further analysis.

The competition saw William Congreve's masque libretto *The Judgement of Paris* set by John Eccles, Daniel Purcell, Gottfried Finger, and the eventual winner, John Weldon. The story is based on the incident that instigated the Trojan War, in which Paris is requested by Zeus to judge a beauty contest between three rival goddesses—Juno, Pallas Athena, and Venus—the last of whom is crowned queen of love and beauty after offering Paris the love of Helen.

Sponsored exclusively by liberal-oriented Whig party members (Lord Halifax, the Duke of Somerset, Anthony Henley, and Congreve himself), the event ostensibly presented an allegory of Whig political principles of individual liberty and freedom of choice. These principles were manifest both in Paris's autonomous judgment and in the judgment of the concert subscribers, who analogously decided the outcome of the competition through their applause. Weldon's surprising victory was contested by the other, more experienced composers. Notably, John Eccles, who came second, protested the outcome, claiming that he had been cheated by a faction of the audience that was predisposed to vote against him from the outset.

In Congreve's libretto, Paris's deliberations form the central part of the work. Unable to decide after each goddess has introduced herself, he asks them to disrobe, declaring that, "when each is undressed I'll judge of the best … since a gay Robe an ill shape may disguise … "[28] Thereupon each goddess attempts to influence Paris's judgment through various bribes. Roger Fiske speculates that during the performance, subsequent to Paris's request, the actresses actually disrobed to some extent.[29]

In typical fashion it is the male characters, Paris and Mercury (through Jove's authority), who control the destiny of the female goddesses and who thus wield

---

[26]   Letter dated January 16, 1782, reproduced in Robert Spaethling (ed./trans.), *Mozart's Letters, Mozart's Life* (New York: W.W. Norton & Co., 2000), 301.

[27]   Ibid.

[28]   Stoddard Lincoln, "The librettos and lyrics of William Congreve," *British Theatre and the Other Arts*, Shirley Strum Kenny (ed.) (Washington D.C.: Folger Shakespeare Libraries, 1984) 116–32.

[29]   Roger Fisk, *English Theatre Music in the Eighteenth Century* (London: Oxford University Press, 1986).

the real power. The goddesses are all portrayed as being manipulative, deceitful, and overly concerned with physical beauty, ultimately lowering themselves to the pastoral equivalent of a cat fight to decide the issue. In contrast to the irrationality displayed by the goddesses, Paris assumes the practical and traditionally patriarchal role of the judge. Venus wins the competition by offering Paris true love in the form of Helen of Sparta, the epitome of mortal feminine beauty. Paris is helpless to resist Venus's offer, and he awards her "the Prize" of a golden apple.

The sexual politics of Paris's judgment resonates strongly with Naomi Wolf's definition of the "beauty myth": "The qualities that a given period calls beautiful in women are merely symbols of the female behavior that period considers desirable: *the beauty myth is always actually prescribing behavior and not appearance.* Competition between women is part of the myth so that women will be divided from one another."[30]

As such, *The Judgement of Paris* and the Prize Musick competition reinforce a long tradition that has stereotypically sexualized the nature of female competition. Picasso's *The Race* (1922), for example, depicts two women runners whose tops have slipped down to reveal a breast, and Canadian painter Alex Colville's *Skater* (1964) invites the viewer to gaze at the female skater's conspicuous Lycra-clad buttocks. Reinforced by scenarios outlined in the Prize Musick competition and in the rivalries engendered by operatic divas, and epitomized in the competition between Faustina and Cuzzoni, these depictions reinforce an artistic and theatrical tradition that depicts women engaged in competition but positioned, dressed, or undressed in a way that tempts salacity.

A more direct, yet extremely rare, example of a sports-related theme involving music from this period can be found in Pietro Metastasio and Antonio Caldara's opera *L'Olimpiade*, which premiered in Venice in 1733. The opening scene of Act I, for example, is a descriptive evocation of the Olympic atmosphere of ancient Greece, portraying the religious rituals, the mass excitement, the sports, the rules, and the prizes. Act II specifically opens at the ruins of an ancient hippodrome. The Olympic site serves mostly as a backdrop to the typical *opera seria* plot devices of courtly conflict between honor and friendship. The ideals embodied in this opera, however, highly influenced Baron de Courbertin's vision of the modern Olympic Games and his subsequent desire to see music integrated into the event.[31]

Eighteenth-century Sportization

In keeping with the neo-Cartesian idea that music and the arts edify the mind while sports edify the body, the pursuit of sports is often thought of as antithetical

---

[30]   Naomi Wolf, *The Beauty Myth* (Toronto: Random House, 1990), 4.

[31]   Jeffrey O. Segrave, "Music as sport history: The special case of Pietro Metastasio's L'Olimpiade and the story of the Olympic Games," in *Sporting Sounds: Relationships Between Sports and Music*, Anthony Bateman and John Bale (eds) (London: Routledge, 2009), 113–27.

to and a diversion from the scientific rationality of other areas of human activity. However, this dichotomy was challenged in the eighteenth century, when sports began to be influenced by the same technologies and rational controls that were influencing industry. Sports theorist Norbert Elias has referred to this development as "sportization"—the process through which precise rules governing contests arose to ensure fairness.[32] The eighteenth century witnessed the advent of self-restraint and government-imposed order to combat violence and social chaos, which in turn brought about the rise of impersonal organizations to maintain rules and govern personal behavior. This development reflected a general tendency in Europe toward interdependence, as people began to orient their activities to each other and to rely less on their own individual subsistence efforts and more on the efforts of others, whose tasks would be specialized and geared toward increasingly narrow objectives. In effect, it was a team mentality, a collectivity of individual contribution toward group subsistence, that began to take effect. Something of this same "team building" mentality can also be found in the rise of orchestras in the mid-eighteenth century in places such as the court of Mannheim, which saw increasingly refined instrumental specialists brought from all over Europe to perform together as coherent integrated units.

In England the industrial revolution ushered in an era of commercialized leisure that saw an expansion in the audiences and venues for both music and sports. An increasingly wealthy populace prized leisure more as its prosperity grew. As such, the growing popularity of social clubs, coffeehouses, and holiday activities (such as swimming and boating), as well as various organized sports and musical activities, demonstrated how Britons increasingly spent their surplus time and wealth in the pursuit of pleasurable leisure pursuits.

Hugh Cunningham, in his book *Leisure in the Industrial Revolution*, particularly cites the influence of alcohol sales—specifically competition among public houses—as the reason for an expansion in blood-sport facilities.[33] The construction of cockpits in inns and taverns illustrates the burgeoning opportunity for profiting from spectatorship during this period. In similar fashion, the late seventeenth and early eighteenth centuries saw the first public music rooms and pleasure gardens being established, also often in conjunction with alcohol sales. As social historian Geoffrey Holmes states, "By the 1720s taverns had entered the serious music business, as they had much else; not even an oratorio was beyond the ambition of London's largest inns."[34] Moreover, in 1726 one of the earliest societies dedicated to the preservation of older styles of music, the Academy of Ancient Music, began meeting at the Crown and Anchor tavern in the Strand, while other musical societies met at a variety of different taverns. It should be

---

[32] Elias, 151.

[33] Hugh Cunningham, *Leisure in the Industrial Revolution, c. 1780–1880* (New York: St. Martin's Press, 1980).

[34] Geoffrey Holmes and Daniel Szechi, *The Age of Oligarchy: Pre-industrial Britain 1722–1783* (London: Longman, 1993), 208.

recognized, of course, that even in today's marketplace alcohol sales still remain a significant commonality in both the music and sports industries. Nonetheless, throughout the eighteenth and nineteenth centuries, both sports and music gained substantial audiences and infrastructure from Britain's increasing cult of leisure.

That the organization of many sports (such as football, rugby, boxing, and tennis) and a fascination with various musical contests arose in England at this time, and were subsequently exported to other European nations, has been the topic of considerable conjecture. Though he has been criticized for being somewhat Anglocentric in his views,[35] sports theorist Norbert Elias provides perhaps the most plausible explanation. Elias traces the English proclivity for nonviolent, rules-oriented competition to the rise of parliament and the pacification of the aristocracy and upper classes:

> ... since sustained tensions form an integral part of a parliamentary regime with its numerous non-violent battles according to firmly established rules, the level of tension-tolerance as part of the social habitus of a people has some bearing on the functioning of such a regime. In that respect, a parliamentary regime shows affinity with sport-games.[36]

Parliament, in addition to curbing the power of the monarchy, united hostile factions (Whig and Tory political parties) in a gentlemanly code of conduct such that they learned to trust one another sufficiently for a successfully productive form of nonviolent contest. The peaceful surrendering of government from one faction to another presupposed a high level of trust and self-restraint, attributes that were at the heart of the increasingly codified worlds of both the concert hall and sporting events. It is also worth mentioning that one of the significant attributes of the English parliamentary system was the right to free assembly, which in turn led to the formation of numerous "clubs" and societies. Such organizations of like-minded individuals might engage in particular sporting activities but could also be devoted to musical or other cultural or philosophic endeavors. The advent of clubs—sporting, musical, or other—resulted in local codifications of conduct, rules, and traditions. Consequently these clubs not only eventually led to the founding of famous soccer/football teams such as Manchester United, but also, in the case of musical societies such as the Academy of Ancient Music, to the establishment of a semi-regularized canon of musical works considered worthy of being preserved and performed—resulting in our modern-day classical concert-going experience.[37]

---

[35] See Richard Giulianotti, *Sport: A Critical Sociology* (Cambridge, UK: Polity, 2005), 149.

[36] Elias, 28.

[37] For more on this evolution see William Weber, *The Rise of Musical Classics in Eighteenth-Century England: A Study in Canon, Ritual, and Ideology* (Oxford: Clarendon, 1992).

The increasingly nonviolent and safe nature of the political process resulted in a similar desire to remove the chances of actual violence and injury in sporting contests. Rather than dampening enthusiasm for such apparently conditioned artificial events, these changes brought a marked growth in spectator interest. As in many other leisure activities, including music, sports moved into the realm of providing an imaginary imitation of a real-life setting or situation but without any of the associated dangers or risks. This mimetic experience meant that spectators of a football match could savor the excitement of the ebb and flow of the game, while simultaneously being reassured that little or no harm would come to either the players on the field or themselves. In the words of Elias, the mimetic pleasure associated with sports is that which is achieved by a "controlled de-controlling of emotions."[38]

To a large extent the same holds true of the concert experience that employs an artificial setting (think of the opulence of most symphonic halls or the spectacle of a rock show) in which audience members mimetically experience a wide range of emotions from fear and sorrow to triumph and joy. In the case of a classical music concert, in marked contrast to a sporting event, the physical movements of the performers are highly controlled, as are those of the audience—largely limited to applauding at the end of a work. But looking back to the time of Haydn or Beethoven, many movements and musical effects were specifically designed to elicit applause or other forms of acclamation as pleasurable releases from the tension produced by the music. Though the mimetic experience of a classical music audience is very comparable to that of a sports audience (the thrill of seeing one's team score a goal can be no less profound than that experienced by someone enjoying the climax of a great symphony), the link between motion and emotion is more overt for both audiences and players of popular music, who are much freer to react vocally and bodily to the ebb and flow of the experience. Audiences and performers of popular and dance music styles, with their concomitant freedom to react spontaneously and physically move around either onstage or by dancing, head bobbing, or fist pumping, provide a much closer analogue to the pleasurable decontrolling of the body and emotions experienced in sports.

Throughout the seventeenth and eighteenth centuries, both sports and music evolved from spontaneous amateur activities into increasingly regularized and specialized events. Roger North, writing as early as 1720, lamented the way that music had been driven out of the practical domestic realm of the average citizen and into the hands of technically accomplished professionals, performing to passive audiences.[39] To a large degree both industrialization and sportization, as outlined above, were symptomatic of an underlying transformation of European societies that demanded of their individual members greater regularity and differentiation of conduct.[40] Races, for example, began to be precisely regulated

---

[38]   Elias, 44.

[39]   Holmes, 208.

[40]   Elias, 151.

in terms of distance. Times were also more accurately measured, recorded, and compared. In 1867 the Queensbury Rules were devised to favor the importance of skill in deciding the outcome of boxing matches; the introduction and padding of gloves and the banning of kicking can all be viewed as part of a civilizing process that was at work. The sport of fox hunting, as it arose in the late eighteenth century, was also bound by a strict code of etiquette and idiosyncratic rules, such as the one forbidding the killing of other animals during the hunt.[41] Much as the metronome began to more precisely regulate and control musical time, tempo, and indeed the performing body, the same rational controls, stemming from industrial advances, started to rein in sports. As the scientific impulse to analyze and quantify began to regulate industrial practice, so it influenced the regulation of sports and its concomitant artistic expression.[42]

Nineteenth-century Sportization and Musical Contests

In the nineteenth century the twin forces of industrialization and urbanization reflected an increasingly competitive world-view, as embodied in the increasing fascination with both sporting and musical contests. Perhaps the ultimate manifestation of this need for order and competitive quantification, at least as far as sports are concerned, was Baron de Coubertin's founding of the modern Olympic Games in 1896. The hallmark values of the industrial age were rational progress, uniformity, and standardization. These were also key to de Coubertin's vision of a comprehensive exhibition of sports, with each being quantified, ranked, and rewarded according to objective standards of excellence.[43]

The rebirth of the Olympics also saw a revival of the associated musical festivities of the ancient Greek games. On March 25, 1896, in Athens an orchestra played the first "Olympic Hymn," written by the poet Kostis Palamas and set to music by the well-known Greek composer Spiros Samaras. Samaras's work remained the official Olympic Hymn until 1912, when various new hymns were

---

[41]   Elias, 90.

[42]   Something of this proclivity to analyze and quantify is manifest in the increasingly faithful and detailed artistic representations of sports. Consider, for example, the precise detail found in George Stubbs's *Anatomy of a Horse*, first published 1766. The subsequent fascination in representations of horse racing and horse-related sports such as fox hunting proliferated among English and American artists. In *Sports: A Cultural History of the Mirror of Art*, Peter Kühnst argues that many works of art in the nineteenth century, such as Théodore Géricault's *The Derby at Epsom* (1821), "show the transformation of physical exercises from static exhibitions of skill to lively achievement oriented contests" (Dresden: Verlag der Kühnst, 1996), 140.

[43]   It should be noted that more recently sports models of management, whereby group interaction is solidified and strengthened through the encouragement of individual contributions, has largely replaced the top-down management style. The emphasis on corporate "team building" has become a common workplace mantra.

tried every four years. Samaras's music returned for the games of 1960 and continues to be used today at the opening and closing ceremonies.

In imitation of the ancient Greek games and inspired by Antonio Caldara's opera *L'Olimpiade*, as outlined above, de Coubertin felt the modern games needed to integrate sports and the arts. His zeal led to the creation of Olympic festival competitions in music, sculpture, painting, literature, and architecture in 1912. Winners of the so-called "Pentathlon of the Muses" were, like their athletic counterparts, awarded gold, silver, and bronze medals. The competitions were held in association with the Olympics from 1912 to 1948 (three were cancelled— in 1916, 1940, and 1944—because of war). The first composer to win a gold medal in music was Italy's Ricardo Barthelemy in 1912 for his "Triumphal Olympic March." The fine arts competitions were often extremely well attended. The 1932 festival held in conjunction with the Los Angeles Olympics, for example, occupied 15 galleries, included 1,100 exhibits, and drew crowds in the neighborhood of 384,000 people.[44]

Several of the leading names in music at the time were sought for judging the entries; for instance, Paul Dukas, Maurice Ravel, and Igor Stravinsky were recruited as judges in 1924 for the Paris Competitions. Indeed, some of modern history's best-known composers tried their hand at composing music for particular moments in Olympic ceremonies and rituals, including Richard Strauss with his "Olympische Hymne" (for mixed chorus) for the 1936 Games in Berlin[45] and Jean Sibelius with his "Song of the Athenians" Op. 31, No. 3 (for boys' chorus, male chorus, and orchestra) for the closing ceremonies of Helsinki's 1952 Olympic Games.

The competitions suffered, however, because in addition to increasingly prohibitive costs, judges deemed many of the entries substandard and refused to award medals. Another sticking point was the amateur rule, which forbade professional artists and composers from participating in the games and thereby prevented juried contributions from the artistic elite. After 1948 the arts competitions were abandoned, and the host cities focused instead on the cultural festival held in the run-up to and throughout the games. Music has, nonetheless, remained especially prominent at the opening and closing ceremonies. The opening ceremonies, for example, include a substantial amount of prescribed music. In addition to the ancillary performances by popular entertainers and songs programmed by the local organizers, the Olympic Hymn is sung, as is the national anthem of the host country.

Indeed, new Olympic theme music is produced every four years. Five-time Oscar winner John Williams, famous for scoring movies such as *Star Wars* and

---

[44]   William K. Guegold, *One Hundred Years of Olympic Music: Music and Musicians of the Modern Olympic Games, 1896–1996* (Mantua, Ohio: Golden Clef Publishing, 1996), 6.

[45]   A somewhat abbreviated version of the "Olympische Hymne" can be heard on the soundtrack to the closing sequence of part one of Leni Riefenstahl's *Olympia*, the film of the 1936 Olympics.

E.T., has written four Olympic themes and won an Emmy for "Summon the Heroes," the theme of the 1996 games in Atlanta. Additional Olympic music by Williams includes "Fanfare Olympique" (1984, Los Angeles), "Olympic Spirit" (1988, Seoul), and "Call of the Champions" (2002, Salt Lake City). In talking about his Olympic music, however, Williams reinscribes the traditional binary surrounding music (mind) versus sports (body) that, at least in part, this book seeks to disassemble.

> I think of music and art as being mind/spiritual and sport being physical. Those are dissimilarities. There are strong reflections of artistic or spiritual things that get into athletic performances. They come together in ballet, taking it literally. Ballet is, to us at least, all of these. It is athleticism, it is art and it's all this brought together.[46]

In addition to Olympic hymns and theme music, the games have inspired a variety of other musical connections. The 1988 Games in Seoul, for example, featured a 3-meter-wide and 88-meter high music fountain, which was capable of changing more than 1,400 times and of playing 140 different songs.[47] Perhaps de Coubertin said it best, after the 1896 revival of the Olympic Games, when he remarked, "Fashions [have changed] over two thousand years, but music has remained the factor which best conveys the emotion within a crowd, and which best accompanies the amplitude of a great spectacle."[48] The singing of national anthems before major sporting events that continues to this day would seem to lend considerable credence to this statement.

The fascination with musical contests in their various formats that marked the eighteenth century continued to evolve through the nineteenth century and even to the present day. The nineteenth century saw, for example, the advent of one of the most venerable composition competitions—the prestigious Prix de Rome. The winner of the contest receives a funded period of compositional study in Rome

---

[46] Guegold, xi.

[47] Music was also prominently featured at the most recent 2010 Winter Olympics held in Vancouver Canada. Indeed the opening and closing ceremonies were something of an exercise in nation building through popular music, showcasing many of Canada's biggest recording stars. In addition to Nikki Yanofsky's "I Believe," the official Olympic theme song which went to No. 1 on the Canadian pop singles charts, the opening ceremonies were highlighted by k.d. lang's stirring version of Leonard Cohen's "Hallelujah," Bryan Adams and Nellie Furtado's rendition of "Bang the Drum," an aerial dance number set to Joni Mitchell's "Both Sides Now" and Sarah McLachlan's solo rendition of "Ordinary Miracle." Ann Murray, one of the best selling Canadian pop singers of all time, was one of the notable Canadian personalities chosen to carry the official Olympic flag into the stadium.

[48] As quoted in David Gilman Romano, "Culture and tradition: The ancient Olympic Games," for the Salt Lake City Organizing Committee of the 2002 Winter Olympic Games. www.weberpl.lib.ut.us/roughdraft/2002/RDwinter02/tradition.htm.

awarded by the French Académie des Beaux-Arts. This contest was held annually from 1803 to 1968 with the intent of fostering French culture. Designed to test the competitors' knowledge of music as both an art and a science, it comprised associated exercises in writing counterpoint, fugue, and harmony, with a later round involving a four- or five-week sequestered composition of an operatic scene for one or more voices based on a common text. Notable competitors included Hector Berlioz, who eventually won the event after four attempts, and Maurice Ravel, who competed five times without winning.[49]

The nineteenth century was also the great age of military music, a form that, particularly in North America, stimulated a notable culture of competition. In the wake of the American Civil War, it is estimated that the Union Army had some 500 bands with over 9,000 players. In 1889 *Harper's Weekly* estimated that more than 10,000 military bands were active in the United States, bands that in some cases provided the only source of music available in smaller towns.[50] During this period the participation of bands at sporting events became increasingly important, and at the end of the nineteenth century, pre-game and half-time performances at football games were common. Professional bandmasters at schools such as Cornell, the University of Illinois, and Ohio State soon replaced student directors, and the quality of the performances and transcriptions significantly improved. This popularity declined in the wake of World War I in the face of competition from radio, recordings, and motion pictures. To stimulate consumer demand for their products, a number of musical instrument manufacturers later began to organize the first national school band contest in Chicago in June 1923. Response was such that by 1941, there were some 562 bands (including nearly 34,000 students) participating in contests held under the auspices of the National School Band Association.[51]

Twentieth and Twenty-first Centuries: Increasing Convergences

Following World War II, the notion of "friendly" competition in music continued to exert a hold on the public imagination. In particular, a variety of classical music competitions began during this period. Similar to the proclivity for composition contests, and as presaged in the keyboard battles of Mozart and Handel, contemporary Western culture witnessed the rise of many pressure-packed talent competitions. The International Tchaikovsky Competition in Moscow, for

---

[49]   Among the most high-profile contemporary composition contests is the Eurovision Song Contest. Begun in 1956, this contest sees representative songwriters and performers of various European nations competing on behalf of their nation in an Olympic style event. Perhaps the most notable act to compete to date has been ABBA, whose song "Waterloo" won in April 1974.

[50]   Trevor Herbert, "American wind bands," *Grove Music Online*. L. Macy (ed.), www.grovemusic.com (accessed April 10, 2008).

[51]   Ibid.

example, has been one of the most prestigious classical music competitions in the world since its inception in 1958. Like the modern Olympic Games, it takes place every four years. Prizes are awarded for violin, cello, male vocal, female vocal, and piano. The last category has perhaps produced the most high profile winners, including Van Cliburn in 1958 and Vladimir Ashkenazy in 1962. Rivaling the profile of the Tchaikovsky Competition is the Van Cliburn International Piano Competition, held in Fort Worth, Texas, since 1962. It, too, is held every four years, with the victors winning substantial cash prizes and a concert tour.

The metaphor of athletics has also often been applied to piano competitions. As discussed by Lisa McCormick, the 1977 Van Cliburn competition employed posters and brochures featuring "a time-line of legendary Olympic athletes through history—from Jesse Owens in Berlin 1936 to Nadia Comăneci in Montreal 1976—leading up to the 1977 Cliburn in Fort Worth where the next 'legend' could be found."[52] The same year the composer and jury member, Alberto Ginastera, claimed, "These young pianists [Cliburn competitors] are the athletes of music; competing is their glory."[53]

Such analogies further reinforce the bodily and social connection between musicians and athletes. At their heart the very idea of competition, whether musical or athletic, is a socially acceptable means to construct and systematize inequality—through talent, ability or just mere chance. In all cases a champion is declared, placing them, if only temporarily, on a higher social level than their peers. This sanctioned reinforcement of inequality applies equally well to both musical and athletic competition from any era and influences many of the synergistic music-sport constructions of class, race, and gender identity discussed in this book. Whether it is the bragging rights acquired by winning the World Cup or *American Idol*, such victories can be, and often are, interpreted by audiences as analogous metaphoric proof of the superiority of the winner's nationality, ethnicity, race or gender.

Adding to the largely art-music-based competitions that proliferated in the seventeenth, eighteenth, and nineteenth centuries, the twentieth century witnessed the advent of a plethora of popular musical skills contests. Cutting contests, for example, were originally a regular feature of jazz and featured soloists competing to determine which musician had superior improvisatory skill. Often occurring spontaneously during jam sessions, such competitions later also became a regular feature of hip hop culture. These contests arose in part as a substitute for violent gang disputes, and thus were an extension of the dueling mentality. As discussed in more detail in Chapter 5, the 1930s and 1940s witnessed a particularly fertile period of interaction between African American sports such as boxing, baseball, and basketball and music styles such as jazz and blues.

---

[52]   Lisa McCormick, "Higher, faster, louder: Representations of the international music competition," *Cultural Sociology* 3/1 (2009), 5–30, 11.

[53]   As quoted in McCormick, 11.

The use of organ music to accompany sports such as baseball and hockey was also a tradition stemming from the mid-twentieth century. Music during the course of a sporting event first appeared in the 1800s, when brass bands strolled through the stands at baseball games. Organ music, however, did not debut until 1941 at Chicago's Wrigley Field. Even then, it did not immediately catch on, nor has it been unanimously admired by fans over the years. During the 1970s, the *Sporting News* published letters complaining that organs "detract from the game" and should be "removed and put back in church where they belong."[54] In recent years organists have become relatively rare. They have been largely replaced by recordings, typically of rock classics or current Top 40 hits. Ironically, though, the recordings are sometimes of organ music (often sounding an imitation of a military bugle "charge"), played repeatedly during intermissions and stoppages of play.

The increasing public preoccupation with leisure in the nineteenth and early twentieth centuries, particularly in England and North America, saw the advent of a flourishing tradition of amateur parlor songs devoted to sports and athletic activities. Encompassing a wide variety of sports, the phenomenon spanned a period of some 80 years, generally dying out in the 1930s during the Great Depression.

In England audiences were likely to demand parlor songs dealing with cricket or horse racing, and both sports have a long history of musical settings. Cricketers, for example, appear on the title page of the sheet music for Matthias von Holst's "Village Rondo" written in 1812. There are many cricketing songs, exemplified by "Willow the King (Farmer)" and "The Cricketers of Hambledon" by Peter Warlock, and Alfred Scott-Gatty's "Cricket." Dancers in Victorian ballrooms enjoyed instrumental tunes such as the "Raniitsinhji Waltz," "The Merry Cricketers' Polka," and one dedicated to Dr W.G. Grace, "Cricket Bat Polka." Also, Albert Coates's opera *Pickwick* contained a cricket fugue, and the music for the film *The Final Test*, released in 1953, was by Benjamin Frankel.

Horse racing invaded the lighter musical theater on a surprising number of occasions: *Newmarket* (1896: music by J.M. Capel, John Crook, and others), *The Gentleman Jockey* (1907: music by George Ess), *Derby Day* (1932: composed in tribute to Gilbert and Sullivan by A.P. Herbert and Alfred Reynolds, featuring tipsters, jockeys, and a chorus of Pearly Kings), no fewer than three shows about horse racing with music by Billy Mayerl—*Sporting Love* (1932), *Twenty-to-One* (1935), and *Over She Goes* (1936)—all popular productions, though perhaps none more so than the "Ascot Gavotte" from *My Fair Lady* (1956).

The Derby also figures in William Alwyn's "Derby Day Overture," inspired by Frith's painting, in Robert Farnon's orchestral miniature "Derby Day" and in the similarly titled 1952 film with music by Anthony Collins. Other racing films included *The Galloping Major* (1951) with music by Georges Auric and *Grand*

---

54   Quoted in Roy Rivenburg, "Ballpark organists: They're out," *Los Angeles Times*, Saturday, June 11, 2005.

National Night (1953) with music by John Greenwood. Of all the racing songs, likely the best-known are Stephen Foster's "Camptown Races" (1850) and George "Geordie" Ridley's anthem "Blaydon Races" (1862), which is particularly popular in the north of England.

England was not the only country interested in sports-themed music, however. In the late nineteenth and early twentieth centuries, several art music composers turned their attention to themes revolving around modern contemporary life, including the increasing fascination with sports. Most of these increasingly modernist works were descriptively programmatic in nature, evoking the movements and events of the sports to which their titles allude. Leos Janácek, for example, wrote *Music for Gymnastic Exercises* (1895) and Jean Sibelius composed *Ballspiel in Trianon* (1899). French composer Arthur Honegger wrote an orchestral movement entitled *Rugby* (1928) and the ballet *Skating Rink* (1922). Similarly, Czech composer Bohslav Martinu wrote an orchestral *rondo* entitled *Half-time* (1922), which depicted the events surrounding a football match. Likely the most famous piece of this type, however, is Claude Debussy's *Jeux (Games)* (1912). *Jeux* (originally intended to accompany a ballet) was written for Serge Diaghilev's Ballets Russes to choreography by Nijinsky. The short melodic motives and constantly shifting rhythms are likely meant to be, at least in part, evocative of the flow of a tennis match. To some extent the modernist aesthetic of expanding the traditional notions of beauty and ability—often manifest in the incorporation of both motoristic and extremely flexible rhythmic nuances, and a propensity for crafting moments of palpable harmonic tension—found a natural outlet in the evocation of sports and sports themes.

At much the same time the realm of popular music saw a burgeoning market for sheet music involving sports themes suitable for playing by amateurs. In Canada, for example, a brief survey of the national library and archives turns up the following offerings: John Holt's "La Crosse" (1867), Mrs. H.S. Scadding's "The Cricketers' Waltzes" (1882), Elmer Smith's "Rugby March" (1896), "The Roarin' Game: A Song for Curling" (190?), the golfing ballad "Far and Sure" by Edward Atherton (1903), Charles Wellinger's "Come with Me for a Roller Skate: The Roller Skating Song Craze" (1907), Homer Boucher's "The Baseball Fan" (1912), Dyer Hurden's "Bowling Song" (1917), Ernest Dunn's "Hockey" (1929), and Doug Romaine's ode to one of Canada's favorite figure skaters, Barbara Ann Scott, called "Barbara Ann" (1947).

During the late nineteenth and early twentieth centuries, North America saw the advent of numerous such songs devoted to individual sports such as golf and football (particularly college football "fight songs"). More than any other sport at this time, however, baseball dominated the American musical imagination. Baseball is enmeshed in a history of tradition and ritual, and fans have been enveloped in baseball lore since its invention. The first recorded song referring to baseball was "The Baseball Polka," written in 1858. The Library of Congress has published a bibliography containing over 400 songs dedicated to the subject of baseball.[55]

By far the most popular baseball song and, indeed, one of the most popular sports-themed songs of any kind, is "Take Me Out to the Ball Game." Now considered baseball's unofficial anthem, the song is sung in ballparks throughout the United States. The song was written by Jack Norworth in 1908, beginning life as a poem about baseball, and subsequently set to piano parlor music composed by Tin Pan Alley composer Albert Von Tilzer. The song was popularized by various vaudeville acts and became one of the top-selling songs (in sheet music and piano rolls) of 1908. Though it is sung by baseball fans around the world and at many amateur and major league ballparks, it was the legendary Chicago broadcaster Harry Caray who instigated the song's association with the "seventh inning stretch." First at the Chicago White Sox ballpark Comiskey Park from 1976 to 1981 and then at the Cubs' Wrigley Field from 1982 until his death in 1997, Caray would enthusiastically lead the stadium crowds in a sing-along of the song between the halves of the seventh inning. In what has become one of baseball's most hallowed and beloved traditions, a variety of celebrity guest vocalists—including Bill Murray, Jeff Gordon, Muhammad Ali, Ozzy Osbourne, and Eddie Vedder—continue to lead the fans at Wrigley in singing the anthem.

Such sporting songs reflect a preoccupation with leisure and are, at least in part, the sonic manifestations of a wealthy society whose economic success enables participation in non-essential musical and sporting activities. However, with the onset of the Great Depression in the 1930s, such lighthearted fare as the sports-themed parlor song was no longer appropriate and, denoting a general decline in leisure activities as a whole, the genre essentially died off by the onset of World War II.

Post-World War II Pop/Rock and Sports

Notwithstanding the impressive cross-pollination of African American music and sports (discussed in detail in Chapter 5), and though there are several prominent historical instances of the confluence of sports *themes* in music, notably in baseball as outlined above, sports has only occasionally formed the thematic basis of pop/rock tunes. One can point to Queen's "Bicycle Race," Kraftwerk's "Tour de France," and even the cult Canadian country singer Stompin' Tom Connors's rendition of "The Hockey Song (The Good Old Hockey Game)"—a staple feature of almost every Canadian hockey game—as examples of this type of relatively rare sports–music connection.

As discussed previously, classical music has from time to time incorporated sports themes. In addition to parlor songs, among the more famous works based

---

[55]   Bibliography of published baseball music and songs in the collections of the Music Division at the Library of Congress. www.loc.gov/rr/perform/baseballbib.html (accessed May 13, 2009).

on, or including references to, sports and athletics are the common use of Orff's *Carmina Burana* to rile up basketball crowds during pre-game festivities, Eric Satie's "Sports et Divertissements" (20 piano cameos of various sports including hunting, golf, and tennis), Georges Bizet's *Carmen*, and Mike Reid's contemporary opera *Different Fields*.

Other classical associations include the Three Tenors concerts, which were first held in conjunction with the soccer World Cup tournament of 1990, and Freddie Mercury and Montserrat Caballé's memorable duet "Barcelona," a theme song of the 1992 Barcelona Olympics. Notably, one of the earliest English football chants was also set by Edward Elgar. An avid fan of the Wolverhampton Wanderers, Elgar set the lyrics "He Banged the Leather for Goal!" to a tune that he later reused in his oratorio *Caractacus*. At the risk of stretching the point, one of the most infamous recent sports–classical music connections is by Peter Schickele (a.k.a. PDQ Bach) and his well-known comedy work "New Horizons in Music Appreciation." A perennial favorite of music appreciation instructors, this work consists of a mostly straightforward rendition of the first movement sonata form of Beethoven's *Fifth Symphony* supplemented by two sports commentators providing a play-by-play of the performance, complete with enthusiastic crowd noises. The work (subtitled a "concert cast") is thus comically reinterpreted as a professional athletic competition between the orchestra and conductor.

Though, as has been outlined, connections between classical music and sports are relatively rare, there is evidence that this generalization may be changing. Recently a number of symphony orchestras, largely in attempts to increase their audience bases, have been actively fostering ties with amateur and professional sports. In January 2008, for example, the Topeka Symphony Orchestra presented a program entitled "The Wide World of Sports," a pop concert of musical works inspired by sports and athletic endeavors. The concert was intended to introduce a wider audience, including young people, to classical music.[56] In an interview the director of the symphony, John Strickler, claimed, "Since 2008 is an Olympic year, we'll begin with the fanfare John Williams wrote for the Los Angeles Olympic Games ... From there, we'll explore many different Olympic sports as depicted in music, including skiing, skating, gymnastics, tennis and boxing ... "[57]

---

[56] Bill Blankenship, "Symphony takes swing at music of sports world," *The Capital-Journal*, Sunday, January 6, 2008.

[57] Director John Strickler, as quoted in Blankenship. The Topeka audiences also heard Emile Waldteufel's "Skater's Waltz," Carter Pann's "Slalom," Nikolai Rimsky-Korsakov's "Dance of the Tumblers," Danny Gould's "Tennis, Anyone?" and an arrangement of highlights from Bill Conti's score for the film *Rocky* (1976). The orchestra also played music from *Chariots of Fire* (1981), a film depicting the 1924 Paris Olympics, from the Oscar-winning score by Vangelis. Archery was represented with music from *Robin Hood: Prince of Thieves* (1991) by Michael Kamen, and hiking and mountaineering through the music Tom Myron wrote for the film *Wilderness and Spirit: A Mountain Called Katahdin* (2002). Finally, the orchestra played Randol Alan Bass's musical setting for the Ernest L.

A similar sports-related classical performance occurred on February 20, 2008, when the Montreal Symphony Orchestra staged a concert entitled "Hockey Legends" in tribute to the game of hockey and in honor of the one hundredth anniversary of the home team Montreal Canadians. Montreal Symphony Orchestra music director Kent Nagano conducted the concert, which was described as "an encounter of symphonic music and the collective imagination of Quebec."[58] Nagano justified the concert in the following manner: "All of us need heroes ... heroes inspire us."[59]

The concert featured music by Québécois composer François Dompierre and followed the story of a fictional young man who dreams of being in the National Hockey League. In an unusual twist, and likely an attempt to draw hockey fans into the concert hall, legendary former players of the Canadians, including Guy Lafleur, Henri Richard, Yvan Cournoyer, Pierre Bouchard, Stéphane Quintal, and Réjean Houle, took part in the spoken word portion of the event.

Such intermingling of sports and classical music continues to be somewhat exceptional. As will be discussed in succeeding chapters, vis-à-vis popular music the relationship has been much more closely aligned in terms of mutual aesthetic influences and cross-marketing. Instances of sports themes and subject matter in popular music, however, are strangely few and far between. To some extent this scarcity may be attributed to the fact that the relationship between sports and popular music has been often unstable and at times even antagonistic. The rise of rock 'n' roll saw the advent of a glamorous career choice that, particularly for young men, promised a life of pleasure, adulation, power, and satisfaction previously bestowed only on star professional athletes. The arrival of the Beatles in America and their effeminizing hair length and attention to fashion began to challenge a notion of physical integrity that had previously underpinned both sports and music. The concept of physical integrity, however, was understood differently in the ideologies of rock 'n' roll and sports.[60] Sports, for example, are more often aligned with the military, as both are stereotypically associated with masculine dominance and often patriarchal beliefs and institutional structures.

To a large degree the militarism of American society has been reflected in a sports culture that has reinforced the pressure on American males to live up to a masculine heroic ideal of the "fight." Indeed, American athletes and coaches have often drawn positive parallels between sports and war. The rhetoric of sports like football is rife with terms such as going on "the attack," "blitzing," and "the long bomb"—not to mention the long tradition of college "fight songs" and militaristic

---

Thayer poem, "Casey at the Bat." The concert also was part of a full season of repertoire with the theme "Music in Motion," for which Strickler chose pieces inspired by movement.

[58]   "Hockey greats to take part in Montreal Symphony Orchestra concert," *TheSpec. com*, January 20, 2008. www.thespec.com/article/316130 (accessed May 25, 2010).

[59]   Ibid.

[60]   For more on this concept, see David Zang, *Sports Wars: Athletes in the Age of Aquarius* (Fayetteville: University of Arkansas Press, 2001), 17.

marching bands associated with many university sporting events. Sociologist Sue Curry Jansen, among others, claims that the striking similarities of military and sports terminologies serve to reinforce the masculine goals of "old men seeking to enlist young men (and sometimes women) to fight their wars for them."[61] The celebrated psychologist William James felt that football was the "moral equivalent of war," while journalist Caspar Whitney regarded it as a worthy form of training for the navy and army, believing the game to be "a mimic battlefield."[62] Conflations of war, sports, and music were particularly evident following the first Gulf War, 9/11, and the Iraq War. Many sporting events in the United States staged musical tributes to the armed forces. Whitney Houston's rendition of "The Star-Spangled Banner" at Super Bowl XXV, punctuated by a flyover of F-14s, was a direct response to the beginning of the bombing campaign of the 1991 Gulf War, which had begun just days earlier. The rendition was, incidentally, the first to hit the pop charts since José Feliciano's rendition in 1968. The 2004 Super Bowl will also perhaps be best remembered for its infamous half-time show that, aside from Janet Jackson's legendary "wardrobe malfunction," had controversial "patriotic" performances by Jackson and Kid Rock and numerous tributes to the troops involved in the Iraq War.

Such a warrior ethos and commingling of popular music and sports, however, was substantially questioned in the 1960s with the onset of the Vietnam War. Most rock musicians opposed war of any kind, a fact manifest in lyrics to songs such as Marvin Gaye's "What's Going On," John Lennon's "Give Peace a Chance," and Edwin Starr's 1970 hit "War." Sports, however, doggedly clung to the pristine notion of military heroism, as color guards typically presented flags and warplanes flew overhead at many sporting events.

The late 1960s also saw a shift to a more cerebral, psychedelic experience of music. Previous to the 1967 release of *Sgt Pepper's Lonely Hearts Club Band*, the energy and rhythm of rock music demanded a physical response; it was primarily intended as dance music. In the wake of acts such as the Beatles and Bob Dylan, attention gradually became increasingly focused on the lyrics and the creation of music which promoted more passive, cerebral contemplation, often enhanced by the kinesthetic experience of psychedelic drugs.[63] In something of a dichotomy, rock music and its associated drug imagery fulfilled a need for both physical expression and sensation, reflecting a desire for a more enhanced, connected experience of the world, while simultaneously promoting physical passivity and an escape from apparently oppressive reality. Sports, likewise, entered an era of increasing experimentation with performance enhancing drugs. Few athletes were

---

[61] Sue Curry Jansen, "Football is more than a game: Masculinity, sport and war," *Critical Communication Theory* (New York: Rowman and Littlefield, 2002), 185–210, 186.

[62] As quoted in Steven Riess, "Sport and the redefinition of middle-class masculinity in Victorian America," in *The New American Sport History*, S.W. Pope (ed.) (Chicago: University of Illinois Press, 2005), 187, 188.

[63] Zang, 21.

concerned with passivity or escape, but it can be argued that the very experience of sports, with its suspension of real time and space, already provided the transgressive release from oppressive reality that the counterculture sought in drugs and psychedelic music. Nonetheless, the hedonism associated with late 1960s and early 1970s youth culture and rock music was often contradicted by athletics that fundamentally stressed practice, work, and effort over fun and pleasure. To some extent the dialectic opposition of sports and rock music represented a symbolic battle for the hearts and minds of American youth.

Following the antagonistic relationship between rock and sports in the previous two decades, the 1980s and 1990s saw an increasing alliance as both industries recognized that commercially they had much to gain from each other. By 1992 the sports–music nexus was so ingrained that even independent artists such as New Order were composing sports songs such as "World in Motion," the official theme for the English soccer team's World Cup finals that year—a song that became their first No. 1 hit. The increasing convergence and cross-marketing of these two forms of mass entertainment and leisure culture continues unabated today.[64] Perhaps this is to be expected, given the numerous similarities between rock and sports. Notwithstanding that there are still important instances of resistance between the hedonism of music culture and the discipline of sports, both sports and rock music encourage the pleasures of physical bodily experience through both participation and passive audience consumption; both are preoccupied with disciplined performativity and physical display. Also noteworthy in this regard is Pierre Bourdieu's contention that:

> the near miraculous orchestration of a team strategy [results in] a pleasure no less intense and learned than the pleasure a music-lover derives from a particularly successful rendering of a favorite work. … In other words, everything seems to suggest that, in sports as in music, extension of the public beyond the circle of amateurs helps to reinforce the reign of the pure professionals."[65]

The similarities do not stop there, however, as both sports and popular/rock music are largely driven by and appeal to the energy of youth. Both promote celebrity cults (through similar fanzine culture and fan websites devoted to favorite players/ artists), both have been active vehicles in the promotion of national identity, and both were, and to varying degrees still are, bastions of masculine power and domination. Late twentieth and early twenty-first century corporate marketers

---

[64]   *Unity*, the official album of the 2004 Athens Olympics, spent several weeks at the top of the European and North American pop charts. The work features an eclectic mix of pop-rock and world music artists such as Sting, Moby, and Alice Cooper. Similarly, K'naan's "Wavin' Flag," the official song of the 2010 World Cup, has topped various charts around the globe.

[65]   Pierre Bourdieu, "How can one be a sports fan?" in *Cultural Studies Reader*, Simon During (ed.) (London: Routledge, 1994), 339–56, 347.

have merely exploited these similarities to gain increased market share. Indeed, one of the most overt similarities of sports and popular music is their increasing proclivity to hypercommodification. It is also true, however, that in their common capacity to offer limitless variation, both sports and rock music offer us the opportunity to transcend corporate calculation. Gary Whannel concludes his study of media sports stars by drawing on Roland Barthes's notion of *jouissance* and recognizes that sports are increasingly the "playground of corporate capitalism ... the ability of sport to produce fleeting moments of *jouissance* can always, albeit briefly, escape the calculations of corporate marketeers and entrepreneurs ... for those brief moments, sport provides ... inspirational glimpses of the ability of humans to transcend the calculable."[66]

In addition to transcending packaged outcomes, the notion of *jouissance* also implies an element of pleasurable tension in the liminality and expectation of that outcome. Although there are many differences between the consumption of music and sports, a focused element of pleasurable excitement (including a degree of tension and anxiety) is always present in both experiences. Whether it is the tension or excitement derived from attending the outcome of a World Cup match or the perhaps the more reserved, but no less profound, excitement and tension derived from an orchestral climax, such experiences have driven much of the historical connection between sports and music. From *kithara* competitions to battles of the swing bands, from jousting to basketball, from baroque composition contests to sporting fight songs, the correlation between and cross-pollination of sports and music, though often unrecognized, can be found throughout the annals of both sports and music histories.

Sports and Music: Critical and Theoretical Connections

The connection of sports and music exists on many theoretical and practical levels. The synchronicity of sports, music, and dance forms one of many such relationships. At the most basic level sound, for example, is a part of the fundamental bodily resonance of sports. Attacking martial artists often yell or shout when they engage an opponent in order to focus and maximally release their energy. Shouting ensures that the air in their lungs is quickly and forcefully exhaled, generating the most amount of energy and power in the punch. Almost every sport imaginable involves audible breathing, grunts, or shouting, the associated ambient sounds of feet and bodies hitting the playing surface, and the clatter of various equipment. The "crack" of a ball hitting a bat is one of the most evocative sounds in baseball. The "rattle" of a golf ball in the cup, the "popping" of pads in football, and the "swish" of a basketball through the netting are among the most recognizable and satisfying sounds in their respective sports. Simply

---

[66] Garry Whannel, *Media Sports Stars: Masculinities and Moralities* (London: Routledge, 2002), 216.

hearing the isolated roar of the crowd inside the arena typically elicits chills from both players and spectators alike. Indeed, the naturally occurring "ambient" music of sports may be among the most common exemplifications of aleatoric sonic principles outside John Cage's famous *4'33"*.

Another realm of association—albeit metaphoric—between music and sports occurs in the classroom. Music teachers have long relied on various sports analogies to teach different aspects of musical technique. Perhaps the technique most common in music and sports, apart from similarities of stressing the importance of stretching and warming up before beginning each activity in earnest, is the general process of visualizing a successful performance. Apart from mental and physical preparation, however, specific techniques are often taught with the help of sports analogies. Piano teachers, for example, often teach proper finger action on the keyboard by telling pupils to visualize their fingers as if they were rebounding off a diving springboard. Similarly, students being taught to sight-read are often told to look ahead as if riding a bicycle. Drummers are sometimes told to let their sticks bounce off the drum like a basketball (and they are sometimes even encouraged to bounce a basketball so as to pick up the feel of the percussive bounce).

Yet another often overlooked nexus of sports and music involves the impact on the body of the respective practices. Many musicians, like their athletic counterparts, suffer from physical injuries and fatigue due to the continual and energetic playing of their instruments. Drummers, for example, often develop calluses on their hands, just as guitarists develop blisters on their fingers. But playing any musical instrument, indeed every musical pursuit, carries bodily risk. A variety of other injuries—ranging from muscle aches and pains to hearing disorders, blown blood vessels and injuries relating to repetitive stress and tendon injuries—accompany rigorous practice sessions for nearly every form of instrument imaginable. Some of the more prominent victims of late have been string players: violinists Peter Oundjian and Reinhard Goebel, each of whom suffered permanent loss of fine motor control in his left (fingering) hand, and David Leisner, a guitarist, who sustained a similar injury to his right (plucking) hand.[67]

All of these disabling hand injuries fall into a category called "focal dystonia," which includes a wide range of overuse or repetitive-stress symptoms. Fingers, for example, may involuntarily splay or curl into the palm. Although much remains to be learned about focal dystonia, it is widely thought to be incurable. Such injuries may not directly compare to the severity of the broken bones and concussions that often accompany contact sports. However, they nonetheless attest to the fact that both types of activity are inherently physical and leave their imprint on the body.

Musical performance is, in part, a physical test. It requires agility and coordination, finely honed skills, intense conditioning, brief warm-up and,

---

[67]   Janet Horvath, *An Injury Prevention Guide for Musicians: Playing (less) Hurt* (Kearney, NE: Morris Publishing, 2006), 109.

especially for longer works, considerable stamina. Indeed, sports scientist Steve Draper from the University of Gloucestershire believes drummers have as much stamina as elite athletes. When recently analyzed, the heart rate of Blondie's drummer, Clem Burke, could hit 190 during the peak of a performance, equivalent to that of a top athlete. He also lost about two litres of fluid during a 90-minute show, similar to fluid loss by an athlete running 10,000 meters. According to Draper, "The most startling thing for us was when we first got heart rate traces from Clem's concert ... we looked at them, and they could have been a premiership footballer."[68]

Similar to sports science, there is a burgeoning field of medicine concerned with music injury. Psychologist Dr Kyle Pruett has even called musicians "small-muscle Olympians." Pruett has recently related the seemingly disparate psychologies of music and sports. Although sports are thought by some to instill an unhealthy sense of competitiveness, classical music, with what Pruett called its "early expectation of perfection," may impose on its practitioners an even harsher and more punishing ethic.[69] Whereas for athletes the performance is ultimately focused on winning, for musicians performance is about achieving an ideal of perfection.

While music and sports share basic similarities in sonic content and physical impact on practitioners, the theorization of each activity has also shared a substantial crossover. Though in and of itself this does not prove a direct link, it is an interesting phenomenon that some of the leading theoretical social theories of sports appear to be equally applicable to music. Charles Stevenson, for example, defined five basic functions of modern sports, all of which could also be found in music. First, he identifies a socio-emotional function, with sports contributing to the maintenance of socio-psychological stability. Second, there is a socialization function, with sports aiding the transmission of cultural beliefs and norms. Third, sports provide an integrative function, facilitating the harmonious integration of disparate individuals and groups. Fourth, sports serve a political function in service of ideological needs. Finally, there is a social mobility function, in which sports act as a source of upward mobility.[70] For each point an equally compelling argument can be made that music facilitates the very same function and thus, at least in these terms, functions analogously as a sport itself (or that sports function analogously as music).

---

[68]   "Drummers need the stamina of athletes, U.K. study finds," *CBCnews.ca*, July 25, 2008. www.cbc.ca/arts/music/story/2008/07/25/drummingproject.htmlwww.cbc.ca/arts/music/story/2008/07/25/drumming-project.html (accessed May 25, 2009).

[69]   James Oestreich, "In music as well as sports, injuries can end a career," *New York Times*, Tuesday, August 27, 1996, section C, page 9. www.nytimes.com/1996/08/27/arts/in-music-as-well-as-sports-injuries-can-end-a-career.html.

[70]   Charles Leslie Stevenson, "Sport as contemporary social phenomenon: A functional explanation," in *International Journal of Physical Education*, 11, 8–14; also quoted in Graham Scambler, *Sport and Society: History, Power and Culture* (New York: Open University Press, 2005), 144.

Other sports theorists have looked to Gramscian hegemony theory to understand sports' relationship to society. John Hargreaves in *Sport, Power and Culture*, for example, delineates five different relationships between sports and capital.[71] In each delineation, however, a direct comparison can be made to an analogous relationship in music. First, Hargreaves identifies profit maximizing, as in professional boxing or horse racing. Many sports, like many forms of music and musical organizations, cannot, however, realize a profit. Thus the second relationship between sports and capital occurs when sports only remain financially viable by adopting strategies such as local fundraising. One need only think of community choir and school band fundraisers to see a musical correlative. Third, according to Hargreaves, sports can stimulate the accumulation of capital indirectly, as when they create a market for goods and services such as equipment and clothing. Music similarly generates indirect capital accumulation through the sale of instruments, sound playback equipment, artist T-shirts and clothing lines, ticket agencies, and other ancillary industries directly related to the creation and consumption of music. Fourth, sports can also assist capital accumulation indirectly by affording opportunities for advertisement and sponsorship. The number of recent tours by pop and rock artists sponsored by major corporations provides an obvious musical analogy. Finally, Hargreaves posits that sports can draw in investment for non-economic reasons—as in the financial sponsorship of a team to pursue prestige or local credibility, or to obtain boxes in a stadium for corporate entertainment. One need only glance at any program from a professional symphony orchestra or opera to see instances of similar corporate investment in music.

The ideology of consumerism associated with postmodern culture has led to a raised tolerance for, and hence enhanced profitability of, violence in both sports and music. It is hardly coincidental that the violent lyrics and imagery associated with gangsta rap, death metal, and shock rock have gained popularity at a time when people have likewise decried both player and fan violence in basketball, football, soccer, and hockey.[72] It has long been thought that sports and music have been active contributors to the civilization of the human species. Though empirical evidence is lacking, the idea that we are perhaps on the cusp of a process of decivilization, driven at least in part by sports and music, would seem to warrant further investigation. Some theorists, notably Jürgen Habermas, have noted the contradictions of postmodern cultural accounts, particularly of the self-refuting character of relativism, which betray a deeper and more insidious form of neo-conservatism. Postmodern rejections of metanarratives of progress—informed by bourgeois, masculine, and white structuralist perspectives that have

---

[71]   John Hargreaves, *Sport, Power and Culture: A Social and Historical Analysis of Popular Sports in Britain* (Cambridge, UK: Polity, 1986).

[72]   Such violence is not limited to sports and music. Movies, video games, and other media have also become increasingly consumed with violence. Though not overtly violent, the associated competitiveness of American society has, perhaps, its most overt musical manifestation in shows like *American Idol*.

been long taken for granted—have emancipated marginalized narratives that have undoubtedly promoted innovative and liberating perspectives.

However, such liberation is in itself a metanarrative of progress, and there is some danger that the lack of an overarching metanarrative of modernism has in fact served to divide, and to some extent institutionally remarginalize, voices outside the mainstream. As Habermas puts it, there is a "performative contradiction" to postmodernist, post-structuralist forms of interpretative critical theory.[73] Habermas views most postmodern or post-structuralist perspectives, for all their capacity to disinhibit, as insidious forms of neo-conservatism, and thus he repeatedly seeks to revive and reconstruct the project of modernity, noting its proven capacity to emancipate. To some extent it is easy to dismiss the increasing nexus of sports and music described throughout this book as evidence of the increasing homogenization of culture—the product of hypercommodification that merely serves capitalist corporate goals at the expense of "authentic," and presumably separate, experiences of these forms of entertainment and leisure. Perhaps, however, we might more profitably look upon these conjunctions as new and progressive forms of communication that enhance the physical experience and pleasure of both activities.

Theodore Adorno takes a much more cynical view in his association of sports with music. Adorno equates the dilettantism of the amateur jazz enthusiast with that of the sports fan, claiming "the listening expert who can identify every band and immerses himself in the history of jazz as if it were Holy Writ … is nearest to the sportsman: if not to the football player himself, then to the swaggering fellow who dominates the stands."[74] For Adorno, sports and popular music are not part of "serious" culture and merely serve to distract and thereby maintain an infantilism in mainstream culture and society. Adorno goes on to equate popular music essentially with sports as existing in what he refers to as "music sport." Adorno sees "the playful release from responsibility" through the repetition of prescribed models of popular music as being the "inherent pretense of music sport."[75]

Several theorists have also commented on the common role that both music and sports have played in dealing with race relations in North America. As jazz scholar Gerald Early has stated:

> Where else, other than the popular arenas of sports and music, have the races really come together, really syncretized their being? And has it not been, in many compelling ways, that society has experienced its greatest changes for the

---

[73]   Jurgen Habermas, *The Philosophical Discourse of Modernity* (Cambridge, UK: Polity Press, 1987); see also *The New Conservatism* (Cambridge, UK: Polity, 1989).

[74]   Theodore Adorno, "On the fetish character in music and the regression of listening," in Simon Frith (ed.), *Popular Music: Critical Concepts in Media and Cultural Studies*, Vol. 3 (New York: Routledge, 2004), 325–49, 345.

[75]   Ibid., 347.

better through just these avenues of marginalized culture suddenly taking center
stage in the culture for one crucial moment?[76]

While popular music and sports have been key sites of racial negotiation (indeed
this will be discussed in more detail in Chapters 5 and 7), they are, perhaps on an
even more fundamental level, cultural industries devoted to the cult of youth. On
the level of both participation and spectatorship, both sports and popular music—
particularly rock music and its cousins—share a preoccupation with physical
displays of youth. Thus, to some extent both cultures find their significance,
in Western society in particular, in their mutual ability to signal social health,
vitality, and potential.

At an elemental level Western society is preoccupied with immortality and
the desire to overcome death. As such we are concerned with overcoming and
negotiating the limitations of the mortal body. Such a proposition is reinforced
particularly through our fascination with religion and various theories of attaining
an afterlife. For the ancient Greeks immortality could be ensured through
achievements that would live on in the collective social memory. The structures
associated with such achievements—temples, theatres, arenas—were built
with a permanence and on a scale that would equally ensure that the deeds and
achievements within would be remembered and commemorated for generations
to come. Consequently, much as it does today, the achievement of either sporting
or artistic fame would ensure a form of immortality. The bodily performance of
both sports and music also draw attention to the impermanence of life. The fleeting
moment of athletic achievement can be equated to the ephemeral nature of music,
and thus both activities mirror the ephemeral nature of life itself. The emphasis on
youth that also dominates both athletics and music (particularly popular music)
also reflects the transient nature of life.

In more recent times, following the rise and dominance of capitalism in the
West, we now often attempt to achieve immortality through the accumulation
of capital wealth, such that one might achieve fame simply through one's
level of monetary worth and ability to leave a financial legacy. In today's
hypercommodified worlds of sports and music, the fascination with immortality
seems to operate on two simultaneous levels. As with the ancient Greeks, some
athletes and musicians attempt to achieve immortality through the collective
public acknowledgment of their athletic or artistic skills. At the same time,
as a society, we have endowed those skills with such cultural capital that the
highest echelons of athletes and musicians are also rewarded with the various
manifestations of economic immortality.

The current age of the internet and the concomitant profusion of personal
digital recording devices (cell phones, cameras, and so on) have witnessed
a major increase in the archiving and memorializing of athletic and musical

---

[76]   Gerald Early, *Tuxedo Junction: Essays on American Culture* (New York: Ecco
Press, 1989), 52.

performances. Previously, permanent records of such achievements were limited to the top ranks of music and sports, and were documented through the release, variously, of records, CDs, videotapes, and television broadcasts. In the past several years, however, the profusion of accessible digital recording technologies has allowed the most private athletic and musical moments to become subjects of permanent record that are often, subsequently, given international airing on the internet through venues such as Myspace, Facebook, and YouTube. Such technology has served to immortalize, as it were, even the most seemingly mundane or insignificant achievements. The advent of such technologies has essentially resulted in a democratization of immortality through achievement. Despite our perhaps relatively modest talents in either the arts or athletics, to the extent that we have access to recording devices and the internet, we can all have a permanent record of our achievements, however humble, that will ensure our immortality.

Above all other social, economic and aesthetic connections, sports and popular music are most firmly linked their common appeal to the body and its pleasures by means of both participation and spectatorship. As manifest in our desire for youthful immortality, discussed above, and as recognized by David Rowe, popular music and sports are "key cultural industries of the body, constantly replenishing the stock of corporeal images which also function as metaphors of social and cultural change."[77] Indeed, it is the combined projection of corporeal images that represents much of their combined power to construct and reflect identity as delineated throughout the remainder of this book. Having discussed some of the historical and theoretical similarities and crossovers between sports and popular music, the succeeding chapters will look at how these culture industries have variously combined in the construction of female body image, expressions of hypermasculine homosexual power and African American masculinity, projections of class, national and ethnic identity, and even in promulgating questions surrounding what constitutes "human" performance.

---

[77] Rowe, *Popular Cultures*, 9.

Chapter 2
"Let's Get Physical": Female Identity, Music and the Fitness Industry

This chapter surveys aspects of the confluence of women, sports, and music. Against the backdrop of the increasing cultural fascination with female athletes and athleticism, manifest in the prominence of the fitness and workout industry, and in the athletic female role models found in popular movies such as *Million Dollar Baby* and *Kill Bill*, I will discuss the impact of works by artists such as Toni Basil ("Mickey"), Madonna, Britney Spears, the Spice Girls (including the impact of the Sporty Spice persona), Grace Jones, Olivia Newton-John, and Gwen Stefani. This discussion will generally center on the increasing trend toward athletically empowered presentations in female pop singers and the role of female performers and their videos in constructing and perpetuating stereotypical notions of the "ideal" female body.

Women, Athletics, and Music: A History of Exclusion

Before embarking on an exploration of the confluence of music and sports in constructing female identity, it may be helpful to address briefly the history of female participation in sports and music generally. Though their athletic history has been little studied or understood, women have nonetheless participated in sporting activities since at least the time of the ancient Egyptians. Likely the most famous sportswoman of ancient Greece was Artemis, goddess of the moon, who appeared in ancient literature and art as a huntress. Also identified with the Roman goddess Diana, in later times she would be the subject of musical works by Ben Jonson among others.[1] Even more athletic was Atalanta, whom Ovid depicted in Books VIII and X as a huntress, a wrestler, and a runner.[2] Physically the match of any man she met, she was also famously musically depicted by Handel and others.[3] In ancient Greek life, however, women were forbidden from the gymnasium and

---

[1]   See for example Ben Jonson's "Hymn to Diana" or Thomas Weelkes's English madrigal "From Latmos Hill Descending."

[2]   Indeed, the Italian Serie A football club Atalanta Bergamo (Atlanta BC) takes the goddess's name and image for its team.

[3]   *Atalanta*, an opera seria composed by Handel in 1736.

excluded from even being spectators at the Olympic Games. Nonetheless, there is evidence of the existence of women-only athletic festivals in honor of the goddess Hera.[4] Similarly, there are several accounts of female gladiators from ancient Rome. In the medieval period women from the lower ranks of society, amongst other physical competitions, commonly engaged in forms of football such as the English tradition of Shrovetide football, which pitted married women against maidens and spinsters. Among the upper classes women participated in hunting, archery, and riding activities and competitions. In the eighteenth and nineteenth centuries sports activities for women might include swimming, bicycle races, and tennis. The nineteenth century also saw the introduction of gymnastic drills for women, with instruction in light free-standing exercises that intentionally avoided any strenuous movement thought to overtax the female frame and potentially endanger reproductive ability.[5]

In the early twentieth century women athletes became relatively common, and organized team sports including basketball, lacrosse, and track and field were played, producing such well-known athletes as Helen Wills, Mildred "Babe" Didrikson, and Sonja Henning. More recently, of course, women have been much more actively engaged in participating in and consuming sports through various media. Following the 1972 "Title IX" legislation in the United States that prohibited gender discrimination within sports at high schools and colleges, women have broken many significant barriers. Billie Jean King defeated Bobby Riggs in the "Battle of the Sexes" (1973); Little League allowed girls to play softball and baseball (1974); Janet Guthrie competed in the 1977 Indianapolis 500; Julie Krone became the first female jockey to win a Triple Crown event, the Belmont Stakes (1993); women competed in the same number of team sports as men at the Sydney Olympics (2000); and Annika Sörenstam became the first woman in 58 years to compete on the men's PGA tour (2003).

This brief history barely scratches the surface of female participation in sports and physical competition. However, despite their continuous, if often overlooked, involvement in such activities, throughout history women have been systematically excluded from participating in sports. As late as the nineteenth century, for example, it was even thought that women could only bear healthy children if they exercised in moderation (reflecting a sixteenth-century European fear that excessive exercise would literally turn women into men).

In recent decades women have witnessed a growth in their passive consumption of sports to match the increase in their active participation. As early as 1936, for example, Marjorie Hill's *Live Alone and Like It: A Guide for the Extra Woman* recommended that single women occupy themselves by watching boxing bouts and seeing art exhibitions. By 1995 more women than men in Britain were

---

[4] Allen Guttmann, *Women's Sports: A History* (New York: Columbia University Press, 1991), 20.

[5] See Giulianotti, 83.

watching Wimbledon tennis on television.[6] Similarly, female viewership of the 2002 Korea/Japan World Cup was 49 percent of the total audience.[7]

Historically, women have suffered a similar level of exclusion from active musical careers, as has been well documented in the influential scholarship of Susan McClary, Suzanne Cusick, and others.[8] Though the situation has recently improved, in the recent past the primary manifestation of music–sports interaction that most women experienced was in the form of cheerleading chants.

For much of Western history women were barred from participating in organized physical recreations. The notion of genteel leisure time was essentially a male construction, and few upper-rank women, much less women of lower ranks, had the means for or an interest in constructing and experiencing leisure as men did. Women rarely claimed leisure time at all. Dance was the primary outlet for social, non-work-related exercise for many women in the seventeenth and eighteenth centuries. Women of the upper classes were able to regularly attend races, assemblies, and exhibitions in the pleasure gardens. Previous to this women were primarily spectators of male sports, though they frequently wagered on events such as animal baiting.[9] By the time of the eighteenth century, however, women of the upper ranks of society were marginalized from almost any form of physical competition or performance. They were allowed to walk the paths of the pleasure gardens but not participate in the races. They were allowed to boat and fish though not in any serious or competitive way. Their main role, as far as sports were concerned, was to provide support for the men. Women at this time and place were, essentially, cheerleaders in the making.

The exclusion of women, and other marginalized groups, may in part be explained by cultural critic Pierre Bourdieu's theory of "symbolic violence": "Symbolic violence is the coercion which is set up only through the consent that the dominated cannot fail to give the dominator (and therefore to the domination) when their understanding of the situation and relation can only use instruments of knowledge that they have in common with the dominator."[10] As such, symbolic violence involves the subtle coercion of the dominated group, inculcating the dominant group's values such that the dominated are reduced to collaborating with their coercion. Such symbolic violence marks the exclusion of various

---

[6]   Toby Miller and Alec McHoul, *Popular Culture and Everyday Life* (London: Sage, 1998), 60.

[7]   David Rowe, *Sport, Culture and the Media: The Unruly Trinity* (London: Open University Press, 2004), 172.

[8]   For a particularly informative and well-written summation of the issues and history of female exclusion in music, see Suzanne Cusick, "Gender, musicology, and feminism," in Nicholas Cook and Mark Everist (eds), *Rethinking Music* (Oxford: Oxford University Press, 1999), 471–98.

[9]   Nancy Struna, *People of Prowess: Sport, Leisure, and Labor in Early Anglo-America* (Urbana: University of Illinois Press, 1996), 18.

[10]   Pierre Bourdieu, *Pascalian Meditations* (Cambridge, UK: Polity, 2000), 170.

marginalized groups, particularly women, from participation in certain sports and even musical activities.

The "male model" of sports is perhaps most overt in the Olympic movement. Pierre de Coubertin's exclusion of women from the resurrected Games is telling. In the *Revue Olympique* in 1912 he stated his philosophy that the Games should promote "the solemn and periodic exultation of male athleticism, based on internationalism, by means of fairness, in an artistic setting, *with the applause of women as a reward*" (emphasis added). Later, in a speech in Lausanne from 1928, de Coubertin expounded on the reasons why women should be barred from the Games:

> The ruggedness of male exertion, the basis of athletic education when prudently but resolutely applied, is much to be dreaded when it comes to the female. That ruggedness is achieved physically only when the nerves are stretched beyond their normal capacity, and morally only when the most precious feminine characteristics are nullified ... Add a female element, and the event becomes monstrous ... if women want to play football or box, let them, provided that the event takes place without spectators, because the spectators who flock to such competitions are not there to watch a sport.[11]

Women have subsequently been allowed to compete in some contact sports in the Olympics, such as ice hockey and martial arts, and recently we have witnessed the rise of female football teams and professional women's boxing. Despite these advancements, however, something of de Coubertin's views still taints our view of women's contact and combat sports today. Professional women's boxing, for example, is regarded by many as more of an oddity and a spectacle than a serious athletic activity. Women's boxing and wrestling are still not regarded as suitable for inclusion in the Olympic games—though until the April 6, 2011 decision by the IOC to allow it in the 2014 Sochi games, neither was a non-contact sport such as women's ski jumping.

A significant change in the participation of women in sports occurred in the 1920s. It was at this time that the cultivation of a youthful "athletic" appearance became fashionable. Though the emphasis on actual physical activity was minimal, the promotion of a vivacious, energetic look, as epitomized by actress Clara Bow and others, became a popular trend. It is a trend that has continued in one form or another to the present period. Recent studies have shown that since the 1950s, ideas about body shape have been closely linked with concerns about consumerism and sedentariness and have become inherently linked in Western culture to notions of success, control, and personal worth. As John Horne has commented, "In consumer culture those who can get their body to approximate the idealized images of youth, health, fitness and beauty can realize a higher economic

---

[11]   Pierre de Coubertin, *Olympism: Selected Writings* (Lausanne: International Olympic Committee, 2000), 188. Also cited in Rod Brookes, *Representing Sport* (London: Arnold Press, 2002), 136.

exchange value than those who cannot or who do not wish to."[12] To some extent body image and fitness, it should be noted, are also tied to class, gender, and racial issues. British journalist Polly Toynebee, for example, concludes: "Fat is a class issue ... [It is] inequality and disrespect that makes people fat."[13] Pierre Bourdieu sees a similar relationship. For Bourdieu it is through sports and other cultural practices, including music, that dominant groups construct what will be viewed as the "legitimate body" in opposition to the bodies and cultural practices of lower social strata.[14]

To a far larger degree than in male participation in either sports or music, body image (as experienced by participants and observers) often occupies a central place in female athletics and music. One of the main intersections between female athletics and music occurs in the realm of fitness and exercise and the musical soundtrack that invariably accompanies working out. However, as Susan Willis observes, "many young women today do not realize that exercise for women as a widely available and socially acceptable endeavor represents a recent victory in women's struggle for equality with men."[15] Daily aerobic workouts, jogging programs, strenuous training regimes for women with disabilities, and challenging exercise programs for seniors all attest to the interest in exercise among women, albeit a small (mainly white, middle-class, and professional) segment of the population. To some extent, however, the burgeoning exercise industry is being built on the premise of women's inadequate body image. It is an image that is typically constructed through male, media-driven ideals. Finnish researcher Prikko Markula sums up the problem:

> The public discourses surrounding aerobics evidently emphasize a fragmented view of the self by focusing overtly or covertly on improving one's body shape ... it became obvious in my research that the individual women in exercise classes actively create meanings of their selves, but these meanings continue to be framed and constructed by dominant forces in society ...[16]

Such a proposition is evident when one considers the popularity of workout videos by Jane Fonda, Olivia Newton-John, and other celebrities who already have attained some level of ideal media image.

---

[12]   John Horne, *Sport in Consumer Culture* (New York: Palgrave Macmillan, 2006), 129.

[13]   As quoted in Horne, 130.

[14]   Giulianotti, 104.

[15]   Susan Willis, "Work(ing) out," *Cultural Studies*, 4 (1990), 1–18, 3.

[16]   Pirkko Markula, "Looking good, feeling good: Strengthening mind and body in aerobics," in L. Laine (ed.), *On the Fringes of Sports* (St Augustine, Germany: Academia, 1993), 98.

Aerobics is an activity that spans and transcends cultural categories of sports, dance, and exercise. As such it has become yet another commodity in the highly commercialized beauty culture. Theorist Margaret Morse claims:

> Exercise can be added to the applications of makeup and clothing and to the body-moulding regimes of corseting, diet, and surgical intervention (including plastic surgery and lipo-suction) as a means of achieving femininity. Of these methods, exercise was one of the first brought in service to a feminist alternative ideal of the female body and one of the last to be commercialized ... while dieting shrinks the body and its power both literally and symbolically, exercise prepares a freely-moving subjectivity which can be active in the world. As such it contradicts long-prevailing notions of feminine passivity and stasis.[17]

Related to the commercialization of beauty culture is the idea that consumer culture has long promoted ideals of a fit, tanned, healthy body—ideals endorsed and replicated by athletes and pop musicians around the world. Acquiring such a body involves the active and ongoing consumption of health foods and beauty products, in addition to constant gym workouts and possibly cosmetic surgery. Ironically, given their mass production and consumption, such beauty and health-related products function as signifiers of consumers' "individuality" and ability to shape their inner self through controlling their outward bodily appearance.

The participation by women in such conformity to consumer-driven notions of ideal femininity is perhaps unavoidable. However, what happens when women engage in activities that do not conform to expected embodied gendered practices, such as boxing or heavy metal? Sex differences that reside in the body are typically invoked as the reason for excluding women from a sport or insisting on different sets of regulations for women and men. As Judith Butler argues, "Sexual difference ... is never simply a function of material differences which are not in some way marked by discursive practices ... the category 'sex' is, from the start, normative; it is what Foucault called a 'regulatory ideal.'"[18] Butler's work, which draws heavily on Foucault, focuses on the instability of gender categories that are not tied to the body that enacts them. Despite such appeals to the constructedness of gender, problems remain in constructing heroic narratives, normative in masculine boxing culture and other sports that bring together women and violence. Heroic masculinity is more problematic for women who choose to seek it, as they often have more to fight than merely their opponents in the ring. Such normative masculine heroic narratives are commonly reinforced in music, as in Bonnie Tyler's 1984 hit song "Holding Out for a Hero" (including the first line, "Where have all the good men gone?"[19]). Former professional boxer Laila Ali, however,

---

[17]   Margaret Morse, "Artemis aging: Exercise and the female body on video," *Discourse* 10, 1 (1987/88) 20–54, 24.

[18]   Judith Butler, *Bodies That Matter* (New York: Routledge, 1993), 1.

[19]   Words and music by Dean Pitchford and Jim Steinman,

represents a contemporary woman who is able to take on a heroic identity without the overtones of misogyny and racism while avoiding stereotypical hegemonic masculine performance. The link to her father, Muhammad Ali, opened some positive political associations with the civil rights movement and empowerment, allowing the emergence of a potentially new subject position for women in boxing.

As they do for many men, sports and music provide a form of escape for women. Like gladiators who could achieve liberation from enslavement, modern female athletes and musicians often seek economic freedom. Though economics may be the most prevalent impetus, female liberation can derive from the very participation in activities from which women have been previously marginalized. Like the life of the gladiator, however, the viability of careers in music and sports is often short—and dependent on the resiliency of the body and the fickleness of the public.

Music, Exercise, and Body Image

The remainder of this chapter discusses the multifaceted and growing relationship between exercise and music from the perspective of the medical benefits, the business and marketing of exercise music, and the socio-cultural impact of this negotiation on women. The increasingly ubiquitous presence of various forms of faceless technologies and a neo-puritanical privileging of the intellect has led many recent scholars to decry the gradual marginalization and exscription of the body. In large part facilitated through the increasing encroachment of various technologies such as MP3 and internet file sharing (though even the earlier invention of the phonograph initially removed the need for actual bodies to be present in order to experience musical performances), this increasing marginalization of the body extends to both contemporary popular music discourse and creation. Notwithstanding the merits of many such arguments, a significant repertoire that would seem to resist this categorization is found in music used in exercise activities such as aerobics, step classes, yoga, Tae Bo, and kickboxing (not to mention the plethora of exercise videos, television shows, and so on). The use of music is integrated into these activities to such an extent that it does not merely accompany these forms of exercise but is an integral component of it. The explosion in health consciousness that has been witnessed in recent years—what Pierre Bordieu has termed the "cult of health"—has paralleled a concomitant expansion in the creation and marketing of music to accompany exercise both of mind and body.[20] Rather than marginalizing the body, exercise music directly invokes bodily participation; indeed it is valued precisely because it stimulates and encourages bodily response.

---

[20] Pierre Bourdieu, "Sport and social class," in Chandra Mukerji and Michael Schudson (eds), *Rethinking Popular Culture* (Los Angeles: University of California Press, 1991), 357–73, 371.

The use of music in exercise, of course, is not limited to the synchronous group activities mentioned above. With the advent of personal listening devices, as early as the Sony Walkman introduced in 1979, and particularly in the wake of lightweight digital MP3 players, many people who work out individually—whether on various exercise machines or through jogging, walking, cycling, or even swimming—choose to work out to music. Serving primarily as a motivational mitigation to the pain and repetitive monotony associated with many workout activities, music is a nearly ubiquitous presence in today's obsession with personal fitness and health.

The *function* of the body in contemporary discourse is typically considered through the perspective of health. In a society where health and disease are often framed as matters of individual will, investing in the body through cardiovascular exercise, vitamin supplements, smoking cessation, and the like is increasingly viewed as instrumental to good health and the extension and increased quality of life. Since the 1970s the commercial fitness industry in North America has promoted exercise as an ideal solution to achieving better health and defeating the causes and effects of disease. Fitness programs and products are promoted as ways to help one look and feel good. Predominantly, fitness consumers tend to be women, although this is not true of all aspects of the fitness industry. Health club membership of the two sexes in the United States, for example, is relatively even. Naturally enough, the main readership of health magazines targeting men, such as *Men's Health*, consists of men, but three of the four biggest-selling health magazines expressly target women.[21]

The rise of the market for fitness and exercise stems from a number of factors. In the 1970s many Western governments began to promote the notion of active healthy living as a way to manage and reduce the escalating costs of health care.[22] Also, in keeping with women's ideals of taking control of their bodies promoted by the feminist movement, exercise was promoted not only as a way to improve women's health, but also as a means of literal self-empowerment. Title IX legislation in the United States, as mentioned, was instrumental in opening up women's access to physical culture in the 1970s. This broadening of perspective was culturally reflected in the popularity of television images of female power, embodied in series such as *Wonder Woman*, *The Bionic Woman*, *Police Woman* and *Charlie's Angels*, shows that reflected tensions between traditional ideals of sex appeal, and emergent feminist empowerment.

The rise and increasing power of the "new" female consumer in the 1970s must also be factored into this equation. Between 1970 and 1990, women's participation in the civilian labour force in the United States rose 33.9 percent.[23] The increased

---

[21]   Jennifer Smith Maguire, "Exercising control: Empowerment and the fitness discourse," in Linda K. Fuller (ed.), *Sport, Rhetoric, and Gender* (New York: Palgrave Macmillan, 2006), 119–29, 121.

[22]   Ibid., 122.

[23]   Ibid., 123.

number of women with economic means for leisure and self-improvement was thus in large part responsible for establishing the exercise and fitness industry and was, in effect, a tangible reflection of their new-found independence and power.

Aerobics as an organized form of exercise dates to 1968, when Dr Kenneth Cooper introduced the notion of using exercise to increase and maintain cardiovascular health.[24] His exercise regime led to the popularization of aerobic "dance" in the 1970s, an activity that required participants to follow strict choreography set to music. However, it was women and not men, as Cooper had intended, who became the primary participants in the "modern aerobics" that quickly followed in the wake of the aerobic "dance" movement.[25] Like many sports aerobics focuses on muscle strength, endurance, and flexibility. Unlike most sports, however, it is mostly non-competitive.[26]

Over the years aerobics as a general category has evolved into several major variants, including step aerobics, aqua aerobics, jazzercise, and several related exercise genres such as kickboxing and spinning classes, Pilates, and even some forms of yoga. In each case these activities are typically conducted with the aid of prerecorded music as an integral part of the workout—though different instructors may use it to different ends. In the case of yoga, for example, instructors endeavor to create a serene mood or atmosphere, whereas in a kickboxing or aerobics class the music is primarily intended both as a means to coordinate actions and to provide an emotional stimulant that will distract from the discomfort of exertion.

Conventional aerobics instructors typically prepare a set, or sequence, of moves that will be executed by participants in unison to music. Usually the choreography will be timed to 32 beats in a set, ideally switching legs so that the set can be repeated in a mirrored fashion. A set may consist of many different moves and the various moves may have different durations. For example, a basic step as described above takes four beats (for the four steps that the person takes). Classes vary in the level of choreography. Introductory classes tend to have a series of relatively basic moves strung together into a sequence. More advanced classes incorporate dance elements such as turns, mambos, and stomps. These elements are typically linked together two or three to a class. Participants learn the routines during the class,

---

[24]   Melissa Camacho, "Television and aerobic sport: Empowerment and patriarchy in *Denise Austin's Daily Workouts*," in *Sport, Rhetoric and Gender*, 145–57, 146.

[25]   Ibid.

[26]   It should be noted that 1983 saw the foundation of a new competitive form of aerobics that came to be known as "sport aerobics," which held the first national aerobic championship in 1984. Howard Schwartz subsequently founded the International Competitive Aerobics Federation (ICAF) in 1989, and the first world championships were held at San Diego in March 1990, with athletes from 15 countries competing. Sport aerobics originally featured competition in four categories: individual male and female, mixed pairs, and trio, which can include any three athletes. Competitors are judged on a one-minute, 45-second routine done to music. In much the same manner as figure skating and gymnastics, judges use two criteria: artistic merit and technical merit.

and then all are performed at the end of the class. Regardless of the complexity of the choreography, most instructors offer various options for different fitness levels and/or dance ability while teaching the routines.

Currently the majority of aerobic participants and instructors continue to be women.[27] The fitness industry has experienced tremendous economic growth, with marketing strategies and weight loss products designed primarily to appeal to a female demographic. In addition to informational classes, magazines, diet books, audio-visual workout regimes, and nutritional supplements, the interest in fitness and aerobics has also been responsible for the concomitant rise of a multi-billion-dollar sports apparel industry. While this clothing is theoretically designed to provide comfort, much of the apparel is created to make women look more sexually appealing while wearing it. Brightly colored, tight fitting spandex shorts, thongs, body suits, and navel-baring sports bras and T-shirts seem often purposely designed to accent and draw attention to women's physique while they are participating in the sporting activity as much as facilitating comfort or practicality. Similarly, camera angles on television aerobics programs "fragment" the instructors' bodies, as Melissa Camacho points out:

> Close-up and editing techniques can make an aerobic video seem as if it was intended *only for watching* women engaging in aerobic exercise, as opposed to encouraging participation in the exercise itself. The gaze can relate to the instructor's body, inviting looking, as opposed to participating, seeing her as a sexual object and heightening her sex appeal.[28]

Furthermore, such television programs often contain thinly veiled advertisements for various products or exotic resort locations that promise the participant-viewer entry into idealized environments. Television fitness instructors, such as Jillian Michaels and Bob Harper from NBC's hit reality television show *The Biggest Loser*, additionally go on to serve as commercial spokespeople for different fitness and nutritional products, contributing to the overall commodification of body image and health. To a large extent the messages promoting aerobics and exercise as a tool for female health and empowerment are often overshadowed, or at least problematized, by the rhetoric of the fitness industry that attempts to sell ideas, products, and services that promise women an idealized body and self-image that are still largely defined by patriarchal standards.

The conflation of athletic bodies with sex appeal is, of course, not a new phenomenon and not exclusive to women athletes. Swimmer Johnny Weissmuller, skier Jean-Claude Killy, English soccer player George Best, and American football quarterback Joe Namath, among others, have all been marketed on the basis of their sex appeal. For women, however, sports and exercise are often much more closely aligned with their own body image, and successful female athletes are

---

[27]   Camacho, 147.

[28]   Ibid.,148.

far more subject to commercial objectification than their male counterparts. In the 1970s the Women's Basketball League marketed posters of one of their stars, Molly Bolin, in shorts and a tank top.[29] Skating stars Katarina Witt and Florence Griffith-Joyner have also been subject to sexualized marketing.[30] More recently the sexuality of tennis stars Anna Kournikova and Maria Sharapova have also been used prominently to promote that game. Such "self-sexualization" can be understood as a somewhat questionable strategy to generate male-dominated public interest and even perhaps corporate sponsorship.

To some extent female athletes are more subject to an erotic exchange value that panders to male voyeurism. Helen Lenskyj believes "a woman's conformity to male-defined standards of heterosexual attractiveness signifies her acquiescence to men's rules."[31] Indeed, coverage of sporting events and musical events that concentrates on the appearance of female athletes or musicians at the expense of their performances is to be lamented. The media fixation on attractive athletes such as Anna Kournikova (despite her lack of any major victories) merely serves to trivialize women's athletic abilities and achievements. However, it seems highly unlikely that the physical appearance of an athlete or musician will ever be completely detached from an audience's experience of a performance. It seems unlikely that we can or even should completely separate the performer from the performance.

Both athletes and musicians are fundamentally concerned with bodily expression, though athletes are perhaps more overtly engaged in it. To a large extent this expression is manifest on the playing fields and arenas of sport. It seems somewhat disingenuous, however, to expect such bodily expression be merely confined to the borders of participating in whatever sport they have chosen. Thus the benign objectification (as opposed to a pathological fetishizing) of both male and female athletes in this regard must be considered a natural by-product of this physical display. This is only reinforced in a capitalistic society that, if the process is fully played out, objectifies and commodifies all aspects of society.

To some extent music's role in athletics and exercise is to act as an enhancing supplement to the activity, but it also underscores something of the expressive act of exercise itself. The use of music to supplement and organize exercise is not an isolated Western cultural phenomenon. Throughout history music has been integral to social organization. Military music, sacred music, national anthems, lullabies, drinking songs—these and many other types and styles of music have been used to structure human agency. In the twentieth century, the broadcast and recording industries dramatically increased the accessibility and deployment of music such that today, music is an almost ubiquitous aspect of everyday life

---

[29]   See Allen Guttman, "Sport and Eros," in S.W. Pope (ed.), *The New American Sport History: Recent Approaches and Perspectives* (Chicago: University of Illinois Press, 1997), 217.

[30]   Ibid., 218.

[31]   Helen Lenskyj, *Out of Bounds* (Toronto: The Women's Press, 1986), 56.

that is experienced in restaurants, waiting rooms, the workplace, elevators, and supermarkets. Indeed, it is often difficult in public spaces to escape the tyranny of music impinging on our consciousness. Outside our private musical choices we are daily subjected to an ever-increasing musical bombardment that seeks to promote various commercial and corporate agendas. The quest to understand the social "powers" of music is not new. Despite the philosophical quest to understand the affective power of music from Plato and Aristotle onwards, sociologists and musicologists have not yet fully explored—much less understood—music's role as an active component of social formation. Sociologists Tia DeNora and Sophie Belcher recently began the project of connecting issues of musical style to bodily conduct and activity:

> Music can 'trigger' feeling and point to a range of subject positions, and these may change as quickly and easily as music itself changes from one song or instant to the next. Music is linked therefore to the instantiation of momentary styles of agency and emotional agency, and to live through music in this way is to be a flexible subject.[32]

This "flexibility" in subject positions makes determining the precise role of music in exercise difficult to pin down.

Celebrity fitness videos are often the preferred medium through which North Americans consume exercise culture. Celebrity workout videos have the advantage of disrupting the usual inhibitions of inadequacy or intimidation that might be induced by the awe-inspiring abilities of athletic celebrities. Workout videos by actresses, singers, and models who have high levels of cultural capital in areas other than health and fitness, however, allows the consumer essentially to experience a part of the celebrity's everyday life. To be sure, Jane Fonda's workout tapes set the standard in the early 1980s. By July 1993 Fonda had sold over 10 million units of her varied workout catalogue. Other celebrities from Cindy Crawford to Suzanne Somers have followed in her wake.

One of the most common categories of celebrity fitness and exercise videos, however, consists of those produced by popular singers. Singers, unlike models or actresses, would seem to offer their target audiences an increased identification through the medium of their music. Fans identify with the singer first through the emotions and imagery of a song's lyrics and the accompanying video and also possibly by seeing the singer perform live. This allows singers a sense of enhanced intimacy with their audiences that would normally be unavailable to models and actresses. A brief listing of celebrity vocalist workout videos includes Jessica Simpson's *SpeedFit Workout* (2008), Paula Abdul's *Get Up and Dance!*

---

[32]   Tia DeNora and Sophie Belcher, "'When you're trying something on you picture yourself in a place where they are playing this kind of music'—musically sponsored agency in the British clothing retail sector," *The Sociological Review* 48/1 (February 2000), 80–101, 99.

An Aerobic Dance Workout (1995), Marky Mark's *Workout* (1993), and the Indigo Girls' *Pushing the Needle Too Far: The Indigo Girls Exercise Video* (2002). This brief list speaks, among other issues, to the variety of musics and images that are marketed in the fitness industry and the general increase of cross-marketing ventures between music and sport.

The acknowledged queen of singers with celebrity fitness videos, however, is Cher. Under her CherFitness program label she first released the exercise video *A New Attitude* in 1991 and followed it with *Body Confidence* in 1992. In between these projects she co-wrote a book, *Forever Fit: The Lifetime Plan for Health, Fitness, and Beauty* that was intended to supplement and encourage the purchase of her aerobic system. Cher's exercise videos, like those of many of her competitors, include advertisements for related products. *Body Confidence*, for example, includes advertising for Fox/CBS and Equal Sweetener and concludes with a pitch for more exercise equipment from her own CherFitness brand.

Emphasizing the mediated invitation to participate in the celebrity's life and thereby achieve the celebrity's level of fitness, in her videos Cher is mainly shot using a wide-angle lens that helps reinforce the social atmosphere of the class which the consumer is invited to join. In her study of celebrity fitness videos, Margaret MacNeill points out several negative, possibly even dangerously unhealthy, elements of Cher's workout videos, including the fact that "Obsession with exercise is presented as a positive habit rather than a vice."[33] Cher is well known for her petite physique. She is 5 feet, 8 inches tall and has admitted to weighing as little as 106 pounds.[34] Moreover, Cher clearly falls prey to fitness and health industry body ideals, stating in her book, "I've killed myself in the gym to have this body." It is an image that she seemingly perpetuates through fans of her videos and fitness book, who are invited to remake their bodies in her image.[35]

Perhaps ironically, music per se plays no special role in Cher's fitness videos. It is present but certainly no more so than in celebrity videos by Jane Fonda or Suzanne Somers. The choreography in her *CherFitness: A New Attitude* (1991) video, for example, is led by Doriana Sanchez, Cher's stage choreographer. Cher takes part in the exercises and provides commentary that directly addresses the audience, typically commiserating about how hard some of the exercises are. The accompanying music is not her own but is by well-known mainstream artists such as the Eurythmics ("Missionary Man") and Free ("All Right Now"). The music is mixed at a very prominent dynamic level and typically consists of aggressive guitar-oriented rock with empowering messages. Notably, for the *CherFitness*

---

[33] Margaret MacNeill, "Sex, lies and videotape: The political and cultural economies of celebrity fitness videos," in Geneviève Rail (ed.), *Sport and Postmodern Time* (New York: State University of New York Press, 1998), 163–84, 178.

[34] Ibid., 176.

[35] Cher and Robert Haas, *Forever Fit: The Lifetime Plan for Health, Fitness, and Beauty* (New York: Bantam Books, 1991), 182.

television commercials, Cher resorts to employing her own hit song "If I Could Turn Back Time" (1989) as the hook for her sales pitch.

From the first aerobics classes in the early 1970s it has generally been assumed that musical accompaniment to exercise provides an important beneficial effect to the exercise experience. Today many participants and instructors regard the absence of music, or an inappropriate choice of music, as a recipe for an unsuccessful workout. Despite the widespread use of music to accompany exercise, there is little evidence to support the positive effects of music on physical performance. Very little research, for example, has investigated the influence of music on physical strength. One exception is a 1981 study that used 33 male and 16 female undergraduate students to compare the influence of stimulative music, sedative music, and silence (no music) on measured grip strength. The results concluded that sedative music may actually decrease one's grip strength and hence one's muscular fitness training potential. However, no statistically significant difference was observed between stimulative music and silence.[36] Similar studies on the effects of music on exercise performance have produced inconsistent data. Music has been shown to improve muscular endurance in junior high students doing sit-ups[37] and college women doing push-ups.[38] Similarly, university-aged men and women were able to walk farther and with less effort when exercising to music than they were with no music.[39] However, music was observed to exhibit no significant physiological influence on bicycle performance in untrained university men and women, though the subjects felt they had performed better with music.[40] Indeed, while the actual physiological benefits of exercising to music may be inconclusive, it is through its capacity to increase enjoyment, and hence compliance to a fitness program, that music is likely to contribute to long-term physical benefits. In 1986 one study, for example, found that upbeat music significantly decreased feelings of anger, fatigue, and depression in comparison with slower music.[41] Similarly, another study by Kate Gfeller surveyed aerobic dance classes to determine participants'

---

[36]   K.A. Pearce, "Effects of different types of music on physical strength," *Perceptual and Motor Skills* 53 (1981), 351–2.

[37]   L. Chipman, "The effects of selected music on endurance," MA thesis, Springfield College, from *Completed Research in Health, Physical Education, and Recreation* 9 (1966), Abstract No. 462.

[38]   E.P. Koschak, "The influence of music on physical performance of women," MA thesis, Central Michigan University, from *Completed Research in Health, Physical Education, and Recreation* 19 (1975), Abstract No. 99.

[39]   A. Beckett, "The effects of music on exercise as determined by physiological recovery heart rates and distance," *Journal of Music Therapy* 27 (1990), 126–36.

[40]   S.E. Schartz, B. Fernhall, and S.A. Plowman, "The effects of music on exercise performance," *Journal of Cardiopulmonary Rehabilitation* 10 (1990), 312–16.

[41]   D.N. Wales, "The effects of tempo and disposition in music on perceived exertion, brain waves, and mood during aerobic exercise," MA thesis, Pennsylvania State University,

attitudes toward music and the influence on their experience in aerobic dance.[42] The results revealed that six characteristics of music were identified by 50 percent or more of the participants. The characteristics and percentage of respondents reporting each one were as follows: style (97 percent), tempo (96 percent), rhythm (94 percent), extra-musical association (93 percent), lyrics (77 percent), and volume/intensity (66 percent).[43] A full 91 percent of the participants also reported that music helped to increase their motivation to exercise and also distracted them from the associated physical discomfort.

Another example of the cognitive benefits of music and exercise is provided by the recent well-publicized study by Charles Emory of Ohio State, which suggests that working out to music may give exercisers a positive cognitive boost. According to Emery: "Evidence suggests that exercise improves the cognitive performance of people with coronary artery disease ... and listening to music is thought to enhance brain power. The combination of music and exercise may stimulate and increase cognitive arousal while helping to organize cognitive output."[44] Thus, though more work needs to be done, it appears that while music may not provide direct physiological benefit, it may provide a cognitive boost or improvement that in effect can lead to physiological benefits.

Perhaps the most persuasive evidence of the psychological, psychophysical, and ergogenic effects of music on sports performance is offered in the work of Costas Karageorghis and Peter Terry. They identify music as affecting sporting performance in three main ways: first, as *asynchronous* music, used as background sound to enhance the general environment and experience of a sport; second, as *synchronous* music, where athletes consciously use the rhythmic and other temporal aspects of music to regulate their movement (as in figure skating, gymnastics, or synchronized swimming); and finally, as *pre-task* music, used to stimulate, relax, or generally regulate the mood of an athlete or team before an event. Karageorghis and Terry conclude that indeed synchronous music does yield a significant ergogenic effect on athletic performance.[45] Furthermore, they conclude that pre-task music can be used to manipulate activation states through its arousal control qualities; to facilitate task-relevant imagery or mental rehearsal;

1985, from *Microform Publications*, University of Oregon, Eugene (University Microfiche No. UNIV ORE: U086 251–2).

[42]   Kate Gfeller, "Musical components and styles preferred by young adults for aerobic fitness classes," *Journal of Music Therapy* 25 (1988), 28–43.

[43]   D. Pargman and S. Wininger, "Assessment of factors associated with exercise enjoyment," *Journal of Music Therapy* 40/1 (Spring 2003), 57–73.

[44]   Charles Emery, "A little music with exercise boosts brain power," *Science Blog*. www.scienceblog.com/community/modules (accessed April 5, 2004).

[45]   Costas Karageorghis and Peter C. Terry, "The psychological, psychophysical and ergogenic effects of music in sports," in Athony Bateman and John Bale (eds), *Sporting Sounds: Relationships between Sports and Music* (London: Routledge, 2009), 13–36, 28.

o promote flow; and to enhance perceptions of self-confidence.[46] They further conclude that loud and upbeat music stimulates arousal, while slower, softer music acts as a sedative, and that the "arousal potential" of music (based on tempo, loudness, and so on) also relates to aspects of music preference. Such research would seem to validate the commonly observed use of music by athletes as a synchronous bodily regulator and pre-task routine.[47] Take for example the case of Haile Gebreselassie, the Ethiopian distance runner who smashed the indoor world record for 2,000 meters in 1998 by synchronizing his steps to the techno song "Scatman," played over loudspeakers during the race. Similarly swimmer Michael Phelps primed himself for attaining seven gold medals and five world records at the 2007 World Championships by listening to rap on his iPod before the race. Indeed, elsewhere Karageorghis has claimed that listening to the right music can boost athletic performance by as much as 20 percent.[48]

Regardless of the scientific benefits, music has recently been encroaching into the realm of sports and exercise in some new ways. The Japanese video dance game DDR (*Dance Dance Revolution*), for example, encourages aspects of both team sports and video fitness. As observed by cultural theorist Jacob Smith, the company that produces DDR consciously markets the health aspects of the game in their press releases: "DDR ... is the only game to get players up off the couch, dancing and laughing while burning calories."[49] Indeed, the physical benefits of DDR have prompted up to 1,500 schools in the United States to adopt the game as a supplement to physical education classes.[50] Continuing to blur the line between performance and consumption, such games also create communities of fans (often organized around regional teams) and encourage synchronous behavior in the audiences who watch them. As the player imitates the moves generated by computer, so, too, do audience members imitate the performers playing the game. Redolent of Jean Baudrillard's notions of simulacrum and hyper-reality, DDR is a meta-discourse whereby the audience vicariously participates in the game by watching player-performers reacting to a disembodied digital video code.

Despite its commercial and social significance, workout music of any kind has been almost completely devoid of serious scholarship. The marketing of the genre began in earnest in 1981 with the release of *Jane Fonda's Workout Tape*. The popularity of the tape was such that it spawned a host of imitators, such as

---

[46]   Ibid., 31–2.

[47]   For more on this topic, see Steven Kurutz, "They're playing my song: Time to work out," *New York Times*, January 10, 2008. www.nytimes.com/2008/01/10/fashion/10fitness. html?_r=2&oref=slogin.

[48]   See Sam Lister, "Why music makes you exercise 20% harder," *The Times*, October 21, 2005. www.timesonline.co.uk/tol/news/uk/article581004.ece.

[49]   Jacob Smith, "I can see tomorrow in your dance: A study of *Dance Dance Revolution* and music video games," *Journal of Popular Music Studies* 16/1 (2004), 58–84, 71.

[50]   Seth Schiesel, "P.E. classes turn to video game that works legs," *New York Times*, April 30, 2007.

Richard Simmons's *Sweatin' to the Oldies* series of videos set to classic rock 'n' roll tunes. Other celebrities such as Suzanne Somers and Cindy Crawford were also able to use mass media as a means of converting their personal fitness and weight loss regimes, primarily aimed at women, into commercial successes. Though the use of music as a backdrop for exercise still abounds (sales figures are difficult to estimate as exercise music typically gets lumped together with different genres as "other" in most NARM surveys), possibly the height of the commercial impact of the exercise music craze was reached with Olivia Newton-John's "(Let's Get) Physical," a song which spent 10 weeks at the top of the US charts in 1981. Such music is typically either completely neglected by social commentators or devalued because of its tendency toward seemingly simple, repetitive beats and because, like Muzak and other forms of ambient music, it is music intended for functional use rather than aesthetic contemplation. It should be noted that exercise and strictly health-oriented sports like aerobics or jogging are essentially devoid of external competition and are instead highly rationalized activities, presupposing in the words of Pierre Bourdieu "a resolute faith in reason."[51] Thus, it seems somehow ironic that this type of music consumption encourages both a bodily and often communal experience of music on a scale heretofore unrealized and serves as at least something of a counterbalance to the increasingly virtual, non-bodily experience of music that seems so prevalent in Western society.

A notable exception to the lack of serious scholarship on the relationship of music to exercise is Tia DeNora's work, most thoroughly presented in her book *Music in Everyday Life* (2000). DeNora explores the role of music in contributing to alternately ordered or disordered aerobic workouts in such a way that "it is possible to illuminate the musical characteristics that afford aerobic embodied agency, that enable the particular bodily movements, endurance, motivation, arousal and co-ordination, and that constrain the perception of fatigue."[52] Aerobic sessions are typically structured into regular segments corresponding to the following:[53]

Warm-up (slower tempo with lower-impact movements designed to gently elevate the heart rate)—about 10 min.

Pre-core (faster tempo with higher-impact movements)—about 5 min.

Core (faster, vigorous, high-impact movements)—about 15 min.

Cool-down (slowed tempo and movements)—about 5 min.

Floor exercises (slow toning exercises)—about 5 min.

---

[51] Bourdieu, "Sport and social class," 371.

[52] Tia DeNora, *Music in Everyday Life* (Cambridge: Cambridge University Press, 2000), 89.

[53] Based on categories published in DeNora, 91.

As outlined by DeNora, exercise music is typically produced and distributed by commercial music outlets such as Pure Energy, Music Xpress, Power Productions, Koreography Klub, and Muscle Mixes.[54] The music that they offer is oriented to highly specific circumstances and catalogued by its intended use and effect. For example collections entitled "Motivation," intended for warming up, maintain a beats-per-minute (bpm) ratio of 130 for eight minutes while collections entitled "Energy Workout" or "Body Blitz" use a bpm of 140 for six minutes and are intended for core body training, typically the hardest part of the workout.[55] As DeNora has observed, the music is typically completely synthesized, which allows for an element of hyper-real clarity to the beat patterns. If there are vocal tracks, they are typically sung by females at the upper end of their register. In effect, the higher-pitched melodies and harmonies constantly press upwards, providing a metaphoric and perhaps literal lift in ways that are analogously comparable to the gravity defying, movements of the aerobic workout itself.[56] A typical session will see the music played at full dynamic level throughout the session. As such, music in aerobic workouts provides more than a mere background accompaniment to the physical activity. While the number of beats per minute is an important consideration, the music is purposely foregrounded "as a device of bodily constitution and bodily organization."[57] Music plays a holistic role in the activity, beyond merely providing a beat to synchronize movements and a catchy melody to provide motivation. As Richard Middleton has posited:

> Music is often felt to "symbolize" awareness of time (through tempo and rhythmic structure) and space (through pitch-height relationships, and intensity and textual contrasts). We think of pitch going "up" and "down" … and so on. Connotations relating to other senses are often attached (thus "high" sounds are "light", "bright", "clear") and so are emotions (usually related to tension/ relaxation schemas); and images of movement are usually involved, too; we have already met many "gestures", and equations of musical rhythms and body rhythms (walking, breathing, heartbeat, and so on) are commonplace.[58]

In this manner music acts in a way that literally helps to direct participants of exercise how to move, telling them how fast and how intense the movement should be. Furthermore, within the context of an organized workout, the music helps the participants emotionally and physically locate themselves, albeit in the context of the physical and emotional conformity of the workout class. Thus, as in militaristic marches and most social dancing, music contributes to the disciplining of the body and, by extension, of society as a whole. Not only do musicians and

---

[54]   Ibid.

[55]   Ibid.

[56]   Ibid., 92.

[57]   Ibid.

[58]   Richard Middleton, *Studying Popular Music*, 225. Also cited in DeNora, 92.

performers regulate their bodies through the repetitive patterns (practicing scales, chords, and so on) required in performing on their instruments, but also listener-participants are disciplined, either willingly or not, by being subjected to various musical directives. There is a type of bodily synchronicity at play whereby the music requires certain bodily movements of the performer, who in turn imputes certain bodily movements (though these movements will typically be different) within a listener. In the context of the exercise class, the music thus not only affects the emotional states of participants and synchronizes actions but also can literally help impel them.

One of the underlying marketing agendas of the fitness industry is to sell and perpetuate stereotypical notions of female bodies. The rise of the notion of the "ideal" female body—tall, thin, and athletically toned—and its links to health, success, and productivity is increasingly prevalent in our media driven society. Underlying most scholarly work on this topic is a tacit understanding that messages about the body come from a variety of sources (such as advertising, movies, sports, and music) and are promoted by various celebrities (such as Michael Jordan, Jane Fonda, and Anna Kournikova). As such this ideal image is a hybrid pastiche of images that often relies on intertextual reference in the construction of its meaning. Celebrity female musicians represent one of the prime locations for the marketing and consumption of ideal active bodies. Not "athletes" per se, singers such as Madonna, Cher, Whitney Houston, Mariah Carey, Celine Dion, Britney Spears, Pink, and Gwen Stefani, among others, are nonetheless high profile manifestations of the promotion of the ideal athletic body described above. Their position outside the world of competitive athletics makes them particularly effective agents of identification for young girls and women, who may feel alienated from or intimidated by the world of sports and athletic competition. As musicians, primarily singers, these women participate in a traditionally feminine activity while continuing to project an ideal, athletically toned body image. As has been outlined in Chapter 1, the intertextual linkage of music and sports is in large part, though by no means only, predicated upon the fact that each cultural form centrally involves the body through both participation and spectatorship.

Cheerleaders: Constructing Female Body Image through Music and Sport

One of the most common instances of the mixing of sports and music for many women has been in the realm of cheerleading. Cheering on the accomplishments of athletes dates at least as far back as the ancient Olympics. As an organized pursuit, however, cheerleading was initially a male activity that dates back to the late 1880s, when the first recorded cheer was performed during a Princeton University football game: "Ray, Ray, Ray! TIGER, TIGER, TIGER! SIS, SIS, SIS! BOOM, BOOM, BOOM! Aaaaah! PRINCETON, PRINCETON, PRINCETON!" (*sic*)[59]

---

[59]   K.D. Kuch, *The Cheerleaders Almanac* (New York: Random House, 1996), 8–9.

In 1884 Thomas Peebles, a graduate of Princeton, took this yell to the University of Minnesota, and it was from that campus that organized cheerleading came into being. Cheerleading as we know it today was initiated in 1898 by Johnny Campbell, an undergraduate at the University of Minnesota, who stood before the crowd at a football game and directed them in a famous and still used yell: "Rah, Rah, Rah! Sku-u-mar, Hoo-Rah! Hoo-Rah! Varsity! Varsity! Minn-e-So-Tah!"[60]

It was not until the 1920s that women became active in cheerleading. The University of Minnesota cheerleaders began to incorporate gymnastics and tumbling into their cheers. The first flash-card cheering section was directed by Lindley Bothwell at Oregon State University. Later in the 1930s universities and high schools began performing using paper pom-poms in their routines. By the 1970s, in addition to cheering for the men's football and basketball teams, cheerleaders began supporting all school sports, sometimes selecting several different squads to cheer for wrestling, track, and swimming.

The first nationwide television broadcast of the Collegiate Cheerleading Championships was on CBS-TV in the spring of 1978, initiated by the International Cheerleading Foundation. During this period cheerleading began to receive recognition as a serious athletic activity in itself as the skills level dramatically increased in areas such as gymnastics, partner stunts, pyramids, and advanced jumps. Many high school cheerleading squads began to cheer for female sports (basketball, volleyball) in addition to male sports. Cheerleading involves musical activity both in the actual chanting or leading of cheers and "fight" songs and in organized acrobatic routines that are closely choreographed, typically, to a prerecorded musical soundtrack. In the latter case synchronized group coordination to the music, in the manner of synchronized swimmers or pair skaters, is of paramount importance. There are an estimated 1.5 million participants in cheerleading in the United States alone.[61] Today it is estimated that 97 percent of cheerleaders are female, but 50 percent of college cheerleading squads remain male.[62]

Such statistics reflect an ongoing public interest in cheerleading and its elevation to a sport in its own right. Ironically, an activity that was originally intended, and is often still regarded, as an entertaining sideshow to the main sporting event has evolved into a competitive and highly athletic sport on its own terms. In part the growth of the sport has stemmed from its growing exposure to a global audience. This trend began with the broadcasting of cheerleading competitions by ESPN International starting in 1997 and with the worldwide release of the 2000 film *Bring It On*, starring real-life former cheerleader Kirsten Dunst. In keeping with the historical Madonna/whore binary that has characterized the depiction of women throughout Western history, the image of cheerleaders in popular culture is typically two-sided. On the one hand they are stereotyped as representing youthful

---

[60]   Paul Froiland, *Cheer Magazine* 1/1 (1993), 13, 30–31, 39.

[61]   Arian Campo-Flores, "A world of cheer!" *Newsweek*, May 14, 2007.

[62]   Joel D. Balthaser, "Cheerleading—Oh how far it has come!" *Pop Warner* (January 6, 2005). www.popwarner.com/articles/phenomenon.asp (accessed January 11, 2007).

attractiveness, fitness, leadership, and popularity. On the other hand they are often denigrated as epitomizing mindless enthusiasm, shallow female social hierarchies, hypercompetitiveness, and objectified sexuality. The negative connotations of cheerleading have been fed in part by the media's fixation on stories such as that of Wanda Holloway, the Texas mother whose obsession with her daughter's cheerleading career caused her to hire a hit man to kill her daughter's rival on the cheerleading squad. She became known as the "Texas-Cheerleader-Murdering-Mom," and her story spawned two made-for-television movies: *The Positively True Adventures of the Alleged Texas Cheerleader-Murdering Mom*, starring Holly Hunter in 1993, and *Willing to Kill: The Texas Cheerleader Story*, which aired on NBC in 1992. The cheerleader image has also borne the brunt of much recent comedy, typically emphasizing vacuity. Will Ferrell and Cheri Oteri's overly enthusiastic "Spartan Cheerleaders" skit from *Saturday Night Live*, for example, was one of the most popular recurring sketches in the show's history.

The most famous example of cheerleading stereotypes in music is provided by Toni Basil's hit song "Mickey" and its accompanying video, released in 1982, which precisely reinscribes the limited stereotype described above. Written by Mike Chapman and Nicky Chinn as "Kitty," it was first recorded by UK pop group Racey in 1979. Basil had a crush on actor/singer Micky Dolenz of the Monkees during her work as a choreographer/dancer on the set of the Monkees' 1968 movie *Head*. This prompted her to change the lyrics to "Mickey" and the gender from female to male to better suit her real-life experience. The single reached No. 1 on the US *Billboard* Hot 100 and No. 2 in the UK singles chart. Beyond its chart success, however, the song has had a permanent presence in the world of actual cheerleading and appears on numerous cheerleading mixes.[63] The line "Oh Mickey, you're so fine / You're so fine you blow my mind / Hey Mickey! Hey Mickey!"[64] is a favorite among cheerleaders. The 2000 cheerleading film *Bring It On* featured "Mickey" on its soundtrack sung by Irish girl group B*Witched, and the closing credits had most of the cast lip-synching and dancing to the song while the credits rolled.

The 1982 video, choreographed by Basil, portrays her character in heavy makeup and pigtails and dressed in a typical cheerleading outfit—complete with a short skirt and tight sweater. Against the backdrop of an up-tempo, syncopated cheerleading drumbeat, Basil chants, "Oh, Mickey, you're so fine / You're so fine you blow my mind." As cartoonish as the video may appear, its images are nothing if not stereotypical and unfortunately reinforce and perpetuate a common stereotype in sports that women must be consigned to the sidelines as childlike eye candy that worships the male performance.

More recently we have witnessed an increasing prevalence of female musical artists employing sports themes that represent challenges to masculine hegemony

---

[63] The tune was also prominently used in the chorus of Run-D.M.C.'s "It's Tricky" (1986).

[64] Words and music by Mike Chapman and Nicky Chinn.

and promote a literal female physical and ideological empowerment. Madonna, for example, has been one of the most influential female pop singers for the past three decades. Her music and videos have influenced countless young women in this time period, and she has played a part in several cultural trends. The message to young girls in many of Madonna's early videos, such as "Like a Virgin" and "Express Yourself," was to actively own and control their sexuality for their own personal enjoyment rather than for the sake of giving it over to men. The audience's reaction to and reading of Madonna's early work was certainly strong. There were legions of fans, known as "Madonna wannabes," who dressed like the star and began to similarly flaunt their sexuality and speak their minds in imitation of their idol's self-actualized frankness. This was a catalyst for later generations of artists, from the Spice Girls to Britney Spears, who cite Madonna as an influence. Douglas Kellner uses the Madonna phenomenon as an example of how "considerations of production, textual analysis, and audience readings can fruitfully intersect in cultural studies."[65] When examining the effects of media, specifically the effects of media on gender relations, Jean Kilbourne suggests that media "normalizes" the idea that women are childish and not to be taken seriously; females are gentle and sweet, whereas men are portrayed as strong, physical beings.[66] In her music and videos Madonna has actively challenged this assumption and, apart from her explorations of the feminine and of various gay, Indian, Asian, and Latin cultures, she has also promoted a body image shaped by dance and exercise.

Madonna's videos and live shows introduced a new physicality into female pop performance. Often, as in the videos for "Like a Virgin" and "Holiday," her toned body is foregrounded in midriff-revealing outfits that were immediately emulated by many of her fans. Madonna was originally trained as a dancer, and her concerts are marked by her high-energy choreography, often performed while simultaneously singing. They are performances which demand a high level of aerobic athletic fitness rarely, if ever, previously seen in the annals of female performance. Madonna's attention to fitness and exercise is legendary. According to an article by Richard Price in London's *Daily Mail*, Madonna employs an almost fanatical dedication to working out.

> When it comes to exercise, Madonna can teach professional sportsmen a thing or two. Her dancers call her "the bionic body" and it is easy to see why.
>
> Her regime takes a minimum of three hours of exercise a day, starting with a session of Ashtanga yoga—a high-intensity form for advanced practitioners

---

[65]   Douglas Kellner, "Cultural studies, multiculturalism, and media culture," in Gail Dines and Jean Humez (eds), *Gender, Race, and Class in Media: A Text Reader* (California: Sage Publications, 2003), 1.

[66]   Jean Kilbourne, "The more you subtract, the more you add: Cutting girls down to size," in *Gender, Race, and Class in Media*, 265.

only—which she does in her gym at home, to work on muscle tone and build up her cardio rating …

Before lunch, she has a regular Pilates session at the North London studio of James D'Silva, where she is occasionally joined by Stella McCartney, Gwyneth Paltrow and Julia Carling …

Madonna likes to alternate her third daily session of exercise, choosing from karate at the Budokwai Club in Fulham, swimming, pumping iron, running, cycling and occasionally horse-riding, which she credits with toning up her thighs.

She also has a StairMaster stepping machine in her office, which she often works on as she takes calls. Incredibly, during her pregnancy with Lourdes, she maintained a 45 minute-a-day StairMaster regime right up until the day before she gave birth …

Friends say this level of fitness is not dangerous for Madonna because she has spent the whole of her adult life in peak physical condition. "There has never been a phase in her career when she has been into drink or drugs," says an associate. "She has always been into fitness and exercise. She started off as a dancer and she has always worked on her body. Forget Kabbalah (the mystical form of Judaism she follows), exercise has always been her number one religion …"[67]

The article goes on to describe Madonna's nearly equal obsession with macrobiotic diets and controlled caloric intake. The article sums up the intersection of celebrity (she works out with everyone from fashion designers to movie stars), body image, and media and the intertextual cross-references from the worlds of music, fashion, movies, and athletics that characterize much of our postmodern society. Ironically, in foregrounding the control over her body in her youth, the middle-aged Madonna now appears to be at pains to be able to maintain the same fitness and ideal body image.[68] To some extent she may be viewed as something of a prisoner of her own constructed image.

Britney Spears was the heir—sealed with the infamous kiss during the MTV Video Awards in 2003—to Madonna's popularity among young girls. Prior to her well-documented personal problems, Spears was likely the most influential celebrity of her generation. That influence, unfortunately, has been blamed for

---

[67] Richard Price, "Why is Madonna punishing herself?" *Daily Mail*, January 21, 2006.

[68] Madonna's connection to the fitness industry was further cemented in December 2010 when she opened the first of her proposed chain of "Hard Candy" fitness centers in Mexico City.

increases in body image problems among many of her young fans.[69] In looking at several of Spears's most popular videos, ... *Baby One More Time* (1999), *Oops ... I Did It Again* (2000), *I'm a Slave 4 U* (2001), and a more recent video, *Piece of Me* (2007), a development in the construction of her mediated personality from schoolgirl to adult diva becomes evident.

In ... *Baby One More Time* Spears embodies a character submissive to masculine power as overtly manifested in lines such as "Hit me baby one more time."[70] This sentiment at best implies her desire to have "another chance" to be with a dominant, presumably aggressive male character or, at worst, that she literally looks forward to his violence toward her. The video clearly promotes her as a naive schoolgirl in pigtails and innocent white clothing, practicing her cheerleading routines in the halls of the school, framed by school lockers. Midway through the video her attire changes to a pink athletic sports bra (exhibiting a toned midriff) and workout pants as she dances surrounded by African American basketball players, presumably from her high school team. The video concludes with her cheerleading routine in the gymnasium interspersed with action highlights from the "big game" at which she dances. Much as in "Mickey," Spears's cheerleading role, despite its athletic dance moves, is passive and marked by the overt male voyeurism of the basketball team. Such early images, in addition to promoting a submissive femininity, immediately connect Spears to sports and to the associated connotation of an athletic body.

In contrast to the subservient characterization presented in ... *Baby One More Time*, just one year later the song and video for *Oops ... I Did It Again* places her in a more controlling position. The video begins with Spears descending to the surface of Mars from a spaceship to lead a cast of dancers. Clad in a tight form-fitting red body suit at one point, she restrains a male dancer with chains and essentially ignores the advances of a male astronaut protagonist. Backed by an aggressive downbeat drum and bass punches she aggressively proclaims she's "not that innocent." Such images, however, are somewhat mitigated by other lyrics in the song in which she admits:

> Can't you see, I'm a fool in so many ways
> But to lose all my senses,
> That is just so typically me[71]

Her image as a female in control is even more conflicted in the video for *I'm a Slave 4 U*. Once again, as overtly indicated in the title, the lyrics articulate a message of complete female submission to a male, repeating the lines "I'm a slave for you / I cannot hold it / I cannot control it."[72] The video features

---

[69]   Catherine Sabiston and Brian Wilson, "Britney, the body and the blurring of popular cultures," in *Sport, Rhetoric and Gender*, pp. 199–210, 200.

[70]   Words and music by Max Martin.

[71]   Words and music by Max Martin and Rami Yacoub.

[72]   Written and produced by The Neptunes.

Spears in a futuristic tenement building, again clad in a scanty midriff-revealing outfit. The video foregrounds Spears's body through her sensual dance moves, voyeuristically appreciated by several male characters, that often center on her rubbing her toned stomach. As in *Oops ... I Did It Again*, she again gives the appearance of controlling the men in the room, aggressively pushing one of them away. The theme of unwanted male attention is found in each video except for ... *Baby One More Time*. One of her most recent releases, the video for *Piece of Me* from 2007, takes this issue one step further, emphasizing the unwanted attention of male paparazzi. This video primarily takes place in the voyeuristic setting of a female bathroom. Spears, again with bare midriff, complains of, among other things, the media's seeming obsession with her body image. This is most overtly foregrounded in the opening verse, which Spears sarcastically intones:

> I'm Miss American Dream since I was 17
> Don't matter if I step on the scene
> Or sneak away to the Philippines
> They still gonna put pictures of my derrière in the magazine
> (You want a piece of me?)[73]

These lyrics immediately conjure images of an idealized body associated with a "Miss American Dream" and the objectification of her body parts. Later, in the chorus, the media's critique of her body image is even more overt:

> I'm Mrs. Extra! Extra! This just in
> (You want a piece of me?)
> I'm Mrs. she's too big, now she's too thin
> (You want a piece of me?)

It is clear from the images projected in her songs and videos that Spears's body is foregrounded in the construction of her identity—much as many athletes tend to understand and construct their identities through body image. Her songs and videos evince something of her conflicted identity and evolution from adolescence to adulthood, a theme that has particular resonance for many of her fans. The naiveté evidenced in the high-school themed video for ... *Baby One More Time* is contrasted by a song from her subsequent album, *Oops ... I Did It Again*, and in the video for *Piece of Me*, which shows her to be both an agent and product of change. Prominent images of Spears dressed in red in *Oops ... I Did It Again* project a more powerful "grown-up" character in contrast to her youthful and deceptively innocent appearance from the previous year. This evolution in maturity is also emphasized by the powerful rhythm section and more adult-themed science fiction imagery contained in the video for *Oops ... I Did It Again*.

---

[73]   Written and produced by Bloodshy and Avant.

Though the visual image and lyrics of these videos often contradict each other, the consistent message embedded in all four videos is an emphasis on the appeal of Spears's "ideal" or "idealized" body. The construction of Spears's image in her videos emphasizes athleticism, typically through her dancing and toned, revealed stomach and physique. Such videos, however, simultaneously contribute to a media environment that privileges and promotes an ideal female body. Although there is no direct evidence that such mediated images of Spears and interpretations of her lyrics expressly lead to body image disturbances among young women, it is nonetheless clear that such images and language reflect societal preoccupations with the female body and exercise.[74] In combination with the extreme tabloid media coverage of her family problems and apparent emotional instability, it seems clear that Spears herself has succumbed to the pressures of maintaining the "ideal" which her media image demands.

The idealized female body in music videos is not, of course, limited to Madonna and Britney Spears. One of the most overt athletic cross-pollinations with music occurred through the Spice Girls, in particular the role played by Melanie Chisholm, otherwise known as Sporty Spice. Because she was often dressed in a tracksuit with her hair in a ponytail and projecting a rather "tomboyish" attitude, Chisholm received the nickname "Sporty Spice" from *Top of the Pops* magazine (each member of the group was given a humorous nickname in a small but influential story titled "Spice rack" in 1996). The Spice Girls dominated the late 1990s, selling over 35 million albums in just two years. They went on to become one of the best-selling girl groups of all time, selling more than 55 million records worldwide. They had nine UK No. 1 singles and two No. 1 albums. Sporty Spice epitomized the new empowered athleticism of young girls. Similar to Britney Spears, Melanie Chisholm typically appeared wearing a midriff-revealing workout outfit and was known for her trademark gymnastic dance moves, which included a Sporty Spice back flip. After disbanding in 2001 (and before their reunion tours beginning in 2007), Melanie Chisholm was the best-selling solo act of the group.

The Spice Girls, of course, were more than just Sporty Spice. The group offered girls various images of femininity with which they could identify, from Posh to Sporty. In this sense the Spice Girls carried on the tradition most successfully initiated by the Beatles, of marketing distinct band member identities with which fans could align themselves. It is a marketing practice that has been imitated by countless other pop culture groups appealing to younger audiences, including the Teenage Mutant Ninja Turtles, the Power Rangers, the Powerpuff Girls, and numerous boy bands. For the Spice Girls the empowerment of young girls and women was most prominently manifest in the phrase "Girl Power," which has

---

[74]   Indeed Melanie Lowe argues that young "tweens" actually often distance themselves from Britney Spears's image. See Melanie Lowe, "'Tween' scene: Resistance within the mainstream," in Andy Bennett and Richard Peterson (eds), *Music Scenes: Local, Translocal, and Virtual* (Nashville: Vanderbilt University Press, 2004), 80–95.

become a rallying cry for young women across the Western world. Within the realm of sports, female athletes—such as Brandi Chastain, whose sports bra-clad body was featured on the cover of *Newsweek* after the 1999 US women's soccer team won the World Cup, with the headline "Girls Rule!"—are held up as models for this new form of athletic female empowerment. In the wake of such a movement even Barbie, Mattel's doll designed for young girls and infamous for its disproportionate, idealized body, has recently become a professional basketball player as well as an astronaut, a US president, and a doctor.

To be sure, young women have been empowered by singers such as Madonna, Britney Spears, and Sporty Spice. The stage performances of these artists and others, such as Gwen Stefani, Beyoncé, or Pink, are far more athletically inspired than previous high-profile female pop singers such as Barbra Streisand, Olivia Newton-John, or the lead singers of ABBA. Though images of cheerleaders are still sometimes employed, as in Britney Spears's video ... *Baby One More Time*, the more common image is likely to be one of an athletic, physically fit, and actively empowered body. Nonetheless this empowerment has often come with the attached notions of an idealized, albeit athletic, body.

Just as athletic performances and idealized, physically fit bodies have marked much of the current image of women in popular music, female musical performance has also seen an increasing sense of competition and aggression. The performance practices of many female performers such as Spears are increasingly physical, requiring increased aerobic fitness and athleticism— aspects often reflected in video and marketing images that promote their fit, toned, "idealized" bodies. The association with physical fitness amongst women pop musicians has at times even crossed into masculine identification. Grace Jones is a pop singer, particularly successful in the late 1970s and the 1980s, who was known for her aggressive and physical performances and persona. Jones, a contralto, secured a record deal with Island Records in 1977, which resulted in a string of dance club hits and a large gay following. Her better-known songs include a reworking of David Bowie's "Fame" (1978) and "Slave to the Rhythm" (1986). In partnership with stylist Jean-Paul Goude, Jones adopted a severe, androgynous look with square-cut hair and angular, padded clothes. The iconic cover photographs of *Nightclubbing* (1981) and *Slave to the Rhythm* (1985) exemplified this new identity. Jones's masculine attire and manner were a clear influence on the "power dressing" movement of the 1980s.

Jones's body in her promotional materials is often depicted as muscular and athletically toned, such that she imparts an aggressive, almost physically dangerous persona. Nowhere, perhaps, is this more evident than in the iconic arabesque image used for Jones's 1985 compilation album *Island Life*.[75] The image originated from a 1978 photograph/artistic creation by Jean-Paul Goude. Jones's pose might be considered beautiful; it is also physically impossible. "What I'm interested in is

[75] The image, and its constructed nature, may be viewed at Jones's homepage: "The World of Grace Jones". www.theworldofgracejones.com/48.html (accessed May 6, 2010).

the illusion of reality," claimed Goude, who transformed her from a hard-partying model into an androgynous fantasy image and international superstar. "And unless you are extraordinarily supple, you cannot do this arabesque. The main point is that Grace couldn't do it, and that's the basis of my entire work: creating a credible illusion."[76] As such, Jones and Goude maintain and even extend the notion of the ideal female body into the realm of illusion, even at the expense of accentuating Jones's buttocks, a stereotypical site of black female objectification.

Grace Jones constructed an aggressive and masculine athletic persona in her work that predated the less threatening Sporty Spice image of the Spice Girls. However, the 1980s also witnessed the extreme growth of the fitness and workout video phenomenon. One of the best-known instances of the blending of exercise and music occurred with Olivia Newton-John's song "Physical." In 1981 Newton-John released her most successful studio album, the double platinum *Physical*. The title track, written by Steve Kipner and Terry Shaddick, spent 10 weeks atop the *Billboard* Hot 100, matching the then record for most weeks at No. 1 by a female artist held by Debby Boone's "You Light Up My Life." The single was certified platinum and ultimately ranks as one of the biggest selling songs of the decade. The song and album even earned Newton-John her only placements ever on the R&B Singles (No. 28) and Albums (No. 32) charts.

To counter the song's overtly suggestive tone, Newton-John filmed an exercise-themed video that had the effect of turning the song into an aerobics anthem (and made sweat headbands a fashion accessory outside the gym). Unlike the highly sexualized videos and marketing images of later artists such as Madonna or Britney Spears, Newton-John is clad in a relatively modest workout bodysuit. She is positioned as the fitness instructor for a group of extremely overweight men. As she moves between various pieces of exercise equipment, encouraging the men to work out, she is clearly portrayed as being in control, more athletically fit and powerful than the men she is leading. None too subtle sexual imagery is prevalent as the piston-like pumping of a cross-training machine simulates sex, as does her mounting and riding one man to whom she is supposedly giving a massage. At one point she leads a group aerobics class and the men, all of whom are grossly out of shape, quickly collapse and drop out, leaving her as literally the only person left standing. The climax of the video occurs after the group workout when Newton-John takes a shower. Here the viewer is voyeuristically transported into her shower as she, now naked but strategically covered by steam, daydreams of the overweight men being transformed into muscularly toned "hunks" wearing nothing but thongs. She emerges from the shower dressed in pure tennis whites, ready for a light game of tennis with one of the now physically transformed men. Unfortunately, the men proceed to ignore her as they file past her in pairs, arm in arm. Notably, this "gay" content was edited from the video when it played on MTV.

---

[76]   As quoted by Will Hodgkinson "Snapshot: Grace Jones," *The Guardian*. http://arts. guardian.co.uk/image/0,,1672997,00.html (accessed March 13, 2008).

The popularity of the video seems to have overridden any overly sexual or gay politics that Newton-John may have been flirting with. Even today, as witnessed by the following commentators, discussion of the *Physical* video on YouTube typically focuses on the exercise theme:

Lets all get fit!

C'mon every body, lets get fit and phisical [sic], its good for all of us and it will make us feel great. I like this video because it actually gets me movin' to the beat to dance and because Olivia is soooo cool. But I do think it's a little bit weird at the end about the guys. But I still love the song and I still love Olivias [sic] music. So I don't think that ending is gonna change anything about her graceful fans.

—Wrightbaby123321

What's funny about this video is when this song was written, it was written obviously about sex. But they thought it too direct so they made it about working out. I mean can you imagine? If this came out today you'd have the usual blonde bimbo singers like Britanny [sic] or Paris practically giving BJ's on screen.

—Edhallick

As evidenced by such contemporary discussion of the video, many still only see the work as a call to get fit. Indeed the song subsequently became almost exclusively associated with exercise and became a pop "anthem" largely on those terms. Though the content is a little less serious and more intentionally campy than similar videos by Madonna or Britney Spears, Newton-John's image in the *Physical* video raises many of the same conflicted messages. She is ultimately portrayed as being physically fit and, redolent of Britney's videos, in control of the men who surround her—though this is somewhat contradicted by the lyrics such as the following, which emphasize her seeming lack of control:[77]

I've been patient, I've been good,
Tried to keep my hands on the table
It's getting' hard this holdin' back,
You know what I mean
I'm sure you'll understand my point of view,
We know each other mentally
You gotta know that you're bringin' out
The animal in me[78]

---

[77]   Indeed, as manifest in the preceding YouTube comments, the comparison of Newton-John to more contemporary stars such as Britney Spears is a common subject of discussion.

[78]   Words and music by Steve Kipner and Terry Shaddick.

Newton-John became a pioneer in the nascent music video industry by recording a video album for *Physical*, featuring videos of all the album's tracks as well as three of her older hits. The video album earned her a fourth Grammy and was aired as an ABC prime time special, *Let's Get Physical*, becoming a Top 10 Nielsen hit.[79]

While not as commonly associated as in women's videos, exercise and aerobics have also featured in the videos of several male artists. The alternative pop band OK Go achieved an international hit with their video for the song *Here It Goes Again*. The video, which features a comedic synchronized dance routine on jogging treadmills, was an instant hit on YouTube and gained the band appearances on *David Letterman* and a Grammy for best short form video in 2007. The band is notable for its other sports associations. In 2007, OK Go wrote the fight song for Chicago's Major League Soccer Team, the Chicago Fire. The single "Get Over It" was additionally featured in the EA Sports video games *Triple Play 2003* and *Madden NFL 2003*. Also, their song "Do What You Want" was featured in the video games *EA Sports NHL 06* and *Burnout Revenge.*

Kanye West's song and video *The New Workout Plan* (2004) is also worthy of mention in the context of exercise-themed male music videos. The video revolves around the marketing hype of a television commercial for a fictional workout tape à la Richard Simmons (indeed the song references Simmons at one point with the line, "We ain't sweatin' to the oldies, we jukin' to a cold beat"[80]). The video pokes fun at the fitness and health industry in general as well as sarcastically commenting on how women—African American women in particular—might best attract an NBA star or a rapper such as West. Throughout the song and video West alludes to his preference for women who are not too thin, inverting the normative "ideal" for women as manifest in the songs and videos of Britney Spears and others. The introduction to the song immediately establishes the scenario of an alternative workout plan:

> Now you just popped in the Kanye West
> Get right for the summer workout tape
> And ladies, if you follow these instructions exactly
> You might be able to pull you a rapper, an NBA player …
> So first of all we goin' work on the stomach
> Nobody wants a little tight ass![81]

While such lyrical sentiments might be seen as a welcome relief to the bodily perfection seemingly demanded by many female singers such as Cher or Britney Spears, West's rhetoric seems ultimately misogynistic in tone, advocating an approach to women's body image that is completely predicated on male desire.

---

[79]   In 2010 Billboard named "Physical" the "sexiest song ever written." See "Olivia Newton-John's 'Physical' sexiest song ever" Reuters, February 12, 2010. www.reuters.com/article/idUSTRE61B5H620100212 (accessed June 3, 2010).

[80]   Written by K. West, J.R. Stephens, B. Kante, M. Ben-Ari and S. Rainey.

[81]   Ibid.

The women in the video function almost purely as jiggling eye candy. Women are shown suggestively exercising on a variety of machines and taking part in Pilates and aerobics classes. Following the introduction, the first verse erases any pretense of respect for African American women.

> 1 and 2 and 3 and 4 and get them sit-ups right and
> Tuck your tummy tight and do your crunches like this
> Give head, stop, breathe, get up, check your weave …
> It's a party tonight and ooh she's so excited
> Tell me who's invited: you, your friends and my dick
> What's scary to me henny make girls look like Halle Berry to me
> So excuse me, miss, I forgot your name
> Thank you, God bless you, good night I came …[82]

The only overweight woman depicted in the video is Kanye West himself dressed in drag. There is also a notable cameo by Anna Nicole Smith, filmed in the wake of her substantial weight loss, referencing the fact that she had recently become the spokesmodel for the Nutrisystem diet plan. On one hand the video can be seen as critiquing the shameless hucksterism of much of the diet, weight-loss, and exercise industry. On the other hand, the video reinforces the image of women, African American women in particular, as gullible pawns, willing to believe almost anything, in search of the "ideal" body. The song and video are also, notably, populated by lower-income African American caricatures.

Despite the caricatures present in West's video, media images of women are becoming increasingly athletic. This is particularly evident in the realm of film where such images are also typically cast as overtly violent and dangerous personas. Films such as *Charlie's Angels* (2000), *Kill Bill* Volumes 1 and 2 (2003, 2004), *Crouching Tiger, Hidden Dragon* (2003), and *Million Dollar Baby* (2004), for example, project aggressive, combative, and highly athletic female lead characters. Unfortunately, with the exception of *Million Dollar Baby*, the lead characters in these movies are still portrayed as exemplifying the toned bodies and fashion model looks that reinscribe traditionally idealized body issues for women. Indeed, there is a certain sexual exoticism at play in several of these works. Chinese American actress Lucy Liu, for example, is featured as a dangerous yet beautiful martial artist in both *Charlie's Angels* and *Kill Bill*, and there is a similar portrayal of Michelle Yeoh in *Crouching Tiger* and in a previous role in the James Bond film *Tomorrow Never Dies* (1997). The Lara Croft: Tomb Raider character, popularized in video games but also in the 2001 and 2003 movies starring Angelina Jolie, also focuses on an athletic, gun-toting, hypersexualized female image.

Similar to the overtly aggressive athletic images of women portrayed in recent films, more athletically aggressive stage performances and imagery have been actively cultivated by popular music artists such as Pink and Gwen Stefani.

---

[82] Ibid.

Reacting in part to the earlier passively sexual image of Britney Spears, such artists, though still celebrating physically fit bodies, promote more aggressive, dangerous female images in keeping with the films discussed above. Pink's punk-inflected aggressive imagery and performance is manifest in videos such as *Get the Party Started* (2001) and *So What* (2008). Both videos display her in various hyperactive athletic movements and often focus on her muscular, toned abs. The lyrics for *So What* include "I'm gonna get in trouble / I'm wanna start a fight!"[83] Indeed, Pink's athletic image was foregrounded when she had a cameo appearance in *Charlie's Angels: Full Throttle* (2003) as a motocross race participant.

Perhaps the current queen of athletic female pop performance, however, is Gwen Stefani. As early as her 1995 hit song and video with No Doubt, *Just a Girl*, Stefani was promoting an overtly athletic image as manifested in her sports bra, track pants, and sneakers. In addition the video features her engaging in a series of athletic movements including high kicks, back bends, and push-ups. Musically the song features an upbeat tempo and bouncy melodic riffs in the guitar and bass that break into a faster, aggressive chorus underscoring the anger implicit in the lyrics "I'm just a girl." Indeed, the song was written about Stefani's frustration over female stereotypes portraying women as weak and in need of a man to look after them. This is evident from lyrics such as "Don't you think I know / Exactly where I stand? / This world is forcing me / To hold your hand."[84] Though again promoting an idealized body image, as underlined by the camera's lingering on her well-defined abdominal muscles, the Amazonian athletic image that Stefani employs seems to promote an empowered message of female strength and fitness.

In her solo work, however, Stefani has often seemingly slipped back into stereotypical images of female athleticism. In her well-known song and video *Hollaback Girl* from her 2005 debut solo album *Love. Angel. Music. Baby.* for example, Stefani appears throughout as a cheerleader. The song was supposedly written as a response to Courtney Love's statement that Stefani was a "cheerleader" in an interview with *Seventeen* magazine: "Being famous is just like being in high school. But I'm not interested in being the cheerleader. I'm not interested in being Gwen Stefani. She's the cheerleader, and I'm out in the smoker shed."[85] Stefani responded in the March 2005 issue of *NME*: "Y'know someone one time called me a cheerleader, negatively, and I've never been a cheerleader. So I was, like, 'OK, fuck you. You want me to be a cheerleader? Well, I will be one then. And I'll rule the whole world, just you watch me.'"

The repeated lyric "I ain't no hollaback girl" seemingly suggests that Stefani won't simply verbally holla back at her critics but rather will actively confront them. Other lyrics in the song also address these sentiments and include several cheerleading and football references.

---

[83]   Words and music by Max Martin, Alecia Moore and John Schuster.

[84]   Words and music by Gwen Stefani and Tom Dumont.

[85]   Atoosa Rubenstein, "Courtney Love speaks about Gwen Stefani," *Seventeen* (August 2004), 19.

I heard that you were talking shit
And you didn't think that I would hear it
People hear you talking like that, getting everybody fired up
So I'm ready to attack, gonna lead the pack
Gonna get a touchdown, gonna take you out
That's right, put your pom-poms down, getting everybody fired up ...[86]

The song is in a moderately fast tempo and combines aspects of old-school hip hop and high school drum line beats. Most of the harmonic content of the song revolves around a two-chord alternation between B major and D sharp minor, which music theorists may regard as a leading tone transformation, in which the root of the major chord is lowered by a half-step to form an inverted minor chord on the third scale degree. Perhaps the musical highlight of the song, however, is the musical and lyrical quote of Queen's 1980 hit "Another One Bites the Dust," which occurs about two thirds of the way through. Stefani references the common use of that song at sporting events to humiliate losing opponents to project a similar antagonistic stance, presumably directed at Courtney Love.

So I'm gonna fight, gonna give it my all
Gonna make you fall, gonna sock it to you
That's right, I'm the last one standing, another one bites the dust.

The video, directed by Paul Hunter, features Stefani and her Asian backup singers, the Harajuku Girls, all outfitted in cheerleading uniforms, accompanied by several Californian spirit groups: the Orange Crush All Stars, a cheerleading squad from Orange County; a high school marching band; a pep flag team; and a drill team. Throughout the video, which is set mostly in gymnasiums and football fields, cheerleaders are engaged in highly acrobatic flips and tosses and synchronized cheering—indeed the drum-line beats and cheerleading content of the song and video have led several critics to compare it to Toni Basil's "Mickey."[87] Through such imagery and Stefani's backup singers' suggestive cheerleading outfits, the song seems again to reinforce an idealized and stereotypical image of women as cheerleaders, engaged in what amounts to a cat fight with a fellow performer. Though critics had mixed reviews of "Hollaback Girl," the song was extremely successful and represented Stefani's first chart-topping hit in the United States. The song held the record for most US radio airplay in one week and peaked at No. 1 on the *Billboard* Pop 100 for 8 weeks. Moreover, in October 2005 "Hollaback Girl" was the first single to ever surpass 1 million digital downloads, selling a total of 1.2 million times, and was certified quintuple platinum. The

---

[86] Words and music by Gwen Stefani, Pharrell Williams and Chad Hugo.

[87] R.J. Smith, "Gwen Stefani: *Love. Angel. Music. Baby.*," *Blender*. www.blender.com/guide/new/53197/love-angel-music-baby.html (accessed May 14, 2009); Quentin Huff, "Gwen Stefani: The sweet escape," *PopMatters*, December 14, 2006.

video also held high chart positions on VH1 and MTV's *Total Request Live* and won the MTV video award for best choreography in 2005.[88] Given the exposure and success of the song, it seems likely that such stereotypical images of women, music, and sports will have been well and truly reinforced among Stefani's fans.

The cross-pollination of popular music, athleticism, and exercise is ubiquitous in Western culture. It serves variously to motivate us, direct our emotional and physical responses to exercise activities, and to enable synchronous group movements. As evidenced by the prominent role played by exercise and athletics in various exercise and workout videos, as well as music videos by some of the leading female pop stars of recent years, it also is a powerful co-conspirator, alongside visual stereotyping, in marketing an idealized body image to women. Such images are an extension of both the ancient Greek ideals of body symmetry and, as discussed in relation to Congreve's *Judgement of Paris* in Chapter 1, a long tradition of sexualizing female competition. The cheerleader image is likely the most conspicuous female engagement with sports and music, a role in which ideal body image is also foregrounded. If recent videos by Britney Spears and Gwen Stefani are any indication, it is a role model that is still exerting a heavy influence on popular culture.

As has been mentioned, a central component in the construction of women's images in sports and music lies in the marketing of various personalities and products. As such, the "business" of popular music and sports is of prime importance in understanding how identity is essentially packaged and sold to consumers. The following chapter looks at the convergence of the popular music and sporting industries and, more generally, at the increasingly controversial and influential role played by commercial technology in driving converging issues around authentic human performance in both realms.

---

[88]   Brian Hiatt, "Stefani, Peas lead singles boom," *Rolling Stone*, January 19, 2006.

Chapter 3
"Who Let the Dogs Out?":
Sports Music, Marketing Crossover, and the
Business of Performance Enhancement

While countless people around the globe today consume popular music and sports as pleasurable and distracting entertainments, it is also important to realize—indeed, perhaps often hard to forget—that they are both multi-billion-dollar industries. Expenditure on musical hardware such as CD and MP3 players, software, and downloads; music-related products such as T-shirts, posters, magazines, and books; and attendance at concerts represents a large component of individual leisure consumption. In similar fashion spending on sports culture, including hardware such as big screen televisions, DVD players, and video recorders; software such as cable and cable programming and highlight DVDs; sports-related products such as team jerseys, caps, posters, magazines, and books; and attendance at games represents an equal, if not larger, portion of this consumption.[1] Participants' expenditures on musical instruments and lessons and on sports equipment and team/league fees also represent a considerable economic investment that supports numerous manufacturing and support/service industries in both forums.

Branding and Marketing Crossover in Sports and Music

Both mainstream popular music and professional sports are typically viewed as being driven by commercial gain and so subject to the economic imperatives of capitalist production. These factors essentially shape and co-opt significant

---

[1]   According to charts based on data from the National Sporting Goods Association and published in the 2004–5 Statistical Abstract of the United States, sales for all athletic and sports clothing for 2002 were almost $10 billion dollars, while sales for athletic and sports equipment were over $21 billion. Receipts from spectator sports events for 2002 were over $1.5 billion. See "Sporting goods sales by product category: 1990 to 2003," *Statistical Abstract of the United States, 2004–2005* (Washington D.C.: US Census Bureau, 2004), Table 1247. By comparison, retail music sales (not including concert tickets or music downloads) in the United States for 2005 were estimated at $12.69 billion. See Recording Industry Association of America 2005 Year End Statistics, available at www. riaa.org/aboutus.php.

elements of youth culture—an important demographic common to both sports and music—into dominant institutions and systems of thought. Consumers are forced to pay increasingly higher prices for concert and sports tickets, accompanying refreshments, and memorabilia that reflect increasingly high-paying contracts of the artists and players and, ultimately, higher profit margins for owners. Increased awareness of each sphere of entertainment also inspires greater participation and thus results in improved sales and profitability of the equipment manufacturing companies associated with sports and music. With the widespread availability, particularly in Europe and North America, of specialized sports and music television channels and the increased consumer access via satellite and internet technology, both forms of entertainment and leisure culture have achieved a form of market saturation that has forced them to look outside their own individual markets for opportunities of alliance and mutual benefit. Evidence of this can be found in the increasingly prevalent practice of product placement in movies, a feature that the music industry has exploited to great effect through the marketing of soundtrack albums. While no one, as yet, has offered the world a musical baseball bat or tennis racket that doubles as a guitar, audiences of sports and music are increasingly subject to music–sports interrelationships that are designed to increase and maximize the market share of both industries.

As outlined in Chapter 1, music and sports have had a long and varied interrelationship. It is clear, however, that in the past 20 years popular music and sports have become noticeably more aligned and interconnected as cross-marketed, hypercommodified products of the leisure and entertainment industry.

One of the clearest examples of this increasingly close relationship is found in alternative and so-called "extreme" or "action" sports, such as skateboarding and snowboarding, which have firmly aligned themselves with punk and alternative hip hop. Extreme sport enthusiasts are well known for their suspicion and avoidance of more organized mainstream sports. This spirit of autonomy and resistance to mainstream commercialism is reflected in the movement's alignment with independent alternative rock. Many practitioners of such nontraditional sports are also involved in the independent music scene. A quick online search of extreme sports websites turns up numerous sites linking aggressive punk and alternative bands with various extreme sports. A representative site is "eXtreme Sports Music," the introduction to which emphasizes the connection between extreme sports and the independent alternative music scene:

> Welcome to eXtreme Sports Music, a site dedicated to independent musicians who are also extreme sports enthusiasts. This site was created by a professional musician and lover of extreme sport. We present lifestyle components of each sport as well as music CDs by bands who participate in extreme sports.[2]

---

[2]   www.extremesportsmusic.com (accessed April 5, 2010).

Such concern for independence and for mutual cross-participation in, or at least appreciation of, alternative sports and music is a central feature of the extreme sports movement. In addition, the ethic of active participation versus passive consumption marks the ideologies of both. The two activities are increasingly being viewed as a fused, singular phenomenon.

More mainstream sports are also overtly attempting to align themselves, and thus identify, with various music genres. Typically this involves connecting the sport to a mainstream music audience and attempting to diversify, or reflect the diversity of their potential fan base, by evoking a broad range of musical genres. NASCAR, the fastest-growing professional sport in North America, is famous for its blue-collar Southern white male country music connections. Indeed, The Nashville Network made the conscious decision to broadcast NASCAR alongside country music to appeal to white working-class men.[3] This target demographic and marketing alliance was reinforced through the 2009 Daytona 500 pre-race performances by country music star Keith Urban (though Urban also cultivates a significant female fan base). The significance of creating a musical identity for NASCAR has been underlined in recent deals with Cherry Lane Music Publishing. Cherry Lane president Aida Gurwicz claims that the company's "mission statement is to ... brand NASCAR with a library of music [designated "Motor Music"] that creates another layer of enjoyment for fans and brings in new fans."[4] Indeed, in an effort to broaden its appeal and perhaps reflect something of the diversity of its current fan base, NASCAR has already begun integrating popular music (mostly hard rock and alternative/heavy metal) into its television (TV) broadcasts and is planning to create original musical themes for various drivers, teams, and tracks. NASCAR vice-president of broadcasting, Paul Brooks, notes that NASCAR is already the second most popular sport on television: "We're creating a [musical] NASCAR logo ID and a large library of music with a stronger connection to the sport that all our partners can pull from and that we can integrate into our TV broadcasts."[5] The interest in music among some of the drivers is equally prevalent. Star driver Dale Earnhardt Jr, for example, has been involved in music videos by 3 Doors Down, the Matthew Good Band, and Sheryl Crow.

Not to be outdone, the National Basketball Association is rapidly increasing its ties with record labels and their artists. During any break in current NBA games, the arenas pulsate with a variety of Top 40 singles. Since 2001 half-time shows at playoff games have included concerts from such acts as U2, Destiny's Child, and Sugar Ray. Frequent videos on music networks MTV and BET promote many hip hop artists sporting jerseys and headbands of their favorite teams and often include shots of their favorite players. As part of Jam Session 2003, the interactive fan fair held during All-Star Weekend, artists such as Nelly, Justin Timberlake,

---

[3]   Don Cusic, "NASCAR and country music," *Studies in Popular Culture* 21/1 (1998), 31–40.

[4]   Jim Bessman, "NASCAR revs up Cherry Lane," *Billboard* 115/24 (June 2003): 42.

[5]   Ibid.

Christina Aguilera, and LL Cool J performed in various musical events that were broadcast around the world. In 2002 a number of promotional videos for the NBA were launched, featuring performers such as Lenny Kravitz, Pink, and No Doubt. Randy Miller, senior vice-president of marketing for Jive Records, claims, "For us it's a great opportunity to put new artists and established talent in front of an NBA audience."[6]

While the NBA recently appears to be trying to reach new audiences by associating itself with a variety of musical styles, the crossover between the music industry and professional basketball has traditionally been most pronounced in the use of hip hop. According to Millar, "there is a natural alliance" between hip hop music and basketball: "Hip-hop is a music that comes from urban America, and basketball is a sport that comes from urban America."[7] Indeed, basketball and hip hop share a very similar visual image: headbands, baggy clothing, and running shoes. The slam dunk move has even been described by cultural critic Nelson George as "intimidation through improvisation."[8] Underlining the connection, a significant number of basketball players have attempted to become recording artists. NBA stars such as Shaquille O'Neal, Kobe Bryant, Chris Webber, and Allen Iverson, for example, have all recorded rap albums. None of these musical efforts has been particularly critically or commercially successful, but they have nonetheless reinforced and solidified the close relationship between hip hop or rap and basketball. The NBA, however, is by no means limiting its musical focus to hip hop. Just as NASCAR is attempting to increase its fan base by expanding out from their country music image, NBA league executives have recently been emphasizing a diversity of musical genres. Disco diva Gloria Gaynor and 1970s rock icon Meatloaf, for example, were part of the 2003 all-star events, and acts such as Elton John, Michelle Branch, and the Dave Matthews Band have also performed in conjunction with other NBA events.

Though in recent times basketball has been the sport most closely aligned with music, a number of other sports have had significant musical traditions. The sports music phenomenon has, however unlikely, even penetrated the world of golf. Over the past several decades a number of songwriters, and at least two record companies, have involved themselves in the genre of golf music that typically relies on the theme of golf, rather than a particular sound or musical style. One company, Private Music, believes in the concept enough to have launched a golf label called Teed Off Records, which released the compilation album *Golf's Greatest Hits* in 1996. The compilation featured songs such as Loudon Wainwright III's "Golfin' Blues." This compilation, however, was not the first or only instance of so-called golf music. The soundtrack for Kevin Costner's

---

[6]   Blane Bachelor, "Music industry keeps its eye on the ball," *Billboard* 115/10 (March 2003), 50.

[7]   Ibid.

[8]   Nelson George, *Elevating the Game: Black Men and Basketball* (New York: Harper Collins, 1992), xv.

film *Tin Cup*, for example, made it as high as No. 85 on the *Billboard* 200 and featured songs like Bruce Hornsby's "Big Stick" and Mickey Jones's "Double Bogey Blues." Indeed, the musical golf repertoire has a relatively long history. Sheet music songs about golf date back at least to 1896.[9] Possibly the first golf album was Oscar Brand and his Sandtrappers' *Fore!* released by Elektra in 1956. Huey Lewis and the News later used the same title for their 1986 album. Another album, "Jazz at the 19th Hole," released by Four Leaf Clover in 2001, represented yet another attempt to broaden the marketing net, though this time by linking golf to the specific genre of easy listening jazz.

While golf and basketball have significant musical histories, they both pale in comparison to the particularly rich musical history of baseball. Like golf music, and unlike the targeted use of music by NASCAR and the NBA to market themselves, the music associated with baseball uses the sport itself as thematic lyrical material. In addition to numerous club theme songs, as discussed in Chapter 1, the classic "Take Me Out to the Ball Game" (1908) is a ubiquitous feature of seventh inning stretches in baseball games of every level and location. Though the song is one of the most popular in America (rivaled by the likes of "Happy Birthday" and "The Star-Spangled Banner"), a number of other baseball tunes have also reached iconic status among baseball fans. Such songs include Terry Castleman's 1981 hit "Talkin' Baseball—Willie, Mickey & 'The Duke'" and John Fogerty's "Centerfield" from 1985. Like their basketball brethren, in the past baseball stars such as Mickey Mantle and Les Brown ("Joltin' Joe Di Maggio") have enhanced their public profile by recording songs. Bernie Williams, a former star outfielder for the New York Yankees, even initiated a bona fide career as a classical-jazz guitarist, releasing the album *The Journey Within* in 2003. The phenomenon has even crossed language and cultural divides, as witnessed by the release of *Roberto Clemente—Un Tributo Musical* (1998) in honor of the late star Pittsburgh Pirate fielder Roberto Clemente. The album is notable for featuring a variety of salsa performances by well-known Latin ballplayers such as Dennis Martinez, José Mesa, Javy Lopez, Tony Perez, and Sandy Alomar Jr.

In addition to the numerous songs that take baseball as their lyrical theme, there are many that, though not about baseball per se, are nonetheless strongly associated with the sport. Sister Sledge's "We Are Family," for example, was played throughout every home game of the 1980 Pittsburgh Pirates World Series campaign and hence became integrally linked to the team. This situation was more recently replicated when the alternative pop of the Fratellis' "Chelsea Dagger" was repeatedly played during celebratory moments throughout the Chicago Blackhawks' victorious 2010 Stanley Cup campaign. Similarly, thanks to the popularity of the movie *Major League* (1989), The Troggs's "Wild Thing" has become almost universally associated with the entrance of the closer or a new pitcher. In the film's climactic one-game playoff with the Yankees, Indians pitcher

---

[9]   Craig Rosen, "Golf music: Out of the rough, into the fore," *Billboard* 106/37 (September 1996), 1, 26.

Ricky "Wild Thing" Vaughn, relegated to a relief role, dramatically enters the game to The Troggs's hit song as the crowd cheers wildly and sings along. Today many real-life closers walk or run in from the bull pen accompanied by similarly loud and imposing hard rock or heavy metal.[10] Indeed, the practice of players' choosing "theme" music to accompany them as they walk to the plate is ubiquitous in baseball. As the theme music is chosen by the players themselves, it is typically closely aligned with their identity and often reflects their ethnic or national heritage or else is simply a reflection of their personal musical tastes.[11]

The Baha Men's hit single "Who Let the Dogs Out?" is likely the most conspicuous example of the confluence of sports and music marketing to date. The music distributor Pro Sports Marketing was primarily responsible for the group's breakout hit when they began distributing the single to baseball stadiums and other sporting arenas in 1999. The song achieved widespread popularity in baseball stadiums and was subsequently added to radio station playlists. In this instance it was the song's initial popularity at sporting venues that actually affected its subsequent success on the musical charts.[12]

"Who Let the Dogs Out?," however, is not the only instance of a song gaining popularity through sports. Another instance of a hit tune being created almost entirely through the medium of sports is Eric Idle's comedic song "Always Look on the Bright Side of Life." This song was originally released as part of the soundtrack for Monty Python's film *Life of Brian* in 1979. An inspired moment of black humor, the song is heard at the end of the movie when it is sung to Brian, who is a mistaken Messiah figure, by his fellow sufferers who are being crucified. In the 1990–91 soccer season, however, it became a popular anthem among football supporters, especially those of Manchester United, and as a result the rereleased single achieved considerable success on the pop charts in Britain. A different, and perhaps even more unusual case of sports influencing the charts,

---

[10] In a case of life imitating art, relief pitcher Mitch Williams, whose speed and control problems were similar to Vaughn's, was nicknamed "Wild Thing" after the film came out. Instead of fighting the image, he switched his uniform number from 28 to Vaughn's 99 and wore it for the rest of his career.

[11] An interesting variation on theme music is found in Japanese professional baseball, where fans compose "fight songs" for individual players that are sung as encouragement while they are at bat. The songs are typically approved by the official fan club of the team and are an indication of the player's status. A player might receive a "fight song" only after several years as an indication from the fans that they have become a respected member of the club.

[12] Notably, Pro Sports' other activities include arranging pre-game concerts, disc and concert ticket giveaways at sporting events, and supplying music clips for syndicated radio shows. While the primary repertoire of stadium sports music is rock and R&B with a party vibe, the company recently arranged for the cross-genre act Three Mo' Tenors to perform "The Star-Spangled Banner" and "America the Beautiful" at Cal Ripken's final game in Baltimore. See Catherine Applefeld Olsen, "Pro sports marketing pitches hits for athletic events," *Billboard* 114/39 (September 2002), 59.

is provided by "Nadia's Theme (The Young and the Restless)." This music was originally written by Barry de Vorzon and Perry Botkin Jr in 1971 for the movie *Bless the Beasts and the Children* and subsequently adopted as the theme of the TV soap opera *The Young and the Restless* in 1973. The tune, however, achieved almost universal public recognition only in 1976 after cinematographer/reporter Robert Riger used it on ABC television's *Wide World of Sports* against slow-motion montages of the floor exercise routine of celebrated Romanian gymnast Nadia Comăneci at the Montreal Olympics. The montage captured the public's imagination and the song became a Top 10 single in the fall of 1976, the composer, Barry De Vorzon, renaming it "Nadia's Theme" after her.[13]

The increasing cross-pollination of music and professional sports is largely rooted in commercial and marketing motivations. Sports offer the music industry an alternative market in a time of declining CD sales. Joe DiMuro, vice-president of BMG Music Strategic Marketing, foresees ever-increasing integrations between music and sports: "Let's face it: The music industry is in a declining state. We are acutely aware of that. We need to find new ways of promoting our artists as a way of generating revenues ... "[14] Though this explanation for the phenomenon is almost entirely rooted in the logic of economics and market expansion, it nonetheless also touches on an aspect of postmodern capitalist globalization that, given the recent spate of corporate media mergers, is resulting in more numerous integrations and cross-pollinations of media and content so as to appeal to as large, and therefore diverse, an audience as possible. Thus, the drive for corporate global market share creates new media pastiches and marketing opportunities—such as sports music, film music soundtracks, coffeehouse music, and other non-traditional music genres and sources of revenue.

Though sports may be a new or expanding venue through which to market music, music culture in turn can help to popularize sports. As rap artist Ice Cube explains, "The NBA without hip-hop is just a game. Hip-hop made Michael [Jordan] cool."[15] As evidenced by the plethora of stars lining up to sing at the Super Bowl and other high-profile sorting events, musicians know that sports certainly can make them cool. John Ondrasik of the band Five for Fighting (who take their name from the five-minute penalty incurred for fighting in ice hockey) states, "Bands position [themselves] for sporting events, as they do get you in front of people ... and it's a good time."[16] There is a natural symbiosis between professional athletes and musicians that often results in a mutual admiration. Both

---

[13] Ironically, Comăneci never actually performed to "Nadia's Theme." Her floor exercise music was a medley of the songs "Yes Sir, That's My Baby" and "Jump in the Line," arranged for piano.

[14] Bachelor, 50.

[15] As quoted in John Rolfe, "The music–sports connection is stronger than ever," *Sports Illustrated.com*, http://sportsillustrated.cnn.com/2007/writers/music_sports/09/28/rolfe.essay/index.html (accessed October 1, 2007).

[16] Ibid.

share the pressures of relying on their talent, energy, passion, and concentration under pressure to perform at a consistently high level in front of thousands of people night after night.

The Age of Agents

Among the array of promoters, sponsors, owners, and performers that make up the industries of sports and music, one group seems particularly representative of the triumph of commercialism. These are the agents who, since their rise in the United States in the early 1960s, have greatly increased the level of financial rewards for both their athletic and artistic clients. In the past the agent's primary motivation for maximizing player and performer salaries and contracts was to increase his or her own fee, typically a percentage of the deal negotiated on behalf of the client. Today's agents, and the larger management agencies to which they often belong, while still interested in generating maximum income from their clients' performance contracts, typically perform a variety of functions to derive income activity for clients and can often simultaneously stage, promote, market, televise, and arrange sponsorship and advertising for an event. As such, agents have become one of the prime factors in facilitating and generating sports–music cross-pollinations.

The world's largest sporting agency is International Marketing Group (IMG). The company website outlines the diversified nature of its services, underlining the increasing interconnection between sports and entertainment media.[17]

> IMG connects brands to global opportunities in sports, entertainment and media.
>
> IMG is the world's premier and most diversified sports, entertainment and media company. We partner with the world's leading marketers and media networks to help them grow their businesses through our event properties, media production and distribution, talent brands, sponsorship consulting, brand licensing, sponsorship sales and other services.
>
> From emerging leadership in areas like digital media, licensing and entertainment programming, to our long-standing strength in sports, fashion and traditional media, IMG is committed to providing business-building solutions. Our partners include many of the world's most famous brands, media outlets, sports governing bodies, national and local governments, athletes, entertainers, models and fashion designers.
>
> IMG is the global leader in event management and talent representation across golf, tennis and fashion and has a significant presence in many other sports,

---

[17]   www.imgworld.com/about/default.sps (accessed April 28, 2008).

cultural and lifestyle categories. Our media division is one of the world's top independent producers of sports and entertainment television across multiple genres and is an emerging leader in video and interactive content creation for broadband and mobile platforms.

In addition to the emphasis on its global reach and diversified marketing opportunities offered to their clients, the website states that IMG's areas of expertise include:

- Media production and distribution across multiple platforms
- Event creation, management and sponsorship sales
- Client representation and brand management
- Sponsorship and media consulting
- Global sponsorship and media sales
- Consumer products licensing
- Athlete training

As indicated in this list, the management company has even crossed into the realm of active athletic training. Though such promotion is primarily foregrounding an athletic connection, and indeed music is never specifically mentioned in their list of services, the company nonetheless does actively court musicians. Pop singer Justin Timberlake recently signed with IMG based in part upon its ability to help him develop an eco-friendly golf course in his native Memphis, Tennessee.[18] As evidenced above, IMG emphasizes the global nature of its enterprise, and indeed this cross-promoting trend is not merely limited to North America or to IMG. The Parc Landon Agency, for example, bills itself as a "music, sports, entertainment professional services agency ... that works with and represents more than 300 concert and sports promoters in the Asia territory ... "[19] Essentially the company specializes in brokering live performances throughout Asia by US recording artists and athletes such as Akon, 50 Cent, Martina Hingis, and Pete Sampras. As such, these increasingly diverse management agencies are central players in actively promoting the economic and marketing connection between the worlds of sports and music.

Music, Sports, and Alternative Media

In addition to the shared live performance venues and agency cross-promotions, the marketing nexus of music and sports is also increasingly being found in other

---

[18] Mark Sweeny, "Timberlake signs IMG marketing deal," *Guardian*, Friday, April 18, 2008, available at www.guardian.co.uk/media/2008/apr/18/marketingandpr?gusrc=rss &feed=media (accessed May 15, 2009).

[19] See www.parclandon.com/index_eng.php (accessed April 28, 2008).

media. The subject of the relationship between sports, music, and motion pictures is specifically dealt with in Chapter 7. The video game industry, however, is also increasingly becoming a lucrative venue for music–sports cross-promotion. Major label musical artists are increasingly being associated with sports-related video games. Artists such as Aerosmith (three songs on Tecmo's *Dead or Alive 3* for Xbox), Metallica (featured in Infogrames' *Test Drive Off-Road: Wide Open*), and Blink 182 (one of 12 acts contributing songs to Infogrames' *Splashdown*, a jet-ski action game) have all created music for various sports-related video games. Moreover, some acts have even taken roles in the games themselves. Barenaked Ladies, for example, not only lent their song "It's Only Me (The Wizard of Magic Land)" to the Electronic Arts Sports hockey game *NHL 2002*, but the band even appears in the game via a create-a-player mode. The *NHL 2002* game was released for PC and PS2 to coincide two months before the band's *All Their Greatest Hits* album hit the marketplace.

This tactic is not a new one and is rooted in hybrid marketing strategies, the benefits of which are common to both band and label. Echoing the rationale cited by Joe DiMuro above, Don Terbush, senior director of film and new media advertising for Universal Music Enterprises, states, "Video games such as *Splashdown*, have provided labels with a great alternative means of gaining exposure for new music and even music by more established acts."[20] Dave Warfield, producer of NHL franchise games for EA Sports, however, notes that the general idea of music in video games is what he calls "emotion and recognition."[21] Though this description is open to interpretation, it appears that the music in video games would ideally (at least as far as EA Sports is concerned) evoke an emotion that will be remembered and associated with a particular game and a particular brand. Activision brand manager David Pokress observes, "It's not just about extreme action sports, but it's also about the lifestyle of our games, which are targeted at teens and young adult males who are into music."[22]

As such a statement implies, it is likely no surprise that sports video games are aimed primarily at young males. There are few such games aimed at young women consumers (notably excepting "Mia Hamm's Soccer 64" and "Mia Hamm's Shootout"). But, perhaps notwithstanding the exercise videos, the character of Sporty Spice from the Spice Girls or the general athleticism exhibited by artists such as Gwen Stefani or Pink as discussed in Chapter 2, there have been few consistently definable instances of sports–music confluences marketed specifically to young women.[23]

---

[20]   Steve Traiman, "Video games provide new platform for music promotion," *Billboard* 113/49 (December 2001), 75.

[21]   Ibid.

[22]   Ibid.

[23]   Laura Groppe, "Girls and gaming: Gender and video game marketing," *Children Now*, www.childrennow.org/media/medianow/mnwinter2001.html (accessed August 4, 2006).

While sports organizations such as NASCAR and the NBA have associated themselves with various types and styles of music to forge a wider fan base, establish a recognizable sonic identity, or merely cash in on lucrative cross-marketing potential, the sports music phenomenon has, at times, had an impact on public taste such that some companies have begun to specifically focus on packaging and distributing the music played at sporting events. A result of this has been the formation of a specific "sports rock" genre. The company Tommy Boy, for example, introduced its first "Jock Rock" album in 1994 and has since released a number of dance-oriented *Jock Jams* albums and a *Slam Jams* album of punk and new wave. Tommy Boy president Monica Lynch says she came up with the idea for *Jock* compilations when she realized that a lot of the same music (such as Gary Glitter's "Rock and Roll Part 2" and Queen's "We Will Rock You") was being played at different venues for different sports. The label teamed with ESPN shortly after this realization to create compilations of music. According to Lynch, the albums attracted a much larger audience than anticipated:

> We found that they are attractive not only to people who would go to major league sports, but we also developed a base in colleges and universities that have big athletic programs and in high school and grade schools. These albums basically became the ultimate soundtracks to any sport. Any song we put on these compilations has to pass the lampshade test. Which means if someone got drunk enough, would they put a lampshade on their head and dance around to it?[24]

This latter admission is somewhat troubling given that, in the same breath, she is also talking about developing an underage fan base within high schools and grade schools. Despite this questionable marketing strategy, the Tommy Boy series has resulted in extremely healthy sales. According to Soundscan, the top sellers are *Jock Jams, Volume 1* at 2.3 million units and *Jock Jams, Volume 2* at 1.9 million. Success breeds imitation, and in 1997 K-Tel began a sports music series that it labeled "The Greatest Sports Rock and Jams" and has subsequently released albums inspired by, and catering to fans of, baseball, football, basketball, and professional wrestling.[25] Alphabet City Sports Records has also begun to target regional and local audiences by producing team-specific "greatest hits" albums that feature tracks commonly heard in each team's home arena. Though the popularity of such specific "sports rock" albums has recently somewhat waned, the previous commercial successes of the genre testify to the cross-

---

[24] Catherine Applefeld Olsen, "Labels take a run with sports," *Billboard* 110/35 (August 1998), 77–8.

[25] Unlike many labels, such as Tommy Boy, that merely dabble in the sports marketplace, Alphabet City's entire business is made up of sports compilations. The New York-based company has created 20 albums that are primarily team-specific for a variety of NFL, NBA, NHL, and NCAA franchises. The company's top sellers are the Chicago Bulls albums, one of which has sold over 500,000 units (Olsen, "Labels," 77–8).

marketing potential of and synchronous aesthetic between sports and music in the minds of many consumers.

A variety of artists have composed songs specifically for sports use. Dave Mustaine, lead singer for the metal band Megadeth, for example, wrote "Crush 'Em" in 1999 as an attempt at a hockey anthem. Similarly in 1996 Run-D.M.C. produced a new version of their song "My Adidas," originally recorded in 1986, called "My Yankees," and rapper Jesse Jaymes composed an ode to the New York Knicks called "Go New York Go!" in 1994.

The music and sports industries have consciously allied themselves in a variety of innovative ways. As both industries have continued to grow, the monetary rewards available to star artists and athletes have also increased to heights previously unimaginable. In today's celebrity-obsessed culture, the lifestyle of successful athletes and musicians is seemingly more overtly hedonistic and decadent than ever before. Many people, old and young alike, are drawn to such images of celebrity, and the public is being subjected to a constant barrage of celebrity images through print, broadcast, and online media. As the monetary stakes in both the music and sports industries have risen, so too has the pressure on athletes and performers to succeed and maintain their success. One of the side effects of such an inherently capitalist driven system is increased competition. Along with increased competition in both sports and music, however, comes a concomitantly increased temptation—indeed in many cases mandatory requirement—to use various forms of performance enhancement.

"Take Me Out to the Ball Game"/"I Wanna Be Sedated": Technologies of Performance Enhancement

The remainder of this chapter examines the rise of performance enhancing technologies, including drugs, in sports in the context of the parallel rise of similar performance enhancing technologies in music. The reasons for the growing prevalence of performance enhancing technologies in both sports and music are varied; however, the increasing emphasis on commercial gain must be considered one of the most important. Commenting on the use of drugs in sports, Ellis Cashmore has noted:

> Commercialism is the malefactor here; as sport has slid further from the Corinthian ideal, its passage lubricated by business interests, so the joy of competing for its own sake has been superseded by an unprincipled win-at-all-costs approach … [Drug use] is but one fact of an alliance between sport and business that has developed over the past several decades.[26]

---

[26]   Cashmore, *Making Sense of Sport*, 121–2, 130.

I would posit that the situation is nearly identical in the world of music, and that the drive to find a competitive edge through performance enhancing technologies of any variety is no less commercially driven there.

In the past few years a variety of scandals have shaken both the sporting and musical communities and caused them to re-examine what will count as an "authentic" or legitimate human performance. In sports culture the allegations and revelations of athletes who have consciously cheated through the ingestion of performance enhancing drugs has touched many sports and athletic events, including professional baseball and football, the Tour de France, and the Olympic Games, to name but a few of the most prominent examples. In the culture of popular music drugs have, at least since the 1960s, been commonly viewed as a method of enhancing creativity and as supplements to a stereotypical hedonistic rock 'n' roll lifestyle. Beyond the consumption of illegal drugs, however, aspects of performance in both sports and music have been greatly enhanced by the continual advent and refinement of more traditional technologies relating to equipment and training techniques.

Music and Chemical Enhancement

The problem of illegal drug use in general is one that affects many areas of society but, perhaps because of their high public profile, seems particularly prevalent in sports and music cultures. Stories of athletes and musicians being arrested on drug possession charges litter the headlines. The question of performance enhancement and the pressure to perform (and perhaps the consequent need to escape that pressure through illegal mind- and body-altering drug use), however, has received relatively little attention.

Particularly within the culture of jazz and popular musics, the notion of taking mind-altering, typically illegal drugs is one often connected to notions of experimentalism and creativity. Drug use by musicians and other artists is often viewed as a means to enhance one's creative perspective and is often done to facilitate a literal transcendence of the physical connection to the body into a state of hyper-sensitive awareness. The Beatles' acknowledged experimentation with LSD and marijuana, particularly on the album *Sgt Pepper's Lonely Hearts Club Band*, is likely the best-known example and has helped to solidify and, at least to some extent, justify the practice among many rock and pop artists. Of course many other musicians, from past icons such as the Rolling Stones, Pink Floyd, and Bob Marley, to more recent acts such as Radiohead and Amy Winehouse, have also openly resorted to using drugs as part of their creative lifestyle. One must not overlook the plethora of well-known jazz artists, such as Miles Davis and Charlie Parker, as well as those in other musical genres, who have also turned to this type of creative performance enhancement. The popular music world in particular, however, is littered with a host of infamous drug casualties, from Elvis to Janis Joplin and Jimi Hendrix. The use of mind-altering drugs, including alcohol, in live performance, rather than to stimulate a creative compositional moment, is generally acknowledged to impair a musical performance, though some might claim the relaxing effects of the drugs help to overcome nervousness and thus enhance the playing.[27] Though the use of anabolic steroids among musicians is not widespread and is generally not linked with enhancing musical performance, the use of beta blockers to calm jittery nerves during a performance is not uncommon. Beta blocker use is particularly prevalent in the realm of classical music. Indeed, a 1987 survey claimed that up to 27 percent of classical musicians used beta blockers.[28]

Some cultural critics have argued that drugs in music merely represent one more instance of technological enhancement of the experience of music. Mathew Collins, for example, has argued that drugs can be usefully theorized as a form of technology that should be discussed in relation to culture.[29] Various popular music trends over the past 50 years have been characterized by a concomitant link to particular drugs, from the association of pot with folk music, reggae, and rap, to acid with 1960s psychedelic and acid rock, to cocaine with disco, to heroin and speed with punk, to ecstasy with rave and techno music. To some extent these drugs have become symbolically representative of the musical genre to which they are attached. Of course some drugs, such as alcohol and marijuana, have become far more normalized in contemporary Western society than others, and hence prevalent across many musical cultures. The use of such drugs has arguably become subsumed into what might simply be called "leisure culture." As Jeremy Gilbert and Ewan Pearson claim, such a term implies that: "Music, fashion, club spaces, advertising imagery, ritualistic forms of consumption (of drugs and associated substances—gum, soft drinks, even Vick's Vapo-rub)—constitute a coherent formation which delimits and defines the range of meanings and effects which the particular technology (drugs) can have."[30]

If one accepts that drugs are simply another form of technology that is available to musicians and audiences, the question arises as to why their use has historically been largely tolerated in the music world while not in the sporting world. It is clear that the use of drugs in music, whether as a performance/reception enhancement or simply for recreational pleasure, is far more socially accepted (at times even celebrated) than in the sporting world. As will be discussed below, the reasons

---

[27]   It is arguable that the amount and degree of the drug taken, and hence the level of impairment, is often crucial in determining whether or not a performance has been helped or hindered by the ingestion of drugs.

[28]   Alex Kinsbury, "Performance enhancing drugs: Not just baseball," *U.S. News & World Report*, posted January 29, 2008, at www.usnews.com/articles/news/national/2008/01/29/performance-enhancing-drugs-not-just-baseball.html.

[29]   Mathew Collin, "The technologies of pleasure," in *Alter State: The Story of Ecstasy Culture and Acid House* (London: Serpent's Tail, 1997), 10–44.

[30]   Jeremy Gilbert and Ewan Pearson, "Metal machine musics," in *Discographies: Dance Music, Culture and the Politics of Sound* (London: Routledge, 1999), 110–45, 140.

for this stem at least in part from the fact that music has always relied on and been mediated by some form of technology. The notion of an "authentic" human performance is thus of less concern in the world of music except when, as will also be discussed, there is a performance that purports to be technologically unenhanced.

Sports and Chemical Enhancement

The issue of chemical use by athletes is one that has received significant attention. Though the primary site of controversy has occurred in the context of steroid use and blood doping, other, seemingly more benign uses of drugs have also raised eyebrows. The use of painkillers among athletes, who are often under pressure to continue performing, has at times resulted in negative consequences for them. Brett Favre, the 1995 NFL MVP, for example, was forced to enter an NFL substance abuse program after he suffered several injuries and became addicted to painkillers. Recreational drug use has also often affected the careers of many professional athletes, from the alcohol abuse of soccer stars George Best or Paul Gascoigne to the cocaine problems of Lawrence Taylor in football or Darryl Strawberry in baseball. According to Richard Giulianotti, "Around 70 per cent of NBA players were cocaine-users in the early 1980s, and in 1986 four of the top seven draft picks lost their careers (and in Len Bias's case, his life) to the drug."[31]

In recent years the use of anabolic steroids among athletes of both professional and amateur sports has been a consistent source of negative press coverage.[32] The issue of athletic performance enhancement through steroid use has had its highest-profile public exposure in the wake of the recent investigation into the Bay Area Laboratory Co-operative (BALCO) run by Victor Comte, which allegedly supplied undetectable drugs and anabolic steroids (particularly tetrahydrogestrinone, or "the clear") to a variety of top athletes in sports ranging from baseball and football to track and field.

The investigation of BALCO particularly affected baseball and has called into question the accomplishments of a long list of star players. Jason Giambi, the former American League MVP and current Oakland A's designated hitter, allegedly admitted to steroid use as well as human growth hormone (HGH) use in front of a grand jury in December 2003. The much-publicized leak of court documents which were said to contain this admission led to a tarnishing of Giambi's career, yet because he never actually failed a drug test, Giambi has, thus far, avoided punishment from Major League Baseball.

---

[31] Giulianotti, 113.

[32] For a detailed investigation of the types of performance enhancing drugs and their effects on sports performance, see Ellis Cashmore's chapter "A question of drugs" in *Making Sense of Sport*, 107–31.

By far the highest-profile athlete to be associated with the BALCO debacle is Barry Bonds. The San Francisco Giants outfielder, who holds the major league records for home runs in both a single season and a career, has been routinely linked to steroid use for several years. This is despite never being explicitly caught and steadfastly denying any and all allegations against him. Bonds's many detractors point to his unusual increase in musculature late in his career, as well as the improvement in his power hitting home run numbers, despite his age. Bonds, like Giambi, has never been punished by Major League Baseball in any way because he has never failed a drug test. Though unrelated to the BALCO investigation, in February 2009 Alex Rodriguez, the highest paid player in baseball, publicly admitted to using steroids while with the Texas Rangers from 2001 to 2003.

Though also not directly related to the BALCO affair, similar allegations have also been made against legendary pitcher Roger Clemens. Clemens's name was mentioned 82 times in the Mitchell Report on steroid use in baseball, released in December 2007.[33] In 2009 the bipartisan House committee in front of which Clemens appeared, citing seven apparent inconsistencies in Clemens's testimony, recommended that the Justice Department investigate whether Clemens lied under oath about using performance-enhancing drugs. On August 19, 2010, Clemens was indicted by a federal grand jury on charges that he lied about his steroid use to Congress.[34]

The BALCO scandal was not just limited to baseball and has touched, and tainted, performances in football, cycling, and track and field. The most notable football player to be involved in the BALCO scandal was two-time All-Pro linebacker Bill Romanowski. The 16-year NFL veteran openly advertised Conte's zinc supplement ZMA, and his involvement with BALCO has only further tainted the career of the four-time Super Bowl champion, who was known throughout his career as a punishing and extremely aggressive defender.

The use of steroids, of course, is not limited to men. The most prominent female athlete to be caught up in the BALCO affair was sprinter Marion Jones. Jones achieved star athletic status after winning five medals, including three gold, at the 2000 Summer Olympics in Sydney, Australia. She attended the University of North Carolina, where she met shot-putter and then UNC coach C.J. Hunter, whom she married in 1998 and divorced in 2002. A former world champion, Hunter, also involved with BALCO, was caught using performance enhancing

[33] See "Clemens hit hard in Mitchell Report," December 13, 2007, *SI.COM*, http://sportsillustrated.cnn.com/2007/baseball/mlb/12/13/mitchell.news (accessed May 15, 2009). Also see Associated Press, "Mitchell says naming names was right decision," December 14, 2007, *MSNBC*, http://nbcsports.msnbc.com/id/22189702 (accessed May 15, 2009).

[34] Michael Schmidt, "Clemens lied about doping, indictment charges," *New York Times*, August 19, 2010. Though not associated with BALCO, in a statement to the Associated press on January 11, 2010, home run king Mark McGwire ended more than a decade of speculation and admitted his use of steroids and human growth hormone. See www.sportingnews.com/mlb/article/2010-01-11/mark-mcgwire-admits-using-steroids (accessed March 10, 2010).

drugs. The publicity surrounding this event led many to believe Jones herself used such drugs as well, an accusation she vehemently denied. Jones then began a relationship with American sprinter Tim Montgomery. Montgomery himself benefited from the banned substances he received from BALCO, and the one-time 100 meter dash world record holder has been stripped of his awards and records since admitting to steroid use and is now retired. After news of Montgomery's cheating broke, Jones was again faced with increased doubt as to the integrity of her career, yet she continued to deny any wrongdoing. Finally, in October 2007, Jones admitted to lying to federal agents about her use of performance enhancing drugs, though she still maintains she believed the substances she was using were flaxseed oil, not steroids, at the time. Jones has handed over the five Olympic medals she earned in Sydney and officially retired from the sport.

The BALCO investigation is perhaps the best-known instance of uncovering steroid use in professional sports in North America. Other international sports organizations, however, have had an equally infamous record concerning illegal performance enhancing methods. Allegations of doping, for example, have plagued the Tour de France almost since its beginning in 1903. Early Tour riders were said to have consumed alcohol and used ether, among other substances, as a means of dulling the pain of competing in endurance cycling. As time went by, riders began using substances as a means of increasing performance rather than dulling the senses, and organizing bodies such as the Tour and the International Cycling Union (UCI), as well as government bodies, enacted policies to combat the practice.

At the 1998 Tour de France—dubbed the "Tour of shame"—a doping scandal erupted when Willy Voet of the Festina team was arrested for possession of erythropoietin (EPO), growth hormones, testosterone, and amphetamines. French police raided several teams in their hotels and found doping products in the possession of the TVM team. The riders staged a sit-down strike on stage 17. After mediation by Jean-Marie Leblanc, the director of the Tour, police agreed to limit the most heavy-handed tactics and the riders agreed to continue. Some riders and teams had already abandoned the race, and only 96 riders finished. In a 2000 criminal trial, it became clear that the management and health officials of the Festina team had organized the doping.

The Tour has been plagued by numerous doping cases since 1998, notably the Operación Puerto, when one day before the beginning of the 2006 race, many favorites, such as Jan Ullrich and Ivan Basso, were banned by their teams because of doping allegations. Notably, the doping controversy has even surrounded seven-time Tour champion Lance Armstrong for some time, although there has never been evidence for him to be penalized. In late August 2005, one month after Armstrong's seventh consecutive victory, the French sports newspaper *L'Equipe* claimed to have uncovered evidence that Armstrong had used EPO in the 1999 Tour de France.[35] Armstrong denied using EPO. In response to *L'Equipe*'s allegations, an investigation was begun by the UCI in October 2005. The investigation reported that Armstrong did not engage in doping and that the actions of the World Anti-Doping Agency were "completely inconsistent" with testing rules.[36]

The most serious doping charge in Tour history, however, emerged just four days after the end of the 2006 Tour de France. It was announced that the overall champion, American rider Floyd Landis, had a positive test for a testosterone imbalance in his "A" or initial test sample, after he won stage 17; this was confirmed in his "B" sample result, published on August 5, 2006. On September 20, 2007, Landis was found guilty of doping by an arbitrator's ruling. He was stripped of his 2006 Tour title and received a two-year ban from cycling.[37] In 2010 Landis recanted his previous innocence and accused 16 other Tour riders, including Lance Armstrong, of using illegal performance enhancing methods.[38]

To be sure, athletes have used stimulants of one form or another throughout history. The Olympians of ancient Greece even consumed various herbal compounds to enhance their competitiveness.[39] There are, likewise, many historical accounts of runners and cyclists using caffeine to boost their energy levels. Nonetheless, the recent concentration of public and regulatory attention on the practice underlines the continuing importance of bodily objectification in sports, as athletes subject themselves to greater and greater health risks to increase their chances of a successful performance.

Music and Technological Performance Enhancement

At roughly the same time that the sports world began to experience high-profile problems with steroid use and other doping techniques, the world of music was also beset with a similar issue of performance enhancement—though this was typically associated with the use of increasingly sophisticated musical technologies that could artificially "sweeten" or enhance performers' voices and also propagate the

---

[35]   "Ex-Kelme rider promises doping revelations," *VeloNews: The Journal of Competitive Cycling*, March 20, 2004, http://velonews.competitor.com/2004/03/road/ex-kelme-rider-promises-doping-revelations_5743 (accessed May 27, 2007).

[36]   Juliet Macur and Samuel Abt, "Investigator and anti-doping group clash on Armstrong tests," *New York Times*, May 31, 2006, www.nytimes.com/2006/05/31/sports/othersports/31cnd-lance.html?_r=1&oref=slogin (accessed April 28, 2008).

[37]   "Landis stripped of Tour title for doping, unsure on appeal," ESPN.com news services, http://sports.espn.go.com/oly/cycling/news/story?id=3029089 (accessed April 29, 2008).

[38]   Juliet Macur, "A disgraced rider's admissions, and accusations" *New York Times*, May 20, 2010, www.nytimes.com/2010/05/21/sports/cycling/21cycling.html (accessed June 1, 2010).

[39]   Giulianotti, 113.

practice of lip-synching. The most infamous and egregious cases were provided by Milli Vanilli in the 1980s and in 2005 by Ashlee Simpson's appearance on the television show *Saturday Night Live*.

Milli Vanilli was the brainchild of German producer Frank Farian, who had previously masterminded the European disco group Boney M. and the session-musician rock outfit Far Corporation. In 1988, seeking to fuse European dance-pop with elements of American rap, Farian assembled a number of session musicians and vocalists, including rapper Charles Shaw (an Army veteran) and two middle-aged American singers living in Germany, Johnny Davis and Brad Howell. Realizing that he had a marketable record but a distinctly unmarketable image, Farian hired two aspiring models and former breakdancers, Rob Pilatus and Fabrice Morvan, to pretend to be the group in videos, concerts, interviews, and any other public appearances. After selling millions of records, Pilatus and Morvan were revealed to be models who did no more than publicly lip-synch to tracks prerecorded by anonymous studio vocalists. They became the first act to ever be stripped of a Grammy Award and came to symbolize all that people disliked about synthesizer-based dance-pop. The scandal reinforced the common perception that it was a genre so faceless that every musician involved could remain anonymous without anyone knowing the difference, and that it was so mechanical and artificial that the people who constructed it had to hire models to give it any human appeal.

Milli Vanilli's first album, *All or Nothing*, was released in Europe in 1988 and was an instant success. Retitled *Girl You Know It's True* (after the lead single), the record was reissued in the United States in early 1989. Its catchy, lightweight pop-rap proved equally popular with American audiences. The title song raced up the pop singles charts to No. 2, and the next three Milli Vanilli singles—"Baby Don't Forget My Number," the ballad "Girl I'm Gonna Miss You," and the Diane Warren-penned "Blame It on the Rain"—all hit No. 1. Despite near-universal critical distaste (Farian's productions often recycled the same sounds and drum tracks), *Girl You Know It's True* sold an astounding 7 million copies in the United States alone; internationally, Milli Vanilli sold approximately 30 million singles. In December 1989, as the fifth single, "All or Nothing," was climbing the charts on its way to the Top 5, rapper Charles Shaw revealed to a New York reporter that Pilatus and Morvan had not actually sung any vocals on the album. Shaw quickly retracted his statements, claiming that they were merely a PR stunt for his own album. Soon after this episode Milli Vanilli was nominated for a Grammy for Best New Artist, even though the rumors continued to swirl. In early 1990 they indeed won the Grammy, beating out the Indigo Girls, Neneh Cherry, Soul II Soul, and Tone-Loc.

Farian became increasingly exasperated with the ruse and exposed the whole scheme in November 1990. Pilatus and Morvan were stripped of their Grammy, and a class-action suit was filed against Arista Records, allowing anyone who believed they had been defrauded into purchasing the group's records to apply for a rebate. Arista dropped the group and deleted *Girl You Know It's True* from their catalog, making it the biggest-selling album ever taken out of print.

In a similar, though slightly less controversial situation, Ashlee Simpson was caught lip-synching to a prerecorded vocal track on *Saturday Night Live* in October 2004. Simpson, the younger sister of pop singer Jessica Simpson, rose to prominence in mid-2004 through the success of her number-one debut album *Autobiography* and the accompanying reality series *The Ashlee Simpson Show*.

Simpson appeared as a musical guest on the October 23, 2004 edition of *Saturday Night Live* and, as is customary for musical guests, performed two songs. Her first song, "Pieces of Me," was performed without any problem. However, when she began her second song, "Autobiography," the vocals for the song "Pieces of Me" were heard again—before she had raised the microphone to her mouth. Simpson tried to cover by performing an improvised dance before leaving the stage, while the band (not a recording) continued playing. During the closing of the show Simpson appeared with guest host Jude Law and said: "I'm so sorry. My band started playing the wrong song, and I didn't know what to do, so I thought I'd do a hoe down." Critics such as Jeanette Walls of MSNBC compared the impact of the *SNL* incident to the 1990 Milli Vanilli performance, live on MTV, during which their guide track skipped, revealing that they were also lip-synching.[40] Unlike Milli Vanilli, however, Simpson was the actual singer on her recordings, and the impact of this incident on her career was relatively short-lived. Indeed *The New York Times* said the much-viewed clip of Simpson's SNL appearance "may just be this year's best music video," but dismissed its significance: "one of 2004's most popular new stars had been exposed as … As what, exactly?"[41]

While these are two of the most famous incidents, other artists have certainly relied on lip-synching, and it is a common practice on many pre-taped television performances. Many bands also use backing tracks in live concert performances to play incidental parts (various percussion and string parts for example) in an effort to accurately reproduce a studio performance which would otherwise be logistically and financially impractical. In the 1970s The Who played to a backing track every time they did "Baba O'Riley" and "Won't Get Fooled Again," which were performed with the same taped keyboard parts Pete Townshend laid down for the album *Who's Next*. Likewise, Cheap Trick has been using prerecorded keyboard tracks in its live shows since 1978, when the hit "Surrender" pushed the band beyond its guitar-only instrumentation. During the same period, Queen unapologetically used taped choruses for the big operatic bridge in "Bohemian Rhapsody."

Digital sampling technology in the 1980s made the temptation to rely on prerecorded sound even harder to resist. It was particularly alluring when bands learned that wiring a trigger into the drum kit made playing, or launching, the samples imperceptible to the audience. Even the venerable Charlie Watts took

---

[40]   Jeanette Walls, "Ashlee Simpson just paying lip service to fans," MSNBC, October 26, 2004, www.msnbc.msn.com/id/6329101 (accessed May 1, 2008).

[41]   Kelefa Sanneh. "Rap against rockism," *New York Times*, October 31, 2004.

advantage of this technique, using his drum kit to trigger handclaps while on tour with the Rolling Stones.

New technologies have reconfigured many musicians' relationship to their art. Digital samplers, for example, are regarded by many musicians as instruments rather than as recording devices. Even bands that make a selling point of their musical virtuosity feel no compunction about using digitally recorded "fly-ins" to fill out an arrangement. Geddy Lee, singer and bassist for the acclaimed band Rush, for example, explains, "As our records have become more complex because of overdubs, we go, okay, we can't reproduce that."[42] As for hiring additional musicians to play those parts: "The fans would hate that. They don't want to see some other guy up there!" Some critics may consider this practice cheating, but as Lee elucidates, triggering samples in mid-song is not easily accomplished: "It's so easy to get confused, because you're playing the bass part and you're simultaneously triggering all these different pedals, which are sometimes extra bass parts, sometimes keyboard chords, sometimes guitar arpeggios that are looping plus you're singing."[43] Traditional instrumental virtuosity is rapidly being replaced by technological virtuosity, even if, somewhat ironically, musicians must replicate the physical techniques and mental agility associated with instrumental proficiency to activate it.

Another form of this type of technological performance enhancement is the use of pitch riders, vocoders, Auto-Tune programming, and other forms of studio technology employed to enhance a vocal performance. Performers no longer necessarily have to be able to sing in tune or in time; pitch inaccuracies and rhythmic discrepancies by both singers and instrumentalists can be "fixed in the mix" by producers and engineers independent of the performer. The use of Auto-Tune, a 1990s computer program that allows performers to vocalize melodies perfectly as if on a synthesizer, has recently been the subject of controversy in rap music. Some rappers have prominently foregrounded the device as in Kanye West's *808s and Heartache* (2008), in which it is employed on every track. Rapper Jay-Z, however, responded with the single "D.O.A. (Death of Auto-Tune)" (2009), which decries the overuse of the device.

Compounding the issue of artificial performance enhancement, the previously often separate roles of composer and performer are, with the aid of digital software programs, increasingly being co-opted by and merged into the role of the listener. Audiences of recorded performances have long had the ability to choose when and where they would like to animate a performance, in which order to play certain tracks, and how much reverb, bass, or treble they would like in their personal mix. Increasingly, individual listeners are even now creating their own versions,

---

[42]   J.D. Considine, "Why Ashlee's taking the heat: It's not as if she's the only musician to have used recorded tracks. Even Geddy Lee does it. But Ashlee Simpson's no Geddy Lee," *Globe and Mail* (Toronto), October 30, 2004.

[43]   Ibid., Considine.

or mash-ups, of different songs. Thanks to technology, the listener has essentially become simultaneously the composer, the performer, and the consumer.

A particularly interesting example of the nexus of technical enhancement in music and sports has occurred in the past two Olympic Games. In the opening ceremonies of the 2006 Winter Olympics in Turin it was recently revealed that Luciano Pavarotti's performance was lip-synched to a prerecorded performance. This was among the famed Italian tenor's last major public performances. He was diagnosed with pancreatic cancer later that year and died in September 2007. Pavarotti's acclaimed operatic stage career therefore, somewhat ironically, ended with a virtual performance.

A similar situation occurred during the opening ceremonies of the 2008 Summer Olympics in Beijing. In an interview with Beijing Radio, Chen Qigang, the ceremony's chief music director, admitted that the nine-year-old girl shown singing in the broadcast to an audience of over 1 billion people was in fact lip-synching. The song, "Ode to the Motherland," was actually recorded by another girl, deemed not as pretty but judged to have a more beautiful voice.[44] The Beijing lip-synching controversy also came amid a previous revelation that one of the myriad of fireworks displays during the opening ceremony—the "29 footprints" segment—was also prerecorded and that broadcasters had been provided with, and subsequently aired, a computer enhanced tape.

China was eager to present a flawless Olympics image to the world, expelling migrant workers and so-called petitioners who had come to the central government with grievances from the city, controlling polluting traffic, and shutting down any sign of protest. China also put extraordinary effort into trying to ensure a drug free Games. The Chinese built a state-of-the-art $10 million laboratory with a staff of 150 technicians.[45] Zhao Jian, head of the Anti-Doping Commission of the Chinese Olympic Committee, proudly proclaimed, "The number of doping tests will increase to 4,500 [from 3,700 in Athens] during the Beijing Games."[46] It seems somewhat ironic, that, given the extraordinary lengths that the International Olympic Committee went to in controlling performance enhancing drugs, that among the greatest performance enhancement scandals of the past two Olympics has revolved around the technological enhancement of, not athletic performances, but musical performances.

---

[44]   Jim Yardley, "In grand Olympic show, some sleight of voice," *New York Times*, August 12, 2008.

[45]   Lei Lei, "Beijing to ramp up Olympic doping tests," *China Daily*, July 6, 2007, http://daily.iflove.com/2008/2007-07/06/content_911778.htm (accessed August 12, 2008).

[46]   Ibid.

Sports and Technological Performance Enhancement

Though technological enhancement has often been at the heart of issues surrounding musical authenticity and veracity, whether applied to the individual's health, his or her technique, or equipment characteristics, it has also played various controversial roles within sports culture. As sports have grown increasingly more competitive, the need for better equipment, athletic health care, and instruction has become concomitantly more important. Sports culture has had a long history of technological innovations to equipment that have aided the achievements of the human body. Golf clubs, football helmets, baseball bats, soccer balls, ice skates, and other equipment have all been subject to considerable technological changes in materials, design, and methods of construction that have resulted in improved human performance.

The increasingly competitive atmosphere and the growing financial rewards of professional sports have also placed more emphasis on sustaining athletes' health and longevity. Technology has fueled innovations in athletic health in areas ranging from nutrition to the treatment of injuries. As the knowledge of the human body has deepened over time, an athlete's physical potential has been increased. Athletes are now able to play to an older age, recover more quickly from injuries, and train more effectively than in previous generations. Advances in technology have made it possible to analyze aspects of sports that were previously out of the reach of unaided human comprehension. Being able to use digital motion capture photography to record the minutiae of their movement, or advanced computer simulations to model physical scenarios, has greatly increased athletes' ability to understand what they are doing and how they can improve their performance.

Technology has advanced at such a pace, particularly in the realm of enhancements to equipment—and by extension, enhancements of the human body's natural ability—that numerous controversies and outright bans on various equipment innovations have characterized many sports. Regulatory sporting bodies, acting to forestall a future where possession of the best technology will be the dominant factor in determining the outcomes of athletic events, typically seek to reinforce the role of human agency.[47]

The game of golf has provided one of the most contested sites of technological enhancement in sports. The evolution of golfing equipment from wooden sticks and rocks in the game's original incarnation to today's oversized graphite and titanium drivers and maximum flight golf balls has revolutionized the game. Industry sources claim that average driving distances on the PGA tour have increased by some 30 yards in the past decade.[48] Indeed, the sport of golf, perhaps

---

[47] For more on the ethical dimension of performance enhancement in sports see Dirk Rodenburg, "Resistance is futile: Confronting the ethics of the 'enhanced human' athlete," *The International Journal of Sport and Society* 1/1 (2010), 285–300.

[48] Jaime Diaz, "The growing gap: Driving distances are skyrocketing on the PGA Tour. So why is the average golfer being left behind?" *Golf Digest*, May 2003, available

more than any other, has been forced to put limits on many aspects of technological innovation that affect the game, regulating the materials and methods used in ball construction and the depth and spacing of grooves on irons, as well as banning electronic distance measuring devices in competition.

Similar controversies regarding the unfairness of new sporting technologies have been raised in Formula One and NASCAR racing (restrictor plate limitations of power and constraints on aerodynamic configurations and ground effects), ice hockey (the banning of oversized goaltending equipment), NFL football (the barring of stickum on receivers' hands, tear-away jerseys, and recording devices to spy on opponents' strategies), professional baseball (the rejection of aluminum bats), and innumerable other sports and leagues that have some form of either formal or informal equipment rules and restrictions.[49]

The role of technology in artificially enhancing human performance has recently been the subject of a high-profile debate in Olympic level swimming. Competition swimming pools are much faster than they were 20 years ago. Wave-reduction technology and many other improvements have created "fast" pools. As well, a similar improvement in the technology of swimming gear has created faster swimsuits. Speedo's new high-tech LZR Racer swimsuit, costing nearly US$600, has been criticized for contributing to a recent plethora of world swimming records.[50] Such advancements are regularly faulted for privileging athletes who have economic access. Everyone swims in the same Olympic pool, but not everyone has access to the fast swimsuits.

In addition to revolutionizing the equipment, health, and training of athletes, innovations in technology have also affected the officiating and regulation of many sports. Instant video replay, for example, is a regular tool used in NFL football and NHL hockey to determine the accuracy of an official's on-field decision. Cyclops is a computer system that was used on the ATP and WTA tennis tours to help determine whether a serve was in or out by projecting five or six infrared horizontal beams of light along the court 10 millimeters above the ground. Cyclops has recently been replaced by Hawk-Eye, another computer system used in cricket, tennis, and other sports that is able to digitally track and display the path of the ball in three-dimensional space.

Music itself has also been recently banned and criticized as an artificial or technical form of performance enhancement. In keeping with studies by Costa

---

at http://findarticles.com/p/articles/mi_m0HFI/is_5_54/ai_101967369/ (accessed May 15, 2009).

[49] Ironically, given the sport's typical concern for chemical and physiological performance enhancement, one of the main concerns during the 2010 Tour de France was, somewhat bizarrely, over the possibility of the presence of small mechanical motors in the bike frames that would assist the competitor's natural ability. See Juliet Macur, "No motors, but mistrust at Tour de France," *New York Times*, July 4, 2010. www.nytimes.com/2010/07/04/sports/cycling/04tour.html (accessed August 10, 2010).

[50] James Hooper, "New swimsuits unfair," *The Daily Telegraph*, March 9, 2008.

Karageorghis, which suggest that listening to the right music can enhance athletic ability by up to 20 percent, the consumption of music while performing certain sports is increasingly coming under scrutiny by sporting regulating bodies. The International Amateur Athletics Federation, for example, is considering banning the use of personal music playing devices in all competition.[51] In 2007 the organizers of the New York Marathon banned the use of personal music players for that event, citing safety concerns as well as the work-enhancing effects of the music. Jill Geer, speaking on behalf of USA Track & Field in 2007, claimed that the increasing popularity of headphones was making races more dangerous: "Runners need to be aware of their surroundings. There can be runners coming up behind them, or announcements from race officials … As you get more and more runners wearing headphones in a race, it becomes more of a safety issue."[52]

Though such improvements in equipment have radically changed many sports, it is perhaps the technological hardware enhancement of the human body itself that raises the most concerns for the future of sports and the human condition in general. In director Ridley Scott's cautionary film *Blade Runner* (1982), human-like, genetically engineered beings called replicants are created to perform the most dangerous and degrading work. Unhappy with their lot in life, the replicants rebel, and specialized police units—blade runners—are called upon to wipe out the replicant threat to humanity.

As life imitates art, the blade runner scenario is no longer the stuff of science fiction. New advances in prosthetic enhancement have touched off debates about where human ability ends and technology begins. Oscar Pistorius, nicknamed "the blade runner," is a South African sprinter who holds Paralympic world records in the 100, 200, and 400 meter sprints. Born with deformed feet and without one of the bones in his lower legs, Pistorius had his legs amputated below the knees when he was 11 months old. He quickly learned to walk, and then run, on prosthetic limbs. He currently races on specially designed blade-like carbon fiber prosthetics known as Cheetahs.[53]

Given his success in the Paralympics, Pistorius has turned his attention to competing against able-bodied athletes. Despite this rather modest aim, Pistorius now finds himself at the center of an international debate involving fundamental questions about the nature of sports and, even more fundamentally, what it means to be human. The International Amateur Athletic Federation (IAAF), the governing body of track and field, looked upon Pistorius with suspicion. Although the IAAF does permit the use of prosthetics in certain circumstances, it recently disqualified him from open competition on the grounds that the Cheetahs

---

[51] Costas Karageorghis and Peter C. Terry, "The psychological, psychophysical and ergogenic effects of music in sports," in Bateman, *Sporting Sounds*, 15.

[52] Quoted in James Bone, "Don't stop us now, say marathon runners who plan to defy music ban," *The Times*, November 2, 2007.

[53] Peter McKnight, "Sports, technology and the meaning of 'human,'" *Vancouver Sun*, Saturday, January 26, 2008.

gave him an unfair advantage over other athletes. Pistorius was at first barred from competing in the Beijing Games. Perhaps the ruling is not surprising since the Cheetahs act like springs, allowing Pistorius to exert 25 percent less energy than able-bodied athletes running at the same speed.[54] Pistorius subsequently won his appeal against the IAAF decision in time for the Beijing Olympics but failed to make the 45.55 second Olympic qualifying time in the 400 meters (his best event), despite setting a personal best of 46.25.[55] Still planning to qualify to compete against able-bodied athletes in the 2012 London Olympics, Pistorius, who will only be 25 years old in 2012, has touched off considerable debate over such controversial issues as the rights of disabled athletes and the future of performance enhancing technology in sports.[56]

The use of prosthetics and/or equipment enhancement, nicknamed "techno-doping," will likely become an increasingly contentious issue in athletics. Even if Pistorius is not at an unfair advantage, it is only a matter of time before athletes using prosthetics and other technologies designed to compensate for disabilities will soon surpass any performance of which able-bodied athletes are capable. Pistorius may represent the start of an increasing blurring of the distinction between therapy— that which helps those with disabilities to become "normal"—and enhancement— that which helps people to become something more than normal.[57]

To be sure, athletes, both disabled and able-bodied, have long used technology to enhance their performances, to become better than normal. As discussed, anabolic steroids and other performance enhancing drugs are probably the best-known ergogenic aids, but athletes have also availed themselves of many other performance enhancers that are accepted by sports organizations, including wearing special shoes and aerodynamic running suits, training at high altitude, or sleeping in hypoxic chambers. Indeed, the hypoxic chamber—also known as an altitude tent—is commonly used by many athletes to aid in recovery and boost red blood cells.[58]

---

[54]   Ibid.

[55]   See "Double amputee hurt in boating accident," CBCNews online: www.cbc.ca/ sports/story/2009/02/22/pistorius-accident.html (accessed February 22, 2009).

[56]   Some Paralympic athletes, however, have also been overstating disabilities or using stimulants as performance enhancements, just as able-bodied athletes do. The success of the Paralympics and concomitant competitiveness has engendered the need to exclude able-bodied athletes. In 2002 Adam Sadler, a British wheelchair racer, was banned by the International Paralympic Committee when he was exposed as being fully mobile.

[57]   Indeed, Japan's Cyberdyne Inc. plans to mass-produce its HAL exoskeleton as a way to enhance a wearer's strength, but the technology can also be used to assist people with missing or damaged limbs. Larry Greenemeier, "Real-life Iron Man: A robotic suit that magnifies human strength," *Scientific American*, April 30, 2008, www.sciam.com/article. cfm?id=real-life-iron-man-exoskeleton (accessed March 3, 2009).

[58]   A hypoxic chamber is an enclosed space that simulates high altitude by maintaining a lower oxygen concentration. It is used by athletes and by high-altitude mountain climbers

The medical enhancement of Pistorius must also be placed in the context of more common surgical enhancements of athletes. The formerly near-sighted Tiger Woods raised few eyebrows with his decision to undergo Lasik eye surgery, even though it gave him 20/15 vision—better than normal—which arguably helped his golf game. Similarly it is also not uncommon for baseball pitchers to undergo various arm surgeries to help them endure the rigors of the game. Though many believe that steroid enhanced records should be erased from the record books, few argue that athletes who have undergone performance enhancing—or career extending—surgeries unavailable to previous record holders should likewise have their records expunged.

Technological enhancements of various kinds keep sports organizations busy in their efforts to ensure fairness, but on a more fundamental level they raise profound ethical questions that go far beyond the boundaries of sports. Indeed the emergence of enhancement technologies, including, but not limited to, nanotechnology, biotechnology, information technology, and cognitive science— referred to collectively as NBIC—raise questions about the extent to which we should employ science to improve the human condition in general. To be sure, we have always used technology to allow us to live longer and better lives, but with the rapid progress of science, it is possible that we will soon develop technologies that allow us, not just to run faster or see farther, but to change our very physical and psychological essence—to become, as it were, "post-human."

Popular Music, Technology, and Trans/Post-humanism

Music has always been produced with and mediated by various technologies, involving everything from instruments to music printing and dissemination. However, technology has played a particularly influential role in the evolution and understanding of popular and rock music. The electronic amplification of performance that accompanied pop singers such as Bing Crosby and that later became a hallmark of rock music in combination with the recording process, makes popular music extremely interconnected with high levels of technology. Such symbiosis, however, is not unconflicted. As David Rowe claims, "The machines that are produced by industrial capitalism are also the means by which rock critiques of commercialism and alienation are disseminated, while the humanism of 'rebel rock' often collides with the machine aesthetics of a disengaged avant garde."[59]

The politics of technology in relationship to music have been talked about at length elsewhere, with most authors decrying the increasing disembodiment of popular music and the tendency to submerge the body within the machine in

---

to stimulate the body's natural adaptations to altitude, including an increase in the number of red blood cells and enzymes.

[59] Rowe, *Popular Cultures*, 82.

creating relatively lifeless musical experiences.[60] In the Baudrillardian sense, listening to a musical recording of any kind implies a hyper-real experience. We listen to a disembodied recording of a musical event that likely, with the advent and widespread reliance on multi-tracking and overdubbing, did not actually take place in real time (the various tracks could have been recorded over months or even years and in different locations before being brought together to simulate a singular performance in the final mix). Similarly, in animating any recorded sound we are only listening to a virtual performance of a body. Prior to the advent of recording technology, bodies were inherently present in experiencing a musical performance. Some*body* had to play the music, and people gathered to listen to the performance in real time and space. Such is no longer the case as the musical experience, particularly with the advent of personal listening devices, has become an increasingly non-communal personal experience. The advent of MP3 and file sharing technologies has contributed to the seeming removal of the body from the musical experience in additional ways. In the past one could typically at least look at the record album or CD cover to see the artist(s) who created the music. Downloading an MP3 file however, often denies even this visual reminder of a body in the creation of the work.[61] Many listeners today have no concept of what their favorite artists even look like. To be sure, such anonymity has its advantages and can serve to defeat the potential marginalization of some artists based on their looks, gender, race, ethnicity, age, or other visual attributes. It is also true that a body must always be present to experience music, but nonetheless the reliance on and mediation of music by technology is seemingly becoming more pronounced than ever.

Over the past 50 years or so there have been several notable differences of opinion about the use of technology in popular music. Bob Dylan instigated a rift between fans of folk and rock music when he used an electric guitar, backed by an electric blues band, at the Newport Folk Festival in 1965. More recently country music fans have been divided between traditional acoustic country and so-called "new country" (marked by more pop influenced performance and recording technologies employed by the likes of Shania Twain). Such debates typically center on some concept of one genre employing technologies that are viewed as being more "natural" (typically meaning more overtly connected to the body) than those of another genre and hence judged to be more "authentic."

As in the sports world, music has long relied on prosthetic enhancement to improve performance. Microphones and amplifiers artificially project the human voice. Earphones and headsets allow musicians to hear sounds they otherwise could not. Digital computer technologies and simple software programs now

---

[60]   See, for example, Jeremy Gilbert and Ewan Pearson, "Metal machine musics," in *Discographies*, 110–45. Also see Mark Katz, *Capturing Sound: How Technology Changed Music* (Los Angeles: University of California Press, 2004).

[61]   MP3 file downloads, assuming they are done legally, at best offer the listener a tiny thumbnail image of the album art, which may or may not show the artist in question.

aid us in the creation and animation of any sound that can be imagined. Though such enhancements are nominally more accepted in the music world than in the sports world, the line between the human and the machine and what constitutes an "authentic" human performance seems to be increasingly blurred. In many ways music has already entered the state of the "post-human."

The music and sports worlds are mutually dependent on and obsessed with developments in technology and equipment to achieve better results. The role of technology in facilitating an increasing drive to transcend the limits of bodily ability seems ubiquitous in contemporary society. To some extent, in our reliance on performance enhancing technologies in music and sports, we are progressing to the embodiment of theories regarding a cyborgian future. Perhaps most notable in this respect is Donna Haraway's notion of the "cyborg" as a non-hierarchical image (hybrid human/machine) of transformative science that "can suggest a way out of the maze of dualisms in which we have explained our bodies and our tools to ourselves."[62] Although such a proposition potentially recreates another dualism (man/machine), the increasing reliance on technology at least suggests a solution to the inequities of gender, race, class, and sexual preference that are seemingly so embedded in both sports and musical culture.

Indeed for scholars such as Haraway and Sadie Plant, the male myth of domination is epitomized in the drive to tame nature and to literally break free of the limitations of earthly physicality through technological mastery. To quote Plant, "those who still cherish the patriarchal dream see cyberspace as a new zone of hope for ... escaping the body and sliding into an infinite, transcendent, perfect other world ... the phallic dream of eternal life."[63] Such dreams are of course challenged by the fact that the anonymity of cyberspace often results in the surrender of masculine control and identity. The use of chemical or machine technologies, however, increasingly questions prevailing notions regarding the "naturalness" and "authenticity" of performances in both sports and music.

The heavy reliance on technology in most forms of popular music calls into question the role of human agency in the creation of such music and, in keeping with the theories of Haraway and Plant, conjures up images of cyborgian artists and composers where traditional notions of race, ethnicity, gender, and class are called into question. For example, the common pre-occupation technology and futuristic imagery evident in funk, rap, and other forms of African American music seems, at first appearance, antithetical to the commonly held view of "authentic"

---

[62] Donna Haraway, "A cyborg manifesto: Science, technology, and socialist-feminism in the late twentieth century," in *Simians, Cyborgs, and Women: The Reinvention of Nature* (New York: Routledge, 1991), 149–81. I also discuss this concept in "Space oddities: Aliens, futurism and meaning in rock music," *Popular Music* 23/2 (2003), 315–33.

[63] Sadie Plant, "On the matrix: Cyberfeminist simulations," in Paul Marris and Sue Thornham (eds), *The Media Studies Reader* (New York: New York University Press, 2000), 835–48, 846.

black music as natural, funky, or soulful.[64] However, such images can also be interpreted as merely the result of human interaction with the environment. As Tricia Rose observes in terms of hip hop:

> If we take a kind of Frankfurt School/fascist/industrial regimentation/lack of creativity as our model for the machine, then of course funky cyborgs would seem like an utter contradiction; but if we understand the machine as a product of human creativity whose parameters are always suggesting what's beyond them, then we can read hip-hop as the response of urban people of color to the postindustrial landscape.[65]

The fear of and fascination with the increasing dependence of humans on machines (computers, television, cell phones, and so on) and the influence of machines on the human body (genetic engineering, microchip implants, pacemakers, hearing aids, and prosthetics) is commonly personified in the cyborg concept (popularized by *Star Trek*'s villainous "Borg" characters). To quote Mark Dery, "Cyborgs populate a cultural landscape in which the human body is increasingly the site of what might be called *micropolitical* power struggles between an information-rich, technocratic elite and the information-poor masses."[66] As outlined by Haraway, cyborg imagery suggests alternatives to the many dualisms with which we regard our bodies. However, the masculine coding of machine culture and its associated socio-economic implications also suggests that the "cyborg" concept is potentially merely another location for reinscribing the marginalization of women, homosexuals and disadvantaged economic classes.

Historically, neo-Cartesian rationalism, as emphasized in Norbert Elias's concept of the "civilizing process" and other approaches, has fostered a hierarchical approach to the conception of being human, one in which the physical body is subordinated to the rational mind. Modern science, however, has enabled us to reconfigure our bodies, in essence improving upon their natural abilities in accordance with the mind's imperatives. It seems clear that the debate over what will count as an "authentic" or "natural" human performance is central to our future understanding of both sports and music. In both worlds, though they are increasingly interconnected, the encroachment of technology has resulted in experiences that are increasingly marked by notions of trans-humanism.

The burgeoning philosophy of "trans-humanism" dedicates itself to exploring the scientific and moral questions associated with the impact of technological

---

[64]   See, for example, futuristic and technological themes in George Clinton and Parliament Funkadelic's *Mothership Connection* (1975), Bernie Worell's *Blacktronic Science* (1993) or more, recently, Kanye West's *808s & Heartbreak* (2008).

[65]   Rose as quoted in Mark Dery, "Black to the future: Interviews with Samuel R. Delany, Greg Tate and Tricia Rose," *The South Atlantic Quarterly* 92/4 (1993), 769. Also see "Space oddities," 345.

[66]   Mark Dery, "Cyberculture," *The South Atlantic Quarterly* 91/3 (1992), 507.

development on human beings. The contemporary meaning of "trans-humanism" is a product of the 1980s, when a futurist intelligentsia based in the United States began to organize what has since grown into the trans-humanist movement. Trans-humanist thinkers predict that human beings will eventually be able to transform themselves into beings with such greatly expanded abilities as to merit the label "post-human." Most trans-humanists support the use of technologies to alter the human condition—even to the point where it can no longer be called the human condition—given their belief that biology should not be destiny and that we have a fundamental moral right to sculpt ourselves into whatever shape we prefer.

Many trans-humanist theorists and advocates such as Nick Bostrom, Max More, David Pearce, and Anders Sandberg seek to apply reason, science, and technology for the purposes of reducing poverty, disease, disability, and malnutrition around the globe. Trans-humanism is distinctive, however, in its particular focus on the application of technologies to the improvement of human bodies at the individual level. Trans-humanist philosophers argue that there not only exists a perfectionist ethical imperative for humans to strive for progress and the improvement of the human condition, but that it is possible and desirable for humanity to enter a post-evolutionary phase of existence, in which humans are in control of their own evolution. In such a phase, natural evolution would be replaced with deliberate, conscious change.

Some theorists, such as Raymond Kurzweil, believe that the pace of technological innovation is accelerating and that the next 50 years may yield not only radical technological advances but also possibly a technological singularity that may fundamentally change the nature of human beings.[67] Trans-humanists who foresee this massive technological change generally maintain that it is desirable. However, some are also concerned with the possible dangers of such extremely rapid technological change and propose options for ensuring that advanced technology is used responsibly. Nick Bostrom, for example, has written extensively on existential risks to humanity's future welfare, including risks that could be created by emerging technologies.[68]

In addition to the current debates around performance enhancement in music and sports, trans-humanist themes appear in a variety of visual and performing arts. "Carnal Art," a form of sculpture originated by the French artist Orlan, uses the body as its medium and plastic surgery as its method. Similarly the work of the Australian artist Stelarc centers on the alteration of his body by robotic prostheses and tissue engineering. Other artists whose work coincided with the emergence and flourishing of trans-humanism and who explored themes related to the transformation of the body are the Yugoslavian performance artist Marina Abramovic and the American media artist Matthew Barney. A 2005 show,

---

[67] Raymond Kurzweil, *The Singularity is Near: When Humans Transcend Biology* (New York: Viking, 2005).

[68] Nick Bostrom, *Anthropic Bias: Observation Selection Effects in Science and Philosophy* (New York: Routledge, 2002).

Becoming Animal, at the Massachusetts Museum of Contemporary Art, presented exhibits by 12 artists whose work concerns the effects of technology in erasing boundaries between the human and non-human.

Trans-humanist themes have also become increasingly prominent in various literary forms. Contemporary science fiction often contains positive renditions of technologically enhanced human life, set in utopian (especially techno-utopian) societies. However, science fiction's depictions of enhanced humans or other post-human beings frequently come with a cautionary twist. The more pessimistic scenarios include many horrific or dystopian tales of human bio-engineering gone wrong. In the decades immediately before trans-humanism emerged as an explicit movement, many trans-humanist concepts and themes began appearing in the speculative fiction of authors such as Robert A. Heinlein (*Lazarus Long* series, 1941–87), A.E. van Vogt (*Slan*, 1946), Isaac Asimov (*I, Robot*, 1950), and Arthur C. Clarke (*Childhood's End*, 1953). More recent novels dealing with trans-humanist themes that have stimulated broad discussion of these issues include *Blood Music* (1985) by Greg Bear, the *Xenogenesis* trilogy (1987–9) by Octavia Butler, the "Culture" novels (1987–2008) of Iain Banks; the *Beggars* trilogy (1990–94) by Nancy Kress, much of Greg Egan's *Permutation City* (1994) and *Diaspora* (1997), *Altered Carbon* (2002) by Richard Morgan, *Oryx and Crake* (2003) by Margaret Atwood, and *Glasshouse* (2005) by Charles Stross.

As one would expect from its literary counterpart, a brief look at science fiction film reveals an intense concern with the consequences of trans-humanism, from the development of intelligent machines that could wipe out humanity (the *Terminator* series) to the creation of a multi-tiered hierarchical society, with genetically enhanced "humans" at the top (*Gattaca*), or with genetically engineered "humans" at the bottom (*Blade Runner*). Beyond science fiction films and literature, trans-humanist scenarios have also achieved widespread popularity in numerous other media during the late twentieth and early twenty-first centuries. Such treatments are found in comic books (*Captain America*, 1941; *Transmetropolitan*, 1997), television series (*The Six Million Dollar Man*, 1974; the Borg of *Star Trek: The Next Generation*, 1989; and the Ancients of *Stargate SG-1*, 2000), Japanese *manga* and *anime* (*Appleseed*, 1985; *Gundam Seed*, 2002) and, increasingly, computer games (*Metal Gear Solid*, 1998; *Half-Life 2*, 2004).

Many works involving trans-humanist themes are considered part of the cyberpunk genre. Indeed, musical incarnations of trans-humanism have perhaps found their most overt expression in cyberpunk. "Cyberpunk," a term coined by William Gibson in his novel *Neuromancer* (1984), has particularly been concerned with the modification of human bodies. Musical groups linked to the trans-humanist principles of cyberpunk include Nine Inch Nails, Marilyn Manson, and Skinny Puppy. Such groups typically rely on a significant amount of musical technology (synthesizers, computers, pitch riders, and so on) to realize their typically post-apocalyptic visions of the future.

As has been discussed, music has been increasingly marked by post- or trans-human practices, whether in the common use of microphones and other technologies that enhance bodily performance or in the increasingly technologically mediated act of listening to and experiencing music. Perhaps the most overt exponent, if unintentionally, of trans-humanism was the late Michael Jackson. Jackson used technologies such as plastic surgery, skin-lightening drugs, and hyperbaric oxygen therapy over the course of his career, with the effect of transforming his artistic persona so as to blur identifiers of gender, race, and age. Though in a much less extreme manner, performance artist Laurie Anderson, perhaps most famous for her hit single "O Superman" (1981), also commonly employs technology to alter her voice and blur her identity.

As manifested in local and trans-local fan cultures and scenes, music and sports cultures are intimately preoccupied with notions of community. The idea that machines and technology, whether consisting of equipment or ingestible chemicals, will override the "natural" humanity of the athlete/artist and, in turn, potentially "program" audience expectations and responses, directly calls into question the community and the role of the body in both activities. In popular music, rather than sublimating the body to the technology, technology has rather produced new ways of disciplining the body. In contemporary club/dance music, for example, the use of technology and its attendant hypnotically repetitive beats allows a type of technological spirituality—a literal transference of spirit from the machine to the body. Many forms of technology-centered popular dance music thus challenge and defeat what Adorno saw as the alienating effect of mechanization on the modern consciousness. In reaction to dissatisfaction with the isolating and alienating culture of the everyday outside world, the rave experience creates an enclosed temporary safe communal space (sometimes called a TAZ: temporary autonomous zone) free from judgment and violence. In its anti-materialist stance, rave and techno music attempts to challenge and provide an alternative, if somewhat flawed, to capitalist commodity culture—flawed if only because consumers and producers of such music must of course buy their technology, both of sound production and reproduction, from the same corporate culture from which they attempt to escape.

Norbert Elias's concept of the "civilizing process" traces the gradual process by which Western civilization has intensified its demands for bodily and emotional control.

> To see grown-up men and women shaken by tears and abandon themselves to their bitter sorrow in public ... or beat each other savagely under the impact of their violent excitement [more common in the uncivilized past] has ceased to be regarded as normal. It is usually a matter of embarrassment for the onlooker and often a matter of shame or regret for those who have allowed themselves to be carried away by their excitement.[69]

What appears to be important here is not the intensity of feeling but our discomfort about its spectacular display. Sports and music both operate as sites of

---

[69] Norbert Elias, *The Quest for Excitement*, 64–5.

"pleasurable de-controlling of human feeling" which, however, simultaneously operate in "maintenance of a set of checks to keep the pleasantly de-controlled emotions under control."[70] The application of various performance enhancing technologies in sports and music would seem to continue the civilizing control of the body. The increasing sublimation and hybridization of the human body to and with machines and technology can be understood as representing an ultimate realization of Elias's concept.

It seems unlikely that there will be ultimate answers in the debates over the role of technology, including drugs, in enhancing human performance in either music or sports. What is clear is that technology is continuing to encroach on the human participation in and consumption of both. The two spheres, however, are linked in being central fronts on the border war between humans and machines. Sports and music are increasingly posing questions about precisely what a "human" performance means, or even more broadly, what it means to be human.

[70]   Ibid., 49.

Chapter 4

"We Will Rock You":
Sports Anthems and Hypermasculinity[1]

No cultural arena is as overtly characterized by masculine identity as sports. The history of sports in the West has been rife with masculine constructions from the time of the male-only Olympic Games of ancient Greece[2] to the eighteenth-century chivalric archery confraternities associated with Masonic lodges, which sought to affirm masculinity by excluding women from secret initiation rites and competitions.[3] The first golf clubs, such as the Gentlemen Golfers of Leith (1744), were created specifically as masculine spaces for socializing and playing games—this despite the fact that many women, such as Mary, Queen of Scots, actively participated in the game. Indeed, throughout history women have been systematically excluded from participating in sports. As mentioned in Chapter 2, as recently as the nineteenth century it was thought that immoderate exercise might sabotage healthy childbearing, a belief stemming from the sixteenth-century European notion that excessive exercise could literally cause women to become men. More recently, of course, women have been actively engaged in sports, both as participants and consumers. As early as 1936, Marjorie Hillis's *Live Alone and Like It: A Guide for the Extra Woman* recommends that single women occupy themselves watching boxing matches and art exhibitions.[4]

---

[1]   Portions of this chapter first appeared in my essay "We are the champions: The politics of sports and popular music," *Popular Music and Society* 29/5 (December 2006), 533–49.

[2]   Indeed, married women were barred from even attending the ancient Olympics under penalty of death. Women were similarly barred from competing in the first modern Olympics in 1896, though a few women were subsequently allowed in the Paris Olympics of 1900. Baron de Coubertin nonetheless stubbornly believed that the games should traditionally remain as a "eulogy for men's sport." Indeed, this men-only policy was at least partially maintained by the International Olympic Committee until 1981, when it deigned to elect its first two women members. See "Women in the Olympic Movement," International Olympic Committee Factsheet: http://multimedia.olympic.org/pdf/en_report_846.pdf (accessed March 2011).

[3]   Pierre Beaurepaire, "Nobles jeux de l'arc et loges maçonniques dans la France," *H-France Review* 3/75 (July 2003), 2.

[4]   Women have witnessed a similar growth in their passive consumption of sports. By 1995, for example, more women than men in Britain watched Wimbledon tennis on television. As cited in Toby Miller and Alec McHoul, *Popular Culture and Everyday Life* (London: Sage Publications, 1998), 60.

Despite significant increases in sports participation and consumption by women, the male body remains the principal currency of sports and related commercial industries. As a result of the almost exclusive construction of athleticism as masculine, sports and homophobia have traditionally also been linked. Notwithstanding the stereotypical "butch" connotations of lesbian athletes, homosexuality is, for example, commonly and derisively linked with both physical and emotional frailty.[5]

As with sports, many realms of music have been overtly associated with masculine identity.[6] Notwithstanding important connections to female stereotypes, such as the myth of the sirens' songs, that associate music with the evils of seductive female sensuality, or the increasing visibility of female composers and performers (and at times outright commercial dominance in popular music), the vast majority of the music-making industry has been historically dominated by men. From classical orchestras to jazz and rock ensembles, most forms of Western music have conventionally occurred in homosocial masculine arenas. In recent years, however, both sports and music have begun to be contested as sites of orthodox masculine construction. The increasing visibility of gay athletes has challenged the traditional dominance of heterosexual men in sports, proving invalid the long-held belief that homosexuality is antithetical to athleticism and traditional constructions of "masculine" image.[7] This is to say that many gay athletes compete with and beat heterosexual men at their own game. Sports theorists such as Brian Pronger have suggested that gay men may in fact be attracted to sports because of the heterosexual façade that it provides.[8] Similarly, there is evidence to show that heterosexual men are increasingly attracted to products and services that are typically perceived to be effete or feminine. The popularity of television shows such as *Queer Eye for the Straight Guy* and the common use of the term "metrosexual"—used to describe a heterosexual male who is meticulously concerned about his looks and grooming in a stereotypically gay manner—are significant indicators of this social change.[9] Such trends suggest

---

[5]   Of course some sports, as notably manifest in the liminality of gender codes present in body-building, problematize gender binaries and heighten tensions over the relationship of muscularity and both sexual and gender identity.

[6]   One major exception to this is opera, which, with its history of high-register male voices and generally transgressive plots and gender roles, is often commonly associated with femininity.

[7]   Some of the more famous "out" athletes have included tennis stars Bill Tilden, Martina Navratilova, and Billie Jean King, diver Greg Louganis, NFL players David Kopay and Roy Simmons, skaters Rudy Galindo and Brian Orser, English soccer star Justin Fashanu, and Olympic decathlete Tom Waddell.

[8]   See Eric Anderson, *In the Game: Gay Athletes and the Cult of Masculinity* (Albany, NY: State University of New York Press, 2005), 14.

[9]   Related to this is the increasing colonization of the male body in the form of poster images and sexual marketing of male athletes, such as soccer star and international

that homophobia is becoming less prevalent among heterosexual men and that a softening or reconception of masculinity has even spilled over into sports culture. If, as others such as sports sociologist Eric Anderson have recently argued, "the hegemony sport once maintained over the production of orthodox masculinity … is under contestation," then the relationship between sports and music is also undergoing a similar change in dynamics.[10]

An important feature of the relationship between the realms of sports, music, and sexual identity lies in the division between team and individual sports. Generally mainstream team sports such as baseball, hockey, football, and basketball employ music in various contexts to a far greater extent than solo sports such as golf, tennis, and track—sports in which music plays little or no role in heightening emotions around the event for either audience or participants. In addition, with the notable exception of combat sports such as boxing or wrestling, solo sports often involve little or no bodily contact between participants in comparison with the consistent same-sex bodily contact involved in team sports. Music thus would seem to be more associated with reinforcing and reflecting the communal homosocial rituals and the environments of team sports. Important exceptions to this generality are figure skating and gymnastics, both non-team sports that rely heavily on music as part of the actual competition—rather than as a mere enhancement or accessory to it, as is the case in team sports. As such, it is important to recognize the distinction between primarily athlete-oriented music used in such sports such as figure skating versus the primarily spectator-oriented use of music in team sports. Though they are non-team sports, the use of music in the actual routines of figure skating or gymnastics has, for some, made them more redolent of art or dance, and thus they have traditionally been considered more stereotypically effeminate sports and often as stereotypical bastions of gay participation. The presence of such well-known openly gay athletes as Brian Orser and Rudy Galindo in figure skating would seem to bear this out. Synchronized swimming is another relatively peripheral sport in which the artistic realization of a musical routine plays a central role. Synchronized swimming is also somewhat unique in that there are solo, duet, and team competitions. Compounding the relatively non-traditional aspect of this sport is the fact that, at least at the Olympic level, it is an all-female sport.[11]

Interestingly, the use of dance music, such as the salsa music that accompanies Cleveland Indians catcher Victor Martinez when he approaches the plate in professional baseball, seems to be regarded as a less effeminate and more culturally expressive statement. The use of dance music in such instances is mitigated,

---

"metrosexual" poster boy David Beckham.

[10] Anderson, 16.

[11] It should be recognized, however, that synchronized swimming (like aquatic sports in general) has an increasingly large participation rate among gay men. It was, for example, one of the featured sports at the 2005 International Gay and Lesbian Aquatics Championships (held at the site of the Atlanta 1996 Olympic Games) and at the 2006 World Out Games held in Montreal at the site of the 1976 Olympic swimming events.

perhaps, by the threatening phallic presence of the bat itself. Indeed, it is common for most baseball players to request a theme song when they come up to bat or when relief pitchers make their entrances. In 2004 one of the most requested songs by major league players was Usher's extremely suggestive "Yeah"—a song known for its sexually suggestive content ("Next thing I knew she was all up on me screaming"[12]).[13] The most requested band was Metallica. It is of likely little surprise that both of these artists project overtly orthodox heterosexual masculine images and aggressive musical profiles. If these requested songs, at least in part, represent the self-perceived identity of the players requesting them, it seems that stereotypical anxieties regarding heterosexual masculine hegemony and sexual identity remain largely in place in baseball.

Freestyle skateboarding, snowboarding, and some forms of skiing (such as mogul competitions) present yet other forms of non-physically-interactive sports that nonetheless use music as a seemingly integral feature. In such competitions recorded alternative and punk rock is typically played throughout each contestant's individual freestyle run. The run and associated "tricks," however, may or may not reflect the changes in the music. The music is used primarily to enhance or amplify the atmosphere surrounding the performance; the sport does not represent an aesthetic interpretation of the music, as is the case in figure skating and gymnastic floor routines, which give marks for artistic expression. The fact that freestyle skateboarding, inline skating, skiing, and snowboarding maintain a highly masculine image despite their close association with music seems to stem, in large part, from the presence of the extreme risk of bodily harm associated with these sports. The orthodox masculine code of violent bodily contact with a foe, typical of traditional team sports, has in these instances been replaced with the equally orthodox masculine notion of stoically overcoming fear of physical injury. The conventional masculine aggressive nature of these sports is, in addition, supplemented by the use of typically aggressive alternative and punk rock music. Some sports, such as ski jumping, for example, usually include an artistic impression or stylistic element in the scoring but do not employ musical interpretation of any kind. In these cases the competitor is judged on the ability to exhibit technical mastery and exemplary physical control over the activity itself.

Traditionally boys and young men have been understood to construct their masculinity based on a patriarchal sense of opposition to femininity. In this sense misogyny and homophobia combine in the construction of the idea of the male "masculine" image. According to a recent national study conducted by the Amateur Athletic Foundation of Los Angeles, "Boys are five times more likely than girls to watch sports programs on a regular basis," and 98 percent of US boys of ages

---

12   Words and music by Lil John, Sean Garrett, Patrick J. Que Smith, Ludacris, Robert McDowell, James Phillips and LaMarquis Jefferson.

13   Peter Schrager, "*Total Request Live* at the ballpark," *ESPN Page 3*, Friday, August 6, 2004, http://sports.espn.go.com/espn/page3/story?page=schrager/040806 (accessed May 18, 2009).

eight to 17 consume some form of sports-related media, with 82 percent doing so at least a couple of times a week.[14] With its fundamentally male "cast"—athletes and anchors, coaches and commentators—professional sports and sports programming send uniquely powerful messages about masculine behavior. Through both passive media consumption and active participation in sports, young males often assert a hegemonic oppression over women and homosexual men and are often steeped in the values of physical competition and dominance within and over their peer groups.[15] Nowhere is this more prevalent than in the worlds of sports and music, which encourage both the notion of a "no pain, no gain" approach to practice and a stoic concentration on performance. The competitive nature of music has already been discussed in Chapter 1 in regard to the history of sports–music relationships. However, in the present day everything from band auditions and classical instrumental and marching band competitions to battles of rock bands and *American Idol*-style pop music contests reinforce the need to dominate and eliminate one's competition in much the same manner as in competitive sports. In both sports and music the notion of success is often predicated on notions of divisiveness, where the achievement of one performer (or group of performers) comes only at the expense of another's loss. In this manner, though competitiveness is by no means a purely masculine construct, conventional hegemonic masculinity informs a large part of both sports and music and even acculturates many women to subscribe to such masculine orthodoxies.

Something of this state of affairs can be glimpsed in the "New York, New York" theme music that accompanies the end of every New York Yankees home game. When the team has been victorious, the loudspeakers at Yankee Stadium blare Frank Sinatra's upbeat and defiant version of the song. When they lose, however, it is instead Liza Minnelli's much more morose and subdued version that is played. Sinatra was famous for his macho persona on stage and screen, and his more stereotypically masculine version, with its deeper vocal range and aggressive rhythmic attack, thus becomes associated with winning. Minnelli, however, is well known for her turbulent life as the daughter of Judy Garland and as an icon and high-profile supporter of the gay community. Her more stereotypical feminine or effeminate version of the song in this context thus becomes associated with loss and perhaps even with physical and emotional pain and suffering.

To be sure, music, for all its obsession with competition, does not replicate the physical violence associated with many sports and is thus often considered a more "civilized" or "civilizing" activity—one that supports intellectual

---

[14]   Mike Messner, Darnell Hunt, and Michele Dunbar, *Boys to Men: Sports Media Messages about Masculinity* (*Children Now* and the Amateur Athletic Foundation of Los Angeles, 1999), 3.

[15]   The same study concluded that media messages to young men resulted in aggressive behavior: "Whether he is playing sports or making choices about which products to purchase, his aggressiveness will win him the ultimate prize: the adoring attention of beautiful women and the admiration of other men." Messner, *Boys to Men*, 11.

edification rather than brutal bodily gratification. While contemporary society is obsessed with the perceived negative values of sex and sexuality, it seems by comparison to be relatively tolerant of violence. The violence of sports has become naturalized in our society to a degree that sex and sexuality have not. The partial exposure of Janet Jackson's breast during the 2004 Super Bowl half-time prompted a rash of moral outrage from parents and others, while the violent context of the football game itself went completely uncriticized. Sports and music are linked through their propensity to promote and maintain socially negative attributes, while maintaining a patina of the socially positive. The multiple hegemonic mythoi of both forms of entertainment have enabled them to maintain a relatively unchallenged, socially acceptable and affirmative image, while any negative social side effects are largely overlooked.[16]

Despite their relative exclusion from open involvement in mainstream sports, gays and lesbians regularly participate in and are avid fans of mainstream, stereotypically heterosexual sports like baseball, soccer, and football. At the same time, openly and exclusively gay and lesbian sports are becoming increasingly popular—though there appears to be little evidence of any particularly distinct homosexual competitive ethos[17]—and serve to reflect the diversity of interests of the broader gay and lesbian populations. From the annual Gay Soccer World Championships to the quadrennial Gay Games, and from the numerous gay rodeos in North America to the European gay chess championship, there are organized gay and lesbian competitions in a vast range of sports. As evidenced above, these sports reflect an interest in both traditional sporting events and in newer, non-traditional adaptations, such as gay men's synchronized swimming. Two of the highest-profile gay sporting events are the Gay Games, held in Cologne in 2010, and the new World Out Games, first held in Montreal in 2006. Both of these events attract major international corporate and national government sponsorship and, though gay and lesbian athletes are not openly part of the mainstream Olympic

---

[16]   There are obvious exceptions to this, such as the steroid and doping scandals that have engulfed many sports (as discussed in Chapter 3) and the similar negative public reaction to the objectionable content of videos and lyrics of some popular music artists. Nonetheless, despite some instances of negative reaction, both sports and music maintain largely positive social images.

[17]   Several studies have concluded that it is difficult for gay and lesbian athletes who have been socialized into the ethos of mainstream sport to abandon their acceptance of "survival of the fittest" competitive values for any alternative model that might privilege fun, friendship, and the pure pleasure gleaned from bodily movement. See Helen Lenskyj, "Girl-friendly sport and female values," *Women in Sport and Physical Activity Journal* 3/1 (1994), 35–46, and Helen Lenskyj, "Gay Games or Gay Olympics? Implications for lesbian inclusion," *Canadian Women's Studies* 21/3 (Winter/Spring, 2002), 24–8.

movement, they are indicative of the increasing presence and visibility of gay and lesbian athletics and athletes.[18]

Sports can offer a highly visible challenge to stereotypes of homosexual passivity and bodily repression. The hypermasculine anthems and images of gay pride (manifest in songs like the Village People's "Macho Man") are not dissimilar to the equally hypermasculine pose associated with many black rap artists and athletes—as exemplified in the supposed sexual exploits of Wilt Chamberlain or the stereotypical depictions of hypersexual appetites depicted in numerous rap videos. Ironically, both groups, despite the overtly negative attitudes often shown by heterosexual black men to homosexuality, share the common media stereotype of being "oversexed" or having "hypersexual" appetites and have similarly often been silenced in mainstream heterosexual white society. Openly gay track coach Eric Anderson speculates that the "hypermasculine" pose adopted by many African American athletes may be "partially based on homophobia" or "hyperheterosexuality."[19] As with rap and breakdancing—overtly physical and competitive outlets for African American culture—voguing, drag lip-synch competitions, and the general prominence of gay musicians and singers have offered analogous responses to social repression that combine elements of competitiveness and physicality common to sports. Among the numerous other attributes examined throughout this book, music and sports thus often share the commonality of being transgressively located outside domestic spaces of bodily control. In this aspect the relationship between sports and music would seem to rely on a similar quest to refine physical pleasure and sexual desire. Michel Foucault comments on the pleasurable tension between danger and desire when he speaks of his inability to feel a "complete total pleasure" that he relates to death: "I do not feel *the* pleasure, the complete and total pleasure and, for me, it's related to death. Because I think that the kind of pleasure I would consider as *the* real pleasure, would be so deep, so intense, so overwhelming that I couldn't survive it. I would die."[20] The often dangerous but pleasurable physicality of sports and associated physical pleasures of music can thus be linked through similarly homosocial situations—whether in the same-sex bonding achieved by

---

[18]   One interesting intersection between sports, homosexuality, and popular music has been provided by Sir Elton John, who, in response to a lifelong obsession with soccer, purchased the English League Watford Football Club in 1974. He was chairman and director of this professional club for some 25 years until resigning in May 2002. Under his directorship the team was divisionally promoted several times and even reached the FA Cup finals in 1984.

[19]   See Keith Boykin, "Black gay athletes: Homosexuality and homoeroticism in black sports," Monday, February 3, 2003, www.keithboykin.com/sports/blackgayathletes. html (accessed May 17, 2008).

[20]   Michel Foucault as cited in bell hooks, "Eating the Other: Desire and resistance," in Meenakshi Gigi Durham and Douglass M. Knellner (eds), *Media and Cultural Studies: Keyworks* (Malden Mass.: Blackwell, 2001), 428.

both team sports and musical groups or even through shared communal attendance at sporting and musical events. These characteristics are obviously common to both heterosexual and homosexual communities; however, it can be argued that, similar to the situation with black men described above, the bodily repression experienced by many homosexuals has perhaps heightened the desire for, at least to some degree, such culturally sanctioned moments of physical transgression and expression.

Presaging Foucault's ideas, in ancient Greece and Rome the body was the locus for an ethics of the self, a site of combat between pleasure and pain that enabled people to find truth in the belief that they mastered themselves in the process.[21] This combination of austerity and hedonism could be achieved through training—in essence a training for the controlled governance of mind and body. Such a philosophy understood the disciplining of the body as an internal and external exercise and as an analogous site for the disciplining and governing of the state and society.

Related to this, and as discussed in this book, sports and music are both important locations of national identity and pride. Building community spirit was central to the evolution of sports. Allegiances to the local football or cricket club, for example, were often originally stimulated by factory owners, who supported the clubs in an effort to influence community standards. Factory owners encouraged the spread of organized sport as a means of educating lower-class workers on the virtues of better discipline and the improvement of their health, as well as to encourage their abandonment of non-productive pre-industrial leisure activities such as fighting, gambling, and excessive drinking. While professional sportsmen had existed prior to industrialization in sports such as cricket and golf, they were typically held in low esteem for deigning to play for pay. To some extent organized sport in the nineteenth century was a reflection of the middle-class values that then shaped England's national identity.

Building on a Protestant work ethic, the Victorian role of sports was not merely for entertainment, diversion, and leisure but rather for moral edification— the creation of a morally upright citizenry. To pursue sports for money or as an end in themselves was deemed unacceptable. The extreme manifestation of this ideology was found in the Muscular Christian movement, where sports and athletics were viewed as creating a physically superior male Christian who was better able to serve God. The outward physical manifestation of the individual was a reflection of his internal moral fitness. However, with the rise of factory-

---

[21]   Michel Foucault, *The History of Sexuality: The Use of Pleasure*, Vol. 2, Robert Hurley (trans.) (New York: Vintage, 1986), 66–9. The very concept of "mastery," whether of a sport or a musical instrument, implies a hegemonic masculine construction. In recent years this has perhaps been most publicly demonstrated through the "Masters" tournament annually held at Augusta National Golf Club, which has been boycotted by Martha Burk and the National Council of Women's Organizations for barring women from the club. See "She means business," *Sports Illustrated* July 29/2002, 35–8.

run community club teams, there was an increased demand for success in sport—
to build both a successful franchise through a consistent fan base and to instill
community pride. The earliest cricket matches, for example, occurred primarily
between competing towns and villages, and as early as 1709 the first known
country "fixture" took place between Surrey and Kent.[22] One has only to think
of the extreme celebrations associated with winning any major contemporary
sporting championship to know that such community pride is still a regular
feature of present-day sports. With the advent of the modern Olympic movement
and "World Championships" in almost every sport conceivable, such notions of
civic pride evolved into expressions of national pride, which in extreme cases
demonstrated jingoistic perceptions of superiority. This was particularly manifest
in the US–Soviet Olympic medal rivalry that essentially replicated the Cold War.

Music serves a similar function in community building. This is borne out in the
generic term "British Invasion," used to describe the popularity of English bands
in the United States during the 1960s, and in the pride of place emphasized in
commonly used terms for musical styles such a "Memphis Soul," "The Nashville
Sound," "Seattle Grunge," or "Chicago House." Fan allegiance to particular bands
and styles of music often indicates what "team" one is on. Pride in place and
community was central to the evolution of a heated, and at times even deadly,
stylistic rivalry in rap between "East Coast" and "West Coast" styles—a rivalry
largely played out between the followers of Notorious B.I.G. and Tupac Shakur.
While the consumption of and participation in sports is a prime marker of
communal identity for mainstream society, the gay community, as a marginalized
sector of society, has typically been excluded from such celebrations. To some
extent the notions associated with the Muscular Christian movement, specifically
the idea that the outward physical fitness of an individual reflects inner moral
character, is one that still has a powerful resonance in Western notions of sports, as
manifest in the concept that a strong body builds a strong mind. Gay athletes and
musicians, however, have hardly been regarded as sources of moral fitness or civic
pride in mainstream Western society. Thus the increasing profile of gay culture in
the West, whether in sporting events, music, or other activities, fulfills a desire to
affirm and express a previously denied, or at least repressed, community status.

One of the prime sites in the convergence of sports, music, and gay culture
lies in the prevalence of hypermasculinized sports "anthems" by gay icons such as
Queen, the Village People, the Pet Shop Boys, and others. These songs often openly
espouse the virtues of a gay lifestyle while, seemingly paradoxically, they are most
commonly heard at heterosexual-dominated sporting events. It is well known that
the singing of actual national anthems such as "The Star-Spangled Banner" serves
to reinforce the nationalistic character of most sports—and analogous nationalistic
musico-cultural inferences. Of more interest to the issues of this chapter are songs

---

[22]   See Geoffrey Holmes and Daniel Szechi, *The Age of Oligarchy: Pre-industrial
Britain 1722–1783* (London: Longman, 1993), 212.

such as the Village People's "YMCA" and "Go West," as well as Queen's "We Are the Champions" and "We Will Rock You."

Though they are not the main anthems to be discussed in the remainder of this chapter, other well-known anthems of this type include Gary Glitter's "Rock and Roll Part 2" and Steam's "Na Na Hey Hey Kiss Him Goodbye." Glitter's song was one of the biggest hits of 1972, reaching No. 2 in Britain and the Top 10 in America. Glitter was famous for his outrageous wardrobe that included over 30 glitter suits and 50 pairs of platform boots. Sadly, in the late 1990s Glitter was convicted of child pornography and his career fell apart. Though Glitter himself was not gay, his flamboyant glam rock stage persona and lifestyle made him an icon in the gay community.

Steam's "Na Na Hey Hey Kiss Him Goodbye" is another popular rock anthem commonly heard at sporting events. Released in 1969, the song rose to No. 1 in the United Kingdom and sold over a million copies in the United States alone. The song became a hit all over again when it was covered by the British girl group Bananarama. Notably, however, the song is also the unofficial anthem of the Chicago White Sox and appeared on the *Dallas Cowboys: The Ultimate Team* album. Somewhat ironically, given the hetero-normative masculine sporting environment at which it is most commonly heard, the song celebrates the break-up of a woman from a man. Indeed, the work was also featured on a 1993 album entitled *There Was Love (The Divorce Songs)*.

As such, each of these rock songs, while not originally popularized through sporting events or overtly thematically concerned with sports, has subsequently risen to iconic anthemic status due largely to being played at and associated with sporting events. Notably, all of these sports anthems feature a memorable and easily sung chorus in which fans can readily participate. These chanted choruses, which were a particularly marked feature of 1970s glam rockers such as Gary Glitter, Slade, the Sweet, and Queen, are a direct extension and emulation of the actual sounds of soccer supporters. During the 1970s, soccer also influenced rock fashion and behavior as the fad for tartan scarf waving, associated with acts like the Bay City Rollers and Rod Stewart and the Faces, was directly modeled on the soccer "terrace" culture from the same period.

Perhaps the most universally recognizable of these tunes are Queen's "We Will Rock You" and "We Are the Champions," which first appeared on the album *News of the World* in 1977. Released as a double A-side single (and often played back-to-back by radio stations) they were a Top 10 hit in both North America and Britain when they were first released. These two songs have achieved lasting significance, however, through their subsequent ubiquitous exposure at major sporting events throughout North America and Europe. Both songs are marked by powerful unison choruses, syncopated clapping/stamping, and a defiant tone of mastery and conquest that has made them a favorite of home team sports fans. In a paradox with their overtly orthodox masculine sentiments, however, both of these songs simultaneously espouse pro-gay sentiments, although many, predominantly heterosexual, listeners appear unaware or intentionally choose to ignore this fact.

Lyrics from Freddie Mercury's "We Are the Champions," such as "I've done my sentence but committed no crime" and "We mean to go on and on and on and on," are thinly veiled allusions to Mercury's semi-closeted lifestyle. Queen had, and continues to have, a significant following among adolescent male fans that either have not known or have refused to believe the fact that Freddie Mercury was gay or that many of Queen's songs referenced gay and bisexual themes. Indeed, when Mercury began wearing a closely cropped hairstyle and a thick moustache following the 1980 release of *The Game,* fans feared the new look was too gay and protested by throwing razor blades on stage during concerts, hoping in vain that he would shave off the moustache. Many fans, nonetheless, overlooked such seeming anomalies and were often attracted to the technical virtuosity of the band, including the forceful and quintessentially macho guitar-hero playing of Brian May and the muscular drum and bass patterns of John Deacon and Roger Taylor. Freddie Mercury's flamboyant stage persona and aggressive, if often nearly operatically inspired, coloraturic vocals merely seemed to be a natural extension of the brash, transgressively hypersexual theatrics of Mick Jagger and other lead singers of the day.

Male musical performers have, of course, long cultivated the use of an effeminate image as a means of projecting a transgressive and, therefore, ironically dangerous and acceptably masculine persona. Nineteenth-century performers such as the virtuoso Paganini and, later, Franz Liszt grew their hair long to suggest a romantically sexual wildness in their playing and, by analogy, in themselves. Gender bending images have likewise long been a part of rock music, from Little Richard's flamboyant use of mascara in the 1950s to the Beatles' mop top haircuts in the 1960s (which arguably initiated the long-haired hippie look that followed) to David Bowie's bisexual alien persona of Ziggy Stardust in the 1970s. The trend, still evident in acts such as Marilyn Manson or Adam Lambert, perhaps reached its apex in the early 1980s with a host of gender bending artists such as Boy George, the Cure, Grace Jones, and Annie Lennox.

The fascination with high-pitched, effeminate male voices also has a long history, stretching back at least to the baroque era's preponderance of castrati roles—roles in which the leading male heroic figure sang in the highest, most effeminized register. The allure of high-pitched male singing can be traced to our fascination with youth and the sound of prepubescent sexual potency, and manifests itself in today's preponderance of high-register male vocalists such as Michael Jackson, to say nothing of gay lead singer Jimmy Somerville's falsetto, made famous in the Bronski Beat's 1984 hit "Why?".[23] For many in the gay community, high-pitched singing and the operatic voice represents the triumph and

---

[23]   High-pitched male vocalizations have, of course, been a consistent feature of popular music, including the falsettos associated with Robert Johnson, Little Richard, and Frankie Valli and the Four Seasons, John Lennon's ethereal tenor, or the high-register vocalizations associated with many hard rock and heavy metal singers such as Robert Plant, Geddy Lee, or Steve Perry.

transcendence of emotion and physical vocality over repressive social and moral conventions. The apparent paradox of hypermasculine stage theatrics combined with effeminate hairstyles and clothing is also a common feature of many heavy metal and hard rock bands such as Mötley Crüe, Bon Jovi, and others.[24]

It should be noted that not all of Queen's songs referenced homosexual themes. Indeed one of their most prominent sports anthems, "Another One Bites the Dust," (1980) does not lend itself to any overt homosexual interpretation. Written by bassist John Deacon, the song was a worldwide hit, reaching No. 1 on the US *Billboard* Hot 100, No. 2 on the R&B chart, and No. 7 in the UK singles chart. "Another One Bites the Dust" is one of Queen's best-selling singles and one of their biggest hits, with sales of over 7 million copies. The characteristic throbbing bass line featured in the song was inspired by the song "Good Times" by the disco group Chic. The lyrics, however, simply reference the commonly understood meaning of the title phrase to "bite the dust": to fall and die, like the loser of a gunfight.

> Verse
> Steve walks warily down the street
> With his brim pulled way down low
> Ain't no sound but the sound of his feet
> Machine guns ready to go …

> Chorus
> And another one gone and another one gone
> Another one bites the dust yeah
> Hey I'm gonna get you too
> Another one bites the dust
> Shootout!

Conjuring up stereotypically masculine gunfighter imagery, the "death in a shootout" motif has made the song a staple at North American professional sporting events, either when the game is over or when the score is out of reach in favor of the home side. Similarly, the overtly heterosexual lyrics and videos associated with Queen songs like "Fat Bottomed Girls" or "Crazy Little Thing Called Love" belie any particular homosexual subtext or reference. However, Queen's lyrics in many instances—particularly those written by Mercury—appear to have intentionally been open to a double-sided interpretation. The 1978 video for "Bicycle Race," for example, would appear to project an overtly heterosexist message, featuring lingering camera shots of naked women riding bicycles.

---

[24]   For a more detailed study of this phenomenon, particularly as it relates to heavy metal, see Robert Walser, "Forging masculinity: Heavy metal sounds and images of gender" in Simon Frith, Andrew Goodwin and Lawrence Grossberg (eds), *Sound and Vision: The Music Video Reader* (Routledge, 1993), 153–81.

Notably the song obviously also references a sports-related lyrical theme. However, the apparently heterosexual nature of the song, reinforced by the video images, can be substantially called into question when one considers Mercury's, at times, bisexual lifestyle. In this context, as with "We Are the Champions," lyrics like "I want to ride my bicycle/I want to ride it where I like"[25] take on a meaning completely antithetical to the video's overtly heterosexist images.

The semi-closeted lyrical content of Queen's songs such as "I Want to Break Free," "Innuendo" ("show yourself—destroy our fears—release your mask ... be free"), and "Somebody to Love" ("I just gotta get out of this prison cell/Someday I'm gonna be free") was just sufficiently vague enough to appeal to the pent-up frustrations of heterosexual male adolescents.[26] Ironically, the common theme of freedom could be read equally well as freedom from adolescent repression imposed by parents, school, and other institutional and social oppressions felt by young heterosexual males, rather than as a cry for gay liberation. If heterosexual male fans even considered gay readings of Queen's repertoire, there was enough ambivalence to ensure plausible denial. Indeed, outside Mercury, even the band members themselves often seemingly had little idea of potential gay readings of the songs. In a 2002 interview, Brian May, in response to viewing a clip of the video for "Killer Queen," claimed that since the band members often did their composing on their own, they typically had no idea of what the meanings of the songs were. "Strangely, in those days we didn't really talk about what the songs were about ... in retrospect it might have been quite interesting."[27]

The use of "Bohemian Rhapsody" in the 1992 movie *Wayne's World* highlighted the homosocial masculine appeal of Queen's music. In the famous unison "head banging scene," Wayne, Garth, and three other male friends go out on the town, squeezed into an AMC Pacer, and crank up Queen's "Bohemian Rhapsody" on the car stereo. The boys are lost in dreamlike rapture in the opening ballad section of the song as they tenderly prop up one of their inebriated buddies in the back seat. With the onset of the aggressive "hard rock" portion of the song, they return to reality and are enervated by synchronized unison head banging. As such the moment is a pivotal moment of male bonding—"team-bonding," to use a sports analogy—in the movie.[28] It is an unstable liminal moment that, like "Bohemian Rhapsody" itself, moves transgressively from a tender and stereotypically effeminate lullaby to aggressive and stereotypically masculine hard rock. In the

---

[25]   Lyrics by Freddie Mercury.

[26]   Words and music written by Freddie Mercury and Roger Taylor, and Freddie Mercury, respectively.

[27]   Brian May, transcribed from an interview in *Queen: Greatest Video Hits 1* DVD Collection 2002, Queen Productions Ltd.

[28]   For a more complete reading of the homosocial implications of this song, please see my article "Bohemian Rhapsodies: Operatic influence and crossover in rock music," *Popular Music* 20/2 (Fall 2001), 189–203.

movie, as with Queen's predominantly male fan base in general, the song provides a vehicle for strengthening homosocial relationships.

The homosocial messages of Queen's promotional videos for "We Will Rock You" and "We Are the Champions" are somewhat more incongruous. The promotional video for "We Will Rock You," for example, was filmed outdoors in 1977 on a chilly January day in Roger Taylor's backyard. The relatively sparse video of the band lip-synching the song (including the rather ridiculous sight of hand clapping with gloves and foot stomping in boots on the frozen ground) gives little hint of its later popularity at sporting events, with the possible exception of bassist John Deacon's Chicago Blackhawks hockey jacket. To some extent, however, the video has the effect, even if unintentionally, of toning down Mercury's hypersexualized image. In the early days of Queen, Mercury presented an overtly effeminate image with long hair, makeup, and eyeliner and dressed in flowing gowns, necklaces, and tight fitting sequined body suits. Though his theatrical costuming was not out of character with other glam rockers of the era, such as David Bowie, his style was more conflicted in its merging of feminine and hypermasculine sexuality. Mercury, for example, supplemented his orthodox feminine characteristics with costumes that invariably provided tight contours for his genital area, and that included plunging chest cut-aways which revealed an abundant growth of masculine chest hair. The result was a gender slippage that combined strongly heterosexual masculine visual codes that were decentered through the visual associations of a woman—he presented himself, in terms of his gender, as deliberately hypersexual.

The video for "We Will Rock You," however, negates or at least mitigates such a transgressive image. It was filmed in a stereotypically heterosexual masculine setting: outdoors on a frigid winter day, and with the forces of nature a visible presence that clearly had to be overcome. Instead of the tight fitting, chest revealing outfits and heavy makeup that characterized his stage shows and other videos, Mercury is dressed in a bulky, non-revealing militaristic bomber jacket and loosely fitting pants. His body, as befits the weather conditions, is fully covered down to his bomber jacket, aviator sunglasses, and gloved hands. His liminal and flamboyant sexual image has thus been negated in this setting in favour of a conventionally heterosexual, and hence less sexually threatening, persona—an identity more in keeping with the superficially aggressive masculine stance of the lyrical sentiments and music of "We Will Rock You."

Filmed several months later in 1977, the video for "We Are the Champions" was a more elaborate production. Directed by Derek Burbridge in the New London Theatre, it features the band lip-synching a live performance in front of a wildly enthusiastic crowd. The crowd was actually composed of hundreds of members of Queen's fan club, who began to spontaneously wave their Queen banners and scarves in the manner of English soccer supporters. The video also features Mercury in one of his trademark Harlequin outfits: a skin-tight body suit divided into one white half and one black half, with a low-cut front revealing Mercury's naked chest.[29] The Harlequin character was a favorite of Mercury's and referenced the popular Italian *commedia dell'arte* of the seventeenth and eighteenth centuries. The Harlequin was a stock pantomime character who was a clownish servant known for his wit and acrobatic skills. Such references from classical theatre highlight Mercury's desire to meld "high" art and culture with rock music—a fact sonically manifest in the elaborate choral productions and operatic vocals found in songs such as "Bohemian Rhapsody." "Bohemian Rhapsody" also references a *commedia dell'arte* character in the lyric "Scaramouche, Scaramouche, will you do the fandango?"[30]

In his half-black, half-white body suit for "We Are the Champions," Mercury evinces more of his liminal persona that underlines his simultaneous embodiment of half-man, half-woman, half-gay, half-straight. In combination with the spectacle created by the enthusiastic soccer-like supporters, this video, even more so than the one produced for "We Will Rock You," reveals an enigmatic play between the spectacle of sports culture, hard rock, and Mercury's own sexually decentered persona as manifest in his Harlequin costume. In its employment of sports-related visual imagery and spectacle, and in combination with the aggressive musical and lyrical nature of the song, the video clearly presaged something of the song's later popularity as a sports anthem.

Subsequent to the phenomenal sports arena successes of "We Are the Champions" and "We Will Rock You," guitarist Brian May has recently revisited the theme with an original composition called "Stadium Rock," written and arranged specifically for marching bands. This light rock composition was intended for high school level bands and includes three short pieces incorporating various sports chants, tunes, and (*à la* "We Will Rock You") syncopated handclaps.[31]

One of the more recent instances of the emergence of a sports anthem is the song "Go West." Originally a 1979 disco classic by the Village People, it was made even more famous when it was covered by the Pet Shop Boys in 1993. Particularly in the wake of the Pet Shop Boys' version, the melody has become a staple underpinning for many English soccer chants, including "One–nil, to the Arsenal" and "Go West Bromwich Albion," as well as many more vulgar variations. The chant, in its original lyrical form, received international exposure during the 2002 World Cup, co-hosted by South Korea and Japan, where it was heard at nearly every venue regardless of whether or not England was competing.

Often playing with notions of sexual ambiguity, the Pet Shop Boys—Neil Tennant and Chris Lowe—are well known for cultivating superficiality in opposition to their perception of the pomposity of much rock music. They take an ambiguous aesthetic stance that constantly shifts between stereotypes of "high"

---

[29]   Jennifer de Boer makes this observation in "On the margins of the mainstream: Queen, the rock press, and gender," M.A. thesis, McMaster University 1999, 38.

[30]   Lyrics by Freddie Mercury. Scaramouche was a stock *commedia dell'arte* character very similar to Harlequin.

[31]   "Stadium Rock," Queen Music Ltd, 1996.

art and "low" culture, juxtaposing, for example, classic disco hits with allusions to Shostakovich and scenes of Harold Pinter. Originally a hit song for the Village People in 1979, the Pet Shop Boys' "Go West" was recorded for their album *Very* in 1993, complete with the help of a young all-male chorus. The reference to the gay men's chorus here postdates the Village People's version and transforms the song from its original celebration of a gay American dream epitomized by the desire to "Go West" to a West Coast lifestyle of sunshine, sand, and sex into a haunting but uplifting disco dream, framed by the specter of HIV and AIDS.

The video, however, took an altogether different approach, using the lyrics to portray an ironic comment on the defeat of Soviet communism and the increasing "Westernization" of Russia. Much of the theme of the work is based on the movie *A Matter of Life and Death* (1946), starring David Niven—released in the United States under the title *Stairway to Heaven*—in which a British World War II aviator who cheats death argues for his life in a celestial trial. Produced in the Pet Shop Boys' usual tongue-in-cheek style, the video parodies the notion of a "stairway to heaven" as it sees the Pet Shop Boys ascending an endless staircase under a golden "W"—a take-off on McDonald's Golden Arch and a comment on increasingly ubiquitous signs of (W)estern corporatization.

Sports play a prominent role in the video, which features the buff, athletic bodies of young men resembling Soviet-era gymnasts set against the odd spectacle of the Pet Shop Boys in futuristic suits with militaristic domed helmets on flying surfboards—here again symbolic of the California lifestyle evoked in the original Village People rendition, but also resembling Cold War era intercontinental ballistic missiles. The athletic male chorus's butch intoning of "Go West" is contrasted with Neil Tennant's effete lead vocal, and both are supplemented by the presence of the Statue of Liberty, which has come to life in the form of a black R&B diva.

The carnivalesque inversions at play here are numerous. The presence of a black female icon of liberty representing the West contrasts the athletic white male bodies of the East, while the Pet Shop Boys' futurist outfits enigmatically resist location, perhaps suggesting that they exist on a metaphysical/metamusical plane. Notably, the song ends openly on a dominant seventh chord, reinforcing the ambiguous and open-ended message of the work. In addition, the chord progression of the song references Johann Pachelbel's *Canon*, as emphasized in the opening harmonies. Thus the Pet Shop Boys' version of "Go West" takes on several layers of meaning: gay pride anthem, AIDS lament, and critique of Western society and values. It is a musical pastiche that transfers meaning from Pachelbel through the Village People to the Pet Shop Boys. As such the song, though dealing with serious subject matter, playfully resists a singular interpretation, an approach that decenters a rigidly heterosexual world-view. This layering of meaning was compounded when the song was adopted as a communal football anthem during the 2002 World Cup. Sung in English by tens of thousands of Korean and Japanese fans, the song became an overtly ironic comment on the "far eastern" setting of the tournament, as well as the general globalization and commodification of the game of football itself and its attempt at universal representation with the "World" Cup.[32] Yet another version of "Go West" became the theme of the 2006 World Cup hosted by Germany. Entitled "Stand Up! (Champions Theme)" the song was given new lyrics and sung by Italian pop baritone Patrizio Buanne. It was piped into every stadium during pre- and post-game festivities.

What is undeniable in many of the instances of the sports anthem phenomenon is their open association with gay artists and themes. Precisely why gay anthems by Queen, the Village People, or the Pet Shop Boys have become popular at sporting events that typically overtly affirm a heterosexual world-view is harder to determine. The University of Virginia's football fight song, for example, is regularly altered by fans to reflect anti-gay sentiments. To the lyrics "We come from Old Virginia, where all is bright and gay," the student body enthusiastically ad lib the response "No way!" Despite the often homophobic atmosphere of sporting events, songs like "YMCA," "Go West," or "We Are the Champions"— songs that openly espouse the virtues and pleasures of gay sex—are regularly celebrated and often even physically enacted, in the case of "YMCA," by middle-class heterosexual America at a variety of sporting events.

Despite the increasing visibility of gay and lesbian athletes, as gay sports historian Brian Pronger has recently asserted, "I am aware of no scholarly research that shows mainstream sport to be a significantly welcome environment for sexual minorities."[33] If sports constitute a forum where homosexuality has been traditionally discouraged, then popular music is a forum where it has, at least by comparison, been relatively tolerated and at times even celebrated. The popularity of the hypermasculinized sports anthems described above—gay anthems that use aggressive unison rhythms, muscular bass lines, and male choruses singing in relatively low registers emulating sports chants—would seem simultaneously to celebrate masculine power and performance while also permitting an open communal expression of bodily participation that transcends sexual orientation and gender preferences. Gilles Deleuze and Felix Guattari theorize that the human body's power to move and connect with other bodies is socially organized, and that desire is the very essence of being.[34] Indeed, many scholars suggest that the control of desire is the primary occupation of any society.[35] In this manner the bodily connection of sports can be linked to the bodily connection of music, particularly in

---

[32] The irony of the song being sung at a sporting event in the far east should not be overlooked, and indeed the English comedy duo Ant and Dec released a parody version of the song called "Go East" as part of a World Cup compilation. Also included on this album was a remake of the Village People's "Macho Man" in a parody called "Sumo Man."

[33] Brian Pronger, *The Arena of Masculinity: Sports, Homosexuality, and the Meaning of Sex* (New York: St. Martin's, 1990), 224.

[34] See Gilles Deleuze and Felix Guattari, *A Thousand Plateaus: Capitalism and Schizophrenia* (Minneapolis: University of Minnesota Press, 1987).

[35] See for example Brian Turner, *The Body and Society: Explorations in Social Theory* (Oxford: Blackwell, 1983).

the desire to participate in communal bodily movement such as dancing, "stadium waving," cheering, or chanting. The desire, as exhibited by primarily heterosexual sports fans, to enact the letters of "YMCA" with outstretched arms supersedes any consideration of or interest in discerning the homosexual connotation of the song's lyrics.

The world of 1970s glam rock that spawned many of the most prominent and enduring sports anthems was by no means the only musical stylistic era to transgress orthodox gender and sexual boundaries. An interesting case in point is the gender blurring associated with 1950s rockabilly. As Mary Bufwack and Robert Oermann have stated, "rockabilly threatened social order when men adopted slithering wiggles and emotional sobbing, previously female identified behavior; likewise, women challenged the status quo when they took on sassy manners and musical aggression."[36] Much as male rockabilly artists such as Elvis, Jerry Lee Lewis, Gene Vincent, and Carl Perkins appropriated such stereotypically female behaviors, so too did artists such as Freddie Mercury, the Village People, and the Pet Shop Boys appropriate hypermasculine modes of behavior and musical traits to destabilize and challenge conventional boundaries of gender and sexual identities.

The role of the sports rock anthems such as "We Will Rock You" or "YMCA" directly evokes the relationship to the spectacle surrounding the singing of actual national anthems at sporting events. To a large degree, the role of music in general at sporting events, and national anthems in particular, is to enhance the importance and monumentality of the occasion: to heighten the spectacle of the event. The Olympic Games, World Cups, Super Bowls, and other high-profile sporting events—including almost every American football half-time—stage extravagant musical shows, all ostensibly to hold an audience's attention, whether on a global, national, or local level. Public spectacles, whether sporting, musical, artistic, or of other kinds, have been used to affirm power and prestige throughout history. The gladiatorial spectacles of ancient Rome are analogous to the musico-theatrical spectacles of the court of Louis XIV at Versailles. Both represented a literal spending of wealth that served to underscore the power of the dominant order by intimidating any would-be threat and to provide a communal diversion from potential social concerns. As such, spectacles were, and still are, instrumental in providing legitimating symbols that contribute to the construction and stability of the state. More recently, the employment of musical spectaculars has often transcended the need for any other dramatic or sporting connection. Productions such as Live 8, Live Aid, or the Three Tenors stadium shows (originally held concurrently with World Cup tournaments) have garnered huge international audiences while drawing on the world of sports for their venues. The majority of the arena or stadium rock shows that depend on sporting venues thus function on

---

[36]   Mary A. Bufwack and Robert K. Oermann, *Finding Her Voice: The Saga of Women in Country Music* (New York: Crown, 1993), 216. Also quoted in Michael Bertrand, "I don't think Hank done it that way," in *A Boy Named Sue: Gender and Country Music*, Kristine McCusker and Diane Pecknold (eds) (Jackson: University of Mississippi, 2004), 59–85, 62.

a symbolic level as a type of sporting spectacular. They substitute a larger-than-life theatrical stage show for the gladiators or combatants on the field. Such large-scale spectaculars, whether sporting, musical, or a combination, reflect the sound of Western wealth and are manifestations of an economic capacity for leisure activities on a grand scale.

The singing of national anthems is, of course, a traditional starting point for North American sporting spectacles. This practice serves to reinforce the nationalistic character of most sports, but it is often also the moment when music most actively participates in the sporting spectacle. As such, the singing of an anthem by the audience and players alike is often enhanced through large-screen projections of the performers, military color guards, and flyovers, as well as both vocal and literal fireworks. Indeed, the sports-related term "vocal gymnastics" seems utterly appropriate to describe many of the heavily embellished versions of national anthems that pop singers have recently performed at larger sporting spectaculars.

Likely the most influential theorizing on the subject of spectacle has occurred in Guy Debord's *Society of the Spectacle* (1967) and his later *Comments on the Society of the Spectacle* (1988). In his examination of international football (soccer) on television, Debord sums up his view of spectacle as follows:

> The construction and presentation of the wholly commodified game in a colorful, ritzy yet standardized society of the mediated spectacle: The SPECTACLE is capital accumulated to the point where it becomes image. ... It is not just that the relationship of commodities is now plain to see—commodities are now all that there is to see, the world we see is the world of the commodity.[37]

Drawing on such definitions, the term "spectacle" in contemporary theory evokes a postmodern notion of the constructedness of an event and how it is framed for a mass audience. In this regard, the spectacularization of sports and music must be understood as an outgrowth of an increasingly media-driven society, and thus it has become a type of symbol of the globalized commodity.

Recently Debord's theories have been criticized, among other reasons, for trivializing human agency, for failing to account for the changing historical terms of spectacle, for eliding spectacle with a central dynamic of capitalist social relations, and for a pessimistic failure to take account of the affirming social and pleasurable aspects of spectacle.[38] The conflation of music and sports during half-time spectacles reinforces in particular the last of these critiques. The self-affirming and communal aspect of many half-time shows, of unison chanting, singing, or clapping—think of English football chanting or participating in

---

[37] Guy Debord, *Society of the Spectacle* (New York: Zone Books, 1995), 25, 29.

[38] For a particularly acute criticism of Debord's theories, see A. Tomlinson, "Theorizing spectacle: Beyond Debord," in John Sugden and Alan Tomlinson (eds), *Power Games: A Critical Sociology of Sports* (London: Routledge, 2002).

Queen's "We Will Rock You" or dancing to the Village People's "YMCA"—directly reinforces a collective and affirmative sociability that underscores human agency and participation in the spectacle. Indeed, it is a memory of this communal and overtly human aspect of the spectacle that the marketers of sports music seek to capture. The communal audience's barking and fist rolling to the Baha Men's "Who Let the Dogs Out," for example, physically enacts the sense of both a sporting moment and of a social party atmosphere. Through the confluence of these experiences they thus serve to reinforce each other.

Closely tied to the notion of spectacle is the idea of the carnivalesque, famously described by Mikhail Bakhtin as:

> something that is created when the themes of carnival twist, mutate and invert standard themes of societal make-up ... the extravagant juxtaposition of the grotesque mixing and confrontations of high and low, upper-class and lower-class, spiritual and material, young and old, male and female, daily identity and festive mask, serious conventions and their parodies, gloomy medieval times and joyous utopian visions. The key to carnival culture involves the temporary suspension of all hierarchical distinctions and barriers among men ... and prohibitions of usual life ...[39]

Bakhtin's concept of hierarchical inversion aligns well with the simultaneous juxtaposition of gay and masculine sports anthems.[40] Originally extravagant visions of homosexual utopias, such as "YMCA" and "We Are the Champions," that inverted "normative" heterosexual identity, have been reinverted and juxtaposed with the very ideal of the heterosexual life that these songs initially critiqued. Sporting events often situate dichotomies such as the apparently seamless combination of overtly homosocial anthems, like "Who Let the Dogs Out," side-by-side with gay pride anthems. The carnivalesque spectacle of a large-scale sporting event, however, allows for and encourages such polarities. Furthermore, in the communal celebration of the spectacle, such songs allow for a collective identification with the athletes, a carnivalesque masking of their true identities in which all identities, including social prohibitions regarding sexual preference, are momentarily suspended. Such carnivalesque moments are equally true for athletes on the field as well, particularly during moments of triumph. Normative heterosexual behavior is suspended while athletes celebrate through communal dances, hugging, and even kissing. Thus the "gay" sports anthem reinforces and

---

[39] Mikhail Bakhtin, *Rabelais and His World*, H. Iswolsky (trans.) (Bloomington, IN: Indiana University Press, 1984), 15.

[40] Bakhtin's concept of the carnivalesque has notably also been invoked in relation to the musical component of beach volleyball. See William Klink, "Digging your lips: Foucault, Bakhtin, Lacan, and pro beach volleyball," *Studies in Popular Culture* 21/3 (1999), 1–11.

parallels the transgressive suspension of time and space that sports themselves often engender.

The effective power of the gay sports anthem mimics the tension between power enacted over the body, as exemplified in sports and musical training, and the power enacted by it. Evoking the masculine notion of "mastery," Michel Foucault analyzes this tension as being beyond resolution:

> Mastery and awareness of one's own body can be acquired only through the effect of an investment of power in the body: gymnastics, exercises, muscle-building, nudism, glorification of the body beautiful. All of this belongs to the pathway leading to the desire of one's own body, by way of the insistent, persistent, meticulous work of power on the bodies of children, or soldiers, the healthy bodies. But once power produces this effect, there inevitably emerge the responding claims and affirmations, those of one's own body against power, of health against the economic system, of pleasure against the moral norms of sexuality, marriage, decency. Suddenly what has made power strong becomes used to attack it. Power, after investing itself in the body, finds itself exposed to a counter-attack in that same body.[41]

Gay sports anthems such as "Go West" and "We Are the Champions" exhibit a similar tension by invoking an affective power over the body as manifested in the audience's synchronous bodily response: chanting, clapping, stomping, and so on. Such anthems challenge the hegemonic power of masculinity but are also, in the context of their broadcast at sporting spectacles, co-opted by mainstream society. The co-option of the musical pose of hypermasculinity exhibited in anthems of gay pride inverts the typical power structure, though it in turn is reinverted in the context of the overtly heterosexual sporting event at which it is typically heard. In the employment of hypermasculine musical attributes associated with the sports-chant-inflected unison choruses of "Go West," "YMCA," and "We Are the Champions," lines demarking the distinctions between gay and straight become less obvious and thereby create room for negotiation. As manifested in the transgressive and often enigmatic sexual personae of the artists who create such anthems, it is a liminal space that allows room for many to explore aspects of their identity beyond the normative social conventions of gender and sexuality.

---

[41] Michel Foucault, "Body/Power," Colin Gordon (trans.) in *Power/Knowledge: Selected Interviews and Other Writings 1972–77* (New York: Pantheon, 1980), 56. Also quoted in Miller and McHoul, *Popular Culture*, 71.

Chapter 5

"It's a Man's Man's Man's World": Constructing Male Identity in African American Music and Sports[1]

This chapter concerns itself with the connection between African American sporting and musical styles and the competitive performance traditions that have often characterized and stereotyped images of aggressive African American masculinity. Connections between music and sports include commonalities of aesthetic practices and marketing approaches, and one of the most important of these is that of shared performance strategies. As posited by theorists such as bell hooks and Judith Butler, performance is one of the central characteristics in the construction of gender and racial identity.[2] By looking at the synergies of the performative traditions of music and athletics, a more nuanced understanding of African American male identity emerges, one that is essentially self-created through conscious and unconscious strategies of performance common to both athletics and music.

The first part of this chapter outlines general links between sports, music, and masculinity in North American society. In the second part I discuss some of the most notable connections between sports and music in the African American community, particularly as manifest in individual performers and historical relationships between jazz and boxing, basketball, and baseball. In the third section I analyze links between musical and athletic performance, and improvisation and the relationship to black masculinity. My overarching purpose is to highlight the little-understood connection between sports and music as two forms of entertainment and leisure culture and their synergetic roles in the formation of African American masculine identity.

---

[1]   Portions of this chapter initially appeared in my essay "Constructions of African American Masculinity in Music and Sports," *American Music* 27/2 (Summer 2009), 204–26.

[2]   bell hooks, "Performance practice as a site of opposition," in Catherine Ugwu (ed.), *Let's Get It On: The Politics of Black Performance* (Seattle: Bay Press, 1995); Judith Butler, *Bodies that Matter: On the Discursive Limits of Sex* (New York: Routledge, 1993).

Music, Sports, and Masculinity

As described in Chapter 4, boys and young men have often been understood to construct their masculinity based on a patriarchal opposition to femininity through asserting a hegemonic dominance over women, homosexual men, and their "weaker" heterosexual peers. The competitive nature of sports and music encourages and reinforces stereotypically masculine notions of stoic training regimes and disciplined performances. Like athletes, musicians must perform whether they are having a good day or bad. Both types of performers often undertake ritualistic practices before their performances to loosen themselves up without inhibiting muscle control. Too much tension, in either the musician or the athlete, will interfere with the smooth flow of physical responses to neural stimuli. The concept of getting into "the zone" is one common to both music and sport. In essence this means that the performer achieves such a high level of concentration that anything aside from the immediate aspects of the performance is barred from consciousness. In both sports and music peak performances are marked by players' ecstatic detachment from consciousness (a form of disembodiment), increased energy, and a sense of being at one with their environment.[3] The interrelationship of the sporting and musical cultures, however, extends beyond similarities of physical activity and mental preparation into the realm of shared techniques and aesthetic outlook.

Perhaps the strongest musical connection to sports lies in commonalities of rhythmic activities. Both music and sports such as basketball rely on rhythmic flow, polyrhythms, and syncopations that disrupt and decenter the expectations of audiences or opponents. There is often an increase in the tempo of events and in the dynamic characteristics of both sports and music as the participants approach conclusive points of repose, such as cadences in music or goals or baskets in sports. Both activities, in addition, require similarities of breath and muscle control, memory, and training. Common musical terms such as "walking bass," "melodic leap," and "running sixteenth notes" also underline the physical element of much music. Indeed, many musicians often adopt a physical embodiment of the beat with tapping feet or head bobbing to keep time. As Paul Berliner observes, "as jazz tempos increased, some musicians found that tired ankles caused tempos to slow down or become erratic, and they chose to omit every other beat, tapping on the music's backbeats, or, alternatively, 'one' and 'three.'"[4] The advent of new recording technologies, in part, helped foster a more athletic rhythmic approach to genres such as jazz and swing. As Gina Caponi-Tabery observes:

---

[3]   Psychologist Mihaly Csikszentmihalyi uses the term "flow" to refer to such euphoric performative experiences in sports. See Mihaly and L.S. Csikszentmihalyi, *Optimal Experience: Psychological Studies of Flow in Consciousness* (Cambridge: Cambridge University Press, 1988).

[4]   Paul Berliner, *Thinking in Jazz: The Infinite Art of Improvisation* (Chicago: University of Chicago Press, 1994), 151–2.

> The advent of electrical recording in 1925 made it possible to replace the brassy
> tuba and loud strumming banjo with more nimble string bass and more subtle
> guitar and drums ... The string bass allowed musicians to provide a bottom note
> on every beat, rather than every other beat, as was more common in the tuba ...
> The resulting sound was more driving, forward moving music ...[5]

This more enervated and nuanced approach to rhythm influenced early jump tunes
that relied on a driving 4/4 meter and bouncing backbeats.

In addition to rhythmic similarities, however, there is also a harmonic aspect to
both activities. The vertical alignment of various pitches in music can, particularly
in team sports such as basketball, be roughly equated to the spatial alignment of
players who must literally synchronically harmonize to support whoever has the
ball at any given moment. In this sense, the ball becomes the figurative melody
that is traded between different soloists while being harmonically supported
by the rest of the band/team. In this manner music and sports are linked by a
common communal aesthetic that creates and reinforces physical, artistic, and
competitive agency.

While such characteristics are potentially shared by many sports and musical
forms, the interconnections to African American forms of these cultural expressions
are particularly strong. The relationship between rhythm and melody in much
traditional African music demonstrates interaction in a manner similar to many
sports teams. Consider Richard Waterman's linking of rhythmic accompaniment
and melody in African music:

> Where the accents of European melodies tend to fall only on the thesis or arsis
> of the rhythmic foot, the main accents in African melodies ... fall between
> the down- and the up-beats. The effect thus produced is that of temporal
> displacement of the melodic phrase, in its relationship to the percussion phrase,
> to the extent of a half beat.[6]

As observed by Anne Danielsen, this temporal displacement "makes it possible
to distinguish between the different [rhythmic] figures. At the same time, the
figures are being locked into their positions. They keep each other steady."[7] Such
descriptions of rhythmic interrelationships closely match the interrelationship of
play in many African American dominated sports such as basketball. The physical
embodiment of the beat, as discussed, provides a synchronous reference point but

---

[5]   Gena Caponi-Tabery, *Jump for Joy: Jazz Basketball and Black Culture in 1930s
America* (Amherst: University of Massachusetts Press, 2008), 53.

[6]   Richard Waterman, "Hot rhythm in Negro music," *Journal of the American
Musicological Society* 1/1 (Spring, 1948), 24–37, 25, as quoted in Anne Danielsen,
Presence and Pleasure: The Funk Grooves of James Brown and Parliament (Middletown,
CT: Wesleyan University Press, 2006), 46.

[7]   Danielsen, 46.

also informs the musical content and ideas "by infusing them with appropriate rhythmic vitality."[8] Similarly, as Henry Louis Gates claims, the play of standard patterns or formulas is a common aspect of African American language and culture. Such "repeating with a difference" is also a feature of African American music (as manifested in the concept of a groove) and sports aesthetics (manifested in the slam dunk move).[9] Terms such as playing "in the pocket" or "being in the groove" are common to both jazz and sports and emphasize the ability to produce a fluid enervated repetition—such as is desirable when repeating a bassline, swinging a baseball bat or making a jump shot. Such features, while not exclusive to African American music and sports, would seem to be more highly emphasized in African-based approaches than in other musical genres such as heavy metal or progressive rock.

Indeed, specific links between sports and music in African American society can be found in traditional African rituals. Samuel Floyd, for example, in commenting on nineteenth-century accounts, describes the confluence of physicality and musical intensification that surrounded the "ring shouts" of African American slaves:

> the initially slow tempo of the music, repetitious singing, which gradually increases in tempo and 'spirit,' call and response figures … [some] competitive … with hand clapping and 'the smiting of breasts' serving as substitutes for drum playing … all rising in 'piercing' and 'staccato' intensity to finally reach a sudden climax … we see the shuffling around in a ring, the upper-body dancing of African provenance …[10]

Comparison to the similar physical experiences of the boxing ring and of the musical intensification in jazz improvisation is not difficult to make.[11] In comparable fashion the notion of a "groove," a common terminology in sports and music, encapsulates a similar non-verbal, physical, and sonic aesthetic that is often prevalent in African music.[12]

To understand recent cross-pollinations of sports and music and their relationship to African American masculinity, it is important to consider the interconnection of sports and militarism that underlies American society in general. As has been discussed at various points throughout this book, sports,

---

[8]   Berliner, 152.

[9]   Henry Louis Gates, Jr, *The Signifying Monkey: A Theory of African-American Literary Criticism* (New York: Oxford University Press, 1988), 63–4.

[10]   Samuel Floyd Jr, *The Power of Black Music: Interpreting Its History from Africa to the United States* (New York: Oxford University Press, 1995), 37.

[11]   I would argue that traces of a similar ring shout aesthetic are likely evident in other sports, particularly basketball.

[12]   See, for example, Charles Keil's discussion of "groove" as it relates to processual analysis and "sound gesture" in his chapter "Motion and feeling through music," in Charles Keil and Steven Feld, *Music Grooves* (Chicago: University of Chicago Press, 1994), 53–76.

along with the military, have traditionally been male-dominated, visibly patriarchal spaces. The militarism of American society is openly reflected in its violent sports culture, a culture that only inculcates and increases the pressure on American boys and men to fulfill a seemingly heroic masculine mythos of fighting and aggression. The systematic process of combining patriotic duty with athletic masculinity began in the wake of the Spanish-American War, when the armed services created an athletic program to train their forces. Over the past century almost every significant American sports organization, from NASCAR to the NHL, has trumpeted its patriotism through official statements and on-field salutes to the armed services.

As discussed in Chapter 1, there are many parallels between sports and war. North American football, in particular, with its rhetoric of a "defensive line" and an "offensive line" that is led into the opponents' territory by an "on-field general" is rife with military terminology, some of which is redolent of the trench warfare of World War I. The conflation of military and artistic triumph with masculine ideals has significant precedents throughout history, such as the aristocratic European "dueling culture," and is particularly prevalent in North America. Robert Kennedy once stated, "Except for war there is nothing in American life—nothing—which trains a boy better for life than football."[13]

Such militaristic underpinnings to musical and sporting cultures are primarily the products of white European culture and are particularly prevalent in a sport such as football, which essentially recreates the ideology and tactics of European colonial expansion. Traditionally, white-dominated hard rock, heavy metal, and country music—in addition to marching bands—have been the musical genres most readily identified with football. In recent years, however, the game has been largely dominated by African American players, and concentrated African American musical interaction with football has increased, though its presence there has been limited in comparison to its prominence in the worlds of basketball and baseball. African Americans have, nonetheless, been subject to and participated in the militaristic nature of the game and of American society in general. In commenting on the increasing violence of hip hop, Michael Eric Dyson directly links the genre with football and war, claiming that "violent masculinity is at the heart of American identity ... [and] central to notions of American democracy and cultural self-expression."[14] Notwithstanding their own histories of institutional racism, the AFL and NFL have been open to African Americans, if only the most exceptional players, from their inception in the 1920s. Sports such as baseball and basketball initially barred African Americans from playing on white teams. This resulted in the formation of Negro leagues and teams, which fostered particularly black styles of play that were largely predicated on creative improvisation. Such

[13]   Nancy Gager Clinch, *The Kennedy Neurosis* (New York: Grosset and Dunlap, 1973), 266.

[14]   Michael Eric Dyson, *Know What I Mean? Reflections on Hip Hop* (Philadelphia: Basic Civitas Books, 2007), 93–5.

segregated experiences offered more in the way of concentrated community building opportunities that made them natural allies of concomitant African American musical styles such as jazz, blues, and later, hip hop.

African American Music and Sports Cultures

Musical Contests

One of the prime sites of convergence between music and sports occurs in the considerable aesthetic rapport found between twentieth and twenty-first century African American music and sports cultures. Within the African American community sports such as boxing, basketball, and baseball have been particularly interconnected with jazz, blues, and rap. Though largely unrecognized, this nexus has mutually influenced various styles of, and aesthetic approaches to, playing and performance practices in both sporting and musical cultures. The 1930s, for example, saw the advent of battles of the bands, in which groups of three or four swing bands toured together and staged performance contests at various venues. Many of these battles, particularly those between Chick Webb and Benny Goodman, acquired legendary status. Swing fans were called on to play active roles as critics and connoisseurs in popular plebiscites to decide the winners of the many battles of the bands held in the nation's ballrooms. As a regular part of the entertainment, for instance, Chick Webb battled Benny Goodman in June 1937 at the Savoy; Charlie Barnet fought Louis Armstrong in Washington D.C.; and Count Basie and Jimmie Lunceford sparred at the Larchmont Casino.[15] Such bouts encouraged intense audience involvement. They were advertised for weeks and discussed in the press, and they drew huge audiences eager to cheer on their favorites. Often fans were asked to fill out ballots to determine their selections. At other times, they chose their champions through applause or dancing fervor. However they were decided, the plebiscite lay with the fans. In one battle Ella Fitzgerald, at the time singing for Chick Webb's band, urged listeners in song "to vote for Mr Rhythm [Webb]" because he was "the people's choice."[16] In allowing the often predominantly black audiences to determine the outcome, such events represented a literal and figurative empowerment of the African American community.

Another form of musical competition stemming from jazz was the cutting contest, which featured soloists competing to determine which musician had superior improvisatory skill. Often occurring spontaneously during jam sessions, similar competitions later also became a regular feature of hip hop culture. These contests arose in part as a substitute for violent gang disputes and thus were

---

[15]   Lewis Erenberg, *Swingin' the Dream: Big Band Jazz and the Rebirth of American Culture* (Chicago: University of Chicago Press, 1998), 60.

[16]   Ibid.

an extension of the "duel" mentality that had its roots in European aristocratic culture of the seventeenth through nineteenth centuries.[17] Redolent of the swing band battles of the 1930s and 1940s and particularly prominent in the formative days of hip hop, breakdancers, turntable DJs, and rappers would engage in fierce competitions or "battles" in the service of personal or neighborhood pride. Eminem, for example, schooled himself in urban black rap culture and won several rapping competitions before he was discovered by Dr Dre and subsequently promoted on a national scale. The popular movie *8 Mile* recreates something of this history as Eminem uses freestyle battling (with improvised raps) to win money and respect. It is also important to note that competitive urban word games like "signifying" and doing "the dozens" and, in the case of female rappers, the athletic and musical competition associated with "double Dutch" skipping infuses African American culture, which is heavily invested in the notion of "play."[18] The dozens, for example, is a custom derived from West African oral tradition in which two contestants engage in a battle of personal power, wit, verbal ability, and mental agility by taking turns insulting— or "snapping" on—one another. The competition is usually lighthearted and intended to diffuse conflict nonviolently. This competition in and of itself has been subjected to musical comment, for example popular 1930s blues musician Kokomo Arnold released a hit song called "Twelves (Dirty Dozens)" that incorporates a number of insults.[19]

Much as in a boxing match or other combative or oppositional sporting event, rap battles typically increase in speed, dynamic level (of both competitors and audience members), and lyrical intensity with each verbal exchange by the contestants. As cultural theorist Imani Perry notes, "exhortations of power seduce listeners as much as the cleverness with which the MCs imagine the configuration

---

[17]   European classical music history is rife with examples of musical duels and skill competitions. As outlined in Chapter 1, notable duels have included the keyboard contests between George Frederick Handel and Domenico Scarlatti, and Wolfgang Amadeus Mozart and Muzio Clementi.

[18]   Kyra Gaunt, "Translating double Dutch to hip hop: The musical vernacular of black girls' play," in Murray Forman and Mark Anthony Neal (eds), *That's the Joint! The Hip-Hop Studies Reader* (New York: Routledge, 2004), 251–63.

[19]   Musical dueling is by no means limited to black musical cultures and aesthetics. In a somewhat similar fashion the 1970s and 1980s witnessed a resurgence of battles of the bands typically in association with the alternative or independent rock music scene. Often sponsored by independent or university radio stations, such contests reflected an effort to provide a higher profile to previously unknown bands. Perhaps the ultimate manifestation of the idea of the musical contest has been the phenomenal international success of various versions of the *Pop Idol* and *American Idol* competitions. The success of these shows in Britain and America has largely been due to the acerbic judge Simon Cowell, and there are numerous international versions of this television show in which the winner is ultimately decided by votes cast by the viewing audience.

of competitors."[20] Indeed, in their proclamations of strength and power, rappers often call on the attributes of athletes. Consider, for example, LL Cool J's "I'm Bad," in which he claims, "I'm like Tyson / Icin' / I'm a soldier at war / I'm makin' sure you don't try to battle me no more … "[21] Here LL compares himself to the heavyweight champion boxer Mike Tyson, renowned for his devastating knockouts and intimidating ring persona.

Although previous incarnations of African American music involved stereotypically masculine forms of competition, with the advent of hypermasculine gangsta rap, the playful, competitive nature of much African American culture often spilled over into actual violence. In the 1990s the verbal feud between rappers Ice Cube, who released "King of the Hill," and Cypress Hill, who responded with "Ice Cube Killer," resulted in mutual threats of bodily harm and represented a larger racial division between Latin-Hispanic culture and African American. The infamous clash between Tupac Shakur and Notorious B.I.G., though initially based on a personal dispute, came to represent larger divisions in the black community, such as those between East Coast and West Coast styles, as well as gang rivalries between Crips and Bloods. Thus the dueling ethos that had been a feature of African American music since at least the era of the big band battles of the 1930s and 1940s, and had originally been an effective non-violent model of settling disputes in the African American community, substantially escalated. The community building of previous generations of African American sporting and musical styles has, at least in part, given way to more aggressive and individualistically oriented cross-pollinations of hip hop and athletic cultures. Indeed, Notorious B.I.G. outlines the stakes in the gangsta ethic in terms of sports in his rap "Things Done Changed," proclaiming "Because the streets is a short stop / Either you're slingin' crack rock or you got a wicked jump shot."[22] The hypermasculine gangsta pose, often reinforced with aggressive beats, sinister sounding bass lines, and general production excess, mirrors or perhaps intentionally confronts the stereotypical view of black athletes and masculinity in general.

Boxing and Jazz

Though the gangsta rap duels represent an atypically violent aspect of black musical culture, it is an unfortunate aberration of the utopian mythos of American masculinity in general. The self-determined individual who must fight and overcome his oppressors to achieve success is played out in countless sports films from *The Jackie Robinson Story* (1950) to *Rocky* (1976) or even *Seabiscuit* (2004). Such an ethos may explain why the sport of boxing particularly captured

---

[20]   Imani Perry, *Prophets of the Hood: Politics and Poetics in Hip Hop* (Durham, NC: Duke University Press, 2004), 85.

[21]   Words and music by Bobby Erving, Dwayne Simon and James Todd Smith.

[22]   Words and music by Christopher Wallace, Dominique Owens and Kevin Delance Scott.

the imagination of the African American musical community. In the swing era, bandleaders and musicians were cultural heroes on a par with the sports figures of the day, and no hero stood higher than heavyweight champion Joe Louis. A symbol of racial self-assertion and democratic values, he became a national hero by defeating Nazi Germany's Max Schmeling in 1938. He was deified in blues and folk songs and was also of inestimable importance to black swing entertainers. Louis had a close association with swing, and while living in Harlem, he associated with musicians at the hotels and clubs where they lived and played. Indeed, "as a great patron of swing music," Louis even served as a judge of *Courier* magazine's Swing Poll.[23]

Musicians often idolized Louis as a symbol of their own aspirations. Lena Horne, who dated Louis, was devastated when he lost his initial bout with Schmeling in 1936: "I was near hysteria toward the end of the fight when he was being so badly beaten and some of the men in the band were crying." Dizzy Gillespie noted, "Black people appreciate my playing in the same way I looked up to Paul Robeson or to Joe Louis."[24] Count Basie also worshipped Louis, as evidenced by his recording "King Joe," with lyrics by Richard Wright and Paul Robeson on vocals. As Lewis Erenberg has noted, this recording "immortalized the connections between black sports and music heroes."[25] Music and sports, more so than film or other media, offered black performers the possibility of both bodily and creative freedom. In sports and the arts, a racial self-awareness was building to the political awakening of the civil rights movement that followed World War II.

In addition to the swing era's fascination with Joe Louis, more contemporary associations between boxing and music are not hard to find and are perhaps most obvious in the music used to introduce each fighter and his entourage as they enter the ring. The film industry has also provided several popular musico-boxing imprints.[26] One film that is particularly notable in the creation of black masculine identity is Leon Gast's Academy Award-winning documentary *When We Were*

---

[23]   Erenberg, 117.

[24]   Dizzy Gillespie with Al Fraser, *To Be or Not ... to Bop* (New York: Da Capo Press, 1979), 499.

[25]   Erenberg, 117.

[26]   Possibly the most famous example of a music-boxing intersection is Bill Conti's hit song "Gonna Fly Now (Theme from *Rocky*)" from the Academy Award-winning movie *Rocky*, a song that made it to *Billboard* No. 1 status in July 1977. However, as shown by Apollo Creed's mocking of the icons of white American history (dressing in outlandish George Washington and Uncle Sam costumes), *Rocky* is a film that in part expresses African American disillusionment with the American dream. Nonetheless, in depicting Rocky's triumphant rise, the film dramatizes the issue of upward mobility, which has been a key factor in motivating young black men to pursue both sports and music, and forms a particularly strong link between hip hop and basketball. Both Michael Jordan and the rapper Jay-Z, for example, began as street "players" before moving to the upper levels of ownership and management in basketball and the music industry, respectively. A more in-depth discussion of boxing movie soundtracks is found in Chapter 7.

Kings (1997), which chronicles Muhammad Ali's upset heavyweight title win over George Foreman on October 30, 1974.[27] The film of the infamous "Rumble in the Jungle" intercuts footage of the boxers in training with scenes from James Brown and B.B. King's concert that coincided with the event. James Brown was an ex-boxer and attributed his well known dancing prowess to time spent practicing his boxing footwork. Gast directly compares Brown's physically aggressive performance to that of the two fighters. In so doing, he presents a powerful image of masculinity that, particularly by incorporating several of the most popular and influential icons of the black power movement from sports and music, is primarily based on physical ability and aggression. Ali won the fight by employing his later legendary—though at the time unexpected—"rope-a-dope" tactics, in which Ali lay back on the ropes and encouraged Foreman to exhaust himself. Ali's renowned verbal facility has also been discussed as an influence on hip hop.[28] By juxtaposing Ali's creative strategy and B.B. King's improvisational blues guitar solos, Gast also directly links the improvisatory genius of both artists and reinforces a powerful theme of inventive creativity in African American culture.[29]

The legendary trumpeter Miles Davis provides another instance of the considerable influence of boxing on jazz. In his 1989 autobiography Davis recounts how as a youngster he loved boxing and listened to Joe Louis's bouts on the radio:

> I loved to box … boxing was and is my heart. I just love it. I can't explain why. Man, I would listen to all of Joe Louis's fights like everybody else. We'd be all crowded around the radio waiting to hear the announcer describe Joe knocking some motherfucker out. And when he did, the whole goddamn black community of East St Louis would go crazy, celebrate in the streets, drinking and dancing and making a lot of noise. But it was joyful noise.[30]

Boxing influenced Davis's career and music throughout his life. In 1952 he approached trainer Bobby McQuillen about taking him on as a boxing student. McQuillen told Davis he would not work with an addict and that he should kick his habit first. Inspired in part by the disciplined nature of fighter Sugar Ray Robinson, Davis returned to St Louis, where, with the help of his father,

---

[27]   Although Gast plays off images of African American creativity, his portrayal of indigenous Africans is fraught with elements of Social Darwinism. This film and its somewhat problematic musical soundtrack are discussed in more detail in Chapter 7.

[28]   See, for example, George Lois, (ed.), *Ali Rap: Muhammad Ali, the First Heavyweight Champion of Rap* (Taschen, 2006).

[29]   It is interesting to note that Jack Johnson, the first African American heavyweight champ, began his career playing harmonica and bass fiddle for a traveling white vaudeville troupe. See Nelson George, *Elevating the Game: Black Men and Basketball* (New York: Harper Collins, 1992), 21.

[30]   Miles Davis, *Miles: The Autobiography* (New York: Simon & Schuster, 1989), 18–19.

he managed to kick the heroin habit that had temporarily derailed his career. Robinson, like Joe Louis before him, provided a role model for many African American musicians. For Davis, Robinson provided an inspiration for the understatement, exactitude, and cool persona that later became the hallmarks of his own musical style. Davis states:

> I really kicked my habit because of the example of Sugar Ray Robinson; I figured if he could be as disciplined as he was, then I could do it, too. I always loved boxing, but I really loved and respected Sugar Ray, because he was a great fighter with a lot of class ... Sugar Ray was one of the few idols that I have ever had. Sugar Ray looked like a socialite when you would see him in the papers getting out of limousines with fine women on his arms, sharp as a tack. But when he was training for a fight ... [or] he was in the ring, he was serious, all business ... I decided that that was the way I was going to be, serious about taking care of my business and disciplined ... Sugar Ray was the hero-image that I carried in my mind ... it was his example that pulled me through some real tough days.[31]

By 1954 Davis had quit heroin, formed his Miles Davis All Stars, and was training with McQuillen at Gleason's Gym in midtown Manhattan or, sometimes, at Silverman's Gym in Harlem. He was still working out with McQuillen in 1970 when he recorded his legendary *Jack Johnson Sessions*, a homage to the first black heavyweight champion.[32] In fact, Davis may have been in the best physical shape of his life around this time. He was working out consistently, boxing with McQuillen, eating well, and working to stay off drugs. The clear-mindedness, physical exhilaration, and stamina are evident on *Bitches Brew* as well as on the live recordings of Davis from 1969 and 1970. Davis displayed a new, athletically conditioned breath control, and his trumpet playing had a more aggressive attack that fitted well with the electronics his bands then used.[33]

More than just providing Davis with role models, however, boxing also influenced the sound of his music. Davis's trumpet (historically a military instrument) sonically bobbed and weaved around his fellow band members as if in the ring. At times he would fiercely engage with them with percussive oppositional dissonance, sometimes merely feigning melodic attacks and at other moments harmonizing as if in a clinch. Davis recounted the direct influence that boxing had on his music during the period of the *Jack Johnson Sessions*. "I had that boxer's movement in mind," says Davis, "that shuffling movement like boxers

---

[31]   Davis, 174.

[32]   *A Tribute to Jack Johnson* is a jazz fusion album recorded in 1970 by Miles Davis. It was recorded as the soundtrack for a documentary of the same name by Bill Cayton.

[33]   Though it is not unique to African American musicians, the notion of muscular training and development, be it of fingers, arms, embouchure, or breathing, is integral to all musicians, allowing them to exercise high degrees of technical control and endurance. Musicians, like athletes, can often literally become out of breath if they are not physically fit.

use. They're almost like dance steps, or like the sound of a train … That train image was in my head when I thought about a great boxer like Joe Louis or Jack Johnson. When you think of a big heavyweight coming at you it's like a train."[34] Indeed, the first of the two lengthy pieces found on the original Jack Johnson tribute album, "Right Off," is a shuffle, the kind of bluesy, swinging beat that Count Basie had championed in Kansas City. The second track, "Yesternow," is built around a slightly modified version of the bass line from James Brown's "Say It Loud—I'm Black and I'm Proud", potentially a deliberate allusion to the song's black power theme as it relates to the film's subject. That Davis was so influenced by boxing is also overtly manifest in the titles of pieces named after fighters that were recorded at several of the sessions, both before and after those that resulted in *Jack Johnson*. Such pieces include "Johnny Bratton," "Archie Moore," "Duran," "Sugar Ray," and "Ali."

Whether in the case of James Brown's powerfully physical funk performances or Miles Davis's aggressive trumpeting, one of the central links between music and boxing is the influence of the controlled aggression and improvisatory quality of boxing on black male musicians.

Basketball, Baseball, and Jazz

In addition to the jazz–boxing nexus, the African American community in the 1930s and 1940s also witnessed a particularly fertile interaction between jazz and sports such as basketball and baseball. Many jazz stars of the day, including Louis Armstrong, Fats Waller, Count Basie, Cab Calloway, and Lionel Hampton (an honorary member of the Kansas City Monarchs baseball team) were fascinated by and had an active involvement in sports.[35] Armstrong was particularly devoted to a New Orleans baseball team, Armstrong's Secret Nine, to which he lent his name and financial support.

Basketball and jazz share several stylized nuances of African American culture derived from the musical, dance, and performance traditions associated with slavery and minstrelsy. Both emerged to prominence in the 1920s, when touring black teams were formed and musicians converged on the northern industrial cities of Chicago and New York. Underscoring this relationship is the fact that jump bands would often tour on the same bus as basketball team, with players and musicians regularly fraternizing and attending each other's events. The two activities would thus share the same social space in African American communities, with the games and post-game dances being held in the same venues, such as William Roche's Renaissance Casino and Ballroom or the Savoy.[36]

---

[34]   Davis, 315.

[35]   S.W. Pope, "Decentering 'race' and (re)presenting 'black' performance in sport history," in Murray G. Phillips (ed.), *Deconstructing Sport History: A Postmodern Analysis*. (Albany: State University of New York Press, 2006), 156.

[36]   Pope, 155.

Both jazz and basketball (and later rap music) are predicated upon improvisation and fluid rhythmic exchanges between individuals who, while able to exhibit individual creativity, must coordinate their efforts for the greater good of the overall team or ensemble. Similar to bandleaders, basketball coaches who encouraged an African American style required their players to both improvise as soloists and to collaborate as part of an ensemble. The Harlem Globetrotters perhaps best exemplify this performance style. Before adopting their present name that connected them to the African American cultural renaissance of the 1930s, the team formed in 1926 as the Savoy 5 in honor of their nominal home court of Chicago's Savoy Ballroom. Dominating the pre-NBA basketball world in the 1930s and 1940s, the Trotters were famous for clowning routines during the warm-up and when they had achieved a sizable lead in the game. This practice was also common in early Negro league baseball and had direct ties to the African American minstrelsy tradition. The dominating playing style of the Trotters, however, came to epitomize the modern style of the game. Unlike the slower, more horizontal and regimented style of their white counterparts, the Trotters relied on fast breaks, rapid passing, intricate dribbling, unexpected jump shots, and improvised one-on-one challenges. It was a style that was redolent of jazz ensemble performance practice that sees the group play the main melody (head motive) as a unified ensemble before each musician breaks away to improvise a solo, and then finally come together again for an ensemble conclusion. The song "Sweet Georgia Brown," with its ebullient melodic line, loose syncopations, and solos, is emblematic of this approach and has become forever associated with the Trotters' improvisatory style.

For the sport of basketball, and many others such as ice hockey, a sense of rhythm and flow is an essential aspect of the game. Basketball players typically, for example, dribble the ball several times before taking a foul shot, essentially to re-establish the rhythm that has been disrupted by the penalty. Jazz and basketball are also both polyrhythmic, in the sense that there may be more than one pulse or tempo in effect at any given time. Similarly, the tempo is not fixed and might speed up or slow down at any given time. Cultural critic Nelson George once described Earl Monroe, a star guard for the New York Knicks in the 1970s, as "employing tempo changes only Thelonious Monk would understand."[37] Philosopher Michael Novak took this relationship to be even more explicit, claiming that both basketball and jazz "move in patterns, in rhythms, at high velocity ... have a score, a melody; each team has its own appropriate tempo ... Basketball is Jazz."[38]

Instantaneous wordless communication used to change tempos and rhythm is another common feature of jazz groups and basketball teams. Players in both activities learn how to anticipate one another's moves and objectives. The no-look

---

[37]   As quoted in Larry Blumenfeld, "On bebop & b-ball," *Jazz* 22/9 (September, 2005), 40–41, 41.

[38]   Michael Novak, *The Joy of Sports: End Zones, Bases, Baskets, Balls, and the Consecration of the American Spirit* (New York: Basic Books, 1976), 100–1.

pass from a guard to a cutting forward, for example, is akin to the pianist improvising a bridge to ease the sax player into a solo. Though they were specifically referring to athletic communication, the intuitive nature of improvisation is summed up by Pierre Bourdieu and Loïc Wacquant: "the ball player ... caught in the heat of action, instantaneously intuits the moves of his opponents and teammates, acts and reacts in an 'inspired' manner without the benefit of hindsight and calculative reason."[39] As inventive creativity is central to both sports and music, it is not surprising that they have both produced iconic players who have imprinted their own sense of style on each form. Louis Armstrong, Charlie Parker, Miles Davis, and John Coltrane sounded nothing like their predecessors. Yet they asserted their individuality in ways that elevated everyone with whom they played and in turn influenced the historical development of jazz. Basketball players like Wilt Chamberlain, Julius Erving, Magic Johnson, and Michael Jordan have had very much the same impact.

Perhaps the most obvious correlation between the two activities is to compare the five-player basketball squad to the common jazz quintet. Wynton Marsalis, a basketball fan, even went so far as to compare the positions on a basketball team to the instrumentation of a jazz quintet when he stated: "The point guard has to be a horn player, if he's the leader of the band. He controls the music and what the sound of the band will be. He controls the pace. The center, the big man, is like a drummer. The power forward would be a bass player. The shooting guard would be the trumpet or saxophonist who is the soloist. Your small forward ... is like a piano player."[40] While such an association is subjective, it nonetheless serves to underline the fundamental similarities of the two activities.

In his critically acclaimed study of black men and basketball, cultural critic Nelson George repeatedly compares the role of basketball in the lives of African American men to the similar place of music. George states, "Probably the most appropriate musical analogy to the African-American player's relationship to basketball is the African-American musician's affinity for the saxophone. The saxophone existed from the mid-nineteenth century to the 1930s before African-Americans took up Adolph Sax's invention in large numbers."[41] Later George compares the emergence of black urban basketball to the arrival of bebop: "The 'new' ball was about putting one's personal stamp on any given contest, about using a team sport as a way to tell your story just as beboppers did on bandstands ... in every major city. City ball was faster, louder, more stop-and-go, and like bebop, defiant of established standards of performance."[42] George also makes the point that black basketball players were often subject to the same exploitation

---

[39]   Pierre Bourdieu and Loïc Wacquant, *An Invitation to Reflexive Sociology* (Cambridge, UK: Polity, 1992), 20–21.

[40]   Blumenfield, 42.

[41]   George, *Elevating the Game*, xv.

[42]   Ibid., 72.

at the hands of white promoters as black musicians. In commenting on Abe Saperstein's founding of the Harlem Globetrotters, George declares:

> Saperstein's role in basketball also paralleled that of two South Side Chicago furniture salesmen turned record makers, Phil and Leonard Chess, who in the 1950s, by recording Chuck Berry, Bo Diddley, Muddy Waters, and others, made available a dynamic form of African-American music, yet never fully compensated its creators for the revenue they generated.[43]

Though there has been a significant rise in both black-owned sports teams and record companies (notably Motown), the larger controlling organizations, at the corporate and league level, continue to be dominated by white male ownership. The New York Knicks' former star guard Earl "the Pearl" Monroe represents a rare instance of a black player who, while also an accomplished musician, founded his own record company, Pretty Pearl Records.

One of the more successful basketball players to have an equally accomplished career in jazz was Wayman Tisdale. An electric bass playing power forward, Tisdale averaged 15 points and six rebounds a game over a 12-year NBA career, during which he played with the Indiana Pacers, the Sacramento Kings, and the Phoenix Suns. His jazz recording career began in 1995, two years before his 1997 NBA retirement, with a debut CD that rose to No. 4 on *Billboard*'s contemporary jazz chart and crossed over to the R&B charts. Subsequent songs—including "Ain't No Stopping Us Now," "Can't Hide Love," and "Don't Take Your Love Away"—also enjoyed radio and commercial success. He recorded eight albums in all, with the 2001 release *Face to Face* climbing to No. 1 on *Billboard*'s contemporary jazz chart. Tisdale died of complications related to cancer in May 2009.

In the 1960s and 1970s African American musicians also influenced a variety of fashion trends that found their way into sports—basketball in particular. Many athletes adopted Afro hairstyles, a symbol of militant black pride since the late 1960s but popularized by James Brown, Jimi Hendrix, and Sly Stone. Similarly, both Hendrix and Stone influenced the adoption of headbands worn by many basketball players from Julius Erving to Wilt Chamberlain. Along with the adoption of multi-colored wristbands and decorated knee-high socks, particularly in basketball, funk-influenced fashion and attitude rubbed off on the African American athletic aesthetic. The "in your face" style of black soul and funk embodied in the music of acts such as George Clinton (a.k.a. Dr Funkenstein) was the epitome of black power and community. In basketball it was the "in your face" slam dunk move, most notably popularized by Julius Erving, that provided analogous images of spontaneous black male empowerment. The move was famously described by Nelson George as embodying "the ability to intimidate through improvisation."[44] Thus in the 1960s and 1970s, African American musical forms were linked

---

[43]   Ibid., 46.
[44]   Ibid., 184.

with basketball in much the same manner that early jazz techniques influenced basketball in the 1930s and 1940s.

Though the NBA currently appears to be trying to reach new audiences by associating itself with a variety of musical styles, the close relationship between African American music and basketball continued into the 1980s and 1990s with the increasing popularity of hip hop. Hip hop and basketball share similar urban roots and audiences. Rap artists adopted the oversize basketball and hockey jerseys and, perhaps more overtly, a new aggressive attitude epitomized in the competitive nature of DJ and MC contests discussed earlier. Similarly, many basketball stars saw themselves as rappers when such well known players as Kobe Bryant, Shaquille O'Neal, and Allan Iverson, among others, released rap albums. Though none has garnered significant critical or popular success, their efforts cemented the relationship between hip hop, rap, and basketball. As improvised slam dunk competitions became an increasingly important aspect of basketball, so too were aggressive improvisatory competitions becoming a regular feature of rap. At the same time the two forms of leisure and entertainment were increasingly aligned and perceived as linked emblems of black male urban experience.

Although basketball is likely the sport most often compared to jazz, African American performance styles also cross-pollinated with a variety of other sports. Montye Fuse and Keith Miller claim that many of the tactics of early Negro League baseball players, particularly those of Jackie Robinson, were informed by African American cultural aesthetics primarily as embodied in jazz and blues: "informed by jazz [and] blues ... African American baseball reached its improvisational apotheosis in the careers of Satchel Paige, Cool Papa Bell, and [Jackie] Robinson himself."[45] Negro League baseball was characterized by playful and inventive techniques variously known as "razzle dazzle" and "trickeration." Such techniques, foreign to the white major leagues, included syncopated base running feints, base stealing, bunting at unpredictable times, and a wide variety of unorthodox pitches and deliveries. Regarding the last of these, the legendary Satchel Paige listed "my single windup, my double windup, my triple windup, my hesitation windup and my no windup ... I got bloopers, loopers, and droopers. I got a jump ball, a bee ball, a screw ball, a wobbly ball, a whipsy-dipsey, a hurry-up ball, a nothin' ball and a bat dodger."[46] The improvisatory array of Paige's pitches directly questioned the immutable superiority of white styles of play. In baseball, as in basketball, the creativity of African American athletes helped question and ultimately destroy the myth of white superiority in those sports, much as jazz questioned and exploded the presumed immutable superiority of white symphonic music.

---

[45]   Monteye Fuse and Keith Miller, "Jazzing the basepaths: Jackie Robinson and African American aesthetics," in John Bloom and Michael Nevin Willard (eds), *Sports Matters: Race Recreation and Culture* (New York: New York University Press, 2002), 120.

[46]   Ibid., 124.

With the migration of African American sporting and musical styles to the north and increasing visibility of black athletes and musicians, white basketball and baseball players encountered a quicker game of fast breaks, feints, explosive speed, innovative ball handling, and varied shot and pitch selection. Similarly, white musicians in the north were exposed to and adopted the complex rhythmic variations and improvisations and a hip, cool attitude from the early generation of black jazz pioneers. It is important to recognize the fact that the relationship between African American sporting and musical styles, rather than being the by-product of some reductive racial trait, was largely shaped by the particular trans-historical context in which both styles developed. Jazz and blues are musical styles whose roots reach back to the forced migration of West Africans to North America during the slave trade of the seventeenth through nineteenth centuries. It was music that grew directly out of field hollers, work songs, and spirituals. Stanley Crouch sums up the experiences, explaining, "the demanding duties of hard labor were met with rhythm, and that rhythm ... was the underlying factor that brought together the listeners, that allowed for physical responses in the dance halls and juke joints where blues emerged."[47] African American sports and musical forms such as jazz and hip hop represent social rituals whose participants employ similar strategies of competition, improvisation, affirmation, and communal celebration. Indeed, built into the structure of African American musical genres and sports such as basketball and baseball are complex rhythms, fluid improvisations, call and response patterns (analogous to give-and-go passes), and competitive interaction that require individuals to synchronize and coordinate their efforts. Thus, both music and sports allowed individuals to assert their improvisatory excellence as soloists while simultaneously collaborating as part of a cohesive ensemble, thereby allowing the formation of a powerful social community without diluting individual expression. Jumping swing tunes and jump shots were thus both literally and figuratively uplifting expressions of an African American experience—effective emblems of physical and mental vitality, community health, and individual creativity.

Music, Sports, and Performing African American Masculinity

In their early incarnations jazz and blues were typically male-dominated art forms that often embraced physical and aggressively creative performances. The jazz trumpet, for example, often evokes a particularly masculine connotation. Though firmly disavowing the "trumpet jock," Krin Gabbard has nonetheless recently observed:

---

[47]   Stanley Crouch, *The All American Skin Game, or, The Decoy of Race* (New York: Vintage Press, 1995), 14.

In the early twentieth century, African American men [such as Buddy Bolden and Louis Armstrong] made brilliant use of the trumpet to assert that they were men and not boys. Many of these black men were single mindedly devoted to making great music, but they may also have found the trumpet to be the ideal instrument for telling the world that they were not merely manly but *extremely* manly.[48]

Indeed some scholars maintain that the term "jazz" derives from the Southern expression to "jis it up"—to put a little masculine force or "gism" into one's performance, either athletic or musical.[49] Krin Gabbard posits that it was in "the sports pages" that "jazz" first appeared in print.[50] Though white musicians were also seminal participants in jazz, its liberating performative presence can be understood as representing a general resistance to the repression and silencing of black men. This situation was paralleled in boxing, basketball, and baseball of the 1930s and 1940s, which allowed a similar physical outlet for black male creative expression. The male "team" bonding experience was as present in jazz and blues ensembles as it was on actual sports teams. The two worlds often fraternized and influenced one another, particularly in regards to similar concerns for improvisation, rhythmic fluidity, and ensemble. The term "jamming," denoting instances of fluid behavioral coordination that occur with minimal self-disclosure and limited consensus, is common to both sports and music. The combination of African American sports such as basketball and baseball and musical forms such as jazz, blues, and rap music imparted and mutually reinforced a model of creative competitive performance for African American males.

In its earliest manifestations rap—like jazz and blues before it—was also an overtly male-dominated art form. Indeed, rap emphasized male expression in ways that openly challenged the repression and silencing of black men through overtly physical and often competitive breakdancing and rapping. As bell hooks has stated:

Male creativity, expressed in rap and dancing, required wide-open spaces, symbolic frontiers where the body could do its thing, expand, grow, and move, surrounded by a watching crowd. Domestic space, equated with repression and containment, as well as with the "feminine," was resisted and rejected so that an assertive patriarchal paradigm of competitive masculinity and its concomitant emphasis on physical prowess could emerge.[51]

---

[48]   Krin Gabbard, *Hotter Than That: The Trumpet, Jazz and American Culture* (New York: Faber and Faber, 2008), 62.

[49]   Collier, 169.

[50]   Gabbard, *Hotter Than That*, 8.

[51]   bell hooks, "Eating the Other: Desire and resistance," 435.

Both sports and music thus offer a highly visible challenge to stereotypes of male bodily repression. Indeed, both cultural arenas have been instrumental in driving a hypermasculine image among black men—as exemplified in the media-hyped sexual exploits of Wilt Chamberlain or the stereotypical depictions of hypersexual appetites depicted in numerous rap videos.

It must be acknowledged, however, that the irreverent nature of much black vernacular culture and the overtly heterosexual libidinous nature of many rap videos and songs (not to mention a plethora of earlier rhythm and blues songs like "Sixty-Minute Man" and "Big Ten Inch") may actually be intended to reflect the absurdity of common racial stereotypes. Furthermore, it is clear that many white musicians, such as Elvis and Mick Jagger, adopted the hypermasculine swagger of African American rhythm and blues artists associated with the songs mentioned above. Such transgressive personae were largely predicated on a self-promoted romanticization of the marginalized existence of African American men. As Michael Bertrand has pointed out about African American hypermasculinity: "While definitely a "coping strategy" utilized daily against racism, poverty, and oppression, [the] example of ritualized black masculinity also ... provided a means for [black] men to create an alternate space or identity so they could rest, play, and recuperate under conditions that they controlled.[52] Thus the coping strategies of oppressed African American slaves and sharecroppers became the coping strategy adopted by generations of white rock artists who felt both similarly oppressed, though for different social and economic reasons, and who emulated them and followed in their wake.

There is little doubt that over the past few decades, there has been an increasing level of violence and aggression in both African American sports and music cultures. As discussed earlier in this chapter, Michael Dyson identifies "violent masculinity" as lying at the heart of American identity and suggests that this has subsequently influenced African American approaches to hip hop and sports. Contributing to this image is the fact that the media has fetishized violent images of gangsta rap and similarly aggressive, "hard," or threatening sporting behavior. The media plays an enormous role in the promotion of today's sports and music industry, and in turn media corporations profit from feature articles and documentaries about sports and music personalities. The common exploitation of professional athletes and rap musicians secures TV ratings and sells newspapers, magazines, and books, especially when it comes to the issue of violence and aggression. Violent and rough play is often given more television airtime than normal play, just as rap music is often only in the mainstream headlines when there has been some type of violent or criminal behavior. Given the media fixation on negative or violent images of African American men in sports and music, overt aggression and violence are easily mistaken by some as acceptable means to achieve upward mobility.

---

[52] Michael Bertrand, "I don't think Hank done it that way," 71.

The significant financial rewards associated with athletic and musical success have also resulted in increased pressure on players to be aggressive in attaining their musical or athletic goals. This would seem to lead to a greater chance of highly intense, aggressive content, performance, and personas in sports and music. The combination of media fetishizing of violence and the adoption of that media image by some young black men as a means to achieve success accounts in some part for the continued image of urban aggression that has become a reductive marker of authenticity and masculinity in African American hip hop and sports cultures.[53]

There is some evidence that suggests the hypermasculine pose adopted by many African American athletes is partially based on homophobia or hyperheterosexuality. As discussed in the work of bell hooks (see footnote 51 on page 150) and Michel Foucault (see Chapter 4), among other attributes, music and sports are both often transgressively located outside domestic spaces of bodily control and can be understood as relying on similar quests to refine physical pleasure and sexual desire. It might be argued that the social and bodily repression experienced by many black men has perhaps heightened the desire for culturally sanctioned moments of physical transgression and expression.

To some extent black masculinity in sports and music has been cast as reductively Janus-faced. Particularly in the late 1990s Anglo-American media obsessed over the success of Michael Jackson before exulting in his decline as an alleged molester of young boys. In sports it was the elevation of O.J. Simpson as a football and media hero before his portrayal as a savage murderer. The rise and fall of rap artist Tupac Shakur or, more recently, Tiger Woods or football stars Michael Vick and Adam "Pacman" Jones have been presented in similar terms. The hypervisibility of these "exceptional" black men also serves to reinforce the racist notions that anonymous black men who disappear into the underclass, prison, or an early grave have only themselves to blame.[54] The work of Michelle Wallace is particularly useful in understanding this issue. Wallace suggests that, "a crucial problem for black political and cultural life is the problem we all share: the problem of celebrity."[55] Wallace's issue with celebrity is that it reinforces a binary in which one extreme is high visibility and the other is extreme invisibility that subsequently renders ordinary black masculinity invisible. The issue of black celebrity is increasingly a global phenomenon and, as such, is a form of overdetermination that prevents other forms of black existence from being considered. Often in the case of black athletes and musicians, the media fosters a spectacularization of their abilities

[53]   Adam Krims addresses the rise of the "Urban Ethos" in relation to rap music. See Adam Krims, *Music and Urban Geography* (New York: Routledge, 2007).

[54]   See Marlon B. Ross, "In search of black men's masculinities," *Feminist Studies* 24/3 (Autumn, 1998): 599–626, 606.

[55]   Michelle Wallace, "Masculinity in black popular culture: Could it be that political correctness is the problem?" in M. Berger, B. Wallis, and S. Watson (eds), *Constructing Masculinity* (New York: Routledge, 1995), 301.

and efforts. The careers of Michael Jordan, Tiger Woods, and Muhammad Ali are often portrayed in terms that transcend ordinary athletic ability and emphasize their ability to make spectacular physical moves and plays, often in combination with a certain degree of creative showmanship. Black male musicians such as Miles Davis, Wynton Marsalis, or more recently rappers such as Tupac Shakur or Kanye West, are granted similarly equivalent levels of spectacular ability. The spectactularization of black athletic and musical masculinity is a form of commodity fetishism that renders invisible the labor of black athletes and musicians so they may simply be read as specimens. The divide between the possession of such spectacular talent, abilities, and achievements by these elite artists and athletes and the "average" black male helps maintain white male hegemony in North America. This situation embodies a narrative of social uplift that suggests to young black men the positive merits of capitalist social relations of individualism and heterosexuality.

Such images also promote the increased sale of equipment, clothing, and other accoutrements that elite black male athletes and musicians use or endorse to signify their success. Young black men who may not possess the physical talent of Michael Jordan or the creative ability of Kanye West can nonetheless appropriate, or approximate, a portion of their success for themselves by acquiring their clothing lines and equipment.

African American music and sports are thus also often linked to entrepreneurial achievement. Many black athletes, such as Michael Jordan and Lebron James, have lucrative endorsement and design deals with shoe and clothing companies. Similarly, many rap artists such as Snoop Dogg, 50 Cent, Nelly, and Kanye West have urban clothing lines. Indeed, Sean Puffy Combs has made a fortune based on his creative entrepreneurial talents—talents that have arguably outshone his abilities as a rap artist. In an effort to avoid repeating previous exploitation of images of African Americans by white corporations, it appears that more African American sports and music personalities are attempting to control their own "brand." However, critics have also argued that black culture has merely been turned into a commodity that white culture is only too happy to consume. Kyle Kusz, for example, claims, "Blacks have been permitted to excel in entertainment only on the condition that they conform to whites' image of blacks."[56] Such an argument would help explain, at least in part, the fetishizing by the media of the violent culture in sports and rap music among black men discussed above.

The synergies between African American music and sports have historically been vehicles of community building. Central to both of the activities is the notion of exceptional performance in the face of a dominant white culture. Tyler Stovall argues that, "all aspects of African American life can be seen as performance, because they can never be completely divorced from their context of a minority

---

[56]   Kyle Kusz, "'I want to be the minority': The products of youthful white masculinities in sport and popular culture in 1990s America," in D. Rowe (ed.), *Critical Reading in Sport, Culture and the Media* (Maidenhead: Open University Press, 2004), pp. 261–75.

subculture in a larger white world."[57] bell hooks has recently identified two types of black performance: performance as complicity in racial oppression for the sake of survival and performance as ritual play.[58] The first type of performance involves a display of blackness to be consumed by predominantly non-black spectatorship, whereas the second functions as a liberatory practice that emphasizes the creation of new languages of identity and community consciousness. As manifest in the mixed reactions to gangsta rap in the African American population, there is an interactive but creative tension between aspects of community and spectacular black performance.

The central bond between African American sporting and musical performance is improvisation. Historian James Collier observes that both "the improvising jazz musician and the athlete must train intensely to build up sets of conditioned reflexes that enable them to respond without thinking of events that are unfolding around them in fractions of seconds."[59] In both sports and music the concept of improvisation involves bringing one's personal awareness into "the moment" and developing a profound understanding of the actions one is undertaking. Such self-awareness, one might argue, is central to the notion of African American identity. In its dominant social position, white society, by comparison, is relatively unaware of itself and thus perhaps less likely to find expression through improvisation. Improvisation, however, is also a creative and adaptive response that allows an individual or community to grow in response to imposed rules. As evident in the careers of Joe Louis or Miles Davis as described above, the drive for spectacular improvisational virtuosity that marks much African American sports and music culture aligns with both the need to signify and stand out from one's peers and also as a conditioned response to the rules and cultural strictures under which such performers perceive themselves to live. To some extent, spectacular improvisation thus functions as a form of literal and metaphoric freedom. This explanation, at least in part, accounts for the popular currency of such performances in both black and white society. Spectacular improvisation, perhaps ironically in the case of African Americans, connects with and appeals to the utopian American mythos of the glory of individualism and self-determination that is played out in countless stories and movies.

The characteristics of aggression and improvisation that typify the image of many forms of African American sports and music combine in ways that generate a constant creative evolution in style and technique. In part, such characteristics would seem to be simply spurred by the economic reality of having to be innovative

---

[57]   Tyler Stovall, "Black community, black spectacle: Performance and race in transatlantic perspective," in Harry Elam and Kennel Jackson (eds), *Black Cultural Traffic: Crossroads in Global Performance and Popular Culture* (Ann Arbor: University of Michigan Press, 2005), pp. 221–41, 237.

[58]   bell hooks, "Performance practice as a site of opposition."

[59]   James Lincoln Collier, *Jazz: The American Theme Song* (New York: Oxford University Press, 1995), 53.

and trying to compete and get ahead in white-dominated society. The emphasis on improvisation, however, injects and ensures an ongoing variety and re-imagining of the limits of musical and sporting performance, and hence constantly reinvigorates both musical and sports cultures. Such creativity is not limited to the mere elevation of the techniques of musical and sporting performance but rubs off into the realm of social empowerment. The unified energy of the "team" or "band" of players provides an effective form of group empowerment that models both to and from the larger community. Though such features of the sports–music nexus are by no means limited to African Americans, the exceptionalism which black performers have traditionally required to be accepted by white audiences has marked conceptions of black masculinity and resulted in ongoing, if not increased, expectations of spectacularity and, hence, the seemingly disproportionate creation of new musical and sporting standards by African Americans.

The increasingly media-driven character of our society also helps explain the spectacularization of African American males in sports and music. As discussed in Chapter 4, Guy Debord argued: "The spectacle is capital accumulated to the point where it becomes image ... "[60] Thus, similar to the prominence of gay sports anthems, the spectacularization of African American sports and music can be recognized as an outgrowth of a corporate media-driven society, and thus a prime location of globalized commodity culture. The spectacular nature of the hypermasculine performance in rap and sports by African American males also evokes one of Debord's central beliefs regarding the erosion of communal identity:

> The spectacle originates in the loss of the unity of the world, and the gigantic expansion of the modern spectacle expresses the totality of this loss ... In the spectacle, one part of the world represents itself to the world and is superior to it. The spectacle is nothing more than the common language of this separation. What binds the spectators together is no more than an irreversible relation at the very center which maintains their isolation. The spectacle reunites the separate, but reunites it as separate.[61]

Though it is on a smaller scale than that envisioned by Debord, spectacular black male performance in sports and music can thus be viewed as a unifying salve to black males, yet also simultaneously a reminder of their marginalization and isolation from mainstream society.

Sports and music have long had close and mutually reinforcing ties in shaping African American male experiences and image. Concomitant with these ties has been the marked rise of the visibility of African American males in these two spheres to a far greater extent than their actual proportion of the population. To some extent we may look on the stereotypical images of black men, as promulgated in sports and popular music as well as films and other forms of mass media, as

---

[60]   Guy Debord, *Society of the Spectacle*, 25, 29.

[61]   Guy Debord, *Society of the Spectacle*, 29.

symbolic of aggressive and internationally intimidating American masculinity in general. Whether it is the global export of the hypermasculine "thug" imagery of rap music or of the arrogance and intimidation sometimes exercised by American basketball players (think of recent American Olympic teams), the black male has emerged as a symbol of aggressive American manliness and associated notions of international dominance over smaller entities who might oppose them. Stemming from the camaraderie engendered in the black male experience, the shared aesthetic tendencies, largely revolving around liberatory improvisation, that marked the close union of African American sports and music in the earlier part of the twentieth century have evolved and perhaps degenerated into a means by which to reinforce cultural codes of containment.

Within the African American community, however, the seeming revelry in notions of prison life and the trappings of gangsta existence project a conscious commitment to otherness and nihilist responses to the social containment of black men. Many members of the hip hop community have appropriated and exploited such stereotypically negative images of black males as a means to express power, if only operating through white American fear. In turn, American mass culture manifests a desire for nationalist virility that can dominate the world, not only by highlighting stereotypes of African American aggression, but also by foregrounding the ability to win against the odds by overcoming the impediment of racism. Just as young suburban white males have adopted the hip hop clothing and hypermasculine pose of their African American musical and sports heroes, boys from across the globe have also mimicked the same traits. Despite the creative and liberatory aspects of black performance styles in both music and sports cultures, black masculinity has been promoted in the media and co-opted as a national commodity that serves to reinforce both America's innovative creativity but also a stereotypically aggressive image around the world.

Chapter 6

"Go West":
The Integration of Sports and Music in Constructing National and Transnational Identities

The connections between sports and nationalism have recently received considerable scholarly attention. According to sports theorist Alan Bairner, for example, sports play "a vital role in the construction and reproduction of a national identity or national identities."[1] Often individual athletes are cast as heroes who symbolize the nation as a whole. To realize the validity of this notion, one need only think of Babe Ruth or Joe Dimaggio in the United States, Pelé in Brazil, Maradona in Argentina, David Beckham in the United Kingdom, Alberto Tomba in Italy, or Wayne Gretzky in Canada. It is equally true, however, that musicians can become similar signs of the nation—as with Bruce Springsteen in the United States, Björk in Iceland, ABBA in Sweden, or the Beatles in the UK.

As discussed in Chapter 5, to a large extent the projection of nationalism in both sports and music arises through the cross-pollination of sports and militarism that underlies much of Western society, North American in particular. In America the systematic process of combining patriotic duty with athletic masculinity that began in the wake of the Spanish-American War flowered in the following century as sports called upon military ceremony and iconography to foster and instill a sense of national pride.[2] As has been previously mentioned, one reason that American nationalism and football have worked together so well involves the game's militaristic nature, signified by its co-optation of the language of war. Depending on the context of the contest, sports teams, supported by musical tributes, cheers, and anthems, are fiercely defending and representing imagined ideals of community and country.

---

[1] Alan Bairner, *Sport, Nationalism, and Globalization: European and North American Perspectives* (Albany: State University of New York Press, 2001), 92.

[2] For a more detailed description of this evolution see Charles Hiroshi Garrett, "Struggling to define a nation: American music in the twentieth century," Diss. (University of California Los Angeles, 2004), 216.

Sports, Music, Ritual, and Nationalism

The union of sports and nationalism has received much attention in both the scholarly and the mainstream press; however, the existing literature generally neglects the role of music in reinforcing this bond. Likely the most overt nexus of sports, music, and nationalism occurs at the Olympic Games in the medal ceremonies that are capped by the national anthem of the victorious country. In North America, however, the confluence of music, sports and nationalism occurs at the beginning of almost every sporting event with the performance of "O Canada" or "The Star-Spangled Banner." This latter patriotic ritual began in the United States as a military band tribute to a nation at the end of World War I. According to the *New York Times*, the practice began in the seventh inning stretch of the opening game of the 1918 World Series between the Chicago Cubs and Boston Red Sox:

> As the crowd ... stood up to take their afternoon yawn ... the band broke forth to the strains of "The Star Spangled Banner." The yawn was checked [as] ... first the song was taken up by a few, then others joined [and] at the very end ... onlookers exploded into thunderous applause and rent the air with a cheer that was the high point of the day's enthusiasm.[3]

From that year forward "The Star-Spangled Banner" was performed before all World Series games and on national holidays. It was not until World War II that Canadian NHL teams began to play "God Save the King" before all hockey games following Canada's entry into the war in 1939. Professional baseball clubs in the United States in turn emulated the NHL and began to play "The Star-Spangled Banner" before all regular season games, a practice which subsequently spread to the amateur clubs and other sports.[4] Today in North America anthems are most often performed with a prerecorded soundtrack in an attempt to create a pristine performance free of distracting or offensive musical mistakes (and thereby undermining the efficacy of the nation-building rite), often accompanied by flyovers of military aircraft or color guards presenting flags. As such, these rituals typically function as overt celebrations of the nation—celebrations that become even more patriotically charged during national crises.

The combined spectacle of music and sports serves as an effective tool in nation building and image consolidation. Nowhere is this more evident than in the marketing and culture of American football. The conflicting impulses of transnational commerce and US nationalism that have pervaded the marketing of the game, however, have made for an uneasy negotiation. The Super Bowl, the prime marketing vehicle for the league, is inordinately connected to musical content. Over the course of an 8-hour television broadcast, including pre- and

---

[3]   "Red Sox beat Cubs in initial battle of World's Series," *The New York Times*, September 6, 1918, 14. Also reproduced in Garrett, 218.

[4]   Garrett, 219.

post-game shows and the like, music is heard for approximately one-third of the time (this includes network themes, commercial themes, and dedicated musical production numbers).[5]

Though it is an event centered specifically on American football, the Super Bowl has become an internationally appreciated spectacle. The 2010 Super Bowl, for example, was televised in 232 countries and in 34 languages around the globe. Despite its transnational appeal, however, it is nonetheless often projected by organizers and broadcasters as an expression of American nationalism, albeit one tinged with heavy doses of advertising and commercialism. Indeed, it is often music that mediates, fuses and mitigates the crass commercialism of the event on the one hand and the crass patriotism on the other. In addition to the singing of the national anthem, Super Bowl half-time shows have included American-centric themes entitled "America Thanks" (1969), "Musical America" (1974), "A Tribute to America's Bicentennial," (1976) and numerous salutes to American music of the twentieth century, including Louis Armstrong (1972), Duke Ellington (1975), The Big Band Era (1980) and Motown (1982 and 1998). Similar to the global projection by Olympic host nations of their national musical image through the showcasing of regional music in the opening and closing ceremonies (and to a lesser extent through the anthems played for medal winning athletes), the Super Bowl provides the yearly opportunity for the projection of American nationalism throughout the world on a grand scale.

The NFL, in attempting to reach even broader global markets, is, however, making efforts musically to broaden its primarily North American appeal as outlined above. One of the most notable attempts on this front was the 2000 Super Bowl half-time show entitled "A Tapestry of Nations." The artists featured—including Christina Aguilera, Enrique Iglesias, Phil Collins, and Toni Braxton—represented a diversity of races, ethnicities, geographies, ages, and genders that was seemingly calculated to appeal to a broad spectrum of viewers. In commenting on this event Charles Hiroshi Garrett observes:

> According to the broadcast narration by [Mexican American] actor Edward James Olmos, the show was meant to evoke "an earthly celebration that unites the nations of the world." The actual aesthetic result of the telecast, however, … [was] a muddled cornucopia of eclectic items that brought together quasi-religious imagery from around the globe, a symphony orchestra, an eighty-person [gospel] choir, a team of acrobats, thirty-foot-tall puppets, Vegas-style choreography, a drum corps, exploding fireworks, hundreds of children meant to represent the nations of the world, and four Western pop stars lip-synching Disney tunes on center stage.[6]

---

[5]   Ibid., 212.

[6]   Ibid., 251.

While perhaps simultaneously an overt manifestation of postmodern hybridity, the influence of American corporate commercialism and an awkward attempt at reflecting the global reach of the event, the dominant impression left by this and other Super Bowl half-time shows is one of overwhelming excess and spectacle.[7]

As discussed in Chapter 4 the concept of the "spectacle," whether sporting, musical, artistic, or of other kinds, has been used to affirm power and prestige throughout history. The musical and military pageantry associated with many major sporting events is a symbolic projection of the resources and leisure capacity of the sponsoring state regardless of the overt intentions of the organizers. Thus, even the best intentions of a "Tapestry of Nations" theme of Super Bowl XXXIV become inherently subsumed in the larger project of reinforcing nationalistic American hegemony.

Reflecting the sound of wealth and capacity for military power as outlined above, American nationalism becomes even more pronounced in many sporting spectacles when the nation is under threat. As Garrett has noted, for the opening of the 2002 Super Bowl, some five months after the tragic attack on the World Trade Center of September 11, 2001, the Fox network chose as its introductory music the heroic and widely recognizable theme from *Star Wars*.[8] This martial music, and the concomitant ideological message of the battle between good and evil that came in the wake of George W. Bush's speech condemning the "axis of evil," sent an unmistakable message to the world. Garrett also observes that the *Star Wars* moment was reinforced by an explicit demonstration of US satellite technology. Fox employed an image from an orbiting satellite that slowly focused in on the Louisiana Superdome.[9] Over this image the Fox announcer solemnly proclaimed:

> Way down there is Afghanistan, just off to the right, and our troops are on duty right now in the defense of freedom. Their weapons may be locked and loaded, but their hearts are half a world away back home in the United States. These incredible pictures of our planet come from NASA satellites, and they're focused, like the rest of the world, on a city in Louisiana. That's because nowhere in the world is there a singular sporting event that brings a country closer together than the Super Bowl. Football is America's sporting passion, and this is Super

---

[7]   The corporate nature of the Superbowl has been reinforced in recent years as American Idol allumni, Jordin Sparks, Jennifer Hudson and Carrie Underwood, were chosen to sing the national anthem in 2008, 2009 and 2010 respectively. In 2009 Bruce Springsteen, in an apparent parody of the commercialization of the event, concluded his half-time set with the iconic advertising statement, "I'm going to Disneyland!"

[8]   Garrett, 253.

[9]   Ironically, though the Louisiana Superdome was the site of this celebration of American power, some three years later it was the scene of what has been regarded by many as one of America's greatest failures. In August 2005, approximately 9,000 people were forced to take shelter amidst violence and squalid conditions in the inadequately provisioned building during and following Hurricane Katrina.

Bowl XXXVI. Now keep your eye on the white dot in the center of your screen because that's where today's events will unfold: a celebration of American spirit, the world's biggest musical stars, and of course the biggest football game of the year.[10]

This opening narrative clearly underlines the mutually reinforcing confluence of sports, music, and nationalism. The half-time entertainment was no less patriotic and was headlined by U2, who, in tribute to the victims of the attacks, performed "Beautiful Day" and "MLK," which led directly into "Where the Streets Have No Name." The band performed on a heart-shaped stage as the names of the victims were projected on screens scrolling heavenward throughout the stadium during the latter two songs. Bono finished the performance by revealing an American flag in the lining of his jacket. The commemorative pre-game activities surrounding this game included renditions of "America the Beautiful," as well as the national anthem and the performance of Paul McCartney's "Freedom" and Barry Manilow's "Let Freedom Ring," two songs that were composed as direct responses to 9/11.[11] The cumulative result of the production was both a memorial to the events of 9/11 and a musical exercise in nationalism that presented an image of national unity and military and economic might to viewers both in the United States and around the world. Underscored by fan recognition of and identification with iconic artists such as Mariah Carey, Paul McCartney and U2, popular music served as a vehicle with which to unite audiences around the globe in identifying with a primarily American national crises. Whether in a time of overt national crisis or not, the Superbowl represents one of the most powerful global examples of the convergence of popular music and sports in the service of national identity.

The Super Bowl, the Olympic Games, and other high-profile sporting events—including almost all American football half-times, even at the high school level—ostensibly stage extravagant musical shows to hold an audience's attention, whether on a global or local level. But to some extent, even despite the sometimes overt desire of the organizers to project an international image, they are bound by the national politics of location.

---

[10]   As transcribed in Garrett, 254.

[11]   It is worth noting that the Canadian Football League's Grey Cup half-time festivities are also centered on popular music though on a much smaller scale, devoid of overt political comment (tributes to Canadian troops usually only occur at the outset of the game), and typically featuring a lone musical act. Similar to the Super Bowl, the game is a national institution in Canada but does not have the same international appeal. Hence the game and its associated musical content, while often inherently reflecting Canadian identity, largely lacks the ability to project that identity outside of the country. Recent performers have consequently ranged from primarily Canadian-market artists such as The Tragically Hip and Blue Rodeo to more internationally known stars such as Shania Twain, Lenny Kravitz and The Black Eyed Peas.

The Hockey Night in Canada Theme

The Canadian Broadcasting Corporation's decision to drop the musical theme of their *Hockey Night in Canada* program is one of the more infamous and remarkable instances of the national impact of the sport–music nexus. "The Hockey Theme," a song written in 1968 by Vancouver composer Dolores Claman, had been a longstanding staple of the CBC's hockey broadcasts until June 2008. The theme is, in the words of one author, "burned into the national consciousness—an on-air calling card that has brought the CBC more recognition than … its logo."[12] Though the tune was sometimes referred to as Canada's second national anthem, the CBC refused to renew its license with Claman for the rights to the song, which had been costing the company about $500 (Canadian) in licensing fees per game, or $65,000 each year. To replace this musical icon, the network instituted a nationwide composition contest. "Canada's Hockey Anthem Challenge" solicited compositions from the general public and received entries from symphony orchestras, professional musicians, children, and rank amateurs alike. The field of contenders, which eventually comprised nearly 15,000 entries, was narrowed down to 10 finalists by producer Bob Rock, well known for his elaborate production work with Metallica, Mötley Crüe, and other rock bands. Rock made professional-quality studio re-arrangements of each of the finalist compositions, which were subsequently placed on CBC's website for the public to judge. The eventual winner, as judged by a national online vote much in the manner of *American Idol*, was a Celtic fiddle and bagpipe-inflected tune called "Canadian Gold," written by Colin Oberst, an elementary school teacher from Alberta. Oberst won $100,000 and 50 percent of the performance royalties for three years. The other 50 percent went to charity.

In an informal poll on their website, CBC posed the question "Can Canada go on as we know it without the *Hockey Night in Canada* theme?" A total of 3,361 people, or 84 percent of respondents, said no.[13] The public outcry over the potential absence of the theme music was so intense that the rights to Claman's original were bought by a rival sports network (TSN), where it continues to be heard on their NHL broadcasts. The affair is an unusual and amusing episode in Canada's cultural life, but one that underlines the significant importance of sports–music synergies in constructing national identity.[14]

---

[12]   Charlie Gillis *et al.*,"Dumb-da-dumb-da-dumb!" *Maclean's Magazine* 121/24 (June 23, 2008).

[13]   www.cbc.ca/news/polls/hockey-night-theme.html (accessed November 18, 2008).

[14]   On the heels of CBC's efforts to find a new theme for *Hockey Night in Canada*, in 2009–10 PepsiCo Canada sponsored a similar "Join the Cheer" competition in which participants were encouraged to write and submit group cheers to urge on Canadian athletes during the 2010 Winter Olympics in Vancouver. Canadians saw through this overt attempt at corporate manipulation of their culture and the winning cheer, "Eh! O', Canada Go!," did not catch on. Canada's musical connection to Hockey, however, was firmly reinforced

As exemplified by the Super Bowl broadcast spectacles and the network conflicts around the *Hockey Night in Canada* theme music, television has played a significant role in the projection of national identity. Indeed, Pierre Bourdieu has argued that through television's intervention into global sports events and their associated spectacularization, the "ritual celebration of universal values has become a medium for nationalism."[15] The resulting "mediatization" has increased the international emphasis of sports both by increasing the number of international tournaments and matches and by creating an increasingly cosmopolitan culture of globe-trotting players and supporters. As global flows of sports and music increase, an awareness of the distinct differences between nations and cultural identities also increases.

Sports, Music, and Transnationalism

Despite the national politics of sports spectacles like the Olympics or the Super Bowl, or the national association of a sport to a particular piece of music, it is also true that one of the most notable commonalities of sports and music is their mutual ability to transcend socio-cultural and national borders. They are both predisposed to a type of cultural diffusion that seems to resist simplistic notions of cultural imperialism. Though the influence and dominance of both Western musical styles and various forms of sports cannot be denied, there are many instances were the non-dominant form of music or sports challenges the dominant power structure. This is to say, for example, that the Japanese have appropriated and appreciate baseball much as they have appropriated and appreciate various forms of Western popular music. Jamaicans can, however unlikely, field a bobsledding team in the winter Olympics just as reggae has become popular throughout many other parts of the world. There is little doubt that globalized sports are intimately fused with national identity (think of football and baseball in the United States, hockey in Canada, and soccer in England or Italy). There is equally little doubt that certain forms of popular music, genres that lie outside the conventional national folk or traditional repertoire, are also stereotypically representative of national identity (think reggae with Jamaica or blues and country with the United States). As mentioned earlier, national anthems that begin sporting events in most countries significantly reinforce the event as an expression of national identity—despite the fact that the sport, indeed typically the musical style of the anthem (as is the case with the American adaptation of an English drinking song, 'To Anacreon in Heaven,' for its national anthem), may have been adopted from another region or culture.

---

on March 18, 2010, when Claman's "The Hockey Theme" was inducted into the Canadian Songwriter's Hall of Fame.

[15]   Pierre Bourdieu, "The state, economics and sport," in H. Dauncey and G. Hare (eds), *France and the 1998 World Cup* (London: Frank Cass, 1999), 15–21, 17.

It would seem that neither the intrinsic properties of a sport or a music style nor the relationship to some supposed collective psychological character is enough to account for the diffusion of some sports and music from one nation to another. Some sports, like some music, have spread from dominant cultures to economically disadvantaged ones, but the reverse has also occurred. The diffusion of styles and genres is complex and not as simple as some would believe. Economic power central to Marxist theories of globalization would seem not to be the only story. Take the case of ice hockey, which has successfully spread from its roots in Canada to the point where it is dominated by US teams and populated by star players from the United States, Europe, and Russia. As Allen Guttmann has remarked, "Like cultural imperialism, cultural hegemony implies intentionality which is unfortunate because those who adopt a sport are often the eager initiators of a transaction of which the 'donors' are scarcely aware."[16] This same state must similarly hold for the adoption of various musical styles and practices around the globe where there has been little, if any, actual "intention" of cultural hegemony—though indeed it may have been the perceived result.

Emulation is a powerful motivator in the adoption of sports and music by economically marginal countries. Arguments surrounding notions of "false consciousness" or "colonization of the mind" are not persuasive explanations for countries or groups who have forced themselves into sports from which the dominant group desired to exclude them or who have adopted modes of "Western" musical practice. In these cases the concept of "beating them at their own game" becomes more than just a cliché. The Australian cricket team defeating England at the famous Lord's Cricket Ground, New Zealand's All Blacks defeating England at rugby, the Japanese or Cubans winning the Little League World Series of baseball, or even the so-called "miracle on ice," in which the American hockey team won the gold medal over the Russians in the 1980 Olympics— these examples of major international sports upsets became very actively charged moments of national and cultural pride. Such instances—and there are many others—represent a tangible resistance to, if not outright defeat of, traditional notions of cultural imperialism. To quote Arjun Appadurai, "People, machinery, money, images and ideas now follow increasingly non-isomorphic paths."[17]

In very much the same fashion, music increasingly also flows isomorphically, as witnessed by the fact that Western rock and popular music—music that has been widely accused of homogenizing and threatening cultural diversity—has been at least partially blunted by "traditional" musical forms and the rise of world music, however imperfectly defined or realized. Localized music trends and forms act as sites of resistance to colonizing (typically Western) musical values and instrumentation. While we may not doubt the huge influence of Western musical

---

[16]   Allen Guttman, *Games and Empires: Modern Sports and Cultural Imperialism* (New York: Columbia University Press, 1994), 179.

[17]   Arjun Appadurai, "Disjuncture and difference in the global cultural economy," *Theory Culture and Society* 7 (1990), 301. Also quoted in Guttmann, *Games and Empires*, 173.

trends on various localized musics in non-Western cultures (even if only present in recording practices), there are certainly instances where Western music has been "beaten at its own game," so to speak. Though the paths of influences are complex, one might look to the impact of reggae, bhangra, and Latino influences on Western popular music as examples, not to mention the considerable impact of West African indigenous music on African American styles of popular music. The globalization of both sports and music is uneven, indicating that it is not the product of a single process but rather the outcome of numerous, perhaps infinitely complex, interactions between interdependent political, cultural, and economic forces.

World music, as well as dance, clearly has the potential to transcend both the local and the national. But the initial interest in world music, at least in the West, has seemingly faded for the moment. Something of the problem is outlined by W. Schäfer:

> Not too many people care about global civilization at this moment, in fact, most people are prepared by their local culture to dismiss a singular civilization or consider it a dangerous thing. Yet, world music, global email, human rights, green politics and other global pursuits and holistic interests are sowing the seeds for more intense global identifications ... People could embrace the civilization of this planet with as much loyalty as they now embrace their local culture.[18]

Such comments regarding world music can also logically be connected to global sports and its potentiality. This begs the question whether or not global sports and music cultures are, in essence, building closer international and global relationships or, in fact, creating more conflicts. In contrast to Norbert Elias's notion of sports and music contributing to a "civilizing process," as discussed in Chapter 1, in this scenario the world music and sports cultures are effectively engaged in a decivilizing process. Issues surrounding cultural exploitation and accusations of uncredited or unpaid performances by non-Western artists appearing on Western artists' albums, such as Stewart Copeland's *Rhythmatist* (1985) and Paul Simon's *Graceland* (1986), have engendered tensions in the music industry.[19] Similarly, global sports, as witnessed by violent clashes between fans of various national teams at recent World Cups, can be seen potentially to aggravate international tensions. In commenting upon sporting relations between Australia and England, sports

---

[18]   W. Schäfer, "Global civilization and local cultures: A crude look at the whole," *International Sociology* 16/3 (2001), 301–19, 312.

[19]   See Tim Taylor, "Popular music and globalization," in *Global Pop: World Music, World Markets* (New York: Routledge, 1997), 1–37. Also see Louise Meintjes, "Paul Simon's *Graceland*, South Africa and the mediation of musical meaning," *Ethnomusicology* 34 (1990), 37–73.

historian Adrian Smith writes that the "notorious 1932–33 'bodyline' [cricket] tour provoked a genuine crisis in relations between London and Canberra … "[20]

Despite the potential for engendering such tensions, the flow of musical and sporting capital across national boundaries and between social groups is an unavoidable, and not necessarily undesirable, outcome of our highly intermeshed global economy. The liminal and often contradictory nature of this flow makes any definitive statement on the global relationship between sports and music nearly impossible. To be sure, wherever they are located around the globe, and as discussed elsewhere in this book, sports and music share commonalities such as an investment in bodily control and spectatorship. The world contains a dizzying variety of sporting and musical styles and approaches. Western popular music and methods of production may have exerted some form of postcolonial dominance around the world, but it is far from totalizing or hegemonic. The influence of Western music is, by any measure, global, though it has been altered, mitigated and ultimately transformed by an infinite number of local influences that owe more to the exigencies of particular places than "Western" influence. In the context of our current global-networked world, just as no single musical style predominates in Western culture, neither does any sport.

The possible exception to this statement is the worldwide popularity of soccer, known in most places outside North America as football. Unlike popular music, whose influence has been shaped and shaded by local influences, soccer has been adopted in various countries in a relatively uniform way. This is due in large part to the presence of a worldwide governing organization, the existence of which would be untenable in music. The Fédération Internationale de Football Association (International Federation of Association Football), commonly known by its acronym FIFA, as the international governing body of association football, attempts to ensure a global application of rules and standards for the game. FIFA's headquarters in Zürich, Switzerland, is responsible for the organization and governance of football's major international tournaments, most notably the FIFA World Cup, held every four years since 1930.

Testifying to the global popularity of the sport, FIFA has 208 national member associations, 16 more than the United Nations and three more than the International Olympic Committee.[21] FIFA's supreme body is the FIFA Congress,

---

[20]   Adrian Smith, "Black against gold: New Zealand–Australia sporting rivalry in the modern era," in Adrian Smith and Dilwyn Porter, *Sport and National Identity in the Post-War World* (London: Routledge, 2004), 168–93, 168. The incident involved the English tactic of bowling the cricket ball tightly towards the body of star Australian batsman Don Bradman, a tactic considered by many to be dangerous and outside the rules. In the wake of the tour international tensions, including commercial boycotts, between England and Australia remained high until the outbreak of World War II.

[21]   For more on the organization of FIFA and its role in the globalization of soccer, see John Sugden and Alan Tomlinson, *FIFA and the Contest for World Football* (Cambridge: Polity Press, 1998).

an assembly made up of a representative from each affiliated national federation. The Congress now assembles in ordinary session annually, and extraordinary sessions have been held once a year since 1998 as and when requested. Only the Congress can pass changes to FIFA's bylaws. As evidenced by the global reach of FIFA and the World Cup, soccer, more than any other sport or competition, has become something of a de facto expression of national pride and physical prowess, at least among countries with a significant tradition of playing the game. In this sense soccer—a Western sport—partially through the influence of a strong governing body such as FIFA, has exerted far more homogenizing influence, in terms of commercial marketing, merchandising, and celebrity cult, than any particular style or genre of popular music.

This is to say that many sports, not merely soccer, exist worldwide in a standardized form. The rules, penalties, numbers of players, size of playing field, prescribed clothing rituals, and symbols of many sports are the same from one country to the next. From Toronto to Beijing, tennis players understand the terminology of volleys, smashes, double faults, and the scoring system that counts from love through 15, 30, and 40 to game. Basketball players from São Paulo to Seoul incur personal fouls, make free throws, and score two points for a basket. The meanings of such actions and the responses they elicit are essentially the same, no matter in which country the venue is located. In short, though it was not always the case, a global sporting system now connects many people throughout the world. In the world of music, though there are no federations controlling the rules, the situation is somewhat similar, if only in the fact that practitioners of certain musical styles and genres will have a common frame of reference and therefore a common understanding of the "rules" (be they musical parameters and expectations or dance moves and clothing styles). Thus jazz musicians from Moscow to Bangkok share a common understanding of chord changes, limelight solos, and structures of improvisation. In addition, the notational language, of Western tonal music at least, crosses all borders in which it is adopted. A notated eighth-note is understood as an eighth-note, though it may be called something else such as a quaver, no matter what country it is performed in.

The globalization of sports has been largely attributed to nineteenth-century European imperialism.[22] The nineteenth century was an era during which Europe exported its politics, goods, ideas, customs, and leisure activities to much of the rest of the world. Its sports and musical practices, which were sometime hugely disruptive, were variously assimilated, imitated, occasionally resisted, and often adapted to the local talents and preferences. The expansion of the British Empire and the fact that several influential sports, including soccer, cricket, and rugby, originated there meant that England was in the forefront of this movement. Sports historian Maarten Van Bottenburg claims that, "After 1870 virtually all western countries emulated England in setting up sports clubs and national [sports]

---

[22]   J.A. Mangan, "Prologue: Imperialism, sport, globalization," in J.A. Mangan (ed.), *Europe, Sport, World: Shaping Global Societies* (London: Frank Cass Press, 2001), 1.

organizations."[23] The British educational system, with sports and athleticism at its center, and the training of teachers versed in competitive athletic principles, were one important factor in the evolution of twentieth- and twenty-first-century global sports culture.[24]

A similar story is discernible in regard to classical music, which saw the international export of English musical teaching practices and standards to its colonies, particularly through the exportation of its conservatory system, adopted in Canada and now increasingly recognized and used in the United States. The rise of the conservatory system in England and elsewhere was largely a response to the growing professionalization of musical life during the late nineteenth century. It was in part intended to draw a sharper distinction between the training of professional and amateur musicians. Increasingly, however, there was also a need for teachers to serve the expanding middle-class demand, particularly for piano and voice training.

Originally the conservatory system essentially served as a "conservator" of national or regional styles of performance and composition. This role has gradually declined in the face of the internationalization of musical life and the trend toward standardization of musical pedagogy.[25] The British conservatories of the nineteenth and early twentieth centuries served the growing demand for instruction in piano and singing. They provided a training ground for the growing population of teachers and amateurs and developed systems for testing and licensing them. The main contribution of the London conservatories—the Royal Academy of Music (founded in 1822), the Royal College of Music (1882), the Guildhall School of Music (1880), and Trinity College of Music (1872)— lay in providing the world of amateur music and music teaching with coherent professional standards.[26] The Royal Academy of Music was founded by the same aristocratic gentlemen who governed the Concert of Ancient Music and the Royal Society of Musicians; it was designed to train singers and instrumentalists for the King's Theatre and for teaching in aristocratic families. The failure to obtain adequate funding led the committee of management in 1868 to reorient the academy toward serving the needs of teachers and the public. Thus, in something of the same process that saw the regularization of sports rules through governing societies around the world, the study of music, albeit largely art music, achieved something not unlike the international standards and practices associated with sports. To a certain degree this process is analogous to the "sportization" of

---

[23]   Maarten van Bottenburg, *Global Games* trans. Beverley Jackson (Chicago: University of Illinois Press, 2001), 5.

[24]   Mangan, "Globalization, the games ethic and imperialism: Further aspects of the siffusion of the ideal," *Europe, Sport, World*, 106.

[25]   William Weber *et al.*, "Conservatories," in *Grove Music Online*, Oxford Music Online, www.oxfordmusiconline.com.myaccess.library.utoronto.ca/subscriber/article/grove/music/41225 (accessed May 16, 2009).

[26]   Ibid.

society identified by Norbert Elias and discussed in Chapter 1. The common need to codify the "rules" and "standards" of both sports and music, often on an international scale, helped drive the global expansion of both cultural industries.

The Music and Sports Nexus Around the Globe

Apart from the broader global comparisons that can be made between sports and music cultures, the cross-pollination of music and sports is by no means an inherently Western phenomenon. A myriad of musical cultures from around the globe are actively connected to various aspects of sports and competition. My discussion of the interaction of sports and music outside Europe and North America is intended neither to be exhaustive nor to provide a teleological narrative of stylistic inheritances and influences but, rather, merely to offer an illustration of the breadth and variety of the phenomenon as it exists around the globe.

One of the most exuberant and active cross-pollinations of sports and non-Western music occurs in Balinese gamelan competitions. Often each neighborhood organization (*banjar*) or village (*desa*, a conglomeration of several *banjars*) in Bali has its own gamelan, an orchestra of gongs and metallophones. The performers are typically amateur musicians from that village and members of a particular *sekehe* or club, whose activities might include badminton, dancing, or kite flying in addition to gamelan. Among the most popular style of gamelan in Bali is *beleganjur*, which, from its initial military associations in the past, grew in popularity during the 1980s thanks to a series of competitive events that were set up across the island.[27] Its popularity also stems from its being a prime site of newly created gamelan compositions.

Gamelan competitions have been a regular part of Balinese life since the 1930s and 1940s.[28] The inter-village or inter-organizational rivalry for the best gamelan performance, however, is nothing short of warlike in its intensity. Spectators commonly cheer on their favorites and aggressively jeer mistakes by opposing orchestras, with the same rabid passion exhibited by professional sports fans in North America. Indeed, ethnomusicologist and gamelan scholar Michael Tenzer has described the atmosphere of competitions as "much more reminiscent of a sporting event than a concert," with vendors of various merchandise and crowds overflowing into the streets.[29] The most popular venue for gamelan competition is the Ardha Candra stage at the city of Denpasar's Taman Budaya (Art Center), where thousands of devoted and often boisterous fans attend on the evening of an important match. Fans devise cheers, paint their faces, and actively taunt the opposing orchestras. The outcome of the gamelan battle is decided by a panel of

---

[27] Michael B. Bakan, *The Music of Death and New Creation: Experiences in the World of Balinese Gamelan Beleganjur* (Chicago: University of Chicago Press, 1999), 10.

[28] Michael Tenzer, *Balinese Music* (Singapore: Periplus Editions Ltd, 1991), 110.

[29] Ibid.

expert judges, sometimes celebrities, but often only after the actual competition has concluded and the performers and supporters have retired to their home territory.

The music of the gamelan and its variants is tightly organized and controlled, full of intricately woven rhythmic layering and melodic complexity. It is music that, to some extent, mirrors the sense of community interaction and interdependence that marks ordinary village life in Bali. The gamelan competitions, however, provide the audience with a cathartic release and temporary liberation from the tight reins of social propriety. A similar form of release is, of course, also part of the Western sporting experience. Many Western and non-Western sports fans live for the weekend, so to speak, to experience vicariously a sense of victory and liberation from their ordinary lives. The ferocity of the gamelan battles and the accompanying sense of community pride and identity as lived through music, however, is something rarely, if ever, experienced in the West outside sports culture.

The competitive nature of Balinese gamelan often extends beyond the mere winning or losing of a contest. As Michael Bakan writes, the competition is often used as "an opportunity to settle—or more accurately, to further complicate—a variety of scores ranging from long standing interpersonal and inter-village rivalries to cultural and ideological conflicts of broad, even national, scope and impact."[30] Balinese gamelan contests have even been known to be artificially thrown or manipulated by wealthy patrons, similar to organized crime control of sports betting practices, such as fixing the outcome of a game or fight. As in most subjectively evaluated artistic and sporting events, judging discrepancies and irregularities have also been known to occur.[31]

Comparable to gamelan in its competitiveness, silat is an Indonesian and Malaysian combative art of fighting and survival that evolved over centuries into a social culture and tradition.[32] During the colonization era, throughout the British colonies of Malaya, Singapore, and Brunei Darussalam and the Dutch ones in Indonesia, practitioners used the martial art as a symbolic forum to liberate themselves from foreign authorities. Silat, however, is not only used for combative purposes. When accompanied with traditional instruments, such as the *kendang* (a double-headed drum), silat transforms into a popular folk dance.

To a large extent, many types of non-Western traditional musics are predicated upon notions of stoic bodily control and rigid techniques of performance. Typically such music emphasizes the union of mind and body in a harmony of mutual discipline. The Japanese art of taiko drumming, for example, is notable for its close ties to the martial arts. In fact, some of the earliest recorded uses of taiko drums were on the battlefields of ancient Japan during the Warring States Period. These massive drums could sound a loud boom that could be heard over the noise and echo across the expanse of the battlefield. The booming address would

---

[30]   Bakan, *The Music of Death*, 219–20.

[31]   Ibid., 220–28.

[32]   Sheikh Shamsuddin, *The Malay Art of Self-Defense: Silat Seni Gayong* (North Atlantic Books, 2005), 1.

potentially intimidate the opposing forces and thus provide a useful advantage. In addition, the drums' ability to cover long distances with their rolling sounds meant that many army generals used them to aid in commanding and directing their men on the battlefields.[33]

Japanese culture and identity is intimately bound to notions of discipline and control. The replication of ideal or patterned form (*kata*) is manifested in the disciplined repetition found in origami, tea ceremonies, martial arts, and even karaoke. *Kata,* or the concept of a correct body position associated the martial arts, is central in taiko drumming training. Both Japanese martial artists and taiko drummers train at a *dojo*, a school for formal training. One of the central tenets of the practice is replicating ideal body positions and playing in a lock-step unison ensemble. Several traditionally oriented taiko drum groups insist on mastering the practice of formal kneeling, with the feet fully extended and the buttocks resting on the calves. The position must be held for hours in some instances and is extremely painful. Such aesthetic disciplining of the body resonates with much Western dance training. Ballet dancers, for example, often experience excruciating pain as they attempt to achieve certain desired positions. Athleticism is inherent in the taiko mindset as members (traditionally male, though many women have taken up the art form, particularly in North America) often perform bare-chested, exhibiting typically lean, well-muscled bodies that provide visual testimony to the mental and bodily discipline of the art. As such, an aesthetic of stoic athleticism features prominently in taiko performances.[34]

It is worth noting that, as manifest in the hip hop *anime* film series, *Afro Samurai*, and in the work of artists such as Wu-Tang Clan, many African American rap artists have been influenced by martial arts movies. The affinity of African Americans for Kung Fu movies—in particular those of Bruce Lee—can be seen to lie in the desire, shared by many minorities, for a creative form of self-defense that exercised and liberated both mind and body. In explaining the popularity of Kung Fu movies among black American youths in the 1970s, film scholar Stuart Kaminsky claims, "the fantasy resolution for the ghetto kid is not through

---

[33] Common Western military instruments such as trumpets and bagpipes served similar purposes and often demand a similarly physically demanding degree of breath and muscle control.

[34] One taiko group in particular, Za Ondekoza, is famous in Japan and throughout the taiko world for its philosophy of training, which involves an extraordinary amount of running. Indeed, group members often run from one performance venue to the next, making their North American debut by giving a concert immediately after taking part in the Boston Marathon in 1975. The Za Ondekoza performance is based on the principle of *Sagokuron*— that running and music are one and are both a reflection of the drama and energy of life. The group spent three years (1990–93) running to concerts and performing around the United States, beginning and ending their journey with performances at Carnegie Hall in New York. At the end of the journey the members had run approximately 9,200 miles (roughly 14,900 kilometers).

the law. The fantasy is of being able to right the wrongs of one's personal frustration through one's own limited ability."[35] Kim Hewitt further speculates that the relaxed intensity associated with the "aesthetic of cool" found in African American jazz is also paralleled in martial arts. Quoting Joel Dinerstein, Hewitt opines that: "… the cool aesthetic is 'in one sense, composed violence.' This musical performance style … parallels the martial arts ideal of relaxed intensity in the face of physical and mental challenges. Martial arts in its ideal form is nothing if not cool."[36] Through a common understanding of "cool," martial arts can be linked to African American musical performance aesthetics. In a more general sense the idea of the martial arts hero, typically fighting for family and community, echoes the notion, expressed in Chapter 5, that individual achievement and improvisational skill become particularly meaningful in the context of the community.

Modern forms of martial arts have also adopted musical accompaniment to routines in a fashion similar to Western figure skating or gymnastics.[37] For example, wushu, also known as modern or contemporary wushu, is both an exhibition and a full-contact sport derived. It was created in the People's Republic of China in1949, in an attempt to nationalize the practice of traditional Chinese martial arts.[38] Wushu is composed of two demonstrations of various stylized combat routines similar to and involving martial art patterns and maneuvers that are often accompanied by music, for which competitors are judged and given points according to specific rules. Wushu has become an international sport largely through efforts of the International Wushu Federation (IWUF), which holds the World Wushu Championships every two years; the first of these was in 1991 in Beijing.

Brazilian capoeira is another well-known form of martial art that has an overt musical connection, though one that is tied to issues of African-Brazilian identity. Capoeira has been variously described as a simultaneous fight, dance, and game.[39] Its history is highly contested, but it likely developed in Africa before abducted

---

[35]   As quoted in Kim Hewitt, "Martial arts is nothing if not cool: Speculations on the intersections between martial arts and African American expressive culture," in Fred Ho and Bill Mullen (eds), *Afro Asia: Revolutionary Political & Cultural Connections Between African American and Asian Americans* (Durham NC: Duke University Press, 2008), 263–84, 269.

[36]   Ibid., 273.

[37]   For more on the musical content and relationship to wushu, see G. Cai and B.-S. Xi, "Research on the status quo of incidental music of competitive wushu taolu," *Journal of Beijing University of Physical Education* 30/6 (June 2007), 852–4.

[38]   Zhongwen Fu, *Mastering Yang Style Taijiquan* (Berkeley, California: Blue Snake Books, 2006).

[39]   For more on the history of capoeira see Maya Talmon-Chvaicer, *The Hidden History of Capoeira: A Collision of Cultures in the Brazilian Battle Dance* (Austin: University of Texas Press, 2008).

slaves transported the practice to Brazil. Capoeira was part of the culture of the male African-Brazilian urban underclass by 1900. After a period of illegality and persecution, capoeira was legalized in 1937, when the government of the Brazilian dictator Getúlio Vargas self-consciously created a Brazilian cultural identity around carnival, samba, and other hybridizations of Portuguese and African Brazilian arts. After 1975 capoeira began to spread to the United States and Europe. Today capoeira is even found in the heartlands of the Asian martial arts.[40]

In capoeira musicians form a *roda*, or circle, around the two combatants. Music, created by both instruments and voices, is integral to the sport, setting the tempo and style of game. Instrumentation varies but typically consists of several *berimbaus*, single-string percussion instruments; a *pandeiro*, a type of tambourine-like hand frame drum; an *agogô*, a single or multiple bell; and a conga drum. Many of the songs are sung in a call-and-response format although some are in the form of a narrative. Songs can be about history or stories of famous capoeiristas (players). Other songs attempt to inspire players to play better, while some songs describe what is being enacted or performed within the *roda*. Capoeiristas change their playing style significantly as the song or rhythm from the *berimbau* commands. In this manner it is the music that directly drives and influences the tempo and intensity of capoeira. Though it is increasingly found throughout the world, including North America, the integration of sports and music seen in capoeira is almost unequaled in any Western sports–music practice. As such, capoeira contrasts with the typical neo-Cartesian division of mind and body that has, as outlined throughout this book, largely dictated a separation of sports and music in Western culture.

Many other mock-fight slave dances, similar to capoeira, are found throughout the New World, including the Caribbean and other nations in South America. The island of Martinique, for example, is famous for *danymé* (also known as *ladja*). As with capoeira, there is a ring of spectators and musicians into which each contestant enters, moving in a counter-clockwise direction and dancing toward drummers. In Cuba a mock-combat dance called *mani* is performed to *yuka* drums. A dancer (*manisero*) stands in the middle of a ring of spectator-participants and, moving to the sound of the songs and drums, would pick someone from the circle and attempt to knock them down. Some of the *manisero*'s moves and kicks are comparable to those of capoeira. Also similar to capoeira, the Cuban master drummer's patterns mirror the contestants' actions and supply accents to accompany certain blows.

As seen in capoeira and wushu, many forms of combat arts around the globe involve music on a fundamental level. Drums, for example, give rhythm to various traditional forms of Arab wrestling. Such wrestling, similar to the concept of music and athletics in ancient Greece, promotes the notion of competition as a matter of the harmony of mind and body in the development of good character. The Turkish national sport of oil wrestling, *yağli güreş*, is often accompanied by Janissary bands—originally Persian military bands largely comprising various

---

[40]   Sarah Delamont and Neil Stephens, "Up on the roof: The embodied habitus of diasporic *capoeira*," in *Cultural Sociology* 2/1 (2008), 57–74.

percussion instruments, drums, zil (cymbals), trumpets, and bells. Similarly, the Iranian national sport of *zurkhaneh* wrestling combines club exercises with drums, bells, and chanting. The club game of *Pahlevan* changes to keep pace with the sound of a drum played by the *morshed* or guide, typically seated in an elevated position within the hall.

A fusion of sports and music has also become highlighted through the indigenous Māori culture of New Zealand. The best known form of traditional Māori musical performance is the haka. A form of both tribal dance and chant, haka traditionally have various uses in everyday Māori life.[41] A haka may be used to tell a story or to express emotions and opinions, but they are best known in their most aggressive forms such as the "Ka Mate" war dance. Warriors used the Ka Mate to prepare for a battle; to focus their strength; to proclaim their powers; to celebrate the triumph of life over death; but also to challenge and intimidate the opponent. Haka performers accompany angular and aggressive body moves with rhythmic vocal chanting, yells, and grunting. The typical movements of body percussion (hands slapping the chest and the biceps, feet stamping the ground) are often combined with finer, though often no less threatening, facial expressions such as grimaces, showing teeth and the whites of the eyes, poking out tongues, breathing through flared nostrils, and fierce glaring. Most haka are performed exclusively by men, which has sometimes led to the misconception that only men may perform haka. However, a minority of haka are performed predominantly by women. In many haka, though, the female role, if any, is limited to providing support by singing in the background.

Functioning as a type of national calling card, haka have been used by New Zealand sports teams around the world immediately prior to international matches. The haka reflects the importance of the game, motivates the teams and their supporters to greater efforts, and of course, as in the old days on the Māori battlefield, challenges the opponent in an intimidating way. The International Rugby Union Team of New Zealand, the All Blacks, have been doing haka since 1906 and they provide the most famous and well-known renditions. Sometimes haka are written especially for the occasion but most commonly the Ka Mate war chant is used.

Though often performed by non-native team members, the haka is intimately connected to Māori life. Like the Balinese gamelan competitions, kapa haka also has a competitive side that is the backbone of the art form in modern New Zealand. Māori kapa haka competitions are held at all levels, from pre-schoolers to elders, and are always fiercely contested. Every two years, the premier kapa haka groups from around the country come together to battle for the title of national champion. Inaugurated in 1972, this festival is known as *Te Matatini* (the many

---

[41]   For more information on Māori Haka see Robert Walker, "We all came out of Africa singing and dancing and we have been doing it ever since," in *Research in Music Education* 24 (2005), 4–16.

faces), a name that reflects the diversity of those who attend.[42] The *Te Matatini* is the world's largest celebration of Māori performing arts and attracts more than 40,000 people from throughout New Zealand. Two teams from Australia and 36 teams from 13 regions of New Zealand attended the 2009 event, having first qualified at a series of regional competitions.

Haka are not merely limited to New Zealand rugby. Other Kiwi teams and sports known for doing haka include the Falcons (New Zealand's national Australian-rules football team) and the Tall Blacks (New Zealand's national men's basketball team). Notably, the tradition has even spread to a number of American football teams, including the Brigham Young University Cougars and the University of Hawaii Warriors. Haka popularity is particularly growing in Hawaii because of similarities between Māori and Hawaiian tribal culture.

New Zealand sports teams have recently been accused of overusing the haka and potentially devaluing its importance. At the 2006 Commonwealth games in Melbourne, several countries expressed displeasure at the performances after bronze medal presentations. The Kiwis, however, saw the haka as a way of recognizing, honoring, welcoming, and sending off their teammates, as well as an expression of general emotion. According to the New Zealand chef de mission Dave Currie: "The only thing that it's not is entertainment. We're not entertaining anyone. We don't do it for an audience … It's spontaneous. We don't have an issue with how many haka we do. If we win more medals, we'll do more haka."[43] Despite such controversies, the haka remains intimately fused with New Zealand sporting identity.

Though this survey of non-Western ethnic and folk music styles that are connected to sport is far from complete, several conclusions may be drawn. Perhaps most obvious is the simple observation that the connection between sport and music occurs in cultures across the globe. Unlike most Western comparisons, however, music often plays a far more influential role in either actively influencing the tempo of the sport, as in capoeira, or as a ritual surrounding the sport, as in the haka. In many cases, as in gamelan or taiko drumming, the line between sport and music is almost indistinguishable.

Much as jazz and hip hop have been closely connected to basketball in North America, some sports in non-Western countries are uniquely tied to specific genres of music that seem particularly suited to their rhythms or spirit. The Brazilian national soccer team, for example, is intimately connected to samba music. The team listens to samba in its dressing room as a pre-game focusing exercise and then is continually accompanied by samba drumbeats from supporters in the crowd as it plays. At certain moments it has been observed that the team appears to synchronize communally with the samba beats, just as dancers might synchronize their movements on a dance floor, and the flow of the game becomes influenced

---

[42]   www.newzealand.com/travel/media/features/maori-culture/kapa-haka-performances_feature.cfm (accessed May 11, 2009).

[43]   "Kiwis deny overdoing haka at games," *Sydney Morning Herald*, March 21, 2006.

by the music. Indeed, the team's nickname is the Samba Boys. Samba drumbeats are now also commonly heard supporting Brazilian athletes, no matter the sport, in competitions around the world. Thus samba and soccer have combined to reinforce a particularly Brazilian national identity that is now promoted at international sporting events around the globe.[44]

A similar correspondence with music is found in cricket, which, thanks to the 2007 World Cup's being held in the Caribbean for the first time, is increasingly becoming associated with calypso music. Television coverage of cricket in the United Kingdom and elsewhere uses calypso music in themes and to underscore coverage of games. The West Indies have long been a hotbed of cricket. However, the appropriation of calypso music by English cricket audiences, and its associated notions of exotic, relaxed, carnivalesque atmosphere, is perhaps not without its problems. Indeed, many of the songs associated with the sport, such as Booker T and the M.G.'s calypso inflected song "Soul Dressing," used in BBC television cricket coverage in the United Kingdom, do not originate in the Caribbean at all.[45]

Fan Communities, Fan Nationalism

Nationalism and sports, particularly team sports, encourage a constant production of sameness and consensus, reinforced by an equally constant disavowal of difference. The projection of difference—an "us versus them" binary—onto opponents or rivals is common to both nations and sports. Within the music industry there are similarly "insiders" and "outsiders," but it is likely at the level of fan reception that such divides are most obvious. Taken to extremes by the fans of gangsta rap (the supporters of various rappers have at times inflicted violence on one another), music fan loyalties can be likened to teams or nations. Indeed, the fan club for the rock band Kiss, one of the largest in existence, calls itself the Kiss Army. Many other musical divides such as the mods versus the rockers in 1960s England or East Coast versus West Coast rap in the United States, for example, have nevertheless engendered levels of aesthetic and moral consensus that can be compared to that involved in nation or sports team building. As such, within nations, sports, and musical cultures, questions of social difference are a crucial organizing factor and key to understanding their ready coexistence.

Sports teams represent a central site of—variously—community, regional, and national pride. In a form of neo-tribalism in which the identity of the tribe

---

[44]   The international music community has several sporting musicians who were active soccer players. In the 1960s Latin crooner Julio Iglesias, for example, briefly played goal for the Spanish soccer team Real Madrid. Similarly, reggae legend Bob Marley was an avid and active soccer player and a lifelong fan of the game.

[45]   For more on the relationship of calypso and cricket, see Claire Westall, "This thing goes beyond the boundary: Cricket, calypso, the Caribbean and their heroes," in Bateman, *Sporting Sounds*, 222–36.

members is in constant flux, supporters wear their team colors as proud locational signifiers, emotionally rising and falling on each victory or loss as if it represented the collective comparative worth, not only of themselves, but of the community at large in which they live. As discussed, Balinese gamelan competitions represent a significant non-Western example of such village attachments to musical teams. Some well-known professional teams, to be sure, challenge this singular attachment to a location. A team such as Manchester United, despite being attached to a particular location and community, attracts a fan base of over 50 million people around the globe. Indeed, the level of global fanaticism was made evident when a disgruntled Nigerian Manchester United fan in Ogbo, Nigeria, drove his bus into a crowd of rival Barcelona supporters, killing four people, following Manchester's loss in the 2009 European Champions League final.[46] Similar translocational franchises are found in the NHL's Montreal Canadians and the New York Yankees, both of which boast significant fan support from wherever they play in North America. Such instances of relative translocational fan appeal are somewhat rare and are typically limited to the most successful and historic teams in their leagues.

Nowhere in North American sport, however, is this attachment to the team more evident than in American college sports. Fans of college football, in particular, are often extremely closely tied to their "alma mater" universities. Indeed, the booster clubs associated with the sports teams of the larger universities are often described as consisting of nations. The term "Tide Nation" refers to the supporters of the University of Alabama's football team, nicknamed the Crimson Tide. Members of Tide Nation watch their team in Tuscaloosa, Alabama, in a crowd of 80,000 or more who rile themselves up for the game by listening to legendary Southern rock band Lynyrd Skynyrd's "Sweet Home Alabama."[47] Not to be outdone, the University of Tennessee has recently seen the publication of a book about the fans of their Volunteers football team. *Once a Vol, Always a VOL!: The Proud Men of the Volunteer Nation* underscores the high degree of identification with that particular school sports program.[48] The Volunteers sonically project their identity through the communal singing (over 100,000 fans regularly occupy Neyland Stadium) of one of the best-known university fight songs, "Rocky Top." Though adopted by the University of Tennessee, "Rocky Top" was written in 1967 by Felice and Boudleaux Bryant and achieved mass popularity when it was recorded by Lynn Anderson in 1970, reaching No. 17 on the US country chart. Referencing a peak in Tennessee's Great Smoky Mountains, it has subsequently been recorded

---

[46] "Nigeria United fan kills rivals," *BBC News*, May 28, 2009, http://news.bbc. co.uk/2/hi/africa/8072356.stm (accessed March 9, 2010).

[47] The song also appears in "virtual" sporting events. It was featured on the PS2 and Xbox versions of NASCAR Thunder 2002 because the game creators, EA Sports, had just announced sponsorship of the fall race at Talladega Superspeedway, located in Alabama.

[48] Gus Manning and Haywood Harris, *Once a Vol, Always a VOL! The Proud Men of the Volunteer Nation* (Sports Publishing LCC, 2006).

by Dolly Parton, John Denver, Brad Paisley, Keith Urban, and the group Phish, among others. The Bryants granted the University of Tennessee a perpetual license to play the song as often as success on the field warrants.

One of the most famous examples of this type of university sports nationalism, however, is provided by the University of Florida Gators. The "Inside the Gator Nation" website, for example, offers a Gator Nation newsletter and the opportunity to post letters and videos answering the question "When did you become a Florida Gator?" Fight songs are also prominently featured, including "Gimme a G, Go Gators," "The Orange and the Blue," "Jaws, Go Gators," and "We Are the Boys from Old Florida." Furthermore, the site proudly proclaims the headline "The Gator Nation is Everywhere!!," followed by some spirited text: "There is no bond stronger than the one formed when you become a member of the Gator Nation. In every corner of the globe, Gators accomplish remarkable feats with innovative thinking and inspired collaboration. The Gator Nation knows no boundaries …"[49] American university athletic programs and their supporters, reinforced by supplemental fight songs and music, serve as powerful sites of communal identity. Indeed such fan "nations" are perhaps second in importance only to actual nationality. As the Gator Nation website implies, however, such identification "knows no boundaries" and thus can be seen as transcending actual community, state, or even national borders.

One of the central claims of this book is that the structures of both music and sports (and indeed the concepts of the nation and related institutions such as the military), by virtue of their repressive demand for sameness that are often driven and reinforced by capitalist goals of commodification, are troubled by the reality and complexities of social difference. As such, both sporting and musical cultures, by and large, act as normalizing structures that constantly attempt to produce conformity and sameness and disavow difference and inequality. They can act as synergistic normalizing agents of, among other things, national identity. The confluence of the two phenomena, as discussed throughout this book, often serves to reinforce the production of conformity in both. This is to say, that the use of alternative music to accompany, for example, extreme sports reinforces the cohesion of both the associated sporting and musical cultures.

Nonetheless, in fan cultures in both music and sports it is possible to identify various levels of hierarchy. Richard Giulianotti, for example, identifies four discrete hierarchies of spectator identity within sport: supporters, followers, fans, and flâneurs.[50] Supporters have "relatively fixed forms of team identification," while followers "identify with other clubs for particular biographical (not market) reasons." Fans, on the other hand, "connect to clubs by consuming team paraphernalia" and through identification with star players. The flâneur, in contrast, freely "shifts sporting allegiances … and embodies a fluid transnational consumerism that implies a potential breakdown of national sports

---

[49]   *Inside the Gator Nation*, http://insidethegatornation.com (accessed May 17, 2009).
[50]   Giulianotti, 179.

identification."[51] This last category embodies elements of postmodern hybridity and juxtaposition.

Fans of various bands or popular music styles, I would argue, can be placed into categories similar to those Giulianotti recognizes in sports. Heavy metal listeners, for example, are often passionately linked to that style and have an encyclopedic knowledge of all aspects of their favorite band's career; thus they might be thought of as supporters. Others, who would be deemed followers by Giulianotti, may identify with a style of music simply because they were raised with it or for other particular biographical reasons. Flâneurs are also common in music, as individuals often buy the T-shirts or adopt the look, fashions, and style of various bands without having any particular allegiance to their music. Exposed to an increasingly global buffet of music, such consumers are also free to identify themselves with any number of musical styles and thus re-envision, without eliminating, traditional notions of many subcultural music-fan-based communities.

In addition to the cross-pollinations between non-Western sports and music, and similar to the university fan "nations" outlined above, the songs of soccer supporters around the globe project an important part of their identity.[52] In Scotland, for example, soccer songs often help construct and convey a set of identities that project many of the underlying religious and political aspects of that society. In addition to the common football songs and chants that might be heard in any soccer stadium throughout Britain, songs abusing Catholics and the Irish, songs about the 1314 Battle of Bannockburn, songs of the British Empire, Irish rebel tunes, Scottish rebel tunes, chants about loyalist paramilitaries in Northern Ireland, and songs about the Pope are common and impart a distinctive politicized and nationalistic component to Scottish soccer.[53] The two leading clubs in the country, Glasgow Celtic and Glasgow Rangers, represent not just neighborhood divisions but also, respectively, the Catholic and Protestant religious divide within the community and country at large.

As discussed by Joseph Bradley, one of the most popular Glasgow Rangers chants is the anti-Catholic "Billy Boys":

---

[51]   Ibid., 179–80.

[52]   One of the most powerful examples of building community through popular song in sports is the case of Liverpool Football Club's anthem "You'll Never Walk Alone." Originally written for the Rodgers and Hammerstein musical *Carousel* (1945), in the wake of Gerry and the Pacemaker's 1963 version it was adopted by Liverpool Football Club were terrace supporters continue sing a stirring rendition before every home game. The title of the song even appears on the club crest and over the entrance to their home stadium. The solidarity building popularity of "You'll Never Walk Alone" has lead to its adoption by a number of other football and sports clubs throughout Europe.

[53]   My discussion here draws on the work of Joseph M. Bradley, "'We shall not be moved'! Mere sport, mere songs? A tale of Scottish football," in Adam Brown (ed.), *Fanatics! Power, Identity and Fandom in Football* (London: Routledge, 1998), pp. 203–18.

Hello, hello, we are the Billy Boys.
Hello, hello, you can tell us by our noise.
We're up to our knees in Fenian blood.
Surrender or you'll die,
For we are the "Billy Billy" Boys.[54]

The song, the singing of which UEFA has supposedly banned, celebrates the values of Protestant Billy Boys, and, as Glasgow Celtic fans note, this anti-Catholic song is sung (sometimes with a varied wording) by the followers of a significant number of clubs in Scotland.[55] This chant is far from a lone exception. Songs such as "I Was Born Under a Union Jack," "King Billy's on the Wall," "The Sash My Father Wore (Sure I'm an Ulster Orangeman)" and even "Rule Britannia" are commonly sung by Ranger's supporters and express similar pro-Protestant/anti-Catholic sentiments.

Glasgow Celtic fans similarly sing supportive chants for their club as well as a collection of folk songs, such as "The Fields of Athenrye" and rebel anthems, such as "The Soldier's Song (Irish National Anthem)," that reflect their own and their club's Irish heritage.[56] Through such associations the supporters continue to forefront the legacy of the period during which the club was founded, when Irish immigrants in many countries maintained links to the Irish nationalist cause then being pursued in the home country. Contemporary Celtic supporters thus continue this tradition by demonstrating their desire, through soccer songs and chants, for an independent and united Ireland.[57]

In the case of both Rangers and Celtic it must be noted, however, that the religious/ethnic identities of each side are mitigated by the exigencies of playing competitive professional soccer at an international level. Echoing the isomorphic flows of power and influence discussed earlier in this chapter, both clubs are populated by players and coaches from across Europe and other continents and benefit from international investment and television and merchandising revenues. Thus, while the history of each club, reinforced by song, appeals to distinct audiences, the reality of their existence is much more complicated.

The songs and symbols associated with Scottish soccer remain significant comments on wider social issues. Of course the representation of differing visions of identity promoted through the songs of the respective fans of Rangers and Celtic not only reflects the complexity of the religious politics in Scottish sport and society, but of identity formation itself. Nonetheless, it is clear that the convergence of sport and music in this instance plays a significant and mutually reinforcing role in the construction of these identities. Lubricated, at least in part, through mass musical experiences, the experience of sports, be it national or local,

---

[54]   As transcribed in Bradley, 204.

[55]   Ibid., 204.

[56]   Joseph M. Bradley, *Ethnic and Religious Identity in Modern Scotland* (Aldershot: Avebury Press, 1995), 34–7.

[57]   Bradley, "We shall not be moved," 206.

typically transforms fans into fans of the nation and/or location itself. Though Scotland may be unique in its internal religious divides that play out between two of its most popular sports franchises, this case study nonetheless shows that the songs of supporters of various sports can be powerful agents in national dialogues and in shaping national and local identity.[58]

Of course, likely more than any other sport, soccer has generated an inordinate amount of popular music. Due in large part to the popularity of the World Cup, every four years artists from around the globe decide to record nationalistic songs designed to inspire their country's squad and rally their supporters. In addition to New Order's "World in Motion" discussed in Chapter 4, Rod Stewart recorded Latin tinged "Olé Ola" for Scotland in the 1978 World Cup held in Argentina. The 1990 Irish World Cup team was sent off to Italy with the song "Jack's Heroes" by The Pogues and The Dubliners. In one of the more bizarre instances of such songs, for the 1994 World Cup hosted by the United States, a reunited Village People wrote and recorded "Far Away in America" for the German team. Though most of these songs were not commercial successes, one of the most popular World Cup songs is "Three Lions" by Frank Skinner, David Baddiel and The Lightning Seeds. This song first serenaded the English team for Euro 96 when it went to number one on the British charts. They re-recorded the song for the 1998 World Cup in France and it topped the charts for a second time. The song was re-recorded yet again for World Cup 2010; the new version features Skinner, Baddiel along with Robbie Williams and Russell Brand.

The use of music in Scottish football or in World Cup songs serves to help delineate particular religious and national identities and, indeed, most music that is used in support of a team—be it on a local or national level—typically attempts to reinforce some form of exclusive identification. Nonetheless, music is sometimes used in sport to reflect a trans-national or pan-global universal identity. Somalian-born, Canadian-based hip hop artist K'naan's "Wavin' Flag" was chosen as the official anthem of the 2010 World Cup Trophy Tour. It was performed by the artist at each stop on the cup's world tour prior to the start of the tournament in South Africa in June 2010.[59] K'naan in fact re-recorded a version of "Wavin' Flag" for the tournament after it was first released on his *Troubadour* album in 2009. The song is similar to the original but includes a

---

[58]   Something of this same complexity can be glimpsed in the Barcelona Football Club's Catalonian identity in the midst of the Spanish premier league, La Liga.

[59]   Aside from the myriad of official songs, anthems, pre game concerts and the like, perhaps the most notable musical connection to the 2010 World Cup was the constant drone of the plastic vuvuzela horns, enthusiastically blown by South African fans at every game. The cacophonous buzzing drone was an indelible sonic marker of the location and event. Also of particular note was Latin superstar Shakira's official FIFA World Cup song "Waka Waka (This Time for Africa)." Though many expressed misgivings over a non-African being chosen to record the song it nonetheless became an international hit and one of the most watched videos on Youtube for 2010.

pre-chorus that sets the uplifting, unified tone in keeping with the global appeal of the World Cup, turning the song into one that is, according to K'naan, "more open, more inviting, more celebratory."[60] In addition to this nod to inclusivity, however, numerous foreign language versions of the song were also subsequently recorded. All versions are bi-lingual duets with K'naan and include versions in Arabic, Chinese, French, Greek, Nigerian, Portuguese, Indonesian, Japanese, Spanish, Thai and Vietnamese. While such efforts at global outreach are generally to be applauded, it must also be noted that the remix of "Wavin' Flag" and the FIFA World Cup Trophy Tour was sponsored by Coca-Cola as part of their global integrated marketing campaign.[61] This particular mix of popular music and sport can thus be understood as merely furthering the goals of corporate capitalism in creating uniform global markets.[62]

In a sense, competing with agendas of local or national identity (as promoted by the songs of Scottish soccer supporters), the sporting and musical sponsorship of the business world (as manifest in the "FIFA World Cup Trophy Tour by Coca-Cola"), are often driven by much more homogenizing goals as they relate to national identity and the creation of national markets. Though the corporate hybridization of sports and music is outlined in Chapter 3, corporate agendas are often synonymous with issues affecting national identity, colonization, and globalization. One of the increasingly prevalent issues in sociological studies of sports is that of the influences of capitalism and the relationship of class to our understanding of various sporting agendas. Graham Scambler, for example, has analyzed the 2000 Sydney Olympics in terms of the "role of relations of class … prepotent in the aspirations and machinations of Sydney's construction industry, of national sponsors and of the television networks."[63] Among other issues, Scambler recognizes the role that American television network NBC played in dictating venues and staging various aspects of the games, often over the political and environmental objections of disenfranchised locals. In this manner the games represented a corporate class colonization, albeit a temporary one, of everyday life for many residents of the city. For Scambler, "It is the resurgence of class which has fostered and hastened, *but not determined* … the novel

---

[60]   "K'naancelebrateshisWorldCupanthem,"*Billboard.biz.*(September29,2009)www. billboard.biz/bbbiz/content_display/industry/e3ife9d9d88fcefbcdce6fc9bb98de68870 (accessed May 21, 2010).

[61]   Ibid.

[62]   Indeed, this reading perhaps becomes even more complicated when one realizes that another allstar remix of "Wavin' Flag" has been used in Canada to raise money for Haitian earthquake relief. Dubbing themselves Young Artists for Haiti, those involved in the single, in addition to K'naan, include Drake, Metric's Emily Haines, Avril Lavigne, Justin Bieber, Nelly Furtado, Broken Social Scene and others. The song was recorded by legendary rock producer Bob Ezrin.

[63]   Graham Scambler, *Sport and Society*, 171.

postmodern shape to the culture of the last quarter of the twentieth century."[64] In relation to sports, perhaps more than music in this respect, the mechanisms of the marketplace, within the kaleidoscope of disorganized capitalism, have led to a rapid increase in the rate and scale of sports colonization of culture. Profitable markets have accompanied, and to some extent driven, the recent mass popularity and hypercommodification of both amateur and professional sports and even more overtly fueled the burgeoning exercise and dietary industries. If the ultimate end point of capitalism is the commodification of everything, then the increasing cross-marketing and hypercommodification of almost all aspects of sports and music, including their association with national identity and notions of sovereignty, should come as little surprise.

Issues of national identity tied to commodification are also invoked in the cultural cross-pollinations that occur when cultural products attempt to establish new footholds in other parts of the world. In the United Kingdom, for example, several American sports, such as NFL football and NBA basketball, are attempting to establish a firm audience base. Ironically, as Joseph Maguire and Mark Falcous have discussed, there has been a resurgence of British nationalism in the wake of globalization:

> This perceived or imagined regeneration of plural British national identities is symptomatic of one of the paradoxes of globalization processes. Politically, manifestations of this cultural shift were mobilized by the incumbent Blairite New Labour government of the late 1990s. Most evocatively captured, somewhat ironically, by the term "Cool Britannia," this mediated vision was one of resurgent Britons in fields including fashion, popular music (notably "Britpop"), art, cinema and other zones of prestige.[65]

While globalization could be seen as reinforcing British nationalism, particularly through the rise and international success of Britpop artists such as Blur, Oasis, and the Spice Girls, professional sports leagues from the United States were actively attempting to establish a foothold among British audiences. Maguire and Falcous point out that the NFL was much more successful in this mission than the NBA. The NBA game was seen as literally alien to many in the British media, in part due to the unfamiliar presence of popular music punctuating play and cheerleading squads, both unknown in the long history of British team sports. Consider Lynn Truss's report on the McDonald's Championship held in Paris in 1997. She decries the event as being played by "gigantic men whose shoe size is only one step short of luggage" and complains of the fragmented, stop-start rhythm of the game. For Truss the game was: "The longest 48 minutes you will experience in your life …

---

[64]   Ibid., 176.

[65]   Joseph Maguire and Mark Falcous, "'Making touchdowns and hoop dreams': The NFL and NBA in England," in Joseph Maguire (ed.), *Power and Global Sport: Zones of Prestige, Emulation and Resistance* (London: Routledge, 2005), 34.

every time the play gets interesting in basketball, somebody calls time-out (why?), a pop music introduction (truncated), aerobic jazz dancing or mascot clowning."[66] A further example of the alienating American experience of the NBA is provided by Andrew Longmore, who in his description of the McDonald's Championship, sarcastically described the experience as being "a cross between a rock concert, Baptist rally and children's theatre" and advised his readers to bring "a set of ear plugs due to the loudness of the music."[67] In each of the descriptions, the loudness and presence of popular music is cited as being one of the prime negative features of the experience. Indeed, for an average North American NBA audience, breaking into an English-style soccer anthem might be an equally alienating experience. Thus even between nations as similar, in terms of shared language and development, and as friendly as the United States and Great Britain, national cultural differences often still hinder the establishment of homogeneous global sporting cultures. Even though both cultures actively employ music as part of the sports experience, the type of music and the ways in which it is incorporated into the event represent distinct national differences.

As witnessed by the relative failure of the NBA in Great Britain, music and sporting cultures do not always translate between different parts of the world. Similarly, as discussed earlier in this chapter, power and influence in both cultural realms often flow in complex isomorphic patterns. Nonetheless, even if only in highlighting the differences in identity as manifest in various fan communities, the combined forces of sport and music are clearly powerful synergistic agents in constructing and reflecting locality, national and community affinities both in the West and in many cultures around the globe.

---

[66]   Lynn Truss, "Bulls hit town for a lesson in jargon," *The Times*, October 20, 1997. Also appears in Maguire and Falcous, 37.

[67]   Andrew Longmore, "NBA orders limited retreat from decibel hell," *The Times*, October 19, 1995. Also appears in Maguire and Falcous, 37.

Chapter 7
"Gonna Fly Now":
Visual Media and the Soundtrack of Sports

In addition to the popularity of the sports films genre, sports video games and television programming provide some of the most socially ingrained and synergistic connections between popular music and sports. As such, the combination of sonic and visual reinforcement is particularly powerful in constructing and reflecting identity. Focusing on sports movies, video games and television, this chapter discusses the use of music in visual media to construct and contest various class, ethnic, racial and gender identities.

Sports Films

From the beginning of the motion picture industry, sports have been a frequent thematic subject. Literally thousands of films about sports have been produced, from documentary-style "news films" recounting major prize fights and the World Series to more recent Hollywood blockbusters such as *Rocky* (1976), *Jerry Maguire* (1996), *Seabiscuit* (2003), and *Million Dollar Baby* (2004). Attesting to the ongoing public fascination with sports, by the middle of the 1980s approximately 2,000 feature films had been made based on sports themes and representations of athletes and athletics.[1]

Though the musical soundtracks for many sports films are instrumental in conveying and reinforcing social identities and messages, they often go relatively unnoticed and hence have drawn relatively little scholarly inquiry. However, the repetition of powerful images transmitted through cinema, television, and even the internet, build powerful associative responses to the music that pervasively accompanies these images. Indeed, a small number of sports movies have become indelibly linked with their musical themes. To think of the movie *Chariots of Fire* (1981) without Vangelis' haunting synthesizer melody is virtually impossible. Vangelis won an Oscar for his soundtrack in which, for most of the movie, synthesizers recreated the sound of acoustic instruments. The famous main theme, first heard during the opening credits while Olympic athletes are seen in slow motion running on an English beach, consists of reverberating beats, perhaps suggestive of the repetitiveness of running, and a simple but uplifting

---

[1]   Harvey Marc Zucker and Lawrence J. Babich, *Sports Films: A Complete Reference* (Jefferson, NC: McFarland, 1987), 3.

anthem that suggests the liberating joy of amateur athletics. The use of a synthesized soundtrack for a historical movie about Olympic track athletes lent the work a sense of ethereal stasis, as if the athletes were frozen in time—an apt use of music, given that the film takes place as a series of recalled memories. As such, the soundtrack is immediately evocative of Olympic glory. In a similar manner, the mere mention of *Rocky* or its sequels is virtually impossible without simultaneously hearing Bill Conti's "Gonna Fly Now" or, alternatively, Survivor's Grammy Award-winning "Eye of the Tiger," specifically written at the request of Sylvester Stallone for *Rocky III* in 1982. Songs such as these typically trigger a state of optimism and excitement in the listener that reinforces the paradigmatic heroic narrative of the drama itself.

When Disney purchased Capital Cities/ABC in 1995, the ESPN sports network was a particularly important component of the acquisition. Executives from both ABC and Disney pointed to the "universal appeal" of sports and its benign ability to "offend no political position."[2] Such a statement seems idealistic at best; one need recall only the various political machinations that seem to accompany every Olympics to realize its naiveté. The statement, however, echoes the utopian mythos of sports that likely accounts for much of their popularity and that often gets superficially reinforced in Hollywood representations. The reality, of course, is much more complex. The synergistic combination of sports, film, and music has produced a plethora of memorable representations that have greatly contributed to the contested process of defining social identities.

Social Class and Ethnicity

Because of their inherent connection to the body, athletics have traditionally played an important role in definitions of gender—masculinity in particular. As a result, to some extent every sports-themed movie is about gender, though it may also be about other aspects of social identity. Hollywood, likely in an attempt to avoid alienating various market segments, rarely engages in overt representations of social identity. Depictions of social class, in particular, are usually avoided. When social difference is foregrounded at all in sports films, it is generally depicted as an obstacle to be overcome by individual initiative and force of will. Physical traits, however, often serve as essentialized reminders of racial and gender identity. In films such as *Pride of the Yankees* (1942), *Gentleman Jim* (1942), *The Pride of St. Louis* (1952), *Rocky, All the Right Moves* (1983), *Hoop Dreams* (1994), and *Million Dollar Baby*, sports are valued primarily as vehicles for upward social mobility. In such films the working-class origins of athletes are typically evoked as the roots of their strength, of both body and character, but are ultimately erased in service of the glory of individual self-determination rather

---

    [2]   "The trophy in Eisner's big deal," *New York Times*, August 6, 1995, sec. 3, 1, 11. Also see Aaron Baker, *Contesting Identities: Sports in American Film* (University of Illinois Press, 2003), 1.

than collective teamwork. The emphasis on individualism and self-reliance in sports films can be traced to what Robert Sklar argues is "the myth making role of the movies," an ethos that grew from conservative Hollywood efforts to reaffirm middle-class American faith in the notion that perseverance and hard work will bring success, undermined during and following the Great Depression.[3] Such myth making is central to the utopianism present in so many films about sports and their accompanying soundtracks.

Euro-American Caucasian masculinity has also been clearly delineated through music in sports films. Musical gestures, for example, are often used in sports films to cue various audience reactions. These gestures, moreover, are largely drawn from the musical vocabulary of classical (often post-Romantic) music literature and classic Hollywood genre films themselves. In underscoring heroic athletic action, composers often rely on gestures that employ vigorous rhythms, dramatic intervallic leaps (often fifths or eighths), simple fanfares, and soaring melodic arpeggiations to underscore the exploits of the hero. Such "heroic" musical gestures have their precedence in a variety of classical works, including Strauss's tone poem *Don Juan* and Wagner's *Ring Cycle*, and were later imitated by film composers in works such as Korngold's music for *Captain Blood* and Miklos Rosza's theme for El Cid from the film of the same name. In turn, these expressive gestures have been replicated in a variety of sports film scores to delineate the athletic actions of white male leading men in films such as *The Natural*, *Hoosiers*, and *Rudy*, among others. As such, these gestures, along with others, have essentially become sonic markers of athletic white masculine identity.[4]

Sports films often evoke a historical memory of either real or imaginary events and athletes. In this way they typically seek to document, and in effect artificially concretize, the social and cultural concerns of the time when they were made. Robert Rosenstone identifies several traits shared by most historical sports films. They generally portray a story with a strong sense of closure that leaves the audience with "a moral message and (usually) a feeling of uplift."[5] The acclaimed basketball film *Hoosiers* (1986) achieves this through a climactic contest—a device shared by many sports films—that serves to reestablish moral order by rewarding underdogs for their hard work and determination. A similar plot device is found in all the *Rocky* films. These films optimistically imply that a general sense of social progress is ensured through the price of hard work.

The soundtracks to both *Hoosiers* and *Rocky* would seem to reinforce this somewhat naive view of the world. In *Rocky*, Rocky Balboa's exhausting training sessions, culminating in the iconic climbing of the steps of the Philadelphia

---

[3]   Robert Sklar, *Movie-Made America* (New York: Random House, 1975), 195–6.

[4]   See Timothy Scheurer, "'The best there ever was in the game': Musical mythopoesis and heroism in film scores of recent sports movies," *Journal of Popular Film & Television* 32/4 (Winter 2005): 157–67.

[5]   Robert Rosenstone, *Visions of the Past* (Cambridge, Mass.: Harvard University Press, 1995), 3.

Museum of Art, are accompanied by Conti's "Gonna Fly Now." This song, also known as "Rocky's Theme," is marked by an energetic brass fanfare that evokes the combative masculine heritage of military brass bands. Conti's aggressively percussive fanfare forcefully captures the rawness of boxing and Rocky's fierce determination to succeed. "Rocky's Theme" is in itself a representation of an evolutionary mentality that underlines the film's gradual growth in complexity and energy as Rocky begins to build strength and confidence. In the initial training sequence, a solo French horn first plays a subdued and somewhat muted version of the motive associated with Rocky. The solo horn is replaced by piano and orchestra, which play the theme at a moderate tempo and with soft dynamics as the relatively out-of-shape Rocky struggles up the stairs of the Museum of Art in the darkness of the early morning. In the second training sequence, the now more fit and confident Rocky is energetically accompanied by a full orchestra, and brass and rock instrumentation, culminating in the exhilarating victory dance at the top of the stairs. The music from this sequence is still used to inspire athletes in many disciplines. At this point, aggressive syncopated downbeat "punches" in the brass section are set in opposition to the rest of the orchestra, and both the increased tempo and dynamic levels reflect his newly-gained sense of self. The use of rock instrumentation, typically associated with youthfulness, also imparts a sense of the new vitality of the character. Moreover, the lyrics to the song, heard here for the first time in the film, also serve to reflect Rocky's underdog persona and the notion that through hard work he will ultimately triumph.

> Trying hard now
> It's so hard now
> Trying hard now
>
> Getting strong now
> Won't be long now
> Getting strong now
>
> Gonna fly now
> Flying high now
> Gonna fly, fly, fly ...[6]

The libratory theme of flight was subsequently taken up in other sports movie hit songs. Notably, R.J. Kelly's "I Believe I Can Fly" and Seal's rendition of Steve Miller's "Fly Like an Eagle" are both used in the basketball cartoon movie *Space Jam* (1996). These songs all emphasize the element of literal and figurative elevation and are anthems to optimism that use the connection with sports to reinforce the possibilities of social and class evolution. In addition to framing sports as the main means to ascend the socio-economic ladder of success, such

---

[6]   Lyrics written by Carol Connors and Ayn Robbins.

songs also reinforce the utopian American mythos of the individual's ability to overcome all odds through determined effort.

Gerry Goldsmith's Oscar-nominated score for *Hoosiers* primarily relies on the use of synth-rock music and crowd noises to generate high energy in action montages of basketball games and practices. Goldsmith, like Conti, uses synthesizer melodies, particularly in the extended opening montage, to accompany shots of the scenic Indiana landscape. The score underlines the American heartland setting of the story and inspires a sonic grandeur that is evocative of Aaron Copland's nationalistic orchestrations. The use of high-energy rock music, however, underscores the low-culture working class ethic of the team and its youthful determination to overcome the odds and win the state championship. Much as with the evolutionary development of "Rocky's Theme," the score generally builds in rhythmic and dramatic intensity as the film progresses. It evolves from the sedate heartland music of the opening to more aggressive percussion-oriented music following the town vote to keep their coach, and finally it moves to a concentrated double time rhythm in the percussion when last-minute victories are won by the team in sectional and regional finals. In addition to increasing the tempo, the soundtrack also uses more reverb and echo as it progresses, effectively painting the increasing depth and importance of the achievements of both coach and team.

The most musically dramatic moments occur during the state championship match at the conclusion of the film. The tempo momentarily slows as ominous sounding bass notes in the synthesizer portray the powerful opposing team, a predominantly African American squad from a much larger high school. The only significant appearance of African Americans in the film, the moment is unfortunately sonically painted by a brooding, "darker" tone color that, perhaps unintentionally, reinforces stereotypical notions of the threat of African American masculinity. The musical climax of the film takes place just after the team wins the championship. The rock music and celebratory crowd noises gradually dissipate, giving way to the orchestra alone. A solemn but uplifting victory theme is poignantly rendered by the French horn and then taken up by the strings— essentially using orchestral cachet (and its often stereotypically elitist associations with history, wealth, and edification) to signify the importance of the victory and the reinforcement of the American dream of success achieved through hard work.

Hoosiers, on first impression, may seem to emphasize the effectiveness of teamwork as opposed to the mythos of American individualism, as clearly promoted by *Rocky*. Indeed, Aaron Baker identifies only nine feature films about sports history that are not overtly centered on individualism: *The Harlem Globetrotters* (1951), *The Bingo Long Traveling All-Stars & Motor Kings* (1976), *Miracle on Ice* (1981), *Hoosiers* (1986), *Eight Men Out* (1988), *A League of Their Own* (1992), *When We Were Kings* (1996), *Soul of the Game* (1996), and *Remember the Titans* (2000).[7] Baker notes, "even these focus on two or three main

---

[7]   Baker, *Contesting Identities*, 10.

characters."[8] In the case of *Hoosiers*, the importance of teamwork and small-town community in overcoming the odds is subordinated to the individual heroism of the star player's game-winning basket and the more dominant storyline of the triumphant redemption of the team's coach.

The combined narratives of triumph over adversity and the heroic accomplishment of the individual will serve to reinforce a public perception of the mythos of the indomitability of the American spirit. For all the studio attempts to use sports as apolitical subject matter, these films can be read as fostering quasi-nationalistic agendas. On another level, however, such films can be viewed as devolving into a form of Social Darwinism.[9] They represent a reinforcement of the "survival of the fittest" ideal that veers dangerously into loaded territory, given the preponderance of white, male, heterosexual heroes celebrated in such films. The musical evolution that occurs in both *Rocky* and *Hoosiers* literally and figuratively underscores such Darwinist content.

One of the most celebrated boxing movies to inculcate musically the notion of ethnic upward mobility is *Gentleman Jim* (1942). Starring Errol Flynn in the title role, the movie recounts the story of 1890s boxer "Gentleman" Jim Corbett's rise to the heavyweight title. The film glorifies Corbett's individualism but at the same time actively negotiates through various notions of masculinity, ethnicity, and social class. Set in the context of the class tumult associated with the Gilded Age, the film depicts Corbett's Horatio Alger-like attempt to gain upper-class respectability. Unlike his contemporaries, Corbett was known for promoting himself as a gentleman and actively cultivated sophisticated manners, a charismatic personality, and a stylish fashion sense. These traits were carried into the ring and further promoted in his development of a "scientific" approach to boxing. Corbett renounced the working-class brawling-style masculinity of his Irish-American heritage, epitomized by his rival, John L. Sullivan, in an attempt to define a more respectable type of prizefighter. In essence Corbett, through employing Marquis of Queensbury rules, a cerebral boxing methodology, and polished manners, presented himself as a more evolved and "civilized" example of Irish masculinity. It was an image that would be judged more acceptable by the upper class to which Corbett aspired.

The film's musical score, directed by Leo Forbstein and composed by Heinz Roenheld, actively reinforces and underlines such evolutionary features. Though the boxing footage is set realistically without music, the parts of the film that remind the audience of Corbett's Irish heritage are underscored with orchestral arrangements of traditional Irish folk tunes. Of particular note is the use of "Dear Old Donegal," which recurs whenever the Corbett family is featured (inevitably engaged in domestic fisticuffs). The lyrics tell the tale of an Irish immigrant to America and the desire to return to Ireland:

---

[8]   Ibid.

[9]   Please see a more detailed discussion of this concept later in this chapter in regards to my analysis of *When We Were Kings*.

It seems like only yesterday
I sailed from out of Cork.
A wanderer from old Erin's isle,
I landed in New York.
There wasn't a soul to greet me there,
A stranger on your shore,
But Irish luck was with me here,
And riches came galore.
And now that I'm going back again
To dear old Erin's isle ...

Combined with an upbeat jig rhythm, the lyrics, as in many Irish folk songs, highlight both the indelible pull of the home country but also the upward mobility offered by the New World. In contrast to the "primitive" evocation of Irish folk music, a variety of cultured Strauss waltzes—including "Rosen aus dem Süden," Op. 388, and "Kunstlerleben," Op. 316—set in full orchestral string arrangements are used to portray the upper-class world of the Olympia Club to which Corbett aspires.

The musical contrast is most dramatically made when Corbett is depicted at the opera, listening to the overture to *Die Schöne Galathée* (*The Beautiful Galathea*) by Franz von Suppé and suitably attired in a tuxedo, before his fight with the reigning champion John L. Sullivan. This image of high-cultured musical taste is directly juxtaposed with a montage of images showing Sullivan, the quintessential Irish brawler, in rigorous physical training sessions that included chopping wood. In contrast to Corbett's operatic pre-fight routine, Sullivan's "primitive" training techniques are underscored by more Irish folk music. The montage is concluded with a musical segue to the "Dear Old Donegal" ritornello. Finally, a subdued orchestral arrangement of the well-known Scottish tune "Auld Lang Syne" is used to highlight the poignancy of the moment Sullivan surrenders his championship belt to Corbett. The haunting melody and lyrical references to remembrances of "old times" comments both on the nostalgia for the past champion—Sullivan was a hero to the emerging Irish immigrant community—and also on Corbett's general loss of connection to his Irish ancestry. Moreover, the tune and its lyrics—"Should old acquaintance be forgot and never brought to mind?"—also comment on the social evolution of the immigrant community itself and the need to remember roots. Something of the danger of this loss of connection is embodied in the triumph of Corbett's civilized and "gentlemanly" approach to fighting and association with high-cultured European classical music.

Outside the movie many working class people dreamt of making the same class transition as Corbett succeeded in achieving during the Gilded Age. Indeed, the boxing community and media, who gave him the nickname "Gentleman," both supported Corbett's attempt to give the sport an aura of respectability, even though it was primarily thought of as a lower-class form of entertainment. However, the wealthy boxing fans who came (and still do) to watch members of the lower class literally fight for respectability, both in reality and in the movie, were engaged in their own form of Spencerian Social Darwinism.

The soundtrack to Martin Scorsese's acclaimed *Raging Bull* (1980) exhibits similar traits of Social Darwinism. The score for this violent biopic, starring Robert De Niro as 1949 middleweight champion boxer Jake LaMotta, was produced by popular musician Robbie Robertson. Robertson, who gained fame as the lead guitarist for the Band, wrote the source music, scored three pieces, and helped select additional songs for the film. A wide variety of primarily Italian popular and African American jazz artists were drawn on for background music in the film, including Ella Fitzgerald, the Ink Spots, the Mills Brothers, Tony Bennett, Harry James, Gene Krupa, Nat King Cole, Louis Prima, Perry Como, Russ Colombo, Artie Shaw, Frankie Lane, and Ray Charles.

By far the largest part of the music, however, reflects LaMotta's Italian heritage. In the 2005 DVD release of the film, Robertson quipped, "You could smell the tomato sauce" in the music. Echoing the folk–classical musical divisions present in *Gentleman Jim*, the music in *Raging Bull* alternates between the working-class Italian popular music of Louis Prima or Russ Colombo and high-art Italian opera, the latter accounting for the most striking musical moments in the work. The acclaimed opening and closing credits feature LaMotta, shot in slow motion, warming up in the ring (the camera angle is such that the ropes resemble musical staff lines through which LaMotta dances). A powerful yet heartrending rendition of Pietro Mascagni's *Cavelleria Rusticana Intermezzo* underscores LaMotta's dance and underlines the pathos of his story, perhaps likening his fate to the tragic life and death of the peasant character Turiddu from the opera. Just as Jim Corbett is portrayed in *Gentleman Jim*, LaMotta fights to win respect for his family and his Italian heritage, and the movie documents his meteoric rise, subsequent fall, and ultimate redemption.

Racial Identity

One of the most telling aspects of sports movies is the sheer number of them that are dedicated to white male nostalgia—as opposed to female or black male issues. Given the high profile of African American sports heroes, this would seem something of a major oversight by Hollywood. Sports films featuring African Americans were infrequent until the civil rights era. The 1950s saw the advent of a number of films based on black athletes, such as *The Jackie Robinson Story* (1950), *The Harlem Globetrotters* (1951), and *The Joe Louis Story* (1953), that were inspired by the gradual integration of previously all-white professional sports. Such films, however, emphasized self-reliance and white paternalism, avoiding more problematic notions of socially deterministic features of racial identity. Such films, among other attributes, were marked by a lack of color photography or lavish sets or production numbers that characterized other popular films of the day, such as *Singin' in the Rain* (1952). The absence of visual spectacle and elaborate production values underlined a strategy of conservative self-denial and reserve that characterized the public persona of African American advancement in general. Such reserve was, of course, in marked contrast to the exuberant creativity that often marked the athletic performance styles of black athletes such as the Harlem Globetrotters.

The soundtracks to these movies were similarly reserved in nature. Rather than embracing the improvisational flamboyance and virtuosity of African American musical styles, characteristic of jazz or rhythm and blues, the music was typically a conservative, if at times dramatic, romantic symphonic score. Such soundtracks, as with the overall production value of the films themselves, reflected the need for restraint and reserve that was prescribed for and expected of African Americans in a white-controlled market.

The relatively recent popularity of basketball changed this dynamic in African American sports films. Since the 1980s, basketball has become an increasingly high-profile part of American popular culture. During this period Michael Jordan replaced Muhammad Ali as America's best-known athlete, and broadcast revenues for the NBA climbed 1,000 percent from 1986 to 1998.[10] The growing popularity of basketball in North America saw a concomitant increase in films about the sport, the majority of which played off white fascination with African American culture. Films such as *White Men Can't Jump* (1992), *The Air Up There* (1994), *Hoop Dreams*, *Above the Rim* (1994), *Space Jam*, *He Got Game* (1998), *Coach Carter* (2005), *Glory Road* (2006), and *Semi-Pro* (2008) attest to Hollywood's relatively recent fascination with the game.

Michael Jordan features prominently in several of these movies, appearing in *Space Jam* and *He Got Game* and being referenced in many others. In his description of a *Sports Illustrated* advertisement that played on ESPN featuring Michael Jordan, John Edgar Wideman points out the NBA's calculated interest in fostering a white audience:

> ... a gallery of young people, male and female, express their wonder, admiration awe and identification with Michael Jordan's supernatural basketball prowess. He can truly fly. The chorus is all white, good looking, clean cut, casually but hiply dressed. An audience of consumers the ad both targets and embodies. A very calculated kind of wish fulfillment at work. A premeditated attempt to bond MJ with these middle-class white kids with highly disposable incomes.[11]

The advertisement exemplifies what Nelson George referred to as a "Black [athletic] aesthetic" in its construction of a black masculinity that aligns with traditional notions of identity in the African American community.[12] There is

---

[10]   Baker, *Contesting Identities*, 30.

[11]   John Edgar Wideman, "Michael Jordan leaps the great divide," *Esquire*, November 1990, 210. Also see Baker, *Contesting Identities*, 31.

[12]   George, *Elevating the Game*, 240.

living proof, and therefore reassurance to both blacks and whites, that at least some African Americans have access to the economic advantages of the white community. However, as discussed in Chapter 5, there is also an undercurrent of a hypermasculine, intimidating menace stereotypically embodied in the black male athlete. This is an image personified in basketball by players such as Charles Barkley or Allen Iverson and other players who, at least superficially, embody attributes of a threatening "gangsta" persona. This more threatening form of blackness is also reinforced and replicated by certain rap artists. Michael Jordan, however, as evidenced by this advertisement and through the first-name familiarity engendered by Gatorade's "Be like Mike" campaign, has been corporately elevated to represent a raceless utopia. He has essentially been commodified, such that our apparent friendship with and consumption of him contributes to a sense of raceless social harmony.

Basketball films such as *Hoosiers*, in which a rural all-white team overcomes the threatening Other of an urban all-black team to reaffirm what are stereotypically regarded as traditional white values, often take underlying racial issues as their focus. In contrast to *Hoosiers*, *White Men Can't Jump*, for example, uses African American prowess at basketball to help a white man realize his own identity. Musically the film is dominated by the presence of iconic African American performers such as Duke Ellington ("Mood Indigo"), James Brown ("I Got You [I Feel Good]" and "Super Bad"), Aretha Franklin, ("If I Lose"), Jimi Hendrix ("Purple Haze"), and rappers Cypress Hill and Queen Latifah. White performers are represented in the movie by country music artist George Jones's "Help Me Make It Through the Night" and the "Jeopardy Theme" (written by Merv Griffin). The film thus traverses a variety of "stereotypically" African American musical styles from rap and funk to R&B, as well as the purportedly white styles of "country and western" and television jingles. As such, *White Men Can't Jump* plays with musical stereotypes as much as it does racial stereotypes. Notably the film features artists such as Boyz II Men, James Brown, and Ray Charles, who achieved success in both black and white communities and thereby reinforces the movie's theme of the importance of interracial friendship to the ultimate benefit of individuals from both races. Indeed, listening to Ray Charles's rendition of "Careless Love" prompts the white character Billy to proclaim, tongue in cheek, "Can somebody tell me why this Negro is singing cowboy music?" Nonetheless, films such as *White Men Can't Jump*, alongside *The Air Up There* and *Above the Rim*—films that also ostensibly promote the benefits of interracial friendship— simultaneously reaffirm conventions of black representation.

In *White Men Can't Jump*, Sidney, played by Wesley Snipes, is an African American street basketball player who, though physically unintimidating, plays a Michael Jordanesque creative form of the game and teams up with an unassuming white player, Billy, played by Woody Harrelson. In contrast to Sidney, Billy plays a conservative textbook brand of basketball that stresses conventional skills and avoids Sidney's more improvisational approach. Billy and Sidney initially gain the advantage over opponents by superficially looking vulnerable so that the opposition initially underestimates their abilities based on physical appearance, i.e., short and white. Though initially successful together, the two teammates run into friction because of their different playing styles and ideas on racial identity. It is a musical discussion in Billy's car that brings these cultural differences to a head. When Billy plays a tape of Jimi Hendrix's "Purple Haze," Sidney derisively tells him that as a white person he might listen to the music but he does not "hear" it. Sidney is trying to point out that, much as Billy cannot appreciate improvisation on the court, he likewise does not hear the improvisation in Hendrix's guitar solo.[13] In what Stuart Hall calls "the metaphorical use of the musical vocabulary" of black popular culture, Sidney implies that Billy is incapable of appreciating the broader cultural significance of improvisation.[14]

Throughout the movie the soundtrack reinforces the notion that the improvisatory style of basketball, which is practised by numerous other black players in the film, has its roots in music. The admonition that you can listen without hearing forms a recurring theme in the movie. And Billy repeats the same adage to Sidney when he plays a George Jones tune. Underlining the association of white people with country music, Billy wins back his girlfriend by playing her a country and western ballad, co-written in real life by Woody Harrelson, on his acoustic guitar. The virtuosity of Sidney's play is directly underscored by that of various African American musical performances, notably James Brown's in "Super Bad," which marks the aggressive trash talking of the final two-on-two championship which Billy and Sidney ultimately win. Likewise, the film ends with the Venice Beach Boys, a group of African American street corner *a cappella* singers improvising a rendition of "A Closer Walk with Thee" as the screen fades to black. Stereotypical black images are also prominent in the film, however, as in the case of one defeated black opponent whose first reaction is to threateningly produce a knife and then go for his gun. Thus, while promoting the benefits of interracial relationships, *White Men Can't Jump* nonetheless simultaneously promulgates two formulaic stereotypes of African American men—that of the violent gangsta and that of the exceptional athlete.

The cartoon basketball movie *Space Jam* provides yet another musical reinforcement of African American masculine norms. The film revolves around a fantastical plot that sees five small aliens who, intimidated by their boss, arrive on earth to abduct Warner Brothers cartoon characters to have them appear at an amusement park in outer space. The cartoon characters challenge the aliens to a basketball game for their freedom. The aliens arrive for the game with gangsta identities stolen from actual NBA players and the Looney Tunes characters attempt to fight fire with fire by abducting Michael Jordan to play for their team. The alien "Monstars," as they are dubbed, consist mostly of the abducted black

---

[13]   See Baker, *Contesting Identities*, 37.

[14]   Stuart Hall, "What is this 'black' in black popular culture?" in David Morely and Kuan-Hsing Chen (eds), *Stuart Hall: Critical Dialogues in Popular Culture* (New York: Routledge, 1996), 473. Also see Baker, *Contesting Identities*, 37.

NBA players Charles Barkley, Muggsy Bogues, Larry Johnson, and Patrick Ewing; the lone exception is the abducted white player Shawn Bradley. The aliens take to the court accompanied by the rap song "Hit 'Em High (The Monstars Anthem)," performed by Busta Rhymes, Coolio, LL Cool J, Method Man, and B-Real, cementing the gangsta personae of the alien players with aggressive gangsta rap. Though the aliens, underscored by rap music, dominate the first half, the inevitable victory by the Looney Tunes characters in the second half reiterates both the utopian view of basketball and the mythos of the individual, as Jordan is largely responsible for their victory. *Space Jam* as such depoliticizes the gangsta stereotype, providing a comical comment on the aliens' desire to exploit others, in contrast to the generosity and self-reliant talent of Jordan.[15]

The NBA player characters also make several insider jokes that to some degree reinforce racial stereotypes. When Barkley prays to God to give him back his skill, he swears to stop his trash talk and no longer have affairs with Madonna, sending up his image as a tough trash talker and in reference to his own real-life affair with the singer. Also, Bradley contemplates becoming a missionary once again, in reference to his own experiences as a Mormon missionary. Thus, though they are linked in their mutual appeals to God, we are presented with the stereotypical image of an aggressive libido-driven black man on the one hand and a clean-cut white missionary on the other. Similarly, when Larry Bird responds negatively to Bill Murray's question as to whether he might potentially be able to play in the NBA, Murray jokes, "It's because I'm white, isn't it?" Indeed, other than Shawn Bradley, white men in the movie are portrayed as un-athletic and appear only as either team owners (Danny DeVito), doctors, or, most significantly, in the grossly overweight character of Jordan's bumbling new manager, Stan Podlack (Wayne Knight). Such images are contrasted with the spectacular, indeed seemingly superhuman alien, abilities of the black basketball players.

The *Space Jam* soundtrack was one of the most successful in sports film history. Consisting exclusively of performances by African American artists, in addition to the rap artists of "Hit 'Em High," it included performances of "Fly Like an Eagle" by Seal, "For You I Will" by Monica, "The Winner" by Coolio, and "I Believe I Can Fly" by Robert Kelly that all charted as singles on the *Billboard* charts. Other notable performances include "Basketball Jones" by Barry White and "Upside Down (Round and Round)" by Salt-n-Pepa. The soundtrack earned good reviews and peaked on the *Billboard* 200 chart at No. 2. Going double platinum less than two months after its release in January 1997, it was certified six times platinum in 2001.

By far the album's biggest hit, however, was Robert Kelly's "I Believe I Can Fly," which went to No. 1 around the world and won the 1998 Grammy Award for best song written specifically for a motion picture. The song bookends the movie. It is heard at the beginning of the film to underscore a flashback of the young Michael Jordan dreaming of playing in the NBA and at the end after the

---

15   Baker, 40.

Monstars have been defeated. The end of the verse and chorus proclaim: "If I can see it, then I can do it / If I just believe it, there's nothing to it / I believe I can fly / I believe I can touch the sky / I think about it every night and day / Spread my wings and fly away / I believe I can soar / I see me running through that open door / I believe I can fly …"[16] In addition to framing sports as the main means to ascend the socio-economic ladder of success, the song also reinforces the notion of the utopian belief in the individual to overcome all odds (gravity being not the least of which) in the manner of a Michael Jordan. As previously mentioned, the theme of flight is also taken up in another hit song from the movie, Seal's rendition of Steve Miller's "Fly Like an Eagle," which is also used to underscore some of Jordan's extraordinary jumping ability.

The use of gangsterized aliens in *Space Jam* also plays into something of a common trope in African American popular culture—that of Afro-futurism. As coined by cultural critic Mark Dery, the term "Afro-futurism" refers to African American signification that appropriates images of advanced technology and alien and/or prosthetically enhanced (cyborg) futures.[17] Though found in science fiction and films, Afro-futurism has been particularly prominent in music, as reflected in the experimental cosmological jazz of Sun Ra. Similarly, George Clinton's futuristic funk stylings on *Mothership Connection*, the techno-tribalism of Miles Davis's *On the Corner*, Herbie Hancock's jazz-cyber funk on *Future Shock*, and Bernie Worrell's *Blacktronic Science* all manifest a fusion of science fiction, techno-futurism, and a mystical African heritage. More recently artists such as OutKast (*ATLiens*), Kanye West ("Stronger" and "RoboCop"), and Janelle Monáe ("Many Moons") have continued the idea of alien Afro-futurism.[18]

Such Afro-futuristic musical and artistic expressions are typically concerned with the creation of mythologies based on confrontations between historical prophetic imagination, such as Egyptian theories of the afterlife, and modern alienated black existence stemming from slavery. As such, Afro-futurism often taps into a black diasporic consciousness that seeks to return to an inaccessible utopian homeland that outer space metaphorically represents. In this sense, black artists employing tropes of science fiction imagery created powerful images of the potential for black wealth and power—a futuristic vision in which the previously marginalized aliens assume control of the world. In *Space Jam*, of course, this vision is ultimately and perhaps ironically thwarted in part by Michael Jordan. Indeed, as Wideman points out above, Michael Jordan's popularity is predicated on his "supernatural basketball prowess. He can truly fly."[19] The Afro-futuristic

---

[16] Words and music by R. Kelly.

[17] Mark Dery, "Black to the future: Interviews with Samuel R. Delany, Greg Tate, and Tricia Rose," *South Atlantic Quarterly* 92/4 (1993), 735–78, 736.

[18] For more on the musical implications of Afro-futurism, see Ken McLeod, "Space oddities: Aliens, futurism and meaning in rock music," *Popular Music* 23/2 (Fall 2003), 315–33.

[19] See footnote 11.

notion of flight and literal escape from Earth can be understood as reaching as far back as nineteenth-century Negro spirituals. Many spirituals reflect a desire to reject Earth and the hardship and suffering it contains. "Swing Low, Sweet Chariot," "All God's Chillun Got Wings," and "This World Is Not My Home" are all thematically based on rejecting and taking flight from the material world. Equating these spiritual journeys to extraterrestrial travel and analogous themes of escaping Earth through superhuman athletic flight as described above is not difficult. Indeed, the parallels can be glimpsed in other films such as *Hancock* (2008), starring Will Smith. In this film an African American is endowed with superhuman powers, including supersonic flight, invulnerability, and immortality.

The basketball film genre, perhaps more than any other media form, has cemented the relationship between sports and rap music and images of African American masculinity. From Tupac Shakur's appearance in *Above the Rim* to the cartoon gangsta fantasy of *Space Jam*, basketball is explicitly linked to rap music as a co-signifier of struggle, creativity, and extraordinary ability for both the African American and white communities. As such, rap and basketball combine to produce a utopian vision of success in contemporary urban society.

Boxing Movies, Masculinity and Race

One of the fundamental and recurring issues in sports films is the conflict between the body and the mind, the inherent tension between the physical and the metaphysical. Such tensions are evident in the game fixing of *Eight Men Out* (1988), the metaphysical qualities of *Field of Dreams* (1989), and the transcendence of physical and class limitations in innumerable films such as *Rocky*, *Chariots of Fire*, *Seabiscuit*, *Cinderella Man* (2005), or *The Wrestler* (2008).

Boxing films, however, foreground the body, the male body in particular. In addition, more consistently than other films, and as demonstrated in the previous discussion of *Gentleman Jim*, *Rocky*, and *Raging Bull*, boxing movies call into question issues surrounding race and class conflict. Joyce Carol Oates has proclaimed that boxing is "the most tragic of all sports because more than any human activity it consumes the very excellence it displays—its drama is this very consumption."[20] To some extent the boxing movie, with its evocation of physical decline, also implies a direct confrontation with death. In some part this may account for the fact that more Hollywood movies have been devoted to boxing than any other sport.[21]

---

[20]   Joyce Carol Oates, *On Boxing* (London: Bloomsbury, 1987), 16.

[21]   See Aaron Baker, "… A left/right combination," in Aaron Baker and Todd Boyd (eds), *Out of Bounds: Sports, Media and the Politics of Identity* (Bloomington IN: Indiana University Press, 1997), 161. Baker notes that a program called *Knockout! Hollywood's Love Affair with Boxing* shown on American Movie Classics in 1992 claimed that as of 1992 more than 400 films had been devoted to boxing since 1910.

The typical narrative in boxing movies is of the boxer's quick rise from economic disadvantage to the title, followed by an equally fast fall from grace that is typically precipitated by the seduction of wealth and fame, followed by some type of final redemption.[22] This relatively simple heroic narrative schema, as such, provides one of the most overt replications and reinforcements of the utopian mythos of American individualism and helps explain why so many boxing movies have been made and why the roles have appealed to some of the biggest box office stars. Jimmy Cagney, John Garfield, Errol Flynn, Kirk Douglas, Burt Lancaster, Paul Newman, Tony Curtis, James Earl Jones, Robert De Niro, Tom Cruise, Antonio Banderas, Denzel Washington, Will Smith, Russell Crowe and, of course, Sylvester Stallone, have all indulged in prizefighting roles. One of the most notable musical connections in this regard is Elvis Presley's role as a boxer in *Kid Galahad* (1962), regarded by many as one of his best performances.

As discussed in relation to *Gentleman Jim*, *Rocky* and *Raging Bull*, boxing movies often speak more directly to issues of class and capitalism than other sports film genres. In most boxing films, a young man (or more recently a young woman) chooses to fight, as boxing appears to be the only means to escape a life of economic hardship and disadvantage. Professional boxing in North America has always relied on youth from marginalized communities with limited opportunities for self-determination. Until World War I, Irish and Jewish boxers dominated the professional prizefighting ranks. Following that war, Italians and fighters of Eastern European extraction became dominant. After World War II it was African American and Chicano boxers who inherited the inner city ghettos and consequently assumed dominance in the boxing world. Members of all these ethnic groups still continued to fight, however, often in the lower weight classes, and promoters would often set up matches between ethnic groups and bill the contests as struggles for national or religious pride.[23]

Boxing movies by their very nature involve the notion of conflict, be it the conflict between individuals; between mind/soul and body; between good and evil; or between opportunity and ethnic, racial, or economic difference. All sports movies to some extent involve conflict, though typically in a far less overt manner and to a more subtle degree than boxing films. The boxer, not unlike similar portrayals of gangsters, is driven to achieve material success by a desire for integration into the dominant culture—a desire that often alienates him from his family and community. As has been discussed earlier in this chapter, boxing movies typically depict the struggle of the underclass as a physical, psychological, and moral battle for success. At their core many boxing films thus question the notion that money and fame are the only standards by which self-improvement can be socially recognized. These problems point back to the basic conflict between body and soul and a need for the integration of the sensual and the psychic. Fight

---

[22] Baker, *Contesting Identities*, 101.

[23] Steven Reiss, *City Games: The Evolution of American Urban Society and the Rise of Sports* (Urbana: University of Illinois Press, 1989), 110–16.

films are also, however, a metaphor for the condition of modernity that sees the increasingly complex forces of our institutional society oppress and overwhelm the individual. The genre, therefore, can be read as expressing a thinly veiled critique of social conditions and the success ethic that dominates the modern Western consciousness.

As previously mentioned, the need to integrate the sensual and psychic is a fundamental conflict in boxing films, and one that to a lesser degree underlies all sports films. Music is one of the key means by which this integration is negotiated. The inherent rhythmic and melodic tensions and resolutions of music often naturally parallel the dramatic trajectories of the character's story.

Roland Barthes, in his essay "The World of Wrestling," compares the sport of wrestling to boxing. According to Barthes, "The gesture of the vanquished wrestler [signifies] to the world a defeat, which far from disguising, he emphasizes and holds like a pause in music … "[24] Barthes here recognizes the metaphoric dramatic similarities of music and the drama involved in wrestling. The comparison elevates wrestlers, as opposed to boxers, to the realm of actors in ancient Greek drama who "reflect the intelligible representation of moral situations which are usually private … "[25] Barthes concludes:

> When the hero or villain of the drama, the man who was seen a few minutes earlier possessed by moral rage … leaves the wrestling hall, impassive, anonymous, carrying a small suitcase and arm-in-arm with his wife, no one can doubt that wrestling holds that power of transmutation which is common to the Spectacle and to Religious Worship. In the ring … wrestlers remain gods because they are, for a few moments, the key which opens Nature, the pure gesture which separates Good from Evil, and unveils a form of Justice which is at last intelligible.[26]

Barthes believes that, distinct from the theatricality associated with wrestling, boxers are required to prove and reveal their actual moral character during the confrontation. As Aaron Baker has argued, however, "the slugger style of prizefighting popularized by television during the late 1940s and 1950s represented an uncritical spectacle of masculinity much like what Barthes describes in wrestling.[27] To a large extent the theatricality of boxing, influenced by the well-known pre-fight antics of Muhammad Ali, is represented in *Rocky*, particularly through the actions of Apollo Creed. Creed, like subsequent opponents in the *Rocky* sequels, is overtly set up as the personification of Evil— the African American threat to the American dream of self-determination and

---

[24]   Roland Barthes, *Mythologies* (London: Vintage Books, 1993), 16.
[25]   Ibid., 18.
[26]   Ibid., 25.
[27]   Baker, *Contesting Identities*, 125.

upward mobility. As such, he is presented as physically but not morally superior to Rocky. A similar plot device is found in all of the *Rocky* sequels.

As manifested in the 1910 heavyweight championship bout between Jim Jeffries and the black champion Jack Johnson, early twentieth-century Western culture identified the heavyweight prizefighter as the personification of manhood and, by extension, of evolution. Johnson's victory, and thus the possibility that a black male could be the epitome of evolution, caused widespread consternation across white America, such that Johnson was infamously forced into exile on concocted charges of consorting with white women. Later in the century, after African American fighters came to dominate the ranks of heavyweight title holders, a long list of "Great White Hopes," stretching from Max Schmeling to Gerry Coony, carried the "white hopes" of regaining supreme masculinity. Such thinking was, in effect, merely an extension of the commonly held belief in Social Darwinism, a term that became popular following the publication of Herbert Spencer's *Principles of Biology* (1864) and Richard Hofstader's *Social Darwinism in American Thought* (1944). The concept extends Darwin's idea that competition between organisms drives biological evolutionary change into the notion that a "survival of the fittest" competition between individuals, ethnic groups, or nations also drives human social evolution. When misapplied to race, as it often was, the logic of Social Darwinian speciously held that the Anglo-Saxon race led the world and was hence the most highly evolved. In the arena of boxing, the heavyweight champion was construed as the most dangerous man on the planet and the peak of evolution; thus the necessity to maintain a white champion.

Against this infamous backdrop of racially loaded incarnations of masculinity perhaps nowhere has a connection between African American sports and music been more closely drawn than in Leon Gast's Academy Award-winning documentary of 1996, *When We Were Kings*. The film documents the "Rumble in the Jungle" heavyweight title bout held in Kinshasa, Zaire, between George Foreman and Muhammad Ali on October 30, 1974, and the elaborate musical festival that accompanied the bout. Ali was a three-to-one underdog to the then-undefeated and seemingly invincible world champion George Foreman. Foreman was physically larger, more powerful, and seven years younger. Nonetheless, Ali won the fight by repeatedly leaning on the ropes and allowing Foreman to punch himself out and, in the process, elevating the term "rope-a-dope" into popular consciousness.

In addition to receiving the Academy Award for best documentary feature in 1997, the film was almost universally acclaimed as, in the words of *Variety* critic Todd McCarthy, "a watershed moment in modern black culture and history."[28] The film is undeniably entertaining and well-crafted and presents an interesting perspective on an important moment in both sports and African American social

---

[28] Todd McCarthy, "When we were kings," *Variety*, Monday, February 12, 1996; also see the *San Francisco Examiner*, Friday, February 14, 1997.

history. Nonetheless the film betrays some of its idealism through its construction that, perhaps unwittingly, often resorts to the tenets of Social Darwinism.[29]

Gast's documentary records the crowning of the latest incarnation of supreme masculinity and, in so doing, revisits notions of racial superiority. Of course this was not a fight between members of different races; however, the film reconstitutes the black–white dichotomy that had been familiar to fight fans for decades. Aside from brief comments from director Spike Lee, the film's primary narrators are Norman Mailer and George Plimpton, and by extension Gast himself. As Julio Rodriguez has recognized, both Plimpton and Mailer were authors associated with the white liberal left, then under assault by opponents of affirmative action, who termed the practice reverse discrimination.[30] Both authors, in attempting to connect to a notion of working-class authenticity that would avoid charges of overly elitist and cerebral journalism, sought to bring their social activism to the realm of the black sporting body. Mailer, in his book *White Negro*, particularly appropriated the black body, claiming:

> The Negro had stayed alive and begun to grow by following the needs of his body … relinquishing the pleasures of the mind for the more obligatory pleasures of the body, and in his music he gave voice to … his rage and the infinite variations of joy, lust … [and the] scream and despair of his orgasm.[31]

Mailer's characterization is, however, merely an extension of the reductive racist binary that associates white with the mind and black with the body. In keeping with this dichotomy Gast associates the white narrators with Ali himself. Framing the events through the memories of white male narrators (rather than the living participants) allows for the victorious Ali to become an embodiment of white masculinity. As Julio Rodriquez has observed of this documentary, "There is no real Ali in the film, only white writers."[32]

The film opens with images of African children dancing and singing in the streets in combination with clips of Ali's career and scenes of Zaire's revolution juxtaposed against stills from a KKK rally and civil rights demonstrations in the United States. Set to the Jazz Crusaders' energetically muscular festival performance of "Young Rabbits," an aggressive "masculine" musical stance to the film is immediately established as the sharply percussive syncopated breaks underscore the opening credits and simulate punches. The visual montage of the

---

[29]   The observation of Social Darwinism in this work was first made by Julio Rodriguez, "Documenting myth: racial representation in Leon Gast's *When We Were Kings*," in John Bloom, *Sports Matters*: *Race, Recreation, and Culture* (New York: New York University Press, 2002), 209–22.

[30]   Rodriguez, 213.

[31]   Norman Mailer, *The White Negro: Superficial Reflections on the Hipster* (San Francisco: City Lights Books, 1957), 4; also quoted in Rodriguez, 213.

[32]   Rodriguez, 214.

opening sequences effectively establishes Ali as an intermediary figure on the continuum between the struggles of blacks in the United States and in Africa. It is a relationship that is underscored throughout the film. Ali views the upcoming fight as a type of homecoming. He bonds with the black pilots that fly his plane to Zaire, shadow boxes with locals on a training run, and exhorts fans to shout "Ali bome aye" (Ali kill him), a chant which was intoned by thousands on the night of the fight. Indeed, Ali is identified by African artist Malik Bowens in the film as being the "more African" of the two boxers.

George Foreman, on the other hand, is clearly identified with the First World, in particular with the former Belgian overlords. Malik Bowens claimed, "Before he arrived in Africa, we thought Foreman was a white man." As Rodriguez has pointed out, Foreman stepped off the plane with a German shepherd, the same dog used to police the populace when Zaire was a Belgian colony, and he is depicted valiantly trying to learn French in a forlorn attempt to connect with his African audience.[33] Foreman's negative portrayal is furthered by his manager, Dick Sadler, who notes the unfamiliar landscape, the poverty, and the heat of Zaire and derisively comments, "Thank God our grandpappies caught that boat!"[34] Ali, quick to seize on the negative press coverage of Foreman, immediately played up his own connection to Africa and labeled Foreman as a "Belgian oppressor," taunting him with statements such as "If you behave like that my African friends will put you in a pot."[35] Foreman is at once characterized as a First World oppressor, dangerous, mean, powerful, and threatening, a persona that according to Norman Mailer "embodied Negritude." On the other hand, Ali mediates the connection between stereotypes of primitive barbarous black Africans and the more evolved, Americanized Africans.

Though evident in the narrative and visual imagery, the dichotomy between "evolved" African Americans and "primitive" Africans is particularly highlighted through the use of music in the documentary. Described by one critic as a "black Woodstock," the fight was originally intended to be the culmination of a three-day African and soul music festival. Promoters enlisted James Brown and B.B. King to headline the event along with an all-star lineup of African and African American artists. Gast's comments to the DVD release of the film note that it was the music, not boxing, that originally inspired the documentary: "What most intrigued [me] … was the unique opportunity to open the world's eyes and ears to 18 of the best musical acts on the African continent." The reality of Gast's film is, however, quite different. With the exception of a performance by Miriam Makeba, African artists are almost completely overlooked, and the few shots of their performances that get used are uncredited. In addition, the African performances are completely absent from the film's subsequent soundtrack CD release. Gast characterizes the

---

[33]   Rodriguez, 215.

[34]   "It takes a heap of Salongo," *Newsweek*, September 23, 1974, 72; also see Rodriguez, 215.

[35]   "Five minute massacre," *Time*, April 8, 1974, 57.

African American performers as being, for the most part, dismissive of the country in which they were going to perform. Several of the African American musicians, preparing to depart, are shown to be unable to pronounce the word "Zaire" in a moment that Gast, ungenerously at best, sets against the Spinners' festival rendition of "I'm Coming Home."

Throughout the film African American musicians are presented as symbolically colonizing their nameless African counterparts while hypermasculinized soul, funk, and blues are projected as more evolved forms of native styles. As such the musical language of the movie is framed in the rhetoric of Social Darwinism. African musicians are cast as primitive versions of their more evolved American counterparts. Shots of Western black musicians rehearsing, performing, traveling, and partying are repeatedly juxtaposed with images of Africans dancing, singing, drumming, and transporting goods on their heads.[36] The seemingly sophisticated decadence of the Western musician is thus played against images of Zairians that are constructed as "primitive." Furthering this evolutionary message, Gast casts Zaire in the light of romantic primitivism, typically presenting native Africans as either violent or childlike in comparison with the more sophisticated representations of the visiting African Americans—particularly as embodied in the charismatic wit of both Ali and Don King, the promoter of the fight. Don King at one point is depicted quoting Shakespeare to George Plimpton. However, when Norman Mailer discusses the political situation in Zaire and President Mobutu's dictatorial killings, we are presented with an uncredited festival performance by an African dance troupe singing an ode to Mobutu. As this is one of the few African performances to be shown at all, indigenous African music is thus rendered as primitive and barbaric as Mobutu's actions themselves.

At several points in the movie Ali engages in musical discussions. After a morning workout he gives a short speech on the importance of soul and funk music to black Americans, and later he attends the concert. Earlier Ali had greeted the musicians on their arrival in Zaire, and his speech on the importance of black music is juxtaposed with clips of B.B. King's concert performance of "Sweet Sixteen." Apart from some reductive stereotyping of Chinese music, Ali here also stereotypes African American women, claiming "your [white] women didn't slip out on you like our women"—sentiments underscored by King's lyric to "Sweet Sixteen": "You wouldn't do nothing for me baby, and now you wanna run away from old me too."[37] Despite these moments, throughout the film Ali plays the part of the stereotypical congenial black male entertainer, more disarming with his wit, charm, and charisma than threatening with his fists. Collectively Gast depicts the musicians, Africans, and Ali as child-like and "primitive."

One of the most powerful musical moments in the work is James Brown's festival performance of "Gonna Have a Funky Good Time." Once again this performance is intercut with depictions of African American wealth and technology

---

[36]   See Rodriquez, 217.
[37]   Words and music by B.B. King and Joe Josea.

juxtaposed against African poverty, children playing, unnamed African street musicians, and overtly objectified images of women—children, women, and native Africans all cast as colonized forerunners of a more evolved masculine music. James Brown was a former amateur boxer and attributed his well-known dancing prowess to his boxing training. His physical performance combined with his aggressive soul-funk style, with its heavily emphasized downbeats and percussive instrumental and melodic attacks, lends a stereotypically masculine stance to the song. Such performances are positioned alongside the physically aggressive performances of the two fighters, and thus Gast presents the audience with an image of black masculinity that seems primarily based on physical ability and aggression. Contrasted against the cerebral white narration of Plimpton and Mailer, this stereotype is only reinforced. Indeed, at one point in the documentary Brown playfully compares his own long hair and moustache to a werewolf comic-book cover and, in so doing, invites and challenges mainstream fears and myths of both masculine and African American primality.

Female voices are almost entirely absent from the documentary. When they are present they are almost always used to reproduce stereotypes of African women. Among the shots connecting musicians to Africa and Ali is one detailing the baring of a Western performer's breasts to the audience. The display reinscribes a profoundly racist and sexual stereotype about over-sexualized black females. In another episode Miriam Makeba, among the first artists to bridge African and American sounds, is portrayed as a "succubus" (a common figure in blues) who symbolically robs the otherwise "awesome" Foreman of his strength before the fight. Clips of Foreman training are intercut with her concert performance of "Am Am Pondo," a song describing the bravery and breathy vocalizations of the Pondo people in their revolt against the government of South Africa in the late 1950s. What is essentially a folk protest song, however, is exoticized in Gast's editing such that the performance is seen as foreshadowing Foreman's injury in training and his eventual defeat. Makeba's succubus image recurs five times throughout the film, including the very first shot and at its conclusion. Based on these images the *International Review for the Sociology of Sport* actually mistook Makeba for a "real witch doctor ... chanting various African curses."[38] Though she is essentially the lone African performer and sole female included in the film credits, nothing of her considerable significance as an artist is mentioned in the film itself.[39]

The absent or negative presentations of women in the film, to some extent, parallel the history of many African American sports and musical forms. As discussed in Chapter 5, in their early incarnations jazz and blues emphasized a

[38] Ben Carrington, review of *When We Were Kings*, in *The International Review for the Sociology of Sport* 33/1 (1998), 76.

[39] Miriam Makeba, nicknamed "The voice of Africa," was a Grammy Award-winning singer from South Africa who recorded more than 50 albums. She was extremely influential in the struggle against apartheid and well known for her humanitarian work. Makeba died following a concert on November 10, 2008.

particularly masculine expression in ways that openly challenged the repression and silencing of black men through overtly physical and often competitive performance. This situation was paralleled in boxing, basketball, and baseball, which allowed a similar physical outlet for black male creative expression.[40] To some extent, Muhammad Ali is the embodiment of such creativity. An anachronistic and liminal figure, he refused to be inducted into the United States military based on his religious beliefs and opposition to the Vietnam War, yet he engaged in one of the most violent sports imaginable. An outspoken advocate for racial equality, he nonetheless used the rhetoric of racist whites to berate his black opponents (he once called Joe Frazier an Uncle Tom and an "Honorary White"). As Rodriguez observes, "to further his career, he played up both his blackness as well as his appeal to mainstream white America … In 1984 he backed Reagan for office, but in 1988 he was in Jesse Jackson's camp."[41] *When We Were Kings*, however, fixes Ali in time, framed by the rhetoric of white commentators and filmmakers. Ali is firmly connected to "primitive" Africans and "barbarous" musicians as an evolutionary rung on the ladder to a more civilized and evolved human state—that of the white male. In the context of the mid-1990s, when the film was made, masculinity was under attack. The February 14, 1994 issue of *Time* reported, "masculinity is in disrepute. Men have become the Germans of gender … the manly virtues (bravery, strength, discipline and egad, machismo itself) remain admirable only by being quietly reassigned to women."[42] Through their co-option of Ali, Plimpton, Mailer, and Gast can be viewed as attempting to defend besieged white masculinity.

Social Darwinism has slowly lost much of its influence on the rhetoric of race and civilization. However, in the boxing ring as well as in the musical arena, the notion of the "survival of the fittest" has retained a certain cogency. Indeed, only one year after the release of *When We Were Kings*, the December 1997 *Sports Illustrated* cover story reflected a veritably panic-stricken narrative. The article lamented the decline in the number of whites (read white heterosexual men) on the most visible stages of American professional sports, even going so far as to claim that whites have "become second class citizens in contemporary sports."[43] Similar to *Gentleman Jim*, *Rocky* or *Raging Bull*, *When We Were Kings* plays to such nostalgia for the mythic supremacy of white masculinity and replicates the reconstruction of an idealized fictional past found in many feature-length sports films such as *Chariots of Fire*, *Bull Durham* (1988), and more recently, *Seabiscuit*. The images and ideologies projected through sports films such as *When We Were Kings* essentially co-opt the past in the service of legitimizing white-male American hegemony. Film theorist Fatimah Romy terms the impulse to capture

---

40   See bell hooks's comments regarding this subject cited in Chapter 5 (footnote 51).

41   Rodriguez, 220.

42   "Are men really that bad?" February 14, 1994, 54.

43   S. Price "Whatever happened to the white athlete?" *Sports Illustrated* (December 6, 1997), 32–51.

things as they were perceived to have been by the filmmaker as "taxidermy or an attempt to make the dead look as if it were still living."[44] By identifying with Ali, Gast, Mailer, Plimpton, and "evolved" African American musical styles, white male middle-aged film viewers are able to maintain something of the notion that they can come off the socio-cultural ropes, so to speak, to retain their mythic championship status as the epitome of evolution.

The 1996 soundtrack recording of the documentary featured several new pieces by leading African American acts of the mid-1990s, though the majority of the album is reproduced from the concert performances of 1974. Among the new works, rap artists the Fugees, A Tribe Called Quest, Busta Rhymes, and Forte combine on the track "Rumble in the Jungle." The song offers a tribute to the bout and helps confirm the display of black kinship and solidarity that the original festival may have been intended to promote. Brian McKnight and Diana King also deliver a retro-soul duet for the soundtrack's title song, which plays during the documentary's closing credits. While some attempt has been made to address the absence of female voices in the original concert and documentary, such as the presence of Zelma Davis's "I'm Calling," none of the more than 18 African acts that performed at the original festival is included on the soundtrack album. As in 1974, however, rap, R&B, and soul, in combination with the masculine funk and blues of the original acts such as James Brown and B.B. King, are presented as more evolved than, or at least more commercially preferable to, black African music.

The Social Darwinism manifest in *When We Were Kings* and the general notion of the survival of the fittest as an analogy for competitive sports in general is increasingly prevalent in popular music today. The popularity of television shows such as *American Idol*, *Star Search*, and *American Bandstand* that place considerable emphasis on judging the value and abilities of competing artists, seems to underscore the competitive nature of the music industry in general. Elayne Rapping, a professor of American studies at the University of Buffalo, claims that *Idol*, which topped the Nielsen ratings for six straight seasons from 2004–10, has become "a national obsession in the same way that maybe baseball used to be or the Super Bowl."[45] In the case of *American Idol* and *Star Search* in particular, the notion of a survival of the fittest gets repeatedly reinforced as contestants are voted off by judges and the public until a lone champion remains. Such a Darwinistic concept also applies to the music industry at large, however, as smaller record companies are regularly bought out or absorbed by larger ones and new technologies win out and replace older ones, as in the case of CDs replacing records or MP3 files replacing CDs. Of course, these latter evolutionary scenarios

---

[44]   Fatimah Romy, *The Third Eye: Race, Cinema, and Ethnographic Spectacle* (Duke: Duke University Press, 1996), 7, 107. Also see Rodriguez, 212.

[45]   Lisa Respers France, "Finale stuns 'Idol' worshippers," *CNN.com*, www.cnn.com/2009/SHOWBIZ/TV/05/21/american.idol.reaction/index.htmlwww.cnn.com/2009/SHOWBIZ/TV/05/21/american.idol.reaction/index.html (accessed May 21, 2009).

apply equally as well to other areas of our socio-industrial state and are likely a general by-product of our capitalist, consumer-driven world.

One of the more overt incarnations of this trend is the continued existence of Social Darwinism in white rap. White rap artists such as Vanilla Ice, Snow, and most recently Eminem, have variously been tagged with the label of "Great White Hope." The white fascination with black rap culture, however, was perhaps most evident in the reality television series *The (White) Rapper*, broadcast in 2007 on the VH1 cable network. In this show, based on much the same format as *American Idol*, 10 white rappers competed with each other for the chance at a $100,000 grand prize. The show was set in the South Bronx, with MC Serch (from the inter-racial rap group 3rd Bass) serving as the host. At the end of each show one rapper was eliminated. Each episode followed a different theme in hip hop culture and music, evolving the contestants from wannabe white rappers to fully-fledged and multi-faceted hip hop acts. Successful contestants won "ghetto passes" each week. At first glance the show may seem to have been a crude reinforcement of racial stereotypes. However, through the use of humorous and over-the-top confrontations of such stereotypes, the show was actually intended as a serious attempt to address and overcome racial divides in rap.[46] Nonetheless the show maintained an aura of Social Darwinism and troped a common boxing theme, as its website proudly announced that the show would "go where no man has gone before … to find rap's next great white hopes."

Although Social Darwinism has long been discredited, in its place we have what Nathaniel Comfort has recently termed "Cultural Darwinism." As Comfort argues: "Social Darwinism applied evolutionary thinking to social and economic problems. Cultural Darwinism applies it to almost any aspect of modern culture."[47] In the realm of culture, Darwinism itself has been engaged in a natural selection of ideas, ideologies, and critical approaches such that many authors have applied Darwinism to a variety of fields outside biology. Given the recent attacks on Darwin's theories of evolution by proponents of intelligent design, it behooves us to understand that the pernicious remains of Social Darwinism continue to be an ongoing, albeit often covert, presence in popular culture. In *Gentleman Jim*, *Raging Bull* or *When We Were Kings*, the "pinnacle" of masculinity, personified by the heavyweight champion, was attained by different ethnic or racial representatives at different periods in North American history. Such films and their soundtracks have underlined notions of upward mobility, often associated with the American dream, tacitly depicted in terms of evolutionary natural selection of variously Irish, Italian, or African Americans. Music is an effective form of evoking past feelings

---

[46]   See *The (White) Rapper*'s official VH1 website: www.vh1.com/shows/dyn/white_rapper/series_about.jhtml (accessed July 27, 2008). Also see an interview with the show's producer, Elliott Wilson: www.craveonline.com/articles/filmtv/04647505/ego_trippin.html (accessed July 27, 2008).

[47]   Nathaniel Comfort, "Cultural Darwinism," *The European Legacy* 13/5 (2008), 623–37, 631.

and ways of being and has been described as a "device for the reflexive process of remembering/constructing who one is."[48] Couched in historical nostalgia amplified by period settings and their soundtracks, these films each ultimately evoke a nostalgic longing for the superiority of white masculine hegemony.

Female Identities in Sports Movie Soundtracks

The utopian narrative of American sports films repeatedly projects a singular vision of ideal masculinity. The heroic individual, white or black, overcomes all physical, social, and cultural barriers through determination and self-reliance. As such, this individual is representative of the American dream that promises to reward the most deserving individuals. Differences in social position are typically naturalized as evolutionary, a momentary obstacle to success that can be overcome by beating the competition through hard work. Sports films rarely acknowledge the gender gap that exists between the competitive opportunities afforded men and those afforded women in our society. When the subject of gender discrimination, like racial discrimination, is raised, it is typically portrayed as merely another challenge to be overcome by the individual, rather than as an endemic flaw in athletics or society. Female characters in many sports movies are relegated to non-athletic roles. In movies such as *Bull Durham* or *White Men Can't Jump*, for example, women are often portrayed as relatively assertive individuals who challenge the masculinity of the male protagonists and serve as inspiration for the male character's ultimate triumph. In films such as *A League of Their Own* (1992) or *Million Dollar Baby* (2004), hypermasculine, ex-athlete male coaches and managers ultimately shape their female athletes into competitive winners.

In the case of *Million Dollar Baby*, as with his previous movies such as *Mystic River* (2003) and *Unforgiven* (1992), director Clint Eastwood's life-long love of music led him to score the film himself. Winner of the 2004 Academy Award for best picture, it narrates the story of a hard-bitten boxing trainer, his elusive past, and his quest for atonement by helping an underdog amateur female boxer (the film's title character)—Maggie Fitzgerald, played by Hilary Swank—to achieve her dream of becoming a professional. The film thus deals with an unconventional female athletic hero and would seem to be an admirable exception to the plethora of sports films featuring stereotypical male heroes who overcome social obstacles to reach their goals. Nonetheless, is it largely through the inspiration and talents of her male trainer, Frankie Dunn, played by Eastwood, that her dream is achieved. Furthermore, she tragically expires as a result of injuries suffered in the ring. As is the case in many operas that feature powerful amazons or warrior women, she seemingly must die for transgressing the stereotypical nature of her sex. Anchored by elegiac figures for solo acoustic guitar and piano, the soundtrack, like the movie, is marked by subtle introspection. But it is also occasionally seasoned

---

[48] Tia DeNora, "Music and self identity," in Andy Bennett *et al.* (eds), *The Popular Music Studies Reader* (Routledge, 2006), pp. 141–7, 141.

with moments of more up-tempo jazz and blues, the by-product of Eastwood's longstanding love affair with American roots music. Its haunting, gently yearning string arrangements lack the bombast and overwrought melodicism that fuel many Hollywood sports films. The understated nature of the score subverts the exuberant pop aesthetic of most masculine sports film soundtracks, much as the tragic outcome subverts the expectations of traditional sports movie heroes. Unlike many of the films previously discussed, there is seemingly no utopian ending for a female athlete. The situation has an eerie parallel with operatic heroines who, as discussed by Catherine Clément, also often must pay with their lives for transgressing the stereotypical boundaries of their sex.[49] Ultimately one might argue that the final message of *Million Dollar Baby* is that the sport of female boxing itself must, like the main character, die. Maggie, however, dies on her own terms and pursues her dreams against all advice and against all social prohibitions of female combat. Again we are thus presented with the mythos of the rugged individual—though one whose triumph is only realized in death.

The narratives of the relatively few feature films about female athletes often center on how women can participate in athletics yet retain a femininity that is largely predicated on their relationships with men or children.[50] As depicted in *A League of Their Own*, women athletes are more likely to be portrayed as "team players" than their male counterparts. Strong, athletically accomplished female athletes subvert dominant assumptions regarding the division between masculinity and femininity. In addition to engaging in what is traditionally considered the overtly male sport of boxing, Hilary Swank's character in *Million Dollar Baby* heightens this division by wearing her hair short. The binary male–female division is, however, typically reinscribed by the end of the film, thereby removing any possibility of a socially transgressive transgendered identity. Something of this is also evident in *A League of Their Own*. Penny Marshall's film portrays something of the masculine athleticism and mannerisms of players in the real-life All-American Girls Professional Baseball League (AAGPBL) but ultimately, rather than focusing on a more masculine character such as the third baseman Doris, portrayed by Rosie O'Donnell, focuses on the more stereotypically feminine main character, the catcher Dottie, played by Gina Davis.

Reinforcing the emphasis on femininity, the real women behind the *A League of Their Own* were required to maintain a certain standard of feminine conduct. Below is an excerpt from the Official AAGPBL Charm School Guide, which specified appropriate beauty routines, clothes, and etiquette. The beauty guidelines were as follows:

---

[49]   See Catherine Clément, *Opera, or, The Undoing of Women* (trans.) Betsy Wing (Minneapolis: University of Minnesota Press, 1988).

[50]   Sports films involving relationships between women, such as *Personal Best* (1982) starring Mariel Hemingway, are even more infrequent.

You should be the best judge of your own beauty requirements. Keep your own kit replenished with the things you need for your own toilette and your beauty culture and care. Remember the skin, the hair, the teeth and the eyes. It is most desirable in your own interests, that of your teammates and fellow players, as well as from the standpoint of the public relations of the league, that each girl be at all times presentable and attractive, whether on the playing field or at leisure. Study your own beauty culture possibilities and without overdoing your beauty treatment at the risk of attaining gaudiness, practice the little measure that will reflect well on your appearance and personality as a real All-American girl.[51]

The *A League of Their Own* soundtrack is largely composed of non-threatening contemporary covers of period works by adult-oriented artists. Works include Manhattan Transfer's rendition of "Choo Choo Ch'Boogie," Carole King's "Now and Forever," James Taylor's "Its Only a Paper Moon," Art Garfunkel's "Two Sleepy People," and Billy Joel's "In a Sentimental Mood." One of the more notable musical moments in the work is "The Victory Song," written and performed by the actual AAGPBL team the Rockford Peaches. The lyrics reinforce the camaraderie and international make-up of the team and pay tribute to their male manager:

Batter up! Hear that call!
The time has come for one and all
To play ball.

We come from cities near and far.
We've got Canadians, Irishmen and Swedes,
We're all for one, we're one for all
We're All-Americans!

Each girl stands, her head so proudly high,
Her motto "Do or Die."
She's not the one to use or need an alibi.

Our chaperones are not too soft,
They're not too tough,
Our managers are on the ball.
We've got a president who really knows his stuff,
We're all for one, we're one for all,
We're All-Americans!

Aside from the somewhat fawning references to their male handlers, the lyrics overtly play up the notion of team spirit. Whatever their background and nationality they were born into, they are ultimately "one for all" and "All-Americans."

Of course the unity implied by "All-Americans" was hardly all-inclusive. In life, as in the movie, there were no black women in the League because they were not allowed to play. The only mention of an African American woman in the movie is when one in the stands throws the ball back to Kit, played by Lori Petty. Kit proclaims it a "Nice throw," seemingly surprised that a black woman had such a strong and accurate arm. Ultimately the music in the movie does little to promote the cause of women, in either sports or music, and, echoing the white nostalgia associated with many male dominated sports movies, serves more as a sentimental reminder of a historical moment in American history.

Sports Video Games

While sports film soundtracks are amongst the most high profile interactions of sports and music it is, however, often rarely groundbreaking in terms of its content or approach. One of the more important and innovative arenas for new music generation in the past 30 years has been the realm of video game music. Though long overlooked by critical theory, video game music has had an extraordinary impact on contemporary aural culture around the world. The global phenomenon of video gaming has ensured that the accompanying soundtracks have transcended and, in the process, destabilized many previous conceptions of music's relation to place and location and to socio-economic, gender, racial, and cultural identities. The approach to game music in the early 1980s usually involved simple tone generation and/or frequency modulation synthesis and was often limited to electronic beeps, squelches, and simple melodies. Nonetheless the significance of music in these early games is evident in Pac-Man (1980), likely the most popular game of all time (at least in terms of its impact on pop culture consciousness). The sound of Pac-Man's insatiable appetite for dots has become synonymous with the sound of consumerism run amok, just as the sound of Pac-Man dying has become a universally recognizable marker of defeat. Released even earlier than Pac-Man, a large part of the appeal of Space Invaders stems from the sonic tension induced by its menacing soundtrack, in which electronic bass squelches accelerate in tempo as the enemy aliens draw nearer. In such games the fantastical nature of the characters obviates much of the need for, or use of, many (though often not all) of the traditional visual or musical markers of class, gender, racial or locational identity.

The leading sports video game manufacturer is the Canadian-based EA Sports (short for Electronic Arts), who are responsible for such popular game series as Madden NFL, Tiger Woods PGA Tour, NBA Live, and NHL. The music in these games has evolved from mere introductory background to simulations of music heard at actual sporting events, in between plays, during half-time shows, and so on. As mentioned in Chapter 3 (see "Music, Sports, and Alternative Media"), many influential bands such as Barenaked Ladies and Aerosmith have contributed music to these games. The presence of music in these games, however, is merely to enhance the overall experience of the sports simulation and to provide what Dave Warfield, producer of NHL franchise games for EA Sports, calls "emotion and recognition."[52] In essence music's role is thus to evoke an emotion that will be remembered and associated with a particular game and video game brand. Music is essentially a passive, if subconsciously influential, background to the onscreen activity. Increasingly, however, interactive or participatory music simulation video games, games that place music at the center of the experience, are becoming popular.

Sports-themed video games are among the most popular video game genres. However, the recent soaring popularity of music simulation games like Rock Band and Guitar Hero has recently surpassed that of sports themed games. Market researchers at Odyssey recently released the results of their "Homefront" study, a quarterly tracking study of ownership and usage of home media products and services among American households, conducted since 1994. While action games, played by 65 percent of gamers, are the most popular genre played on consoles, the soaring popularity of the music genre has pushed it past sports; 58 percent of gamers are playing music titles, compared with 50 percent for sports titles. Rounding out the top five genres are adventure role playing games at 36 percent and "other simulations" at 32 percent.[53]

To understand this trend it may be helpful to describe one of the more recent and most popular releases, Guitar Hero World Tour. The game consists entirely of master recordings from classic and contemporary rock bands including Van Halen, Linkin Park, and the Eagles. Additionally, the game offers localized downloadable music such that the musical experience can be tailored to better reflect the tastes of various regions. Essentially the game is a more involved form of precursor musical memory games such as Simon; players are scored on their ability to follow accurately onscreen patterns that outline various guitar solos. Budding rock stars are also given creative license to customize fully everything from the characters' appearance and instruments to the band's logo and album covers. Enabled to live out their rock fantasies, virtual musicians can play either a single instrument or any combination of instruments, in addition to the full band experience. As well as the online game-play modes, there is also a Battle of the Bands mode that allows eight players to join online and challenge each other band-to-band to determine who is the best. In the Band modes, up to four players can jam together, online or off, as they progress through the game. In single-player Career mode, players can jam on any of the instruments in branching venue progression.

---

[52]   Steve Traiman, "Video games provide new platform for music promotion," *Billboard* 113/49 (December 2001), 75.

[53]   James Brightman, "Music video games now more popular than sports games, says study," *Game Daily*, Tuesday, October 21, 2008, www.gamedaily.com/articles/news/music-video-games-now-more-popular-than-sports-games-says-study/?biz=1 (accessed April 2, 2009).

The popular Wii platform has also adopted an increasingly popular game entitled Wii Music. In contrast to Rock Band and Guitar Hero, Wii Music doesn't have any faux instruments. Players use the Wii remote control to act as if they are playing various instruments such as the saxophone (there are over 60 instruments from which to choose). Unlike Rock Band or Guitar Hero, the game is uncompetitive and forgiving, allowing children and novices to play without concern that their music will be judged. Player-performers hear the results coming from the television and see their avatar characters act out their motions on screen. Players can also make a video out of their performance and then create an album cover.

The future of musical simulation games has continued to seem bright, as Disney recently released the interactive music game Ultimate Band and announced its forthcoming *High School Musical 3*. In the latter case it is worth noting the three-way cross-marketing of music, video games, and film.

A particularly noteworthy statistic from the "Homefront" Odyssey study is that the majority of gamers playing music titles are actually female, which is not the case for other video game genres; 53 percent of music game players were found to be female. According to Erik Whiteford, Odyssey's managing director, "Typically males have dominated the major console game genres. The fact that females make up the majority of a key category may be the first meaningful indication that console gaming is beginning to expand its audience, but it is too soon to tell."[54]

Another factor that may be influencing the surge in popularity of interactive music games is the increasing awareness of the health benefits of such games. Perhaps counter-intuitively, increasing evidence is emerging from the medical community that such interactive video games are actually improving aspects of the players' health, mobility, and welfare. Furthermore, such games are often seen as having a particular benefit for those with limited mobility or restricted access to traditional forms of exercise.[55]

Further evidence that the health benefits of video gaming are becoming a marketable commodity is provided by the fact that EA Sports has recently released a game called Sports Active: Personal Trainer for the Wii console (released in North America November 19, 2009).[56] Along with an arm strap pouch to hold the

---

[54]   As quoted in Brightman.

[55]   Such studies include Lee Graves, N.D. Ridgers, and G. Stratton, "The contribution of upper limb and total body movement to adolescents' energy expenditure whilst playing Nintendo Wii," *European Journal of Applied Physiology* 104/4 (2008), 617–23; Michael Tlauka, Jennifer Williams, and Paul Williamson, "Spatial ability in secondary school students: Intra-sex differences based on self-selection for physical education," *British Journal of Psychology* 99/3 (August 2008), 427–40; and Lee Graves, Gareth Stratton, N.D. Ridgers, and N.T. Cable, "Energy expenditure in adolescents playing new generation computer games," *British Journal of Sports Medicine* 42/7 (2008), 592–94.

[56]   See EA Sports press release: www.easportsactive.com/home.action?id=Active%20 Press%20Release-20081112111814201.xml (accessed April 3, 2009).

Wii remote, the game also ships with a resistance band and a booklet on nutrition. The game is expected to be the first in a line of EA Sports Active branded games and related peripherals. Notably, the game is apparently being marketed mostly to women. EA's website, for example, features all-female fitness models and satisfaction testimonials, rose-pink background coloring, and rhetoric redolent of women's fitness magazines about receiving "exclusive healthy-living tips ... useful exercise techniques from ... the EA SPORTS Active fitness consultant, secret tips and tricks from Kathryn, our editor, and fresh EA SPORTS Active news." The exercises are timed to sync-up with the upbeat soundtrack that accompanies each exercise. It seems clear that video game exercise, with its accompanying musical soundtrack, is set to replace the previous generation of VHS workout videos described in Chapter 2.

The fact that more and more actual physical exercise is reliant on virtual technology reinforces Baudrillardian notions of the spread of hyper-real simulacra of reality. The increasing integration of digital media and the body also recalls the increasing contestation of the human, and the resulting emphasis on notions of the trans-human, that have destabilized both sports and music. Given the increasing participation by both females and people with health issues or disabilities, video gaming—interactive music gaming in particular—is becoming an increasingly democratizing source of both music and exercise—at least in so far as people have economic access to this technology.

Sports Television

Music and sports are linked in every entertainment media imaginable, from film and video games to radio and the internet. Television, however, perhaps provides the most overt and ubiquitous instances of this interrelationship. Not only is music used to underscore sports highlights on the nightly news, but theme music announces the plethora of sports talk shows and sports highlight shows, not to mention the regularly scheduled NFL, NBA, NHL, MLB, PGA, and NASCAR events and other more intensively covered but intermittently scheduled events such as the Olympics, Wimbledon, or the World Cup. Much of the relationship between music and sports on television is based on the commodification of various networks and sports leagues. Indeed, Steven Miles claims that television has likely represented "the single most influential driving force underlying the commodification of sports."[57] The revenues generated from advertising rights to various sports and sporting events are enormous and continue to grow. The American network NBC paid $1.18 billion US for the rights to broadcast the 2012 London Olympics, more than double what they paid in 1996 for the Atlanta

---

[57] Steven Miles, *Consumerism As a Way of Life* (London: Sage, 1997), 140.

games.[58] Music typically plays into the strategies used in the process of packaging events for television consumers.

Television, however, has also had an impact on the presence of music at live sporting events. Since the advent of televised sports programming in the 1960s, opportunities to play music, either live or recorded, during sports events have substantially increased due to longer and more frequent breaks necessary to accommodate television commercials. The "television timeout" is a common feature of many televised sports. Indeed, the ubiquitous presence of such "incidental" music during stoppages of play has, somewhat ironically, become vital to the "live" experience of the event. It serves to make attending a game seem familiar to spectators who have become accustomed to sports television viewing. The vicarious experience of watching sports on television, marked by a constant barrage of sounds, music, and media information, has been replicated in the live event itself, during which the fans experience a constant stream of ancillary entertainment. Also the music in live sporting events serves to mask the artificial silences created by the commercial time-outs in the first place. Aided by the latest in digital programming, sound systems, and score-board projection technologies, professional sports franchises typically deliver a dazzling multimedia sensory extravaganza, combining live and recorded music, video features (including commercials for various corporate sponsors), promotional contests, mascot antics, recorded chants and applause, and instant replays. The advertising and instant replays that take place in the arenas, of course, particularly mimic the home television experience of the event. In many ways attending a live sporting event is becoming more and more a mediated simulacrum of the real event.[59]

A central component of all such sports television broadcasts is the theme music, whether it is a pre-existent pop song or a newly composed tag. Television sports show theme music, such as the *Hockey Night in Canada* theme discussed in Chapter 6, indicates the beginning and the ending of a broadcast and punctuates the material in between. Indeed, Malcolm MacLean discusses sports television music in terms of "framing:" how it delineates the show from others and sets the tone of its content.[60] Theme music associated with televised sporting events is often an essential indicator of meaning and of the terms of audience engagement. As such, the theme music becomes an integral part of the broadcast text and functions in a manner similar to a book cover; it advertises the contents within and acts as an

---

[58]   John Horne, "Sport, consumerism and the mass media," in *Sport in Consumer Culture* (New York: Palgrave MacMillan, 2006), 53

[59]   Indeed the use of music during breaks of play in most sports has become so common that sports, such as tennis or golf, that do not feature recorded music are seen as exceptional. See John Wertheim, "The quiet sounds of tennis," *Cnnsi*, January 14, 2002. http://sportsillustrated.cnn.com/inside_game/jon_wertheim/news/2002/01/14/wertheim_ viewpoint/ (accessed June 16, 2010).

[60]   Malcolm MacLean, "Bouts of Kiwi loyalty: Musical frames and televised sport," *Sporting Sounds*, 237–50.

osmotic barrier between the game and non-game world. Quoting literary theorist John Frow, MacLean describes such framing: "the song holds the game 'in a kind of suspension such that the framed word is, in Mikhail Bakhtin's terminology, a 'represented word': the word represents itself *cites* itself as a fictive word, a word which cannot be accepted directly.'"[61]

In North America the major television networks often delineate their sporting broadcasts, whether basketball, football, or baseball, with particular music that signals the type and atmosphere of the sporting content to follow. Such pieces are often replayed over the course of several days in the case of multi-day events such as the World Cup, the Olympics, or golf or tennis tournaments. For many years, from the mid-1970s through the late 1980s, the theme music associated with ABC sports golf coverage was Barry White's "Love's Theme" (1973). "Love's Theme," recorded by White and his 40-piece Love Unlimited Orchestra, was the first purely orchestral work to reach No. 1 on *Billboard*'s Hot 100 Chart in 1974. The lush orchestral arrangements supplemented by heavy wah-wah and production effects resulted in an opulent sound. In troping high-end studio production values and orchestral arrangements, it was a representation of the sound of black wealth. In the late 1960s and early 1970s, African American performers such as Marvin Gaye, Isaac Hayes, and Barry White sought to compete with the studio experimentation and production values of progressive white rock acts, typified in the increasingly orchestral sound of the Beatles. These artists turned to costly studio production and orchestral arrangements, sonically manifesting and projecting the sound of black empowerment and the promise—if not the reality—of economic success associated with control of advanced studio technology and the perception of classical music's stereotypical socio-economic elitism.

Ironically, few African Americans until the advent of Tiger Woods were interested in golf, and many were even still banned from white-only country clubs. Nonetheless Barry White's "Love's Theme" was the most prominent musical association with the game. Indeed the opulent sound of the number, and its association with country club wealth, resulted in its later use as the soundtrack to the television program *Lifestyles of the Rich and Famous* (1984–95). The current theme music used for CBS PGA golf coverage is by the well-known new age artist Yanni and projects a simpler synthesizer arrangement but one that is still relaxed and meditative—presumably linking to the leisurely and meditative connotations of golf.

Golf television theme music is somewhat atypical in its employment of a relaxed musical accompaniment that projects an atmosphere of leisure and wealth, seemingly evoking and connecting it to the country club heritage of the game. The overwhelming majority of television sports music, however, is

---

[61] MacLean, 247; also see John Frow, "The literary frame," *Journal of Aesthetic Education* 16/2 (1982): 25–30, 26.

overtly coded as aggressive and ties into more stereotypical notions of masculine aggression and heroism.

One of the most famous television sports themes is that of *ABC's Wide World of Sports*, which ran from 1961 until 1998. The show was hosted for most of its 37 years by Jim McKay and featured a variety of athletic competitions not traditionally seen on American television, such as surfing, rodeo, and traditional Olympic sports from around the world. The show was introduced by a brassy musical fanfare, composed by Charles Fox, over a montage of sports clips and with a dramatic accompanying voiceover by McKay: "Spanning the globe to bring you the constant variety of sport ... the thrill of victory ... and the agony of defeat ... the human drama of athletic competition ... This is *ABC's Wide World of Sports*." Fox's theme was a stirring orchestral arrangement that, in addition to the unison brass chord opening fanfare, featured aggressive military snare drum beats and harsh downbeat dissonances that sonically painted and highlighted the classic phrase "the agony of defeat." The middle section of the theme transitions to a subdued consonant minor mode before dramatically transitioning to the final triumphant cadence in a major key. The overwhelming aesthetic embodied by the music is one of masculine tension and struggle culminating in heroic martial victory.

Perhaps the most overtly gendered examples of television sports soundtracks are found in the world of NFL football. Television soundtracks typically reinforce and reflect what is already an overtly masculine dominated culture of players, coaches, announcers and color commentators. As such, network football themes rely heavily on musical expressions of power that have been traditionally coded as masculine, including militaristic brass fanfares, aggressive distorted guitar playing and similarly bellicose singing and lyrics. Programmers and composers have seemingly sought to reproduce aurally the tough, combative and macho image of the game. This is despite the fact that approximately 45 percent of the league's fan base are women.[62] Such an image is actively in keeping with the league's marketing image.[63]

---

[62]   "Marketers alter their pitches with more females tuning in," *USA Today*, October 17, 2008 http://www.usatoday.com/sports/2008-09-17-women-marketing_N.htm (accessed June 7, 2010).

[63]   The NFL compilation CD entitled *The Power and the Glory* (1998), for example, declares at the start of the title track that NFL football "is a rare game. The men who play it make it, so ... [it] is a mirror of early America, reflecting toughness, courage, and self-denial." The sentiments are overtly nationalistic but also reinforced by overtly stereotypically masculine coded arrangements. Reinforcing the primordial masculinity of the game, near the end of the track the narrator intones, "Do you fear the force of the wind, the slash of the rain? Go face them and fight them, be savage again!" The remainder of the album repeats themes that glorify militarism, savagery and pain, such as "Westside Rumble," "Classic Battle," "Be Savage Again," "Pain Is Inevitable" and "Cossack's Charge." See *The Power and The Glory: The Original Music and Voices of NFL Films* (1998) distributed by Tommy Boy Records (TBCD 1269). Also discussed in Charles Hiroshi Garrett, Struggling to define a nation," 237.

The soundtrack to *Monday Night Football* provides a prime example of the league's reliance on stereotypically masculine musical content. Before moving to ESPN, *Monday Night Football* aired on ABC from 1970 until 2005, making it the second longest-running prime time show on American network television (after CBS's *60 Minutes*). From 1989 to 2008, Hank Williams Jr's "All My Rowdy Friends Are Here on Monday Night," a remake of his 1984 song "All My Rowdy Friends Are Coming Over Tonight," served as the show's theme song. The hook phrase "Are you ready for some football?" has transcended the show to become part of the lexicon of popular culture.[64]

Predicated on stereotypically masculine sonic markers, the *Monday Night Football* theme song is a rowdy bar-room blues number with frenetic piano and distorted electric guitars overlaid with Williams's aggressive, almost shouted, baritone vocals. In the reworked version Williams describes gathering his friends to watch a football game in terms of hosting a rowdy house party. In keeping with his "Outlaw" persona, Williams projects an overt image of aggressive "Southern good-old-boy" masculinity that is reinforced by his macho stance and by his scruffy beard, sunglasses, jeans, black leather vest and cowboy hat.[65] A version of the song, subtitled "Operation invasion," leads off the 1996 compilation CD *ABC Monday Night Football Official Party Album*.[66] The lyrics overtly reinforce the connection between football and war:

> Well it's Monday night and we're ready to strike!
> Our special forces are in full flight.
> We're coming by air and on the ground,
> Monday night football's takin' over the town.
> We gotta get ready, we gotta get right,
> Its gonna be a battle in the NFL tonight …
> Are you ready for some football!
> A Monday night invasion …

Again the music and lyrics link football to American military might and, if only by inference, patriotism. For *Monday Night Football's* 2006 debut on ESPN, Williams Jr re-recorded the theme with an all-star all-male jam band that included Brian Setzer, Little Richard, Joe Perry, Clarence Clemons, Rick Nielsen, Bootsy Collins, Charlie Daniels, and Steven Van Zandt, among others.

---

[64] Garrett also discusses this song in "Struggling to define a nation," 239–40.

[65] See Garrett, 240.

[66] *ABC Monday Night Football Official Party Album*, Hollywood Records, B0000000G9 1996. The album contains works from a number of other stereotypically macho country artists, including Toby Keith and Jerry Reed, and aggressive masculine themed songs such "Take This Job and Shove It," "Should've Been a Cowboy" and "Soul Man." It should be noted that Williams slightly altered the lyrics to suit the teams and location featured in each week's game.

Though most football broadcasts—indeed, most sports broadcasts of any kind—present an overtly masculine image, there are several notable exceptions. Seemingly in an attempt to register more female viewers, in 2006 the producers of NBC's *Sunday Night Football* opted to use a female vocalist for the show's theme song. The network chose the artist Pink, who claims to be "a huge football fan" and whose "Get the Party Started" was already a staple in sports arenas throughout North America.[67] The resultant "Waiting All Day for Sunday Night" was a slightly more musically aggressive and lyrical revision of "I Hate Myself for Lovin' You," originally released by Joan Jett in 1988. On the selection of Pink, NFL on NBC producer Fred Gaudelli explained:

> A football fan knows the anticipation of waiting all day for the big game. When you hear this song on Sunday nights you'll know the big game is about to kick off. ... We chose Pink as the signature voice because she is a tremendous talent with a crossover appeal that makes her relevant to all segments of our audience.[68]

Pink's appeal apparently did not live up to expectations. Country singer Faith Hill replaced Pink as the singer of the opening theme in the 2007 and 2008 seasons, though the theme still resembles the Joan Jett song. "I'm honored to have been asked," Hill told the Associated Press. "I truly am a football fan. Particularly men find it hard to believe that women can be big fans of football, but I love it. I loved it in junior high and high school, but being married to a man [fellow country singer Tim McGraw] who schedules his life around football games, it makes it a lot easier." Oddly, given her previous attempt to challenge stereotypes of female lack of interest in football, Hill goes on to admit, "I've learned when to ask questions and when not to ask them—like in the middle of a replay."[69]

American television networks that cover NFL football all have similar yet distinctive theme songs that draw on many of the same conventions as *Wide World of Sports* or *Monday Night Football*. However, most networks do not rely on a human voice to brand their football coverage. The characteristic brass fanfare also serves as the leitmotif brand for CBS television's football telecasts. Scored for synthesized brass and percussion, the melody outlines an ascending minor triad before a barrage of percussion sounds adds an intense gladiatorial tone and announces a tonic closure. CBS broadcasts this militaristic fanfare repeatedly throughout the game, before and after every commercial break as well, to announce periodically

---

[67]   "Multi-platinum pop singer Pink performs NBC *Sunday Night Football* opening music," press release issued by NBC, August 30, 2006, www.thefutoncritic.com/news. aspx?id=20060830nbc01 (accessed May 16, 2009).

[68]   "*Sunday Night Football* thinks Pink," *Zap2it.com*, August 30, 2006, www.zap2it. com/tv/news/zap-pinksingssundaynightfootballtheme,0,4215656.story?coll=zap-tv-headlines (accessed May 16, 2009).

[69]   "Faith Hill to sing *Sunday Night Football* theme," *MSNBC* August 30, 2007, http:// nbcsports.msnbc.com/id/20498058 (accessed May 16, 2009).

updates in other games. The audience is virtually continually bombarded by the theme and its attendant violent associations.[70] Fox's theme similarly uses a brass fanfare and a dramatic orchestral arrangement supplemented by digital electronic sounds. Yet again, the aesthetic is of military conquest and aggression. Typically technological industrial sounds, military drumbeats, aggressive downbeats, brass fanfares, loud dynamics featuring thick, heavy, bass-oriented textures, and registers with massive reverb are foregrounded in such tunes. Some themes supplement the aforementioned musical content with recorded game sounds and or announcer voiceovers. Ultimately all of these themes function as a celebration of triumphalism, particularly a cultural validation of the US military industrial complex and of aggressive masculinity in general. Heard dozens of times throughout a typical broadcast, before and after every commercial break, and during pre- and post-game shows, such music subjects the viewer to relentless marketing that approaches brainwashing.

In comparison to the television network sports themes, Olympic television theme songs, with much of the same hypermasculine emphasis on brass fanfares and drumbeats, tend to be less frantic, slower in tempo, and more ceremonial in mood. As such they tend to try to project a more solemn atmosphere that underlines the gravitas of the heritage and global purview of amateur athletics. Much of the recently composed Olympic music, for example, speaks to a mythologized Hellenic past. John Williams particularly evokes this notion in his Olympic works such as "Olympic Spirit" (1988, Seoul), "Summon the Heroes" (1996, Atlanta), and "Call of the Champions" (2002, Salt Lake City).[71] "Summon the Heroes," in particular, has become commonly associated with the Olympic television experience and is now used prevalently by NBC for all their commercial break intros and outros, for both their summer and winter Olympics broadcasts. Williams comments on his evocation of a heroic, mythic past in his Olympic pieces:

> ... This sense of history and heraldic things and pageant things, you get an almost adolescent turn-on with these things in the film world that is fun for the composer and can provide an inspiration for him. That may connect with the Olympic kind of pageant and all of that ... It's all about deities and heroes that lived up in the mountains somewhere ... I really think there is this unbroken mythological thing ... And these games are also contests and that relates to music in as such that it is a contrapuntal competition—that's the whole essence I suppose of polyphony ... Or a concert, which is a competition between a soloist

---

[70]   Charles Garrett counts more the 40 instances of the theme during a broadcast in September 2004. Garret, 241.

[71]   Williams has, notably, also composed the theme music (as distinguished from the theme song sung by Pink and Faith Hill) for NBC's *Sunday Night Football*.

and this huge unbeatable force ... So I think in musical terms it's heroes or things like that which we want to write about in music.[72]

Williams also directly ties his Olympic art to the idea of the "audiovisual," stating, "I live with visual [filmic] distractions every day and they usually cover up whatever good phrases I can conjure ... But I'm attracted to it because it's a source of rich imagery in the visual sense and in the spooky mythological sense that we feel."[73]

The repeated use of musical themes in television sports broadcasts ties in to the production ethos of television in general. Many television series, whether dramatic, comedic, or sports-based, adopt an assembly-line style of production—a repetition exacerbated through the recurring regularity of scheduling time slots, duration, and character types to convey images of social stability.[74] Moreover, sports often reinforce the standard curve of narrative action, including stock characters (heroes and villains) who encounter new versions of stock situations, opposition, conflict, and victorious resolution for one side or the other. In typical dramatic television shows the plot resolves over 30 or 60 minutes and, in itself, becomes a source of hegemonic rigidity and forced regularity. Though sports are often exceptions to the durational regularity of television scheduling—overtimes and extra innings can often extend broadcast times—the broadcasts are nonetheless framed, through commercial time-outs and the like, to resolve, and therefore conform as closely as possible to their advertised length.

The use of musical themes that punctuate every commercial break plays into the hegemonic regularity of network television culture. In this way televised sports programs and their musical themes rehearse and reinforce social fixity; they represent and cement the obduracy of an audience and consumer society that has become resistant to substantial change. Indeed, popular music associated with television sports marketing campaigns—perhaps most infamously manifest in Nike's controversial use of the Beatles' "Revolution" in 1987—is yet another component of the reinforcement of social fixity and, in the case of the Nike advertisement, a classic example of the commodification of dissent.[75] The repetitive

---

[72]   William K. Guegold, *One Hundred Years of Olympic Music: Music and Musicians of the Modern Olympic Games, 1896–1996* (Mantua, Ohio: Golden Clef Publishing, 1996), xiii, xiv, xv.

[73]   Ibid., xii.

[74]   For a more complete discussion of this understanding of television see Todd Gitlin, "Prime time ideology: The hegemonic process in television entertainment," *Social Problems* 26/3 (February, 1979), 251–66.

[75]   "Revolution" was the first Beatles recording to be used in a television commercial. The campaign was criticized by the surviving Beatles and their fans felt it was an over-commercialization of their music, particularly in the wake of controversies surrounding Nike's use of sweatshop labor. The Beatles brought a lawsuit against Nike and their ad agency that was settled out of court in 1989 with undisclosed terms.

nature of popular music, amplified through continual television commercial circulation, has been theorized by Jacques Attali, and others as a form of silencing of dissent as it creates, in effect, a consumer desire for conformity.[76]

Nonetheless, in sports broadcasting, standardization and the threat of evanescence due to cancellation are ironically often entwined: they mirror the enmeshed processes of commodity production, predictability, and obsolescence in a high-consumption society. They may help convince audiences of "the rightness and naturalness of a world that, in only an apparent paradox, regularly requires an irregularity—an unreliability that it calls progress."[77] In this way the regular variegation of games and outcomes, like shifting television programming in general, seem to affirm the sovereignty of the audience while keeping more substantive alternatives out of mainstream public purview. In this manner, elite authority and consumer choice are simultaneously affirmed to reinforce a central operation of hegemonic liberal capitalist ideology. Televised sports are often constructed and presented in such a way as to reproduce dominant American values surrounding capitalist consumerism and stability ensured through repetition and rhetorical and physical aggression. The repetitive and overtly (masculine?) aggressive musical themes that frame and punctuate the broadcasts are one more important method by which this is accomplished.

---

[76] See "Repeating" in Jacques Attali, *Noise: The Political Economy of Music* (Minneapolis MN: University of Minnesota Press, 1989), 87–132. Also see Robert Fink's discussion linking minimalist music to the "repetitive excess of consumerism" in *Repeating Ourselves: American Music as Cultural Practice* (Los Angeles: University of California Press, 2005), xi. The similarities of repetitive action and aesthetics in music and sports are discussed in Chapter 5.

[77] Gitlin, "Prime time ideology," 5.

Conclusion
"Na Na Hey Hey Kiss Him Goodbye": Codas and Overtimes

This book has examined the significant links between the realms of popular music and sports. In particular, I have underlined their shared and often mutually reinforcing roles in delineating and reflecting identity. From the sanctioned social conditioning of inequality fostered in both sporting and musical competitions to the singing of national anthems and team chants, the nexus of music and sports is too often overlooked as a location in the construction, contestation and promotion of identity. Common markers of youth as well as physical and performative display, these typically discreetly studied realms of entertainment and leisure culture are also interconnected in significant ways in regards to constructions of African American masculinity, female body image, sexual identity, class, nationalism and location. They are even on the frontlines of debates surrounding questions of performance enhancement and what it means to be human.

Due to our ever increasing focus on youth and commercialism in Western society, popular music, as distinct from other forms of music, has been harnessed to sport and vice versa. Aside from being strong allies in the construction of identity, popular music and sports have also actively affected the practical components of each activity. More than just symbolic icons associated with supporting various teams and sporting events, as in gymnastics and figure skating, music often plays an active role in the sport itself. Similarly, as witnessed in the improvisatory links between African American jazz and both basketball and baseball, sports and music have at times mutually influenced each other's performative and aesthetic content.

To state the obvious, however, sports and popular music are not the same activities, and never will be. The intent of this book was not necessarily to demonstrate how similar they are, though as participatory or passively consumed activities they certainly evince more similarities than one might suspect and I have endeavored to underline many of these moments. My goal, instead, has been to examine and understand how these two activities have been combined, often compounding their individual influence, to construct and reflect identity in our increasingly hybridized world.

It is my hope that this study will open up further avenues of research concerning the connections between sports and music. This study, though extensive, is far from comprehensive and there is much work that remains to be done. The extent of the relationship between sports and the literally thousands of nineteenth- and early twentieth-century parlour songs has only been briefly suggested in this book. A comprehensive cataloging and analysis of these works would, I believe, tell us much about leisure patterns and social and class constructions during these eras. Similarly, far more work needs to be done on the presence of sports themes in classical music. A focused in-depth analysis of sports and music in non-Western cultures would certainly yield valuable insights into the construction of identities in many cultures. Though I have spent some time discussing the relationship of music and sports in the construction of male, female and gay identities, there is still work to be done regarding often overlooked lesbian, transgendered and bi-sexual identities. Other areas, such as a focused inquiry into the intersections of music and sport in promoting aggression and violence, would also prove to be extremely fruitful avenues of research.

At the time of writing the signature omnipresent drone of the vuvuzelas are still ringing in the ears of all who took in World Cup South Africa 2010. To some extent the vuvuzela, though reviled by many (including several teams who protested its presence in stadiums as it impeded hearing coaching instructions on the field), sums up the nexus of music, sports and identity that is central to this book. No arguably musical sound, in the near future at least, will ever be so indelibly linked to a sporting event nor so representative of locational identity. Underlining the common commercial connections between sports and music, the plastic horn was also an economic boon to the plastic company who manufactured it and the many local vendors who sold them to fans.

While this particular study has reached its culmination, as is exemplified by the impact of the vuvuzela on the 2010 World Cup, new examples of the sports–music nexus are occurring with virtually every new major sporting event. The 2012 London Olympics have already signed a deal with Universal Music that grants them exclusive rights to release all London 2012-branded music.[1] Fans and players of the 2010 Stanley Cup Champion Chicago Blackhawks revelled to the Scottish alternative pop of The Fratellis' "Chelsea Dagger" after every goal and in their numerous post-championship victory celebrations. Similarly, sporting organizations continue to associate themselves with various types of music and musicians (for example, hip hop mogul Jay Z has been part-owner of the New Jersey Nets since 2004) and sports films and television soundtracks associated with sports will undoubtedly continue to proliferate. Some of the more prominent sports-related movies released in 2010 included *Secretariat*, *Invictus*, and a remake of *The Karate Kid* (featuring a theme song by teen sensation Justin Bieber), to name a few. The 2010 Toronto International Film Festival was launched with *Score: A Hockey Musical* featuring Olivia Newton John and Nellie Furtado. As we become more and more attached to our iPods and MP3 players, music will also continue to permeate our individual exercise regimes, serving to both motivate and distract us from the fatigue and pain. In short, the connections between music and sport will continue to develop and flourish and, likewise, they will continue to combine in new delineations of identity.

---

[1]   "London Olympics ink deal with Universal Music" *CBCSports.ca*, www.cbc.ca/sports/amateur/story/2010/05/24/sp-universal-london.html (accessed July 10, 2010).

Given the extensive history and manifestation of the cross-pollinations of popular music and sport as outlined in this study, it is unclear why the topic has been relatively neglected. It is increasingly curious, given the recent interest in interdisciplinarity that has consumed much humanistic inquiry. I suspect that the reasons stem from lingering biases in the study of both discreet areas that refuses to take either popular music studies seriously or, alternatively, finds sports to be an equally unworthy topic for consequential scholarly inquiry. One of the underlying goals of this study has been to dismantle further the mind–body duality that has often stereotyped and characterized both athletes and musicians. The stereotypical high school mentality of divisions between the marching band (geeks) and football team (jocks) needs to be unequivocally dismantled.

The intersection of music and athletics resonates deeply within all of us in a type of nascent sonic enervation. Both music and sports are inherently connected to the body. On the most basic level sports and music are interconnected aspects of human existence. From the earliest age, whether in the womb listening to our mother's heartbeat or as we crawl on the floor as babies, human beings associate sound, rhythm and music with bodily movement. Indeed, music is typically described in terms of its affective properties, its ability to be both emotionally and corporally "moving." It is likely no accident that the concept of "play" is central to both activities. In keeping with the ideals of the ancient Greeks, both music and athletics—even if only in the service of distracting entertainment—evince a common ability to simultaneously enervate both the mind and the body. Increasingly interconnected modes of social practice, the confluence of music and sports simultaneously combine to provide a powerful nexus of identity formation that must no longer be overlooked. Given the near universal exposure to both sports and popular music, it would seem that all our identities are, at least in some small way, influenced by the confluence of these cultural forms. To the extent that we proclaim ourselves through sports and music connections—be it in aligning ourselves with the musical culture of various teams or in the music to which we listen while exercising—to paraphrase the words of Queen's classic sports anthem, "we are all the champions!"

Bibliography

Adorno, Theodore, "On the fetish character in music and the regression of listening," in Simon Frith (ed.), *Popular Music: Critical Concepts in Media and Cultural Studies*, Vol. 3 (New York: Routledge, 2004), pp. 325–49.

Anderson, Eric, *In the Game: Gay Athletes and the Cult of Masculinity* (Albany, NY: State University of New York Press, 2005).

Appadurai, Arjun, "Disjuncture and difference in the global cultural economy," *Theory Culture and Society* 7 (1990), p. 301.

Aristotle, *Politics*, Book 8, Part IV, trans. H. Rackham (Cambridge, Mass.: Harvard University Press, 1990).

Attali, Jacques, *Noise: The Political Economy of Music* (Minneapolis MN: University of Minnesota Press, 1989).

Bachelor, Blane, "Music industry keeps its eye on the ball," *Billboard* 115/10 (March 2003), p. 50.

Bairner, Alan, *Sport, Nationalism, and Globalization: European and North American Perspectives* (Albany: State University of New York Press, 2001).

Bakan, Michael B., *The Music of Death and New Creation: Experiences in the World of Balinese Gamelan Beleganjur* (Chicago: University of Chicago Press, 1999).

Baker, Aaron, *Contesting Identities: Sports in American Film* (University of Illinois Press, 2003).

Baker, Aaron and Todd Boyd (eds), *Out of Bounds: Sports, Media and the Politics of Identity* (Bloomington IN: Indiana University Press, 1997).

Bakhtin, Mikhail, *Rabelais and His World*, trans. H. Iswolsky (Bloomington, Ind: Indiana University Press, 1984).

Baldick, Robert, *The Duel: A History of Dueling* (London: Chapman & Hall, 1965).

Balthaser, Joel D., "Cheerleading—Oh how far it has come!," *Pop Warner*. January 6, 2005. www.popwarner.com/articles/phenomenon.asp (accessed on January 11, 2007).

Barthes, Roland, *Mythologies* (London: Vintage Books, 1993).

Bateman, Anthony and John Bale (eds), *Sporting Sounds: Relationships Between Sports and Music* (London: Routledge, 2009).

Beaurepaire, Pierre, 'Nobles jeux de l'arc et loges maçonniques dans la France,' *H-France Review* 3/75 (July 2003).

Beckett, A., "The effects of music on exercise as determined by physiological recovery heart rates and distance," *Journal of Music Therapy* 27 (1990), pp. 126–36.

Beebe, Roger, Denise Fulbrook and Ben Saunders (eds), *Rock Over the Edge: Transformations in Popular Music Culture* (Durham, NC: Duke University Press, 2002).

Bennett, Andy and Richard Peterson (eds), *Music Scenes: Local, Translocal, and Virtual* (Nashville: Vanderbilt University Press, 2004).

Bennett, Andy, Barry Shank and Jason Toynbee (eds), *The Popular Music Studies Reader* (New York: Routledge, 2006).

Berger, Maurice, Brian Wallis and Simon Watson (eds), *Constructing Masculinity* (New York: Routledge, 1995).

Berliner, Paul, *Thinking in Jazz: The Infinite Art of Improvisation* (Chicago: University of Chicago Press, 1994).

Bessman, Jim, "NASCAR revs up Cherry Lane," *Billboard* 115/24 (June 2003), p. 43.

Blain, Neil, Raymond Boyle and Hugh O'Donnell, *Sport and National Identity in European Media* (Leicester: Leicester University Press, 1993).

Blankenship, Bill, "Symphony takes swing at music of sports world," *The Capital-Journal*, Sunday, January 6, 2008.

Bloom, John, and Michael Nevin Willard (eds), *Sports Matters: Race Recreation and Culture* (New York: New York University Press, 2002).

Blumenfield, Larry, "On bebop & b-ball," *Jazz* 22/9 (September 2005), pp. 40–42.

Bone, James, "Don't stop us now, say marathon runners who plan to defy music ban," *The Times*, November 2, 2007.

Bostrom, Nick, *Anthropic Bias: Observation Selection Effects in Science and Philosophy* (New York: Routledge, 2002).

Bourdieu, Pierre, "Sport and social class," in Chandra Mukerji and Michael Schudson (eds), *Rethinking Popular Culture* (Los Angeles: University of California Press, 1991), pp. 357–73.

_____, "How can one be a sports fan?," in Simon During (ed.), *A Cultural Studies Reader* (London: Routledge, 1994), pp. 339–56.

_____, "The state, economics and sport," in H. Dauncey and G. Hare (eds), *France and the 1998 World Cup* (London: Frank Cass, 1999), pp. 15–21.

_____, *Pascalian Meditations* (Cambridge, UK: Polity, 2000).

Bourdieu, Pierre, and Loïc Wacquant, *An Invitation to Reflexive Sociology* (Cambridge, UK: Polity, 1992).

Boyd, Todd, *The Rise of the NBA, The Hip Hop Invasion and the Transformation of American Culture* (New York: Doubleday, 2003).

Boykin, Keith, "Black gay athletes: Homosexuality and homoeroticism in black sports" (website), Monday, February 3, 2003. www.keithboykin.com/sports/blackgayathletes.html (accessed May 17, 2008).

Brackett, David, *Interpreting Popular Music* (New York : Cambridge University Press, 1995).

Bradley, Joseph M., *Ethnic and Religious Identity in Modern Scotland* (Aldershot: Avebury Press, 1995).

_____, "We shall not be moved'! Mere sport, mere songs? A tale of Scottish football," in Adam Brown (ed.), *Fanatics!: Power, Identity and Fandom in Football* (London: Routledge, 1998), pp. 203–18.

Brightman, James, "Music video games now more popular than sports games, says study," *Game Daily*, Tuesday, October 21, 2008. www.gamedaily.com/articles/news/music-video-games-now-more-popular-than-sports-games-says-study/?biz=1 (accessed April 2, 2009).

Brookes, Rod, *Representing Sport* (London: Arnold Press, 2002).

Bufwack, Mary A. and Robert K. Oermann, *Finding Her Voice: The Saga of Women in Country Music* (New York: Crown, 1993).

Butler, Judith, *Bodies that Matter: On the Discursive Limits of Sex* (New York: Routledge, 1993).

Cai, G., and Xi, B.-S., "Research on the status quo of incidental music of competitive wushu taolu," *Journal of Beijing University of Physical Education* 30/6 (2007), pp. 852–4.

Campo-Flores, Arian, "A world of cheer!," *Newsweek*, May 14, 2007.

Caponi-Tabery, Gina, *Jump for Joy: Jazz, Basketball & Black Culture in 1930s America* (Amherst: University of Massachusetts Press, 2008).

Carrington, Ben, review of *When We Were Kings*, in *The International Review for the Sociology of Sport* 33/1 (1998), p. 76.

Cashmore, Ellis, *Making Sense of Sports* (London: Routledge, 2000).

Chipman, L. "The effects of selected music on endurance," MA thesis, Springfield College. From *Completed Research in Health, Physical Education, and Recreation* 9 (1966), Abstract No. 462.

Clément, Catherine, *Opera, or, The Undoing of Women*, trans. Betsy Wing (Minneapolis: University of Minnesota Press, 1988).

Collier, James Lincoln, *Jazz: The American Theme Song* (New York: Oxford University Press, 1993).

Collin, Mathew, "The technologies of pleasure," in *Alter State: The Story of Ecstasy Culture and Acid House* (London: Serpent's Tail, 1997), pp. 10–44.

Comfort, Nathaniel, "Cultural Darwinism," *The European Legacy* 13/5 (2008), pp. 623–37.

Considine, J.D., "Why Ashlee's taking the heat: It's not as if she's the only musician to have used recorded tracks. Even Geddy Lee does it. But Ashlee Simpson's no Geddy Lee," *Globe and Mail* (Toronto), October 30, 2004.

Crouch, Stanley, *The All American Skin Game, or, The Decoy of Race* (New York: Vintage Press, 1995).

Csikszentmihalyi, Mihaly and L.S., *Optimal Experience: Psychological Studies of Flow in Consciousness* (Cambridge: Cambridge University Press, 1988).

Cunningham, Hugh, *Leisure in the Industrial Revolution, c. 1780–1880* (New York: St Martin's Press, 1980).

Cusic, Don, "NASCAR and country music," *Studies in Popular Culture* 21/1 (1998), pp. 31–40.

_____, *Baseball and Country Music* (Madison WI: University of Wisconsin Press, 2003).

Cusick, Suzanne G., "Caccini," *Grove Music Online*. L. Macy (ed.), www.grovemusic.com (accessed January 24, 2006).

_____, "Gender, musicology, and feminism," in Nicholas Cook and Mark Everist (eds), *Rethinking Music* (Oxford: Oxford University Press, 1999).

Danielsen, Anne, Presence and Pleasure: *The Funk Grooves of James Brown and Parliament* (Middletown, CT: Wesleyan University Press, 2006).

Davis, Miles, *Miles: The Autobiography* (New York: Simon & Schuster, 1989).

de Boer, Jennifer, "On the margins of the mainstream: Queen, the rock press, and gender," MA thesis, McMaster University, 1999.

Debord, Guy, *The Society of Spectacle* (New York: Zone Books, 1995).

de Coubertin, Pierre, *Olympism: Selected Writings* (Lausanne: International Olympic Committee, 2000).

Delamont, Sarah, and Neil Stephens, "Up on the roof: The embodied habitus of diasporic *capoeira*," *Cultural Sociology* 2/1 (2008), pp. 57–74.

Deleuze, Gilles and Felix Guattari, *A Thousand Plateaus: Capitalism and Schizophrenia* (Minneapolis: University of Minnesota Press, 1987).

DeNora, Tia, *Music in Everyday Life* (Cambridge: Cambridge University Press, 2000).

DeNora, Tia, and Sophie Belcher, "'When you're trying something on you picture yourself in a place where they are playing this kind of music'—musically sponsored agency in the British clothing retail sector," *The Sociological Review* 48/1 (February 2000), pp. 80–101.

Dery, Mark, "Cyberculture," *The South Atlantic Quarterly* 91/3 (Summer 1992), pp. 501–23.

_____, "Black to the future: Interviews with Samuel R. Delany, Greg Tate and Tricia Rose," *The South Atlantic Quarterly* 92/4 (Fall 1993), pp. 735–78.

Diaz, Jaime, "The growing gap: Driving distances are skyrocketing on the PGA Tour. So why is the average golfer being left behind?" *Golf Digest*, May 2003. http://findarticles.com/p/articles/mi_m0HFI/is_5_54/ai_101967369/ (accessed May 15, 2009).

Dines, Gail and Jean Humez (eds), *Gender, Race, and Class in Media: A Text Reader* (California: Sage Publications, 2003).

Dyson, Michael Eric, *Know What I Mean? Reflections on Hip Hop* (Philadelphia: Basic Civitas Books, 2007).

Early, Gerald, *Tuxedo Junction: Essays on American Culture* (New York: Ecco Press, 1989).

Eitzen, D. Stanley (ed.), *Sport in Contemporary Society* (New York: Worth, 2001).

Elam, Harry and Kennel Jackson (eds), *Black Cultural Traffic: Crossroads in Global Performance and Popular Culture* (Ann Arbor: University of Michigan Press, 2005).

Elias, Norbert, *The Quest for Excitement: Sport and Leisure in the Civilizing Process* (Oxford: Blackwell, 1986).

Emery, Charles, "A little music with exercise boosts brain power," *Science Blog*. www.scienceblog.com/community/modules (accessed April 5, 2004).

Epstein, Jonathon, *Youth Culture: Identity in a Postmodern World* (Oxford: Blackwell, 1998).

Erenberg, Lewis, *Swingin' the Dream: Big Band Jazz and the Rebirth of American Culture* (Chicago: University of Chicago Press, 1998).

Fairs, J.R., "When was the golden age of the body?," *Journal of the Canadian Association of Health, Physical Education and Recreation* 37/1 (1970), pp. 11–24.

Fink, Robert, *Repeating Ourselves: American Music as Cultural Practice* (Los Angeles: University of California Press, 2005).

Fisk, Roger, *English Theatre Music in the Eighteenth Century* (London: Oxford University Press, 1986).

Floyd, Samuel A., *The Power of Black Music: Interpreting its History from Africa to the United States* (New York: Oxford University Press, 1995).

Forman, Murray and Mark Anthony Neal (eds), *That's the Joint! The Hip-Hop Studies Reader* (New York: Routledge, 2004).

Foucault, Michel, "Body/Power," in Colin Gordon, trans., *Power/Knowledge: Selected Interviews and Other Writings 1972–77* (New York: Pantheon, 1980).
_____, *The History of Sexuality: The Use of Pleasure*, Vol. 2, trans. Robert Hurley (New York: Vintage, 1986).

France, Lisa Respers, "Finale stuns 'Idol' worshippers," *CNN.com*. www.cnn.com/2009/SHOWBIZ/TV/05/21/american.idol.reaction/index.html (accessed May 21, 2009).

Frith, Simon, *Performing Rites: On the Value of Popular Music* (Cambridge, Mass.: Harvard University Press, 1996).

Frith, Simon, Andrew Goodwin and Lawrence Grossberg (eds), *Sound and Vision: The Music Video Reader* (London: Routledge, 1993).

Froiland, Paul, *Cheer Magazine* 1/1 (1993), pp. 13, 30–31, 39.

Frow, John, "The literary frame," *Journal of Aesthetic Education* 16/2 (1982), pp. 25–30.

Fu, Zhongwen, *Mastering Yang Style Taijiquan* (Berkeley, California: Blue Snake Books: 2006).

Fuller, Linda K. (ed.), *Sport, Rhetoric, and Gender: Historical Perspectives and Media Representations* (New York: Palgrave Macmillan, 2006).

Gabbard, Krin, *Hotter than That: The Trumpet, Jazz and American Culture* (New York: Faber and Faber, 2008).

Gager Clinch, Nancy, *The Kennedy Neurosis* (New York: Grosset and Dunlap, 1973).

Garrett, Charles Hiroshi, "Struggling to define a nation: American music in the twentieth century," Diss., University of California Los Angeles, 2004.

Gates, Henry Louis Jr, *The Signifying Monkey: A Theory of African-American Literary Criticism* (New York: Oxford University Press, 1988).

Gaunt, Kyra, "Translating Double Dutch to hip hop: The musical vernacular of black girls' play," in Murray Forman and Mark Anthony Neal (eds), *That's the Joint!: The Hip-Hop Studies Reader* (New York: Routledge, 2004), pp. 251–63.

George, Nelson, *Elevating the Game: Black Men and Basketball* (New York: Harper Collins, 1992).

Gfeller, Kate, "Musical components and styles preferred by young adults for aerobic fitness classes," *Journal of Music Therapy* 25 (1988), pp. 28–43.

Gilbert, Jeremy and Ewan Pearson, *Discographies: Dance Music, Culture and the Politics of Sound* (London: Routledge, 1999).

Gillespie, Dizzie and Al Fraser, *To Be or Not ... to Bop* (New York: Da Capo Press, 1979).

Gillis, Charlie, "Dumb-da-dumb-da-dumb!," *Maclean's Magazine* 21/24 June 23, 2008.

Gitlin, Todd, "Prime time ideology: The hegemonic process in television entertainment," *Social Problems* 26/3 (February, 1979), pp. 251–66.

Giulianotti, Richard, *Sport: A Critical Sociology* (Cambridge, UK: Polity, 2005).

Gracyk, Theodore, *I Wanna Be Me: Politics and Identity in Rock Music* (Temple University Press: 2001).

Graves, Lee, N.D. Ridgers and G. Stratton, "The contribution of upper limb and total body movement to adolescents' energy expenditure whilst playing Nintendo Wii," *European Journal of Applied Physiology* 104/ 4 (2008), pp. 617–23.

Graves, Lee, G. Stratton, N.D. Ridgers, and N.T. Cable, "Energy expenditure in adolescents playing new generation computer games," *British Journal of Sports Medicine* 42/7 (2008), pp. 592–4.

Green, Geoffrey, *Soccer: The World Game* (London: The Phoenix House, 1953).

Greenemeier, Larry, "Real-life Iron Man: A robotic suit that magnifies human strength," *Scientific American*, April 30, 2008. www.sciam.com/article.cfm?id=real-life-iron-man-exoskeleton.

Groppe, Laura, "Girls and gaming: Gender and video game marketing," *Children Now*. www.childrennow.org/media/medianow/mnwinter2001.html (accessed Aug 4, 2006).

Guegold, William K., *One Hundred Years of Olympic Music: Music and Musicians of the Modern Olympic Games, 1896–1996* (Mantua, Ohio: Golden Clef Publishing, 1996).

Guttman, Allen, *Women's Sports: A History* (New York: Columbia University Press, 1991).

———, *Games and Empires: Modern Sports and Cultural Imperialism* (New York: Columbia University Press, 1994).

Haas, Cher and Robert, *Forever Fit: The Lifetime Plan for Health, Fitness, and Beauty* (New York: Bantam Books, 1991).

Habermas, Jurgen, *The Philosophical Discourse of Modernity* (Cambridge, UK: Polity Press, 1987).

———, *The New Conservatism* (Cambridge, UK: Polity Press, 1989).

Hall, Stuart, "What is this 'black' in black popular culture?," in David Morely and Kuan-Hsing Chen (eds), *Stuart Hall: Critical Dialogues in Popular Culture* (New York: Routledge, 1996).

Haraway, Donna, "A cyborg manifesto: Science, technology, and socialist-feminism in the late twentieth century," in *Simians, Cyborgs, and Women: The Reinvention of Nature* (New York: Routledge, 1991), pp. 149–81.

Hargreaves, John, *Sport, Power and Culture: A Social and Historical Analysis of Popular Sports in Britain* (Cambridge, UK: Polity Press, 1986).

Herbert, Trevor, "American wind bands," *Grove Music Online*. L. Macy (ed.), www.grovemusic.com (accessed April 10, 2008).

Hiatt, Brian, "Stefani, Peas lead singles boom," *Rolling Stone*, January 19, 2006.

Ho, Fred, and Bill Mullen (eds), *Afro Asia: Revolutionary Political & Cultural Connections Between African American and Asian Americans* (Durham NC: Duke University Press, 2008).

Hodgkinson, Will, "Snapshot: Grace Jones," *Guardian Unlimited Online*. http://arts.guardian.co.uk/image/0,,1672997,00.html (accessed March 13, 2008).

Holmes, Geoffrey, and Daniel Szechi, *The Age of Oligarchy: Pre-industrial Britain 1722–1783* (London: Longman, 1993).

hooks, bell, "Performance practice as a site of opposition," in Catherine Ugwu (ed.), *Let's Get It On: The Politics of Black Performance* (Seattle: Bay Press, 1995).

———, "Eating the Other: Desire and resistance," in Meenakshi Gigi Durham and Douglas M. Kellner (eds), *Media and Cultural Studies: Keyworks* (Malden Mass.: Blackwell, 2001).

Hooper, James, "New swimsuits unfair," *Daily Telegraph*, March 9, 2008.

Horne, John, *Sport in Consumer Culture* (New York: Palgrave Macmillan, 2006).

Horvath, Janet, *An Injury Prevention Guide for Musicians: Playing (less) Hurt* (Kearney, NE: Morris Publishing, 2006).

Huff, Quentin, "Gwen Stefani: The sweet escape," *PopMatters*, December 14, 2006.

Jansen, Sue Curry, "Football is more than a game: Masculinity, sport and war," *Critical Communication Theory* (New York: Rowman and Littlefield, 2002), pp. 185–210.

Katz, Mark, *Capturing Sound: How Technology Changed Music* (Los Angeles: University of California Press, 2004).

Keil, Charles, and Steven Feld, *Music Grooves* (Chicago: University of Chicago Press, 1994).

Klink, William, "Digging your lips: Foucault, Bakhtin, Lacan, and pro beach volleyball," *Studies in Popular Culture* 21/3 (1999), pp. 1–11.

Kinsbury, Alex, "Performance enhancing drugs: Not just baseball," *U.S. News & World Report*, January 29, 2008. www.usnews.com/articles/news/national/2008/01/29/performance-enhancing-drugs-not-just-baseball.html (accessed March 7, 2010).

Koschak, E.P., "The influence of music on physical performance of women," MA thesis, Central Michigan University. From *Completed Research in Health, Physical Education, and Recreation* 19 (1975), Abstract No. 99.

Krims, Adam, *Music and Urban Geography* (New York: Routledge, 2007).

Kuch, K.D., *The Cheerleaders Almanac* (New York: Random House, 1996).

Kühnst, Peter, *Sports: A Cultural History of the Mirror of Art* (Dresden: Verlag der Kühnst, 1996).

Kurutz, Steven, "They're playing my song: Time to work out," *New York Times*, January 10, 2008.

Kurzweil, Raymond, *The Singularity is Near: When Humans Transcend Biology* (New York: Viking, 2005).

Kusz, Kyle, "'I want to be the minority': The products of youthful white masculinities in sport and popular culture in 1990s America," in David Rowe (ed.), *Critical Reading in Sport, Culture and the Media* (Maidenhead: Open University Press, 2004), pp. 261–75.

Laine, L. (ed.), *On the Fringes of Sports* (St Augustine, Germany: Academia, 1993).

Lei, Lei, "Beijing to ramp up Olympic doping tests," *China Daily*, July 6, 2007. http://daily.iflove.com/2008/2007-07/06/content_911778.htm (accessed August 12, 2008).

Lenskyj, Helen, *Out of Bounds* (Toronto: The Women's Press, 1986), 56.

_____, "Girl-friendly sport and female values," *Women in Sport and Physical Activity Journal* 3/1 (1994), pp. 35–46.

_____, "Gay Games or Gay Olympics? Implications for lesbian inclusion," *Canadian Women's Studies* 21/ 3 (Winter/Spring 2002), pp. 24–8.

Lincoln, Stoddard, "The librettos and lyrics of William Congreve," in Shirley Strum Kenny (ed.), *British Theatre and the Other Arts, 1660–1800* (Washington D.C.: Folger Shakespeare Libraries, 1984), pp. 116–32.

Lister, Sam, "Why music makes you exercise 20% harder," *The Times*, October 21, 2005.

Lois, George (ed.), *Ali Rap: Muhammad Ali, the First Heavyweight Champion of Rap* (Taschen, 2006).

Longmore, Andrew, "NBA orders limited retreat from decibel hell," *The Times*, October 19, 1995.

Lowe, Benjamin, *The Beauty of Sport: A Cross-Disciplinary Inquiry* (Englewood Cliffs, New Jersey: Prentice Hall, 1977).

Lowe, Melanie, "'Tween' scene: Resistance within the mainstream," in Andy Bennett and Richard Peterson (eds), *Music Scenes: Local, Translocal, and Virtual* (Nashville: Vanderbilt University Press, 2004), pp. 80–95.

MacNeill, Margaret, "Sex, lies and videotape: The political and cultural economies of celebrity fitness videos," in Geneviève Rail (ed.), *Sport and Postmodern Time* (New York: State University of New York Press, 1998), pp. 163–84.

Macur, Juliet, "A disgraced rider's admissions, and accusations," *New York Times*, May 20, 2010. www.nytimes.com/2010/05/21/sports/cycling/21cycling.html (accessed June 1, 2010).

_____, "No motors, but mistrust at Tour de France," *New York Times*, July 4, 2010. www.nytimes.com/2010/07/04/sports/cycling/04tour.html (accessed August 10, 2010).

Macur, Juliet, and Samuel Abt, "Investigator and anti-doping group clash on Armstrong Tests," *New York Times*, May 31, 2006. www.nytimes. com/2006/05/31/sports/othersports/31cnd-lance.html?_r=1&oref=slogin (accessed April 28, 2008).

Maguire, Jennifer Smith, "Exercising control: empowerment and the fitness discourse," in Linda K. Fuller (ed.), *Sport, Rhetoric, and Gender* (New York: Palgrave Macmillan, 2006), pp. 119–29.

Maguire, Joseph (ed.), *Power and Global Sport: Zones of Prestige, Emulation and Resistance* (London: Routledge, 2005).

Mailer, Norman, *The White Negro: Superficial Reflections on the Hipster* (San Francisco: City Lights Books, 1957).

Mainwaring, John, *Memoirs of the Life of the Late George Frederick Handel* (London, 1760).

Mandell, Richard, *Sport: A Cultural History* (New York: Columbia Press, 1984).

Mangan, J.A. (ed.), *Europe, Sport, World: Shaping Global Societies* (London: Frank Cass Press, 2001).

Manning, Gus, and Haywood Harris, *Once a Vol, Always a VOL! The Proud Men of the Volunteer Nation* (Sports Publishing LCC, 2006).

Marris, Paul, and Sue Thornham (eds), *The Media Studies Reader* (New York: New York University Press, 2000).

Mathiesen, Thomas, "Nomos," *Grove Music Online*. L. Macy (ed.), www. grovemusic.com (accessed March 5, 2006).

Maus, Fred E., "Glamour and evasion: the fabulous ambivalence of the Pet Shop Boys," *Popular Music* 20/3 (2001), pp. 379–93.

McBride, James, *War, Battering and Other Sports: The Gulf Between American Men and Women* (Atlantic Highland: Humanities Press, 1995).

McCarthy, Todd, "When we were kings," *Variety*, Monday, February 12, 1996.

McClary, Susan, *Feminine Endings: Music, Gender, and Sexuality* (Minneapolis: University of Minnesota Press, 1995).

McCormick, Lisa, "Higher, faster, louder: Representations of the international music competition," *Cultural Sociology* 3/1 (2009), pp. 5–30.

McCusker, Kristine, and Diane Pecknold (eds), *A Boy Named Sue: Gender and Country Music* (Jackson: University of Mississippi, 2004).

McKay, Jim, and David Rowe, "Ideology, the media, and Australian sport," *Sociology of Sport Journal* 4 (1997), pp. 258–73.

McKay, Jim, Michael Messner and Don Sabo (eds), *Masculinities, Gender Relations, and Sport* (New York: Sage, 2000), pp. 222–44.

McLeod, Ken, "Bohemian Rhapsodies: Operatic influence and crossover in rock music," *Popular Music* 20/2 (2001), pp. 189–203.

_____, "Space oddities: Aliens, futurism and meaning in rock music," *Popular Music* 23/2 (Fall 2003), pp. 315–33.

_____, "We are the champions: The politics of sports and popular music," *Popular Music and Society* 29/5 (December 2006), pp. 533–49.

_____, "Constructions of African American masculinity in music and sports," *American Music* 27/2 (2009), pp. 204–26.

McKnight, Peter, "Sports, technology and the meaning of 'human,'" *Vancouver Sun*, Saturday, January 26, 2008.

McNeill, William, *Keeping Together in Time: Dance and Drill in Human History* (Cambridge, Mass.: Harvard University Press, 1995).

Meintjes, Louise, "Paul Simon's *Graceland*, South Africa and the mediation of musical meaning," *Ethnomusicology* 34 (1990), pp. 37–73.

Messner, Mike, Darnell Hunt and Michele Dunbar, *Boys to Men: Sports Media Messages about Masculinity* (*Children Now* and the Amateur Athletic Foundation of Los Angeles, 1999).

Middleton, Richard, *Studying Popular Music* (Milton Keynes: Open University Press, 1990).

_____, *Reading Pop: Approaches to Textual Analysis in Popular Music* (New York: Oxford University Press, 2000).

Miles, Steven, *Consumerism as a Way of Life* (London: Sage, 1997).

Miller, Toby, and Alec McHoul, *Popular Culture and Everyday Life* (London: Sage Publications, 1998).

Morse, Margaret, "Artemis aging: Exercise and the female body on video," *Discourse* 10/1 (1987/1988), pp. 20–54.

Nixon, Howard L., *Sport in a Changing World* (London: Paradigm, 2008).

Novak, Michael, *The Joy of Sports: End Zones, Bases, Baskets, Balls, and the Consecration of the American Spirit* (New York: Basic Books, 1976).

Oates, Joyce Carol, *On Boxing* (London: Bloomsbury, 1987).

Oestreich, James, "In music as well as sports, injuries can end a career," *New York Times*, Tuesday, August 27, 1996.

Olsen, Catherine Applefeld, "Labels take a run with sports," *Billboard* 110/35 (August 1998), pp. 77–8.

_____, "Pro sports marketing pitches hits for athletic events," *Billboard* 114/39 (September 2002), p. 59.

Organizing Committee for the Games of the XXth Olympiad, Munich, 1972, *The Scientific View of Sport* (New York: Springer Verlag, 1972).

Pargman, D., and S. Wininger, "Assessment of factors associated with exercise enjoyment," *Journal of Music Therapy* 40/1 (2003), pp. 57–73.

Pearce, K.A., "Effects of different types of music on physical strength," *Perceptual and Motor Skills* 53 (1981), pp. 351–2.

Perry, Imani, *Prophets of the Hood: Politics and Poetics in Hip Hop* (Durham NC: Duke University Press, 2004).

Picart, Caroline Joan, *From Ballroom to DanceSport: Aesthetics, Athletics, and Body Culture* (New York: State University of New York Press, 2006).

Phillips, Murray G. (ed.), *Deconstructing Sport History: A Postmodern Analysis* (Albany: State University of New York Press, 2006).

Pope, S.W. (ed.), *The New American Sport History: Recent Approaches and Perspectives* (Chicago: University of Illinois Press, 1997).

Price, Richard, "Why is Madonna punishing herself?" *Daily Mail*, January 21, 2006.

Price, Scott, "Whatever happened to the white athlete?" *Sports Illustrated* (December 6, 1997), pp. 32–51.

Pronger, Brian, *The Arena of Masculinity: Sports, Homosexuality, and the Meaning of Sex* (New York: St. Martin's, 1990).

Rail, Geneviève (ed.), *Sport and Postmodern Times* (New York: State University of New York Press, 1998).

Ramano, David Gilman, "Culture and tradition: The ancient Olympic Games." Article written for the Salt Lake City Organizing Committee of the 2002 Winter Olympic Games. www.weberpl.lib.ut.us/roughdraft/2002/RDwinter02/tradition.htm (accessed April 20, 2010).

Redhead, Steve, Derek Wynne, and Justin O'Connor (eds), *The ClubCultures Reader: Reading in Popular Cultural Studies* (Oxford: Blackwell, 1997).

Reiss, Steven, *City Games: The Evolution of American Urban Society and the Rise of Sports* (Urbana: University of Illinois Press, 1989).

Rivenburg, Roy, "Ballpark organists: They're out," *Los Angeles Times*, Saturday, June 11, 2005.

Rodenburg, Dirk, "Resistance is futile: Confronting the ethics of the 'enhanced human' athlete," *The International Journal of Sport and Society* 1/1 (2010), pp. 285–300.

Rolfe, John, "The music–sports connection is stronger than ever," *Sports Illustrated. com.* http://sportsillustrated.cnn.com/2007/writers/music_sports/09/28/rolfe.essay/index.html (accessed October 1, 2007).

Romy, Fatimah, *The Third Eye: Race, Cinema, and Ethnographic Spectacle* (Duke: Duke University Press, 1996).

Rosen, Craig, "Golf music: Out of the rough, into the fore," *Billboard* 106/37 (September 1996), pp. 1, 26.

Rosenstone, Robert, *Visions of the Past* (Cambridge, Mass.: Harvard University Press, 1995).

Ross, Marlon B., "In search of black men's masculinities," *Feminist Studies* 24/3 (Autumn 1998), pp. 599–626.

Rowe, David, *Popular Cultures: Rock Music, Sport and the Politics of Pleasure* (London: Sage Publications, 1995).

_____, *Sport, Culture and the Media: The Unruly Trinity* (London: Open University Press, 2004).

_____, (ed.), *Critical Reading in Sport, Culture and the Media* (Maidenhead: Open University Press, 2004).

Rubenstein, Atoosa, "Courtney Love speaks about Gwen Stefani," *Seventeen* (August 2004), p. 19.

Sanneh, Kelefa, "Rap against rockism," *New York Times*, October 31, 2004.

Scambler, Graham, *Sport and Society: History, Power and Culture* (New York: Open University Press, 2005).

Schäfer, W., "Global civilization and local cultures: A crude look at the whole," *International Sociology* 16/3 (2001), pp. 301–19.

Schartz, S.E., B. Fernhall and S.A. Plowman, "The effects of music on exercise performance," *Journal of Cardiopulmonary Rehabilitation* 10 (1990), pp. 312–16.

Scheurer, Timothy, "'The best there ever was in the game': Musical mythopoesis and heroism in film scores of recent sports movies," *Journal of Popular Film & Television* 32/4 (Winter 2005), pp. 157–67.

Schiesel, Seth, "P.E. classes turn to video game that works legs," *New York Times*, April 30, 2007.

Schmidt, Michael, "Clemens lied about doping, indictment charges," *New York Times*, August 19, 2010.

Schrager, Peter, "*Total Request Live* at the ballpark," *ESPN Page 3*, Friday, August 6, 2004. http://sports.espn.go.com/espn/page3/story?page=schrager/040806 (accessed May 18, 2009).

Shamsuddin, Sheikh, *The Malay Art of Self-Defense: Silat Seni Gayong* (North Atlantic Books, 2005).

Sklar, Robert, *Movie-Made America* (New York: Random House, 1975).

Smith, Adrian and Dilwyn Porter, *Sport and National Identity in the Post-War World* (London: Routledge, 2004).

Smith, Jacob, "I can see tomorrow in your dance: A study of *Dance Dance Revolution* and music video games," *Journal of Popular Music Studies* 16/1 (2004), pp. 58–84.

Smith, R.J., "Gwen Stefani: *Love. Angel. Music. Baby.*," *Blender*. www.blender.com/guide/new/53197/love-angel-music-baby.html (accessed May 14, 2009).

Sugden, John, and Alan Tomlinson (eds), *FIFA and the Contest for World Football* (Cambridge, UK: Polity Press, 1998).

_____, *Power Games: A Critical Sociology of Sports* (London: Routledge, 2002).

Spaethling, Robert (ed./trans.), *Mozart's Letters, Mozart's Life* (New York: W.W. Norton & Co., 2000).

Stevenson, Charles Leslie, "Sport as contemporary social phenomenon: A functional explanation," *International Journal of Physical Education* 11, pp. 8–14.

Straw, Will, *Popular Music—Style and Identity* (Montreal: Centre for Research on Canadian Cultural Industries and Institutions, 1995).

Struna, Nancy, *People of Prowess: Sport, Leisure, and Labor in Early Anglo-America* (Urbana: University of Illinois Press, 1996).

Sutton, Julia, "Arbeau, Thoinot," in *Grove Music Online*, Oxford Music Online. www.oxfordmusiconline.com.myaccess.library.utoronto.ca/subscriber/article/grove/music/45795 (accessed May 19, 2009).

Sutton, Julia, *et al.*, "Dance," in *Grove Music Online*, Oxford Music Online. www.oxfordmusiconline.com.myaccess.library.utoronto.ca/subscriber/article/grove/music/01163 (accessed May 18, 2009).

Sweeny, Mark, "Timberlake signs IMG marketing deal," *Guardian*, Friday, April 18, 2008. www.guardian.co.uk/media/2008/apr/18/marketingandpr?gusrc=rss&feed=media (accessed May 15, 2009).

Talmon-Chvaicer, Maya, *The Hidden History of Capoeira: A Collision of Cultures in the Brazilian Battle Dance* (Austin: University of Texas Press, 2008).

Taylor, Timothy, *Global Pop: World Music, World Markets* (New York: Routledge, 1997).

_____, *Strange Sounds: Music, Technology and Culture* (New York: Routledge, 2001).

Tenzer, Michael, *Balinese Music* (Singapore: Periplus Editions Ltd, 1991).

Timms, Colin, "Opera-Torneo," *New Groves Online*. L. Macy (ed.), www.grovemusic.com (accessed May 16, 2006).

Tlauka, Michael, Jennifer Williams and Paul Williamson, "Spatial ability in secondary school students: Intra-sex differences based on self-selection for physical education," *British Journal of Psychology* 99/3 (August 2008), pp. 427–40.

Traiman, Steve, "Video games provide new platform for music promotion," *Billboard* 113/49 (December 2001), p. 75.

Truss, Lynn, "Bulls hit town for a lesson in jargon," *The Times*, October 20, 1997.

Turner, Brian, *The Body and Society: Explorations in Social Theory* (Oxford: Blackwell, 1983).

van Bottenburg, Maarten, *Global Games* (Chicago: University of Illinois Press, 2001).

van Orden, Kate, *Music, Discipline, and Arms in Early Modern France* (Chicago: University of Chicago Press, 2005).

Wales, D.N., "The effects of tempo and disposition in music on perceived exertion, brain waves, and mood during aerobic exercise," MA thesis, Pennsylvania State University, 1985. *Microform Publications*, University of Oregon Eugene, OR (University Microfiche No. UNIV ORE: U086 251–2).

Walker, Robert, "We all came out of Africa singing and dancing and we have been doing it ever since," *Research in Music Education* 24 (2005), pp. 4–16.

Walls, Jeanette, "Ashlee Simpson just paying lip service to fans," *MSNBC*, October 26, 2004. www.msnbc.msn.com/id/6329101 (accessed May 1, 2008).

Walser, Robert, *Running With the Devil: Power, Gender and Madness in Heavy Metal Music* (Hanover, NH : University Press of New England, 1993).

Weber, William, *The Rise of Musical Classics in Eighteenth-Century England: A Study in Canon, Ritual, and Ideology* (Oxford: Clarendon, 1992).

Weber, William, *et al.*, "Conservatories," in *Grove Music Online*, Oxford Music Online. www.oxfordmusiconline.com.myaccess.library.utoronto.ca/subscriber/article/grove/music/41225 (accessed May 16, 2009).

Weiss, Paul, *Sports: A Philosophic Inquiry* (Carbondale: Southern Illinois University Press, 1969).

Wertheim, John, "The quiet sounds of tennis," *Cnnsi*, January 14, 2002. http://sportsillustrated.cnn.com/inside_game/jon_wertheim/news/2002/01/14/wertheim_viewpoint/ (accessed June 16, 2010).

Whannel, Garry, *Media Sports Stars: Masculinities and Moralities* (London: Routledge, 2002).

Whitely, Sheila, *Sexing the Groove: Popular Music and Gender* (New York: Routledge, 1997).

Wideman, John Edgar, "Michael Jordan leaps the great divide," *Esquire*, November 1990, p. 210.

Willis, Susan, "Work(ing) out," *Cultural Studies* 4 (1990), pp. 1–18.

Wolf, Naomi, *The Beauty Myth* (Toronto: Random House, 1990).

Woodward, Kath, "Rumbles in the jungle. Boxing: racialization and the performance of masculinity," *Leisure Studies* 23/1, pp. 1–13.

Yardley, Jim, "In grand Olympic show, some sleight of voice," *New York Times*, August 12, 2008.

Zang, David, *Sports Wars: Athletes in the Age of Aquarius* (Fayetteville: University of Arkansas Press, 2001).

Zucker, Harvey Marc, and Lawrence J. Babich, *Sports Films: A Complete Reference* (Jefferson, NC: McFarland, 1987).

Press and Online Items without Bylines

"Are men really that bad?," *Time*, February 14, 1994.

Bibliography of published baseball music and songs in the collections of the Music Division at the Library of Congress. www.loc.gov/rr/perform/baseballbib.html (accessed May 13, 2009).

"Clemens hit hard in Mitchell Report," *SI.COM*, December 13, 2007. http://sportsillustrated.cnn.com/2007/baseball/mlb/12/13/mitchell.news (accessed May 15, 2009).

"Double amputee hurt in boating accident," *CBCNews online*. www.cbc.ca/sports/story/2009/02/22/pistorius-accident.html (accessed February 22, 2009).

"Drummers need the stamina of athletes, U.K. study finds," *CBCnews.ca*, July 25, 2008. www.cbc.ca/arts/music/story/2008/07/25/drummingproject.htmlwww.cbc.ca/arts/music/story/2008/07/25/drumming-project.html (accessed May 25, 2009).

"Ex-Kelme rider promises doping revelations," *VeloNews*, March 20, 2004. http://velonews.competitor.com/2004/03/road/ex-kelme-rider-promises-doping-revelations_5743 (accessed May 27, 2007).

"Faith Hill to sing 'Sunday Night Football' theme," *MSNBC*, August 30, 2007. http://nbcsports.msnbc.com/id/20498058 (accessed May 16, 2009).

"Five minute massacre," *Time*, April 8, 1974. www.time.com/time/magazine/article/0,9171,908552,00.html (accessed June 1, 2009).

"Hockey greats to take part in Montreal Symphony Orchestra concert," *TheSpec.com*, January 20, 2008. www.thespec.com/article/316130 (accessed May 25, 2010).

"It takes a heap of Salongo," *Newsweek*, September 23, 1974.

"K'naan celebrates his World Cup anthem," *Billboard.biz.* (September 29, 2009). www.billboard.biz/bbbiz/content_display/industrye3ife9d9d88fcefbcdce6fc9bb 98de68870 (accessed May 21, 2010).

"Kiwis deny overdoing haka at games," *Sydney Morning Herald*, March 21, 2006.

"Landis stripped of Tour title for doping, unsure on appeal," *ESPN.com*. http://sports.espn.go.com/oly/cycling/news/story?id=3029089 (accessed April 29, 2008).

"London Olympics ink deal with Universal Music" *CBCSports.ca*. www.cbc.ca/sports/amateur/story/2010/05/24/sp-universal-london.html (accessed July 10, 2010).

"Marketers alter their pitches with more females tuning in," *USA Today*, October 17, 2008. www.usatoday.com/sports/2008-09-17-women-marketing_N.htm (accessed June 7, 2010).

"Multi-platinum pop singer Pink performs NBC *Sunday Night Football* opening music," press release issued by NBC, August 30, 2006, www.thefutoncritic.com/news.aspx?id=20060830nbc01 (accessed May 16, 2009).

"Nigeria United fan kills rivals," *BBC News*, May 28, 2009. http://news.bbc.co.uk/2/hi/africa/8072356.stm (accessed March 9, 2010).

"Olivia Newton-John's 'Physical' sexiest song ever," Reuters (Feb 12, 2010). www.reuters.com/article/idUSTRE61B5H620100212 (accessed June 3, 2010).

Recording Industry Association of America 2005 Year End Statistics: www.riaa.org/aboutus.php.

"Sporting goods sales by product category: 1990 to 2003," *Statistical Abstract of the United States, 2004–2005* (Washington D.C.: US Census Bureau, 2004), Table 1247.

"*Sunday Night Football* thinks Pink," *Zap2it.com*, August 30, 2006. www.zap2it.com/tv/news/zap-pinksingssundaynightfootballtheme,0,4215656.story?coll=zap-tv-headlines (accessed May 16, 2009).

"The trophy in Eisner's big deal," *New York Times*, August 6, 1995.

The (White) Rapper, VH1. www.vh1.com/shows/dyn/white_rapper/series_about.jhtml (accessed July 27, 2008).

"Women in the Olympic Movement," International Olympic Committee Factsheet. http://multimedia.olympic.org/pdf/en_report_846.pdf (accessed March 2011).

CDs and DVD

ABC Monday Night Football Official Party Album, Hollywood Records (1996), B000000OG9.

The Power and The Glory: The Original Music and Voices of NFL Films (1998), Tommy Boy Records (TBCD 1269).

Queen: Greatest Video Hits 1 DVD Collection (2002), Queen Productions Ltd.

Index

Page numbers followed by "n" refer to a note at the bottom of the page, eg. 179n.